W9-BSZ-064

 Atlas of

THE 1990 CENSUS

 Atlas of

THE 1990 CENSUS

Mark T. Mattson

MACMILLAN PUBLISHING COMPANY
NEW YORK

Maxwell Macmillan Canada
TORONTO

Maxwell Macmillan International
NEW YORK   OXFORD   SINGAPORE   SYDNEY

Macmillan Publishing Company   Maxwell Macmillan Canada, Inc.
866 Third Avenue   1200 Eglinton Avenue East, Suite 200
New York, N.Y. 10022   Don Mills, Ontario M3C 3N1

Macmillan Publishing Company is part of the
Maxwell Communication Group of Companies.

Library of Congress Catalog Card Number: 92–24006

Printed in the United States of America

printing number
  2 3 4 5 6 7 8 9 10

Library of Congress Cataloging–in–Publication Data

Mattson, Mark T.
    Atlas of the 1990 census / Mark T. Mattson
          p.   cm.
    Includes glossary.
    ISBN 0–02–897302–X
    1. United States—Census, 21st, 1990—Maps.   2. United States—
Population—Maps.   I. Macmillan Publishing Company.   II. Title.
G1201.E2M3 1992 <G&M>
304.6'0973'09049—dc20   92 24006
                                                CIP
                                                MAP

The paper used in this publication meets the minimum requirements of American National
Standard for Information Sciences—Permanence of Printed Library Materials. ANSI
Z39.48–1984. ⊖™

Contents

Foreword

We Americans define ourselves in terms of place. Whether we are Hoosiers, southern Californians, Manhattanites, or New Englanders, we know that these places convey much about who we are and how we differ from others. Place provides a population profile of our numbers, population composition, family life, and interests; it tells us what we are likely to do for a living and how wealthy we are. Place helps us to know where we stand relative to others and, overtime, from where we have come and where we are likely to go.

We are able to define ourselves in terms of place because of the information collected in the United States Census every ten years. From its mandate in the first article of the U.S. Constitution, the Census is firmly rooted in the concept of place because place is inextricably bound to congressional representation. Thus the decennial Censuses record the evolution of place in America.

This *Atlas of the 1990 Census* is a significant effort to document and help us understand our current position. It focuses on the first tabulations of the 1990 Census of Population and Housing, which total the questions asked of everyone supplemented by some information from other sources, but later printings will incorporate the socioeconomic data which are collected from a sample of the American population. The questions asked of everyone—the 100 percent questions—deal with numbers and the age, gender, racial, ethnic, household, and family composition of the population. Additional data are collected about type, tenure, and cost of housing. And all of the information is arrayed geographically.

The Atlas is both a substantial supplement to and a replacement for material published by the Bureau of the Census in earlier decades. Because the United States Census has never published an atlas of the Census and has issued relatively few maps illustrating its findings, the *Atlas of the 1990 Census* represents a valuable addition to Census publications. Much that is presented here was for earlier censuses only provided in tabular form—a format from which it is difficult to discern spatial relationships. Here we can see the patterns of growth, decline, and change spread across the American landscape.

Less happily, it will also replace some earlier Census publications. One of the ironies of the increasing computerization of the Census is that while it has lowered costs and made publication of tabulations in a variety of forms far easier, the amount of published material has significantly declined over the past two decades. One reason for this change is that the overall cost of the Census has risen substantially with time ($2.6 billion for the 1990 Census), despite efforts to minimize costs with new technologies. With a larger and increasingly diverse population and more household adults working, it is simply an ever larger, more difficult, and costly task. Another reason has been the spread of the concept that users should absorb more of the costs of Census publications. Beginning in the late 1970s and intensifying throughout the 1980s, the dominant view of decision–makers has been that the dissemination of Census information should be increasingly left to the private market. As a result, some publications have been eliminated. Users either have to acquire and tabulate the data themselves or rely on commercial publications like this one. The ultimate effect is, paradoxically, both to restrict and expand the amount and kinds of information required for citizenship and individual, and organizational decision–making to those who can afford to pay.

In this paradoxical situation, the *Atlas of the 1990 Census* substantially expands the available information. More importantly, by combining data from the 1980 and 1990 Censuses, it helps us understand where we are, from where we have come, and where we are headed.

David Elesh
Social Science Data Library
Temple University

Acknowledgments

Working with the United States Census has been a joy throughout this entire project. It has been collected and distributed in a form that many people will find useful and within their means to obtain. It is important to acknowledge the Bureau of the Census for their decision–making over the last 20 years. Not only have they responded to the needs of a countless constituency, they have also set the direction for and created an ever widening base of users through their insight into data–based systems and their geographic implication. For their work, my first gesture of thanks belongs to the United States Bureau of the Census.

At a less global level, I am deeply indebted to several Census Bureau employees. In working with census data, it was my pleasure to be involved with Ann Jeffers and David Lewis. Both fielded any number of phone calls and have alerted me to releases and other matters related to the publication of this book. With respect to Ann, it was a special privilege to share this experience with her and to see her doing so well in her career. Ann is a graduate of our department at Temple University who has gone on to represent our faculty and students in a most professional manner.

Thanks must also be given to David Webb and David Elesh of our Social Science Data Library. It was their network development and supervision that gave us the computer horsepower to make this book possible. Their selfless commitment to collegial empowerment is manifest in this atlas and will be evident in countless future projects throughout the university. Gentlemen, thanks for making my problems yours in the middle of your busy schedules.

No project could run smoothly without the support of a benevolent boss. To Carolyn Adams, our department chair, thanks. Your constant support of our lab has made this atlas and the others preceding it a reality.

Finally, and most importantly, I owe the success of this book to two individuals—Christopher Salvatico and Scott Snyder. They crunched the data, made the maps, and laid the pages out with text and graphics. If I could give my best friends a single gift it would be the pleasure of working with two people such as you. This book simply would not have happened without you. Thank you Scott. Thank you Chris. You know exactly how much you mean to me and how I rely on you, day by day, for almost everything.

Introduction

The U.S. Constitution provides for a census of the population every 10 years primarily to establish a basis for appointment of members to the United States House of Representatives. For more than a century after the first census of 1790, the organization that collected population data was a temporary one. In 1902, the federal government established a permanent agency, which was responsible for enumerating the population and collecting valuable statistics on a wide variety of topics.

During the twentieth century, politicians, social scientists, marketing specialists, students, and any number of other citizens have come to rely heavily on the wealth of information that is made available by the United States Bureau of the Census. Hardly a moment goes by in America when an organization or an individual is not putting "census" information to good use.

There are many censuses. The most well known is the *Census of Housing and Population*, which is conducted at the beginning of each decade. This atlas is a graphic representation of the first information released from the *1990 Census of Population and Housing (STF–1A)*. In subsequent printings of this atlas, other information will be included as it is made available by the government. Until such time, surrogate data from census related sources have been mapped. We have done this so that the STF-1A information—the primary focus of *this* volume—can be viewed within a context that will make it useful and relevant.

The Bureau of the Census collects information at a number of geographic levels. An aggregation process exists that starts from individual responses and works its way to descriptions of phenomena at a national level. Users of census data require information at any number of these levels. One person may wish to see numbers for African Americans for each state while another may wish to focus more closely looking at Black communities in sections of certain cities. The level at which data is mapped for a volume such as this is largely driven by simple mathematics and space. Within an atlas, a balance between the number of variables presented and the level of detail to which those variables can be graphically portrayed must be reached. To this end, we have tried to be as detailed as possible without limiting the number.of subjects that we present; hence the useability of our volume to many potential readers.

In the *Atlas of the 1990 Census,* most variables are presented at three levels of detail. At the first level, state information is presented and comparisons are made between the years of 1980 and 1990. At a second level of detail, subjects are looked at on a regional and national scale. These portrayals are followed by a close–up look at counties for readers who find more generalized information too coarse for adequate or substantive analysis.

The *Atlas of the 1990 Census* is divided into six parts—Population, Households, Housing, Race and Ethnicity, Economy, and Education. These sections are followed by regional county locator maps, a Metro Fact Finder, and a glossary of census terms.

In the first section on population, traditional concepts such as population density, population change, median age, and population projections are followed by more specialized looks at the distribution of those Americans that are 65 years of age and over and that segment of the population that is under 18 years of age. This section concludes with one page treatments on metropolitan/rural population and vital statistics which includes data on births, deaths, infant mortality, and abortions.

The second section is devoted to households. In it, attention is given to the number of households in the United States and the changing nature of American households. A particular emphasis is placed on female heads of household, the emergence of nontraditional households, families, and householders.

Section three deals with housing—its value and characteristics. A particularly strong part of the third section is that which contains county–level choropleth maps that show changes in home values for the entire United States. In addition, household occupancy and vacancy rates are calculated at various levels of detail.

Race and ethnicity are the topics covered in section four. Relying strongly on the use of county–level information about the spatial distribution of various ethnic groups, the beginning of this section shows where Americans come from and discusses patterns of migration.

The fifth section covers the economy. In it, income and the means by which people generate income are examined. Also explored is the distribution of various segments of the U.S. economy, and how those segments relate to population concentrations and housing characteristics and values.

Education is the final section of the *Atlas of the 1990 Census*. Although it is only eight pages in length, it provides valuable information on all levels of geographic detail related to school–age population.

Part One

POPULATION

POPULATION DENSITY

While the population of the United States increases from year to year, the space within which it is contained remains the same. The census of 1790 demonstrated a population of 4.5 persons per square mile. That figure has risen steady to 70.3 in 1990.

Currently, over 250 million people live in the United States. They are overwhelmingly concentrated in a belt that begins in Illinois and works its way east along the Great Lakes through New England and south along the Atlantic coast to Florida. The map on page 5 demonstrates this pattern together with a dark coloration in California indicating its high density.

The District of Columbia, more a city than a state per se, features the most highly concentrated population. The state with the most densely packed residency is New Jersey. Many states in the Midwest and in the Mountain regions have few residents compared to their total land area. Alaska is the least dense state with only one resident per square mile.

POPULATION DISTRIBUTION AND GROWTH

The population of each state, regardless of its overall population density, is located in or around major urban centers. For the purpose of description and analysis, the Bureau of the Census has designated 284 Metropolitan Areas (MSA's and CMSA's). The concept of a metropolitan area is one in which surrounding communities are tied to a major metropolitan nucleus by a high degree of social and economic interaction. Within the United States, 77.5 percent of all persons (192,726,000) live within designated metropolitan areas. That figure is increasing. Between 1980 and 1990, metropolitan population increased by 11.6 percent. Between 1970 and 1980 a similar increase of 16.0 percent was noted.

The largest states, in terms of population, are California and New York. The least populous states are Wyoming and Alaska. The greatest increases between 1980 and 1990 have occurred in Alaska, California, Nevada, Arizona, New Hampshire, and Florida. Several states have decreased population, with West Virginia leading this category at –8.01 percent. North Dakota, Wyoming, and Iowa have also declined.

The Middle Atlantic, the East North Central, the South Atlantic, and the Pacific are the most populated regions. The largest increases in population, since 1980, have occurred in the Pacific (23.0 percent) and the Mountain (20.1 percent) regions. The slowest regional growth rates were calculated for the East

North Central (0.8 percent) and the Middle Atlantic (2.2 percent).

Looking at the county maps on pages 14 through 19, one is immediately confronted with the lack of growth or slow growth exhibited in nearly all New England, Middle Atlantic, and Midwestern states. Conversely, the counties of the Southwestern and the Lower Mountain states, as featured on page 18, are growing rapidly.

COMPONENTS OF POPULATION CHANGE

On a national scale, population has increased at a declining rate since 1960. This trend is expected to continue through the early decades of the twenty–first century. By 2025, U.S. population is expected to be increasing by a rate of only 0.2 percent. This is compared to a yearly rate of increase of 1.6 percent in 1960. This trend is explained by an increase in deaths coupled with a decrease in births and the number of immigrants entering the country.

Overall net civilian immigration is expected to level off at approximately 500,000 by the year 2000. The origins of America's newest citizens can be ascertained by moving ahead to pages 98 and 99.

In the United States, inter–regional migration accounts for much of the changes in state populations. The following table illuminates regional shifts between 1987 and 1988.

	Northeast	Mid West	South	West
Immigrants (000s)	448	741	1,364	627
From Northeast	—	112	444	122
From Midwest	91	—	528	528
From South	250	403	—	294
From West	107	226	393	—
Outmigrants	697	829	946	725
To Northeast	—	91	250	107
To Midwest	112	—	403	226
To South	444	528	—	393
To West	122	210	294	—
Net migration	–231	–88	418	–98

POPULATION INTO THE NEXT CENTURY

By the year 2010, the United States will have anywhere between 264 and 282 million residents, depending on the projection used. By 2025, these figures will increase to 262 to 348 million.

Population growth will be extreme for African Americans and Hispanics, and will virtually come to a

halt for Whites by year 2025. The fastest growing age groups will be those 45 to 54 years old and 75 years old and over between 1990 and year 2000. In the first decade of the next century, the fastest growing group will be between 55 and 64 years of age.

COMPONENTS OF GENDER

Females outnumber males for all age groups except in the Hispanic population. The largest disparity in the sexes is demonstrated in the African American community, where there are barely over nine males for every ten females. Given that women live longer than men (79.0 years as opposed to 72.1 in 1990), this disparity is more pronounced in later years. In 1989, for example, only 68.9 men were alive for every 100 women.

AGE OF POPULATION

The American population is growing older. In 1960, 17.9 percent of the population was over 55 years of age. This figure increased to 21.1 percent in 1989 and is expected to balloon to 26.5 percent by 2010.

Median age for the United States increased from 29.6 years in 1980 to 32.8 years in 1990. The states that are aging most quickly are also the states which are losing population (see pages 12 and 22). This would seem to indicate an outmigration of younger residents, resulting in a decreased rate of birth. Florida, a popular retirement state, has had the oldest population since 1980. Utah, in the last two decennial censuses has been America's youngest state. Population under 5 years of age and under 17 years of age has shown a steady decline since 1960. The graph to the lower left on page 31 shows perfectly the dynamic change in the nation's population in terms of age.

VITAL STATISTICS

Birth rates are down in thirty of the fifty states since 1980. The current national birth rate is 14.9 births per 1,000 population.

The national abortion ratio was 404 per 1,000 live births in 1988 and 1989. In the District of Columbia, 1.26 pregnancies are aborted for every one carried to full term. Between the ages of 15 and 44, 27.3 women of every 1,000 women had an abortion during the same time period.

Of pregnancies carried to full term, 6.9 percent resulted in births to low weight babies, 12.5 percent were to teenage mothers, and 25.7 percent were to unmarried women in 1989.

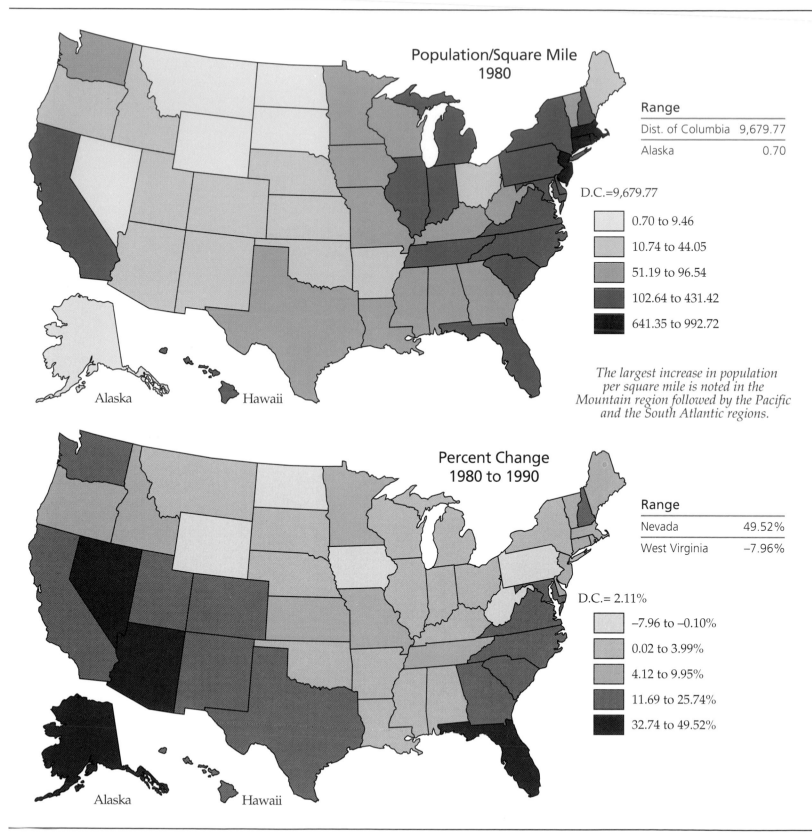

Population/Square Mile 1980

Range

Dist. of Columbia	9,679.77
Alaska	0.70

D.C.=9,679.77

- 0.70 to 9.46
- 10.74 to 44.05
- 51.19 to 96.54
- 102.64 to 431.42
- 641.35 to 992.72

The largest increase in population per square mile is noted in the Mountain region followed by the Pacific and the South Atlantic regions.

Alaska Hawaii

Percent Change 1980 to 1990

Range

Nevada	49.52%
West Virginia	−7.96%

D.C.= 2.11%

- −7.96 to −0.10%
- 0.02 to 3.99%
- 4.12 to 9.95%
- 11.69 to 25.74%
- 32.74 to 49.52%

Alaska Hawaii

Population/Square Mile, 1980

United States	64.00
Alabama	76.73
Alaska	0.70
Arizona	23.92
Arkansas	43.91
California	151.74
Colorado	27.86
Connecticut	641.35
Delaware	326.58
District of Columbia	9,679.77
Florida	180.50
Georgia	94.32
Hawaii	150.18
Idaho	11.41
Illinois	205.56
Indiana	153.06
Iowa	52.15
Kansas	28.89
Kentucky	92.14
Louisiana	96.54
Maine	36.44
Maryland	431.42
Massachusetts	731.95
Michigan	163.04
Minnesota	51.19
Mississippi	52.86
Missouri	71.36
Montana	5.40
Nebraska	20.42
Nevada	7.29
New Hampshire	102.64
New Jersey	992.72
New Mexico	10.74
New York	371.81
North Carolina	120.73
North Dakota	9.46
Ohio	263.66
Oklahoma	44.05
Oregon	27.43
Pennsylvania	265.37
Rhode Island	906.37
South Carolina	103.68
South Dakota	9.10
Tennessee	111.38
Texas	54.33
Utah	17.78
Vermont	55.30
Virginia	135.03
Washington	62.06
West Virginia	80.94
Wisconsin	86.64
Wyoming	4.84

Population/Square Mile, 1990

United States	70.3
Alabama	79.6
Alaska	1.0
Arizona	32.3
Arkansas	45.1
California	190.8
Colorado	31.8
Connecticut	678.4
Delaware	340.8
District of Columbia	9,884.4
Florida	239.6
Georgia	111.9
Hawaii	172.5
Idaho	12.2
Illinois	205.6
Indiana	154.6
Iowa	49.7
Kansas	30.3
Kentucky	92.8
Louisiana	96.9
Maine	39.8
Maryland	489.2
Massachusetts	767.6
Michigan	163.6
Minnesota	55.0
Mississippi	54.0
Missouri	74.3
Montana	5.5
Nebraska	20.5
Nevada	10.9
New Hampshire	123.7
New Jersey	1,042.0
New Mexico	12.5
New York	381.0
North Carolina	136.1
North Dakota	9.3
Ohio	264.9
Oklahoma	45.8
Oregon	29.6
Pennsylvania	265.1
Rhode Island	960.3
South Carolina	115.8
South Dakota	9.2
Tennessee	118.3
Texas	64.9
Utah	21.0
Vermont	60.8
Virginia	156.3
Washington	73.1
West Virginia	74.5
Wisconsin	90.1
Wyoming	4.7

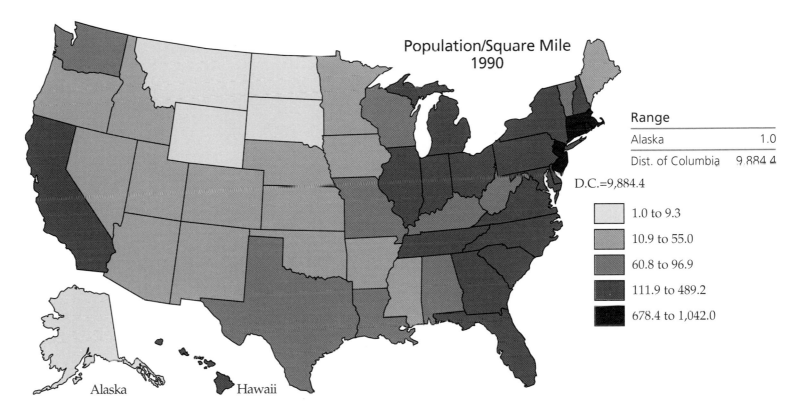

Population/Square Mile
1990

Range

Alaska	1.0
Dist. of Columbia	9,884.4

D.C.=9,884.4

1.0 to 9.3
10.9 to 55.0
60.8 to 96.9
111.9 to 489.2
678.4 to 1,042.0

Alaska   Hawaii

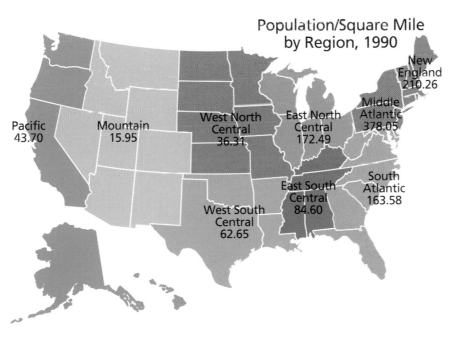

Population/Square Mile
by Region, 1990

Pacific 43.70
Mountain 15.95
West North Central 36.31
East North Central 172.49
Middle Atlantic 378.05
New England 210.26
East South Central 84.60
South Atlantic 163.58
West South Central 62.65

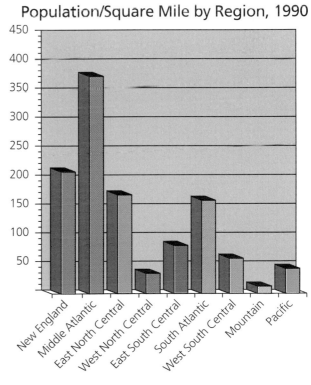

Population/Square Mile by Region, 1990

New England · Middle Atlantic · East North Central · West North Central · East South Central · South Atlantic · West South Central · Mountain · Pacific

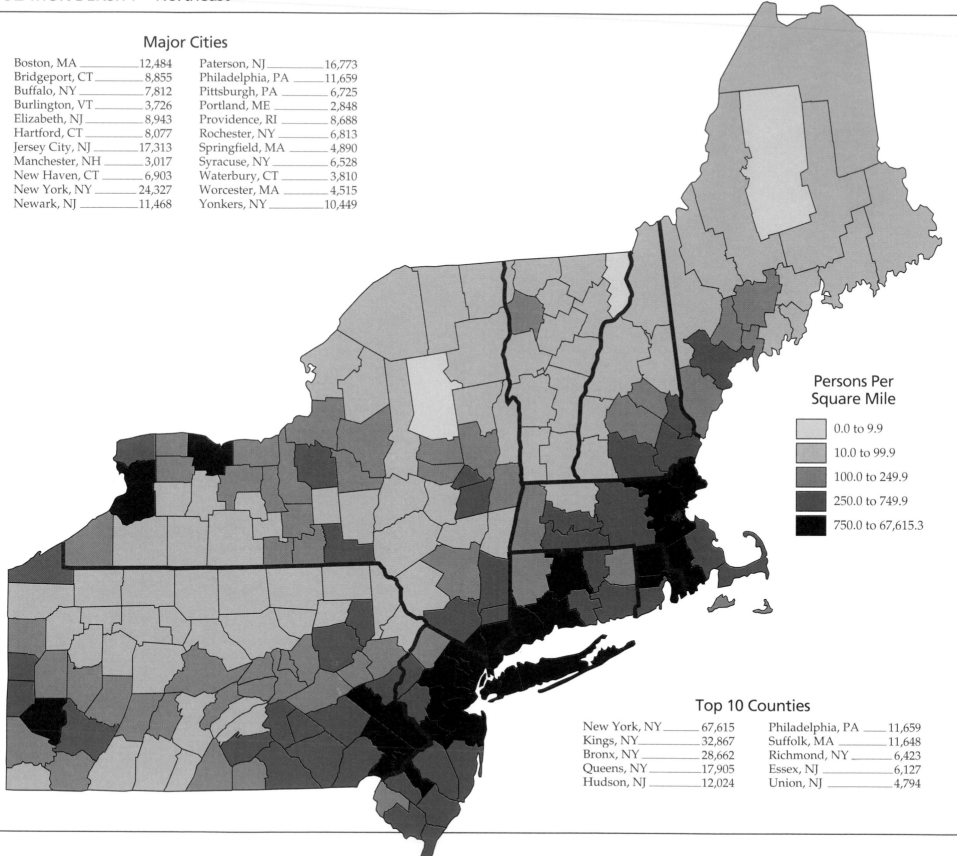

Major Cities

Boston, MA	12,484	Paterson, NJ	16,773
Bridgeport, CT	8,855	Philadelphia, PA	11,659
Buffalo, NY	7,812	Pittsburgh, PA	6,725
Burlington, VT	3,726	Portland, ME	2,848
Elizabeth, NJ	8,943	Providence, RI	8,688
Hartford, CT	8,077	Rochester, NY	6,813
Jersey City, NJ	17,313	Springfield, MA	4,890
Manchester, NH	3,017	Syracuse, NY	6,528
New Haven, CT	6,903	Waterbury, CT	3,810
New York, NY	24,327	Worcester, MA	4,515
Newark, NJ	11,468	Yonkers, NY	10,449

Persons Per Square Mile

- 0.0 to 9.9
- 10.0 to 99.9
- 100.0 to 249.9
- 250.0 to 749.9
- 750.0 to 67,615.3

Top 10 Counties

New York, NY	67,615	Philadelphia, PA	11,659
Kings, NY	32,867	Suffolk, MA	11,648
Bronx, NY	28,662	Richmond, NY	6,423
Queens, NY	17,905	Essex, NJ	6,127
Hudson, NJ	12,024	Union, NJ	4,794

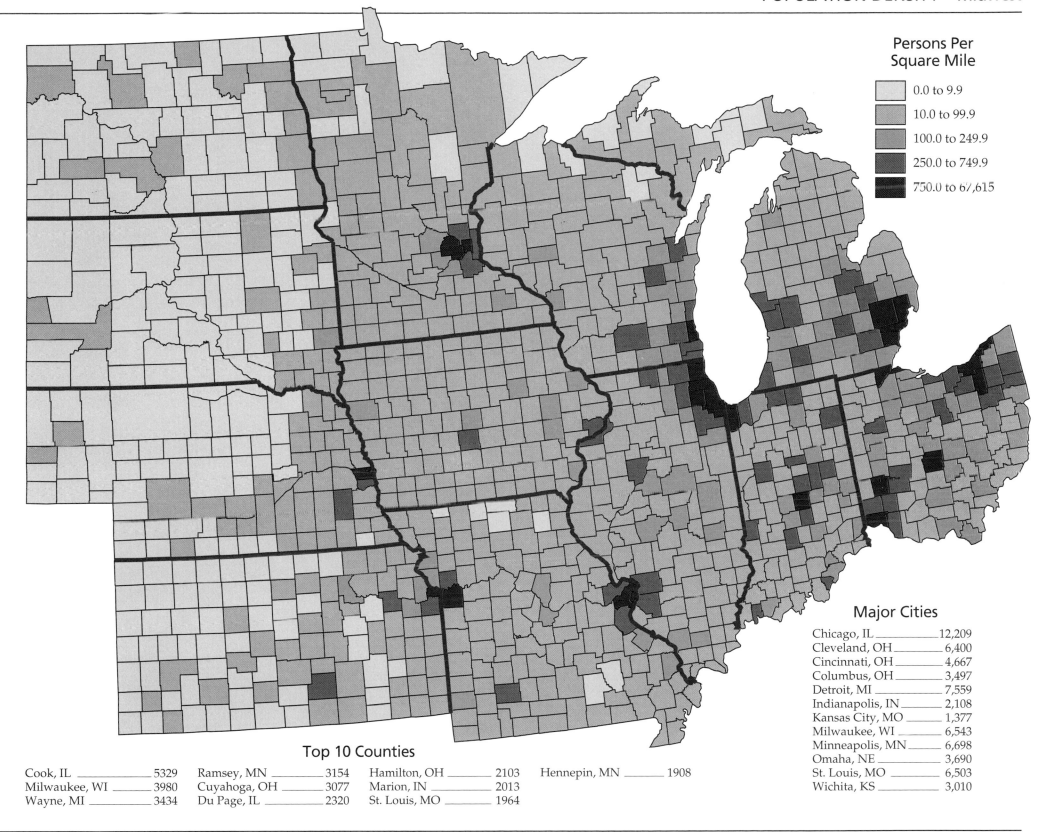

Persons Per
Square Mile

0.0 to 9.9
10.0 to 99.9
100.0 to 249.9
250.0 to 749.9
750.0 to 67,615

Major Cities

Chicago, IL _____ 12,209
Cleveland, OH _____ 6,400
Cincinnati, OH _____ 4,667
Columbus, OH _____ 3,497
Detroit, MI _____ 7,559
Indianapolis, IN _____ 2,108
Kansas City, MO _____ 1,377
Milwaukee, WI _____ 6,543
Minneapolis, MN _____ 6,698
Omaha, NE _____ 3,690
St. Louis, MO _____ 6,503
Wichita, KS _____ 3,010

Top 10 Counties

Cook, IL _____ 5329
Milwaukee, WI ____ 3980
Wayne, MI _____ 3434

Ramsey, MN _____ 3154
Cuyahoga, OH _____ 3077
Du Page, IL _____ 2320

Hamilton, OH _____ 2103
Marion, IN _____ 2013
St. Louis, MO _____ 1964

Hennepin, MN _____ 1908

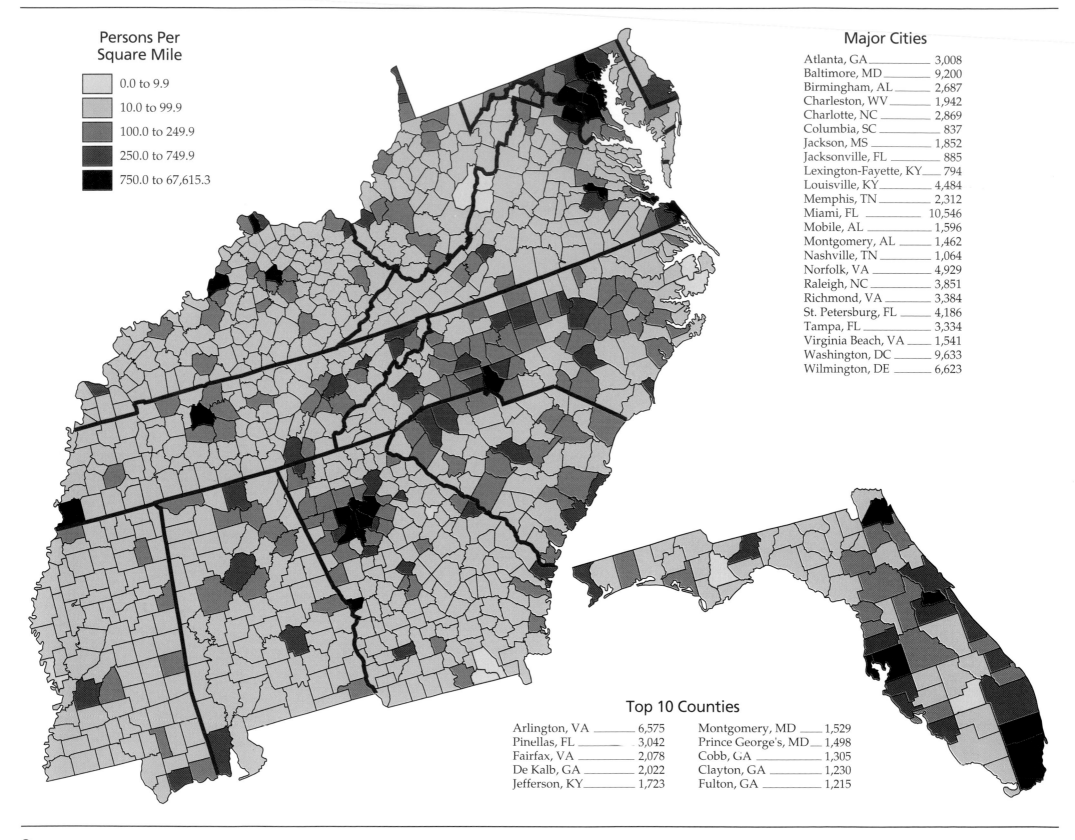

Persons Per Square Mile

- 0.0 to 9.9
- 10.0 to 99.9
- 100.0 to 249.9
- 250.0 to 749.9
- 750.0 to 67,615.3

Major Cities

City	Density
Atlanta, GA	3,008
Baltimore, MD	9,200
Birmingham, AL	2,687
Charleston, WV	1,942
Charlotte, NC	2,869
Columbia, SC	837
Jackson, MS	1,852
Jacksonville, FL	885
Lexington-Fayette, KY	794
Louisville, KY	4,484
Memphis, TN	2,312
Miami, FL	10,546
Mobile, AL	1,596
Montgomery, AL	1,462
Nashville, TN	1,064
Norfolk, VA	4,929
Raleigh, NC	3,851
Richmond, VA	3,384
St. Petersburg, FL	4,186
Tampa, FL	3,334
Virginia Beach, VA	1,541
Washington, DC	9,633
Wilmington, DE	6,623

Top 10 Counties

County	Density	County	Density
Arlington, VA	6,575	Montgomery, MD	1,529
Pinellas, FL	3,042	Prince George's, MD	1,498
Fairfax, VA	2,078	Cobb, GA	1,305
De Kalb, GA	2,022	Clayton, GA	1,230
Jefferson, KY	1,723	Fulton, GA	1,215

Top 10 Counties

County	Density
Orleans, LA	2,497
Dallas, TX	2,106
Harris, TX	1,625
Tarrant, TX	1,348
Jefferson, LA	1,288
Bexar, TX	950
Tulsa, OK	880
Oklahoma, OK	847
East Baton Rouge, LA	830
Lafayette, LA	610

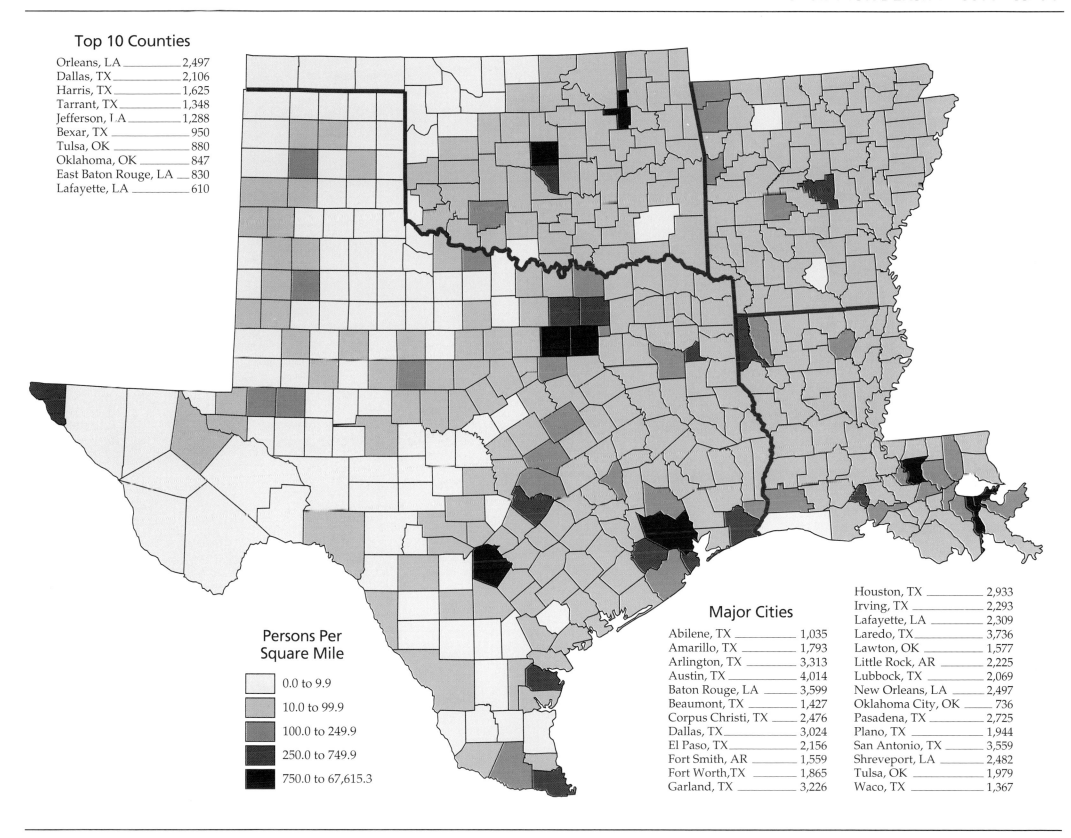

Persons Per Square Mile

- 0.0 to 9.9
- 10.0 to 99.9
- 100.0 to 249.9
- 250.0 to 749.9
- 750.0 to 67,615.3

Major Cities

City	Density
Abilene, TX	1,035
Amarillo, TX	1,793
Arlington, TX	3,313
Austin, TX	4,014
Baton Rouge, LA	3,599
Beaumont, TX	1,427
Corpus Christi, TX	2,476
Dallas, TX	3,024
El Paso, TX	2,156
Fort Smith, AR	1,559
Fort Worth, TX	1,865
Garland, TX	3,226
Houston, TX	2,933
Irving, TX	2,293
Lafayette, LA	2,309
Laredo, TX	3,736
Lawton, OK	1,577
Little Rock, AR	2,225
Lubbock, TX	2,069
New Orleans, LA	2,497
Oklahoma City, OK	736
Pasadena, TX	2,725
Plano, TX	1,944
San Antonio, TX	3,559
Shreveport, LA	2,482
Tulsa, OK	1,979
Waco, TX	1,367

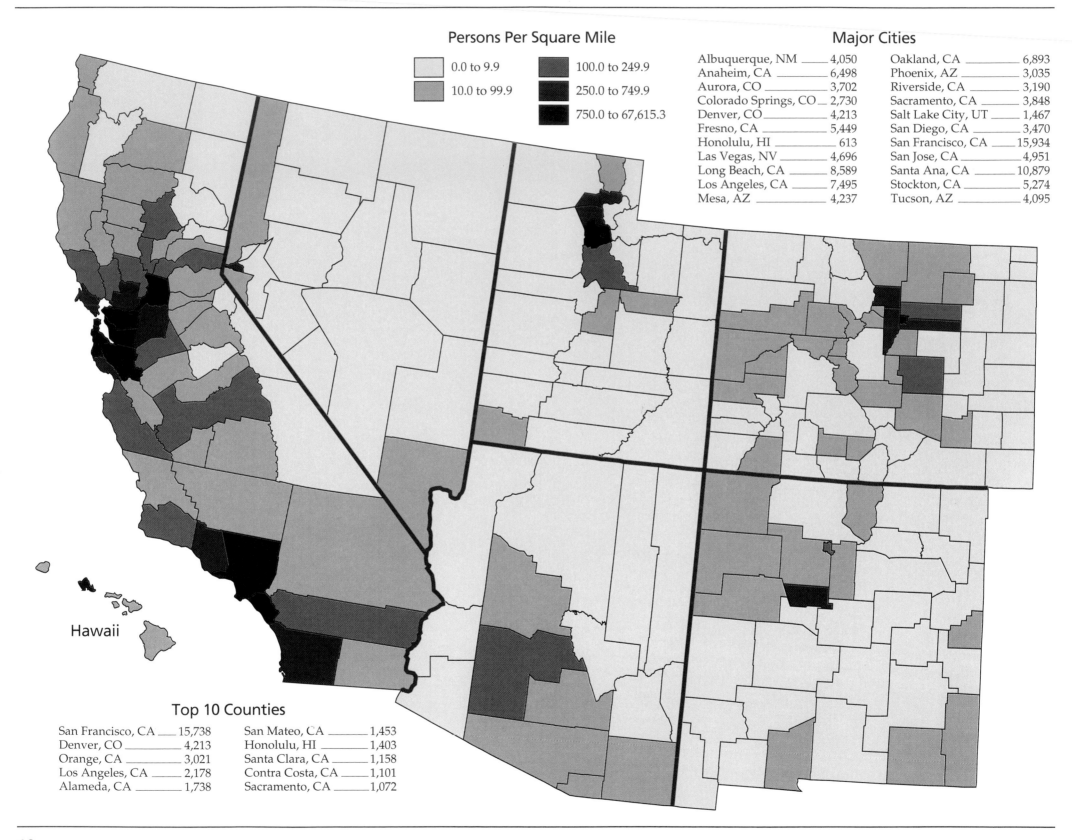

Persons Per Square Mile

- 0.0 to 9.9
- 10.0 to 99.9
- 100.0 to 249.9
- 250.0 to 749.9
- 750.0 to 67,615.3

Major Cities

City	Density
Albuquerque, NM	4,050
Anaheim, CA	6,498
Aurora, CO	3,702
Colorado Springs, CO	2,730
Denver, CO	4,213
Fresno, CA	5,449
Honolulu, HI	613
Las Vegas, NV	4,696
Long Beach, CA	8,589
Los Angeles, CA	7,495
Mesa, AZ	4,237
Oakland, CA	6,893
Phoenix, AZ	3,035
Riverside, CA	3,190
Sacramento, CA	3,848
Salt Lake City, UT	1,467
San Diego, CA	3,470
San Francisco, CA	15,934
San Jose, CA	4,951
Santa Ana, CA	10,879
Stockton, CA	5,274
Tucson, AZ	4,095

Hawaii

Top 10 Counties

County	Density
San Francisco, CA	15,738
Denver, CO	4,213
Orange, CA	3,021
Los Angeles, CA	2,178
Alameda, CA	1,738
San Mateo, CA	1,453
Honolulu, HI	1,403
Santa Clara, CA	1,158
Contra Costa, CA	1,101
Sacramento, CA	1,072

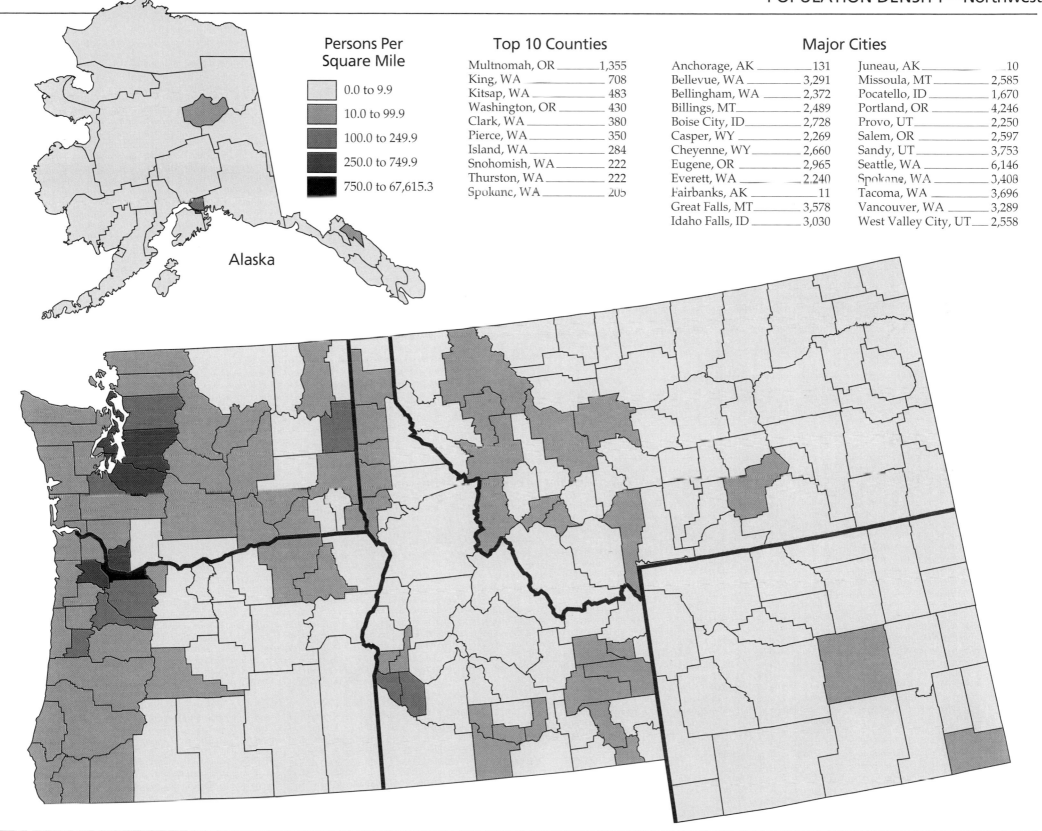

Persons Per Square Mile

- 0.0 to 9.9
- 10.0 to 99.9
- 100.0 to 249.9
- 250.0 to 749.9
- 750.0 to 67,615.3

Alaska

Top 10 Counties

Multnomah, OR	1,355
King, WA	708
Kitsap, WA	483
Washington, OR	430
Clark, WA	380
Pierce, WA	350
Island, WA	284
Snohomish, WA	222
Thurston, WA	222
Spokane, WA	205

Major Cities

Anchorage, AK	131	Juneau, AK	10
Bellevue, WA	3,291	Missoula, MT	2,585
Bellingham, WA	2,372	Pocatello, ID	1,670
Billings, MT	2,489	Portland, OR	4,246
Boise City, ID	2,728	Provo, UT	2,250
Casper, WY	2,269	Salem, OR	2,597
Cheyenne, WY	2,660	Sandy, UT	3,753
Eugene, OR	2,965	Seattle, WA	6,146
Everett, WA	2,240	Spokane, WA	3,408
Fairbanks, AK	11	Tacoma, WA	3,696
Great Falls, MT	3,578	Vancouver, WA	3,289
Idaho Falls, ID	3,030	West Valley City, UT	2,558

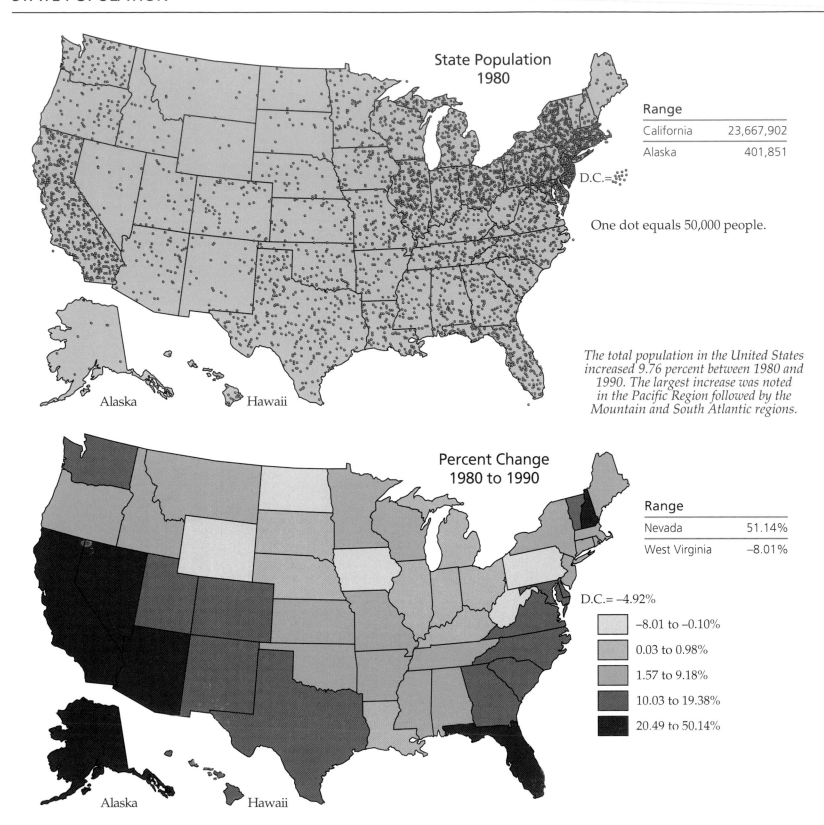

State Population 1980

Range

California	23,667,902
Alaska	401,851

D.C.=

One dot equals 50,000 people.

The total population in the United States increased 9.76 percent between 1980 and 1990. The largest increase was noted in the Pacific Region followed by the Mountain and South Atlantic regions.

Alaska   Hawaii

Percent Change 1980 to 1990

Range

Nevada	51.14%
West Virginia	−8.01%

D.C.= −4.92%

- −8.01 to −0.10%
- 0.03 to 0.98%
- 1.57 to 9.18%
- 10.03 to 19.38%
- 20.49 to 50.14%

Alaska   Hawaii

State Population, 1980

United States	226,576,825
Alabama	3,893,888
Alaska	401,851
Arizona	2,718,215
Arkansas	2,286,435
California	23,667,902
Colorado	2,889,964
Connecticut	3,107,576
Delaware	594,338
District of Columbia	638,333
Florida	9,746,324
Georgia	5,463,105
Hawaii	964,691
Idaho	943,935
Illinois	11,427,518
Indiana	5,490,224
Iowa	2,913,808
Kansas	2,363,679
Kentucky	3,660,777
Louisiana	4,205,900
Maine	1,124,660
Maryland	4,216,975
Massachusetts	5,737,037
Michigan	9,262,078
Minnesota	4,075,970
Mississippi	2,520,638
Missouri	4,916,686
Montana	786,690
Nebraska	1,569,825
Nevada	800,493
New Hampshire	920,610
New Jersey	7,364,823
New Mexico	1,302,894
New York	17,558,072
North Carolina	5,881,766
North Dakota	652,717
Ohio	10,797,630
Oklahoma	3,025,290
Oregon	2,633,105
Pennsylvania	11,893,895
Rhode Island	947,154
South Carolina	3,121,820
South Dakota	690,768
Tennessee	4,591,120
Texas	14,229,191
Utah	1,461,037
Vermont	511,456
Virginia	5,346,818
Washington	4,132,156
West Virginia	1,949,664
Wisconsin	4,705,767
Wyoming	469,557

State Population, 1990

United States	248,691,873
Alabama	4,040,587
Alaska	550,043
Arizona	3,665,228
Arkansas	2,350,725
California	29,760,021
Colorado	3,294,394
Connecticut	3,287,116
Delaware	666,168
District of Columbia	606,900
Florida	12,937,926
Georgia	6,478,216
Hawaii	1,108,229
Idaho	1,006,749
Illinois	11,430,602
Indiana	5,544,159
Iowa	2,776,755
Kansas	2,477,574
Kentucky	3,685,296
Louisiana	4,219,973
Maine	1,227,928
Maryland	4,781,468
Massachusetts	6,016,425
Michigan	9,295,297
Minnesota	4,375,099
Mississippi	2,573,216
Missouri	5,117,073
Montana	799,065
Nebraska	1,578,385
Nevada	1,201,833
New Hampshire	1,109,252
New Jersey	7,730,188
New Mexico	1,515,069
New York	17,990,455
North Carolina	6,628,637
North Dakota	638,800
Ohio	10,847,115
Oklahoma	3,145,585
Oregon	2,842,321
Pennsylvania	11,881,643
Rhode Island	1,003,464
South Carolina	3,468,703
South Dakota	696,004
Tennessee	4,877,185
Texas	16,986,510
Utah	1,722,850
Vermont	562,758
Virginia	6,187,358
Washington	4,866,692
West Virginia	1,793,477
Wisconsin	4,891,769
Wyoming	453,588

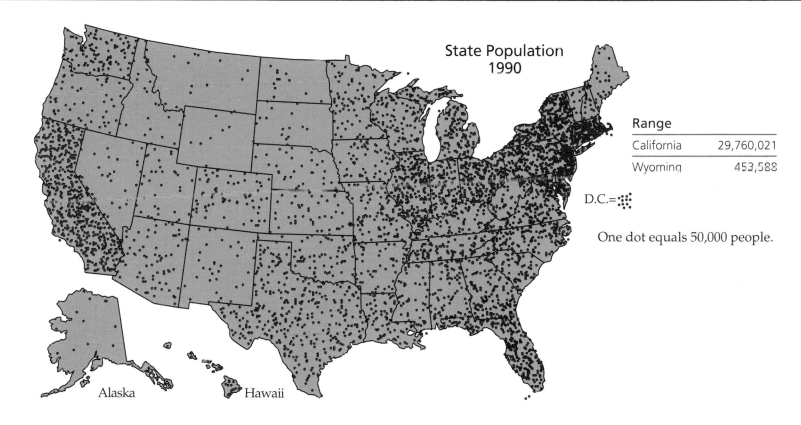

State Population 1990

Range

California	29,760,021
Wyoming	453,588

D.C.=

One dot equals 50,000 people.

Alaska   Hawaii

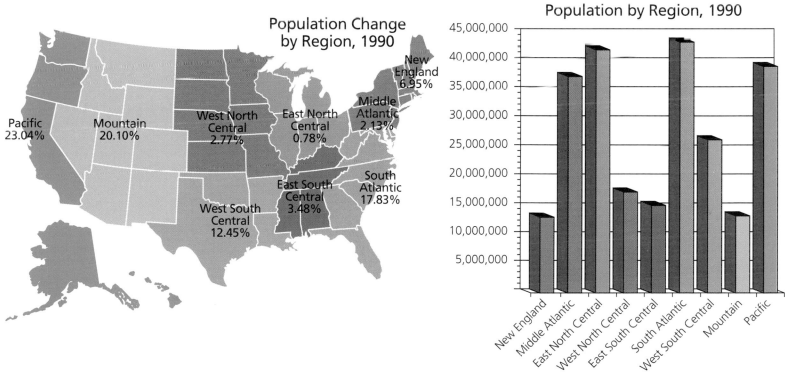

Population Change by Region, 1990

Pacific 23.04%
Mountain 20.10%
West North Central 2.77%
East North Central 0.78%
Middle Atlantic 2.13%
New England 6.95%
South Atlantic 17.83%
East South Central 3.48%
West South Central 12.45%

Population by Region, 1990

New England
Middle Atlantic
East North Central
West North Central
East South Central
South Atlantic
West South Central
Mountain
Pacific

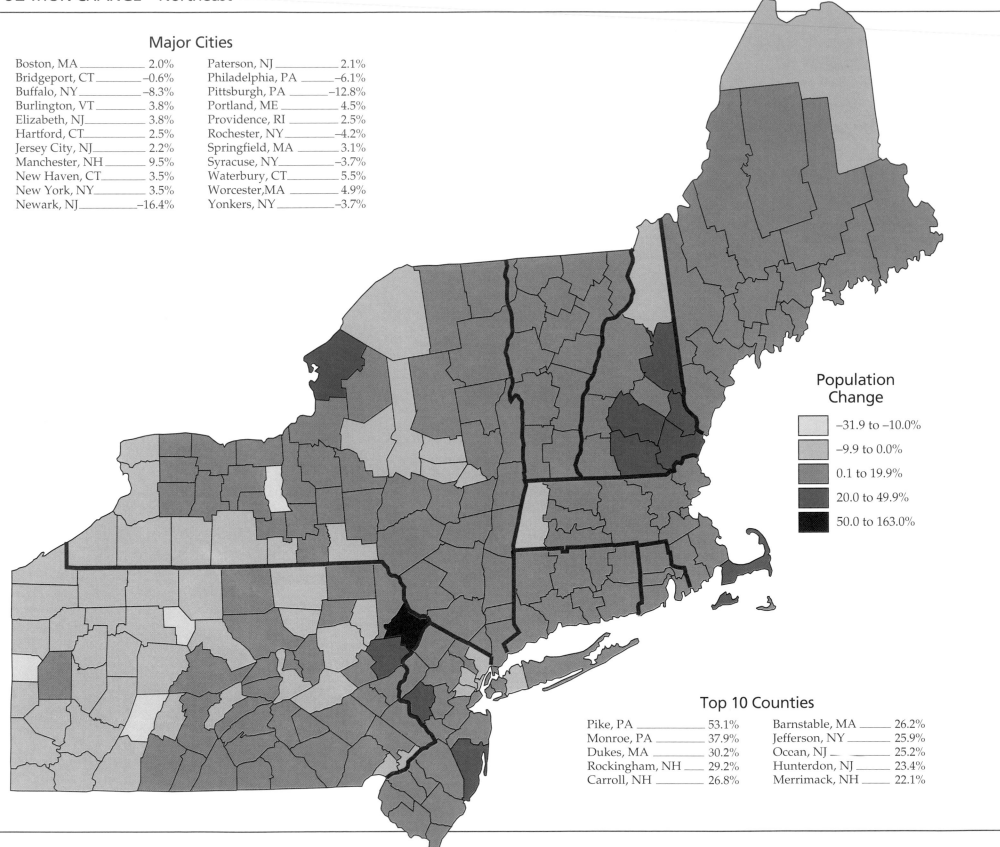

Major Cities

City	%
Boston, MA	2.0%
Bridgeport, CT	–0.6%
Buffalo, NY	–8.3%
Burlington, VT	3.8%
Elizabeth, NJ	3.8%
Hartford, CT	2.5%
Jersey City, NJ	2.2%
Manchester, NH	9.5%
New Haven, CT	3.5%
New York, NY	3.5%
Newark, NJ	–16.4%
Paterson, NJ	2.1%
Philadelphia, PA	–6.1%
Pittsburgh, PA	–12.8%
Portland, ME	4.5%
Providence, RI	2.5%
Rochester, NY	–4.2%
Springfield, MA	3.1%
Syracuse, NY	–3.7%
Waterbury, CT	5.5%
Worcester, MA	4.9%
Yonkers, NY	–3.7%

Population Change

- –31.9 to –10.0%
- –9.9 to 0.0%
- 0.1 to 19.9%
- 20.0 to 49.9%
- 50.0 to 163.0%

Top 10 Counties

County	%	County	%
Pike, PA	53.1%	Barnstable, MA	26.2%
Monroe, PA	37.9%	Jefferson, NY	25.9%
Dukes, MA	30.2%	Ocean, NJ	25.2%
Rockingham, NH	29.2%	Hunterdon, NJ	23.4%
Carroll, NH	26.8%	Merrimack, NH	22.1%

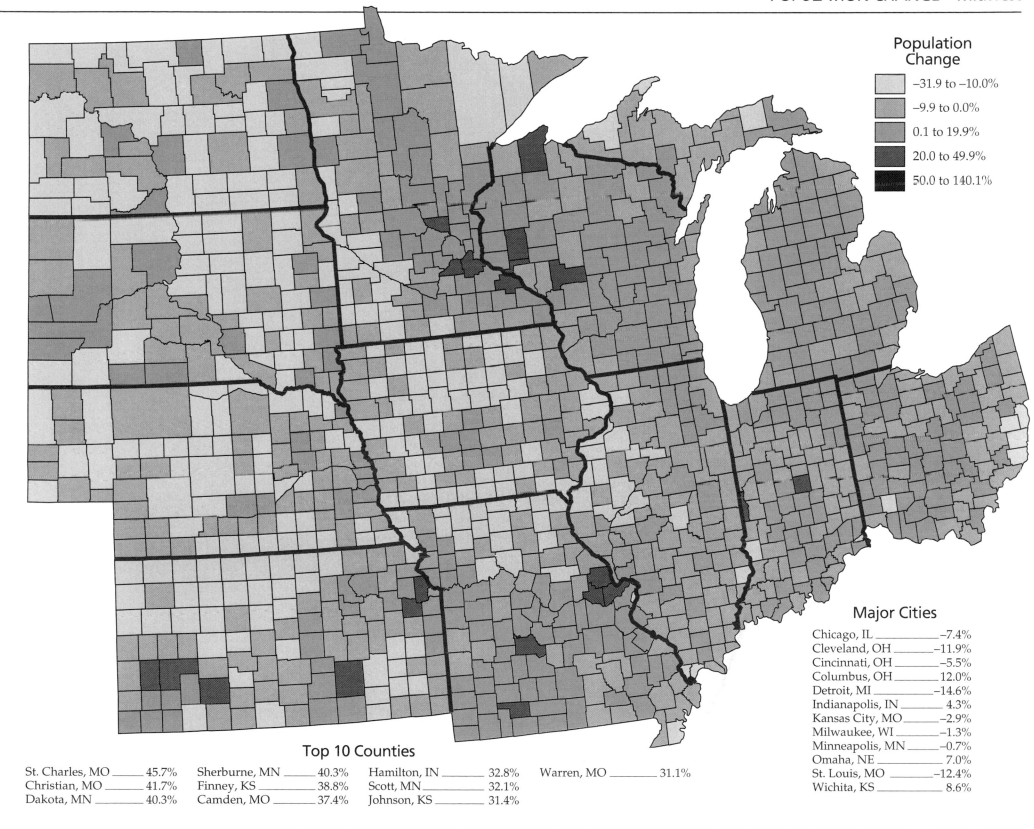

Population
Change

	−31.9 to −10.0%
	−9.9 to 0.0%
	0.1 to 19.9%
	20.0 to 49.9%
	50.0 to 140.1%

Major Cities

Chicago, IL _____ −7.4%
Cleveland, OH _____ −11.9%
Cincinnati, OH _____ −5.5%
Columbus, OH _____ 12.0%
Detroit, MI _____ −14.6%
Indianapolis, IN _____ 4.3%
Kansas City, MO _____ −2.9%
Milwaukee, WI _____ −1.3%
Minneapolis, MN _____ −0.7%
Omaha, NE _____ 7.0%
St. Louis, MO _____ −12.4%
Wichita, KS _____ 8.6%

Top 10 Counties

St. Charles, MO ____ 45.7%	Sherburne, MN ____ 40.3%	Hamilton, IN ____ 32.8%	Warren, MO ____ 31.1%
Christian, MO ____ 41.7%	Finney, KS ____ 38.8%	Scott, MN ____ 32.1%	
Dakota, MN ____ 40.3%	Camden, MO ____ 37.4%	Johnson, KS ____ 31.4%	

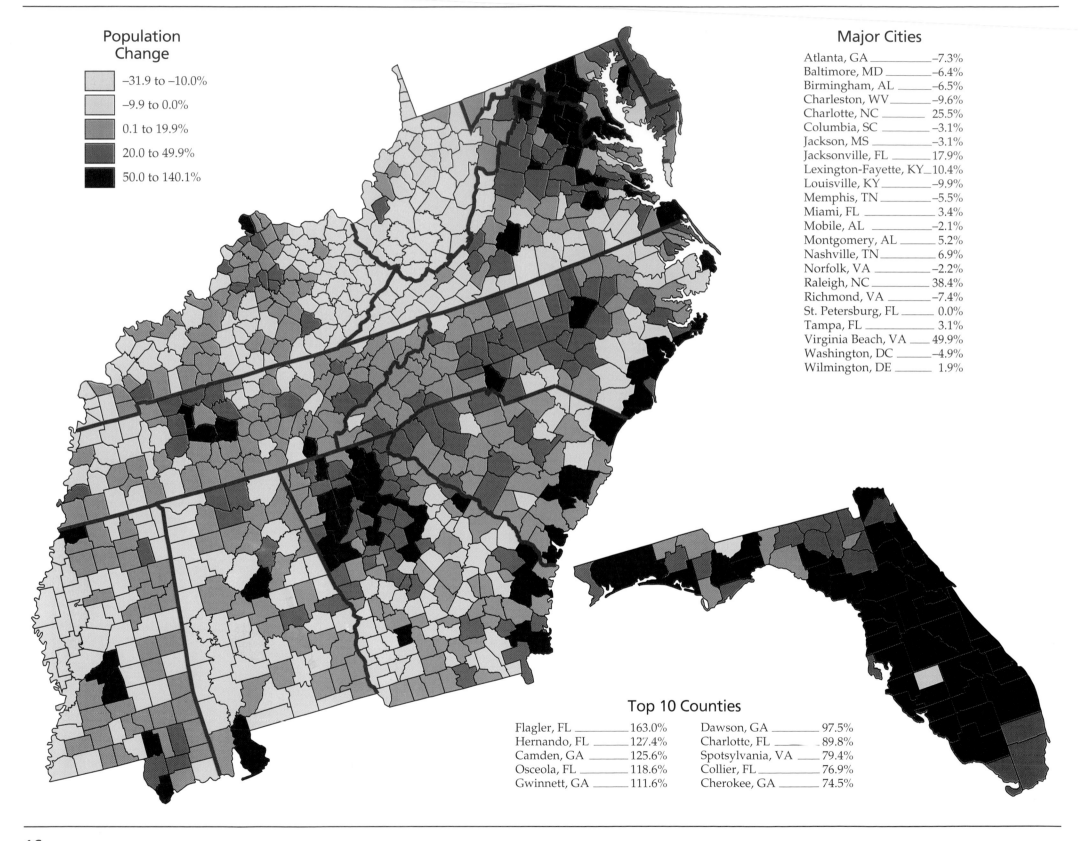

Population Change

- −31.9 to −10.0%
- −9.9 to 0.0%
- 0.1 to 19.9%
- 20.0 to 49.9%
- 50.0 to 140.1%

Major Cities

Atlanta, GA	−7.3%
Baltimore, MD	−6.4%
Birmingham, AL	−6.5%
Charleston, WV	−9.6%
Charlotte, NC	25.5%
Columbia, SC	−3.1%
Jackson, MS	−3.1%
Jacksonville, FL	17.9%
Lexington-Fayette, KY	10.4%
Louisville, KY	−9.9%
Memphis, TN	−5.5%
Miami, FL	3.4%
Mobile, AL	−2.1%
Montgomery, AL	5.2%
Nashville, TN	6.9%
Norfolk, VA	−2.2%
Raleigh, NC	38.4%
Richmond, VA	−7.4%
St. Petersburg, FL	0.0%
Tampa, FL	3.1%
Virginia Beach, VA	49.9%
Washington, DC	−4.9%
Wilmington, DE	1.9%

Top 10 Counties

Flagler, FL	163.0%	Dawson, GA	97.5%
Hernando, FL	127.4%	Charlotte, FL	89.8%
Camden, GA	125.6%	Spotsylvania, VA	79.4%
Osceola, FL	118.6%	Collier, FL	76.9%
Gwinnett, GA	111.6%	Cherokee, GA	74.5%

Top 10 Counties

Denton, TX ————— 91.1%
Collin, TX ————— 82.6%
Williamson, TX ——— 82.4%
Rockwall, TX ———— 76.2%
Fort Bend, TX ———— 72.1%
Hood, TX ———————— 63.6%
Hays, TX —————————— 61.6%
Bastrop, TX————————— 54.8%
Bandera, TX ———————— 49.1%
Starr, TX ————————— 48.6%

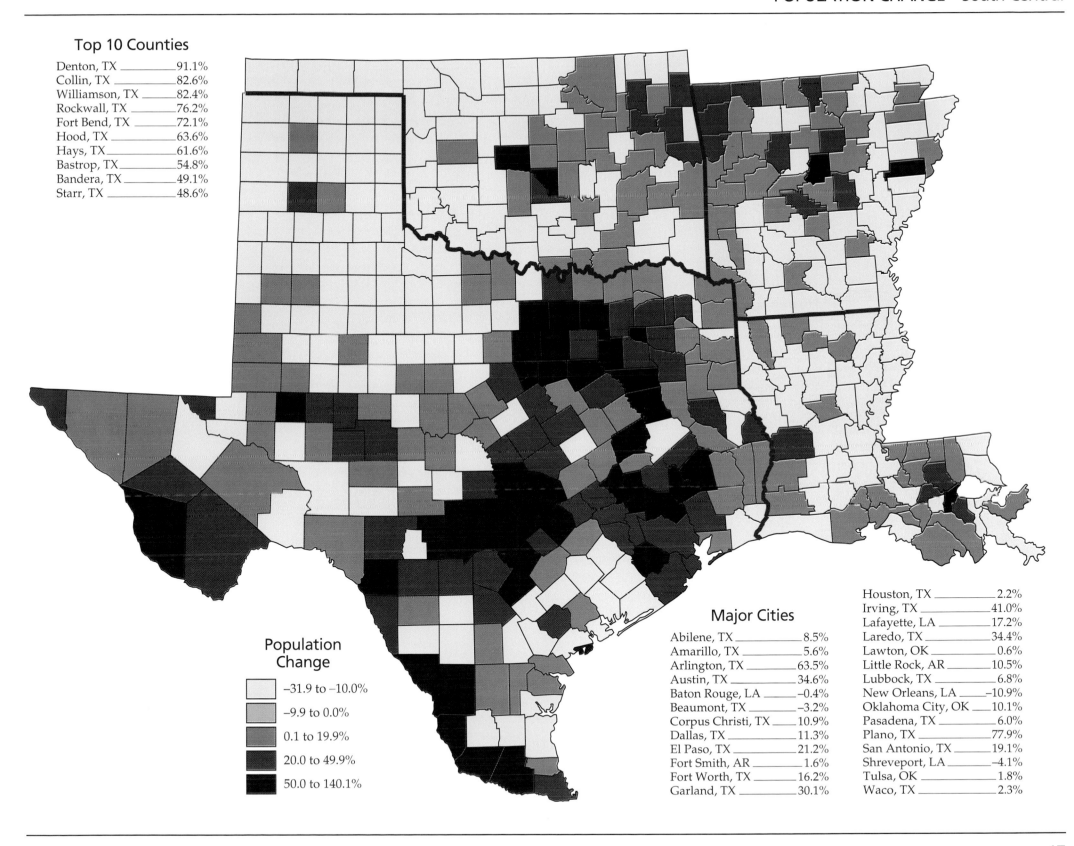

Population Change

- ⬜ −31.9 to −10.0%
- ▨ −9.9 to 0.0%
- ▦ 0.1 to 19.9%
- ▩ 20.0 to 49.9%
- ⬛ 50.0 to 140.1%

Major Cities

Abilene, TX ————— 8.5%
Amarillo, TX ———— 5.6%
Arlington, TX ———— 63.5%
Austin, TX ————— 34.6%
Baton Rouge, LA ——— −0.4%
Beaumont, TX ———— −3.2%
Corpus Christi, TX —— 10.9%
Dallas, TX ————— 11.3%
El Paso, TX ————— 21.2%
Fort Smith, AR ———— 1.6%
Fort Worth, TX ———— 16.2%
Garland, TX ———— 30.1%

Houston, TX ————— 2.2%
Irving, TX ————— 41.0%
Lafayette, LA ———— 17.2%
Laredo, TX ————— 34.4%
Lawton, OK ————— 0.6%
Little Rock, AR ———— 10.5%
Lubbock, TX ————— 6.8%
New Orleans, LA ——— −10.9%
Oklahoma City, OK — 10.1%
Pasadena, TX ———— 6.0%
Plano, TX ————— 77.9%
San Antonio, TX ——— 19.1%
Shreveport, LA ———— −4.1%
Tulsa, OK ————— 1.8%
Waco, TX ————— 2.3%

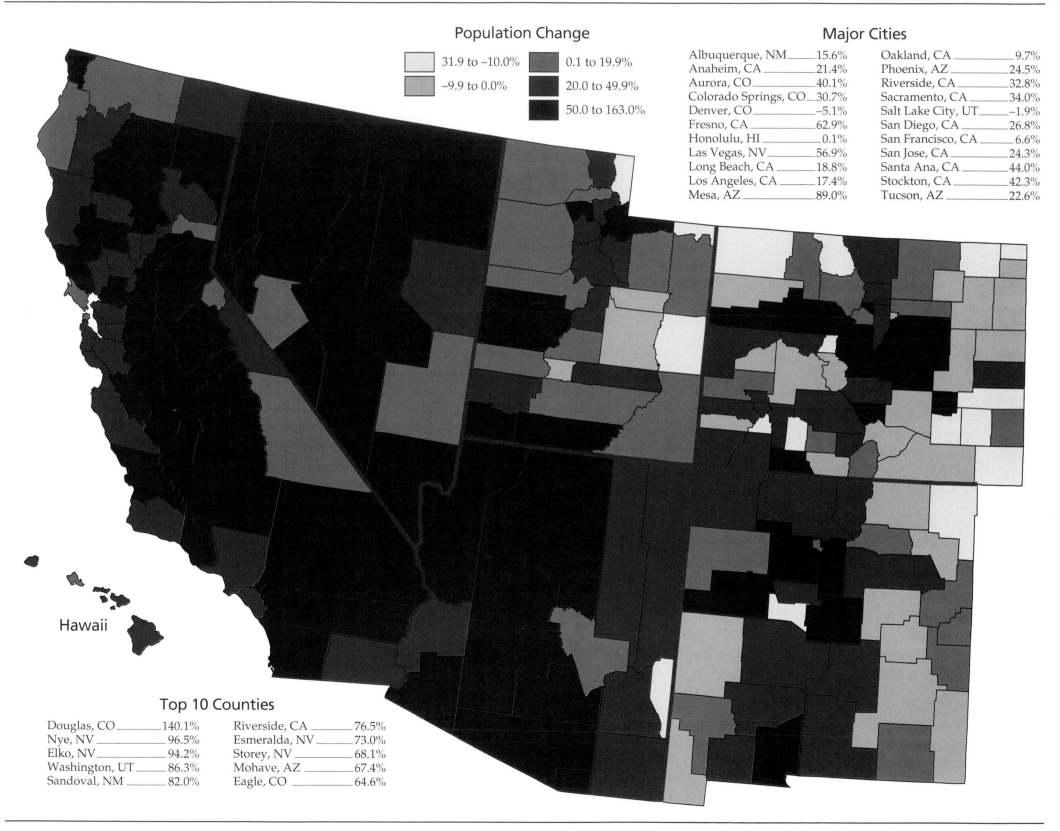

Population Change

- 31.9 to –10.0%
- –9.9 to 0.0%
- 0.1 to 19.9%
- 20.0 to 49.9%
- 50.0 to 163.0%

Major Cities

City	%	City	%
Albuquerque, NM	15.6%	Oakland, CA	9.7%
Anaheim, CA	21.4%	Phoenix, AZ	24.5%
Aurora, CO	40.1%	Riverside, CA	32.8%
Colorado Springs, CO	30.7%	Sacramento, CA	34.0%
Denver, CO	–5.1%	Salt Lake City, UT	–1.9%
Fresno, CA	62.9%	San Diego, CA	26.8%
Honolulu, HI	0.1%	San Francisco, CA	6.6%
Las Vegas, NV	56.9%	San Jose, CA	24.3%
Long Beach, CA	18.8%	Santa Ana, CA	44.0%
Los Angeles, CA	17.4%	Stockton, CA	42.3%
Mesa, AZ	89.0%	Tucson, AZ	22.6%

Hawaii

Top 10 Counties

County	%	County	%
Douglas, CO	140.1%	Riverside, CA	76.5%
Nye, NV	96.5%	Esmeralda, NV	73.0%
Elko, NV	94.2%	Storey, NV	68.1%
Washington, UT	86.3%	Mohave, AZ	67.4%
Sandoval, NM	82.0%	Eagle, CO	64.6%

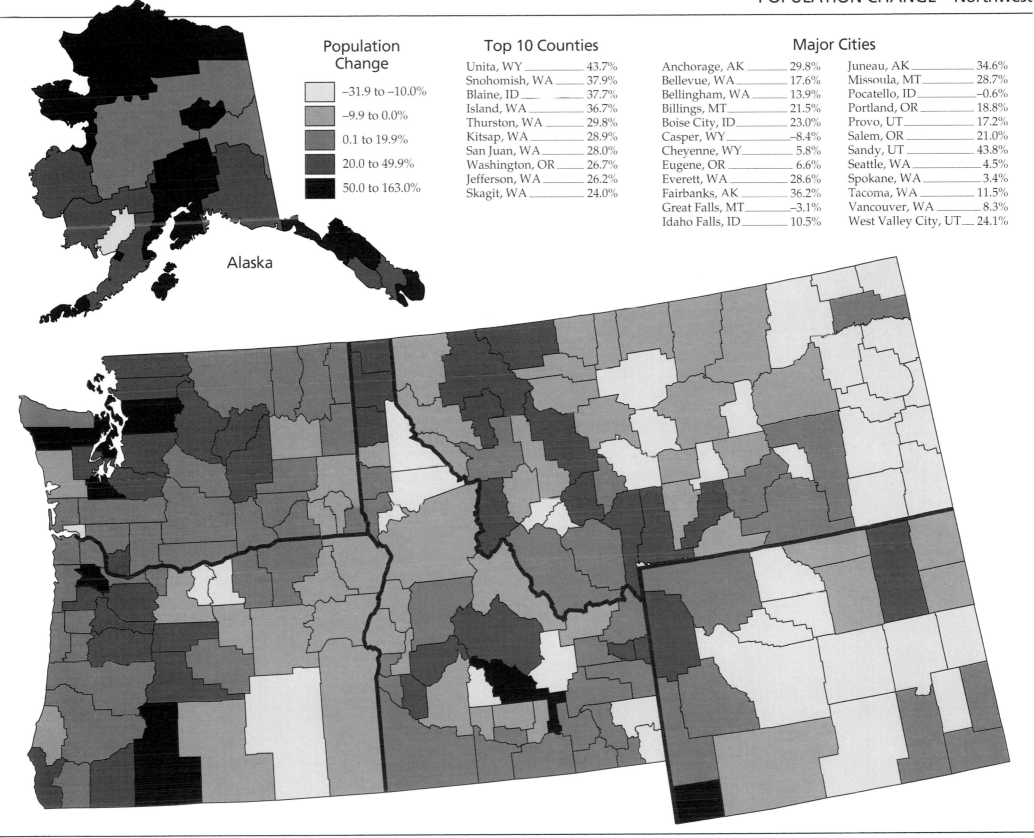

Population Change

- -31.9 to -10.0%
- -9.9 to 0.0%
- 0.1 to 19.9%
- 20.0 to 49.9%
- 50.0 to 163.0%

Top 10 Counties

County	Change
Unita, WY	43.7%
Snohomish, WA	37.9%
Blaine, ID	37.7%
Island, WA	36.7%
Thurston, WA	29.8%
Kitsap, WA	28.9%
San Juan, WA	28.0%
Washington, OR	26.7%
Jefferson, WA	26.2%
Skagit, WA	24.0%

Major Cities

City	Change	City	Change
Anchorage, AK	29.8%	Juneau, AK	34.6%
Bellevue, WA	17.6%	Missoula, MT	28.7%
Bellingham, WA	13.9%	Pocatello, ID	-0.6%
Billings, MT	21.5%	Portland, OR	18.8%
Boise City, ID	23.0%	Provo, UT	17.2%
Casper, WY	-8.4%	Salem, OR	21.0%
Cheyenne, WY	5.8%	Sandy, UT	43.8%
Eugene, OR	6.6%	Seattle, WA	4.5%
Everett, WA	28.6%	Spokane, WA	3.4%
Fairbanks, AK	36.2%	Tacoma, WA	11.5%
Great Falls, MT	-3.1%	Vancouver, WA	8.3%
Idaho Falls, ID	10.5%	West Valley City, UT	24.1%

Alaska

Natural Increase in Population, 1960 to 2025

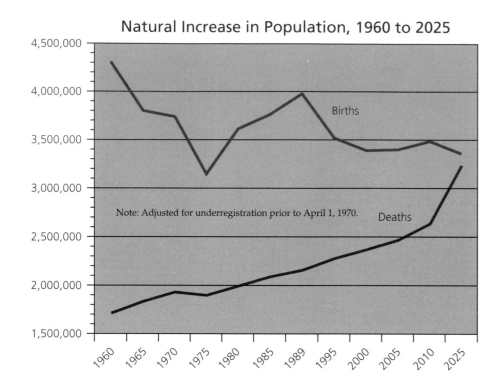

Births

Note: Adjusted for underregistration prior to April 1, 1970.

Deaths

Net Civilian Immigration, 1960 to 2025

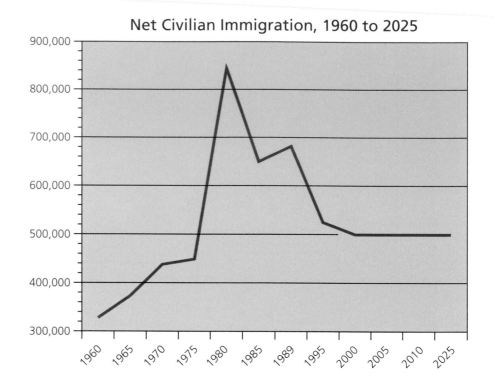

U.S. Bureau of the Census, *Current Population Reports*, series P–25, Nos. 1045 and 1057.

Net Growth Rate, 1960 to 2025

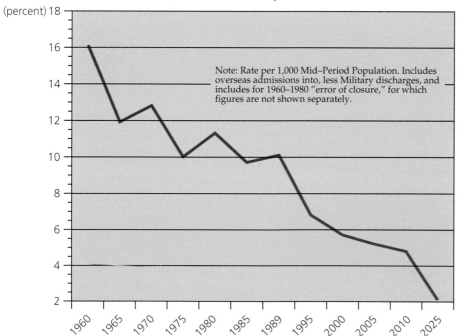

(percent)

Note: Rate per 1,000 Mid–Period Population. Includes overseas admissions into, less Military discharges, and includes for 1960–1980 "error of closure," for which figures are not shown separately.

Net Increase in Population, 1960 to 2025

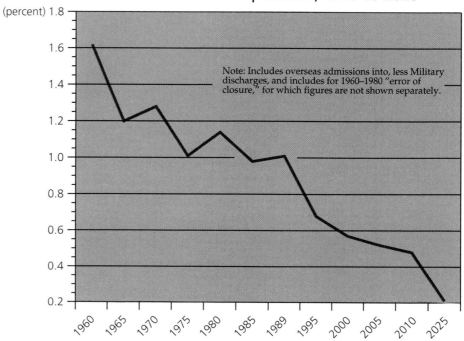

(percent)

Note: Includes overseas admissions into, less Military discharges, and includes for 1960–1980 "error of closure," for which figures are not shown separately.

Projections of the Total Population, by Age, Year 2000 (000s)

Age	Male	Female	White	Black	Other
Under 5 Years	8,661	8,237	13,324	2,748	826
5 to 17 Years	25,027	23,788	38,569	7,895	2,350
18 to 24 Years	12,770	12,461	19,998	3,924	1,309
25 to 34 Years	18,662	18,487	29,988	5,264	1,897
35 to 44 Years	21,945	21,966	36,574	5,481	1,856
45 to 54 Years	18,296	18,927	31,618	4,106	1,500
55 to 64 Years	11,557	12,601	20,667	2,578	912
65 to 74 Years	8,242	10,001	15,811	1,848	584
75+ Years	6,032	10,607	14,965	1,283	391

Source: U.S. Bureau of the Census, *Current Population Reports,* series P–25, No. 1018.

Projections of the Total Population, by Age and Sex, Year 2000

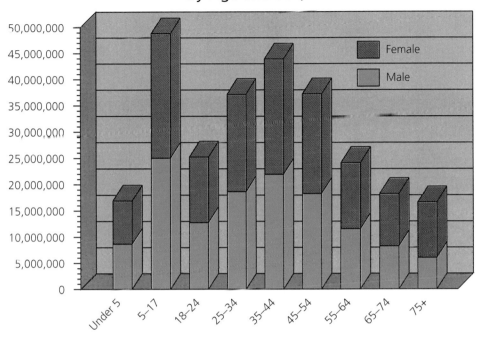

Projections of the Total Population, 1990 to 2010

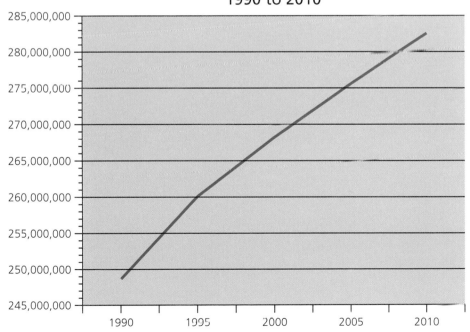

Projections of the Total Population, by Age and Race, Year 2000

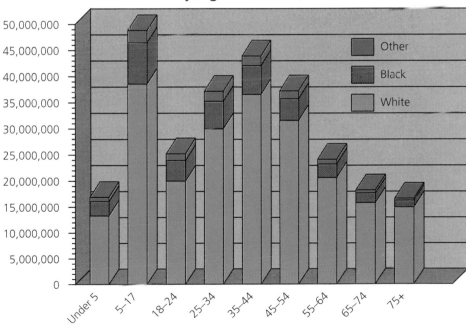

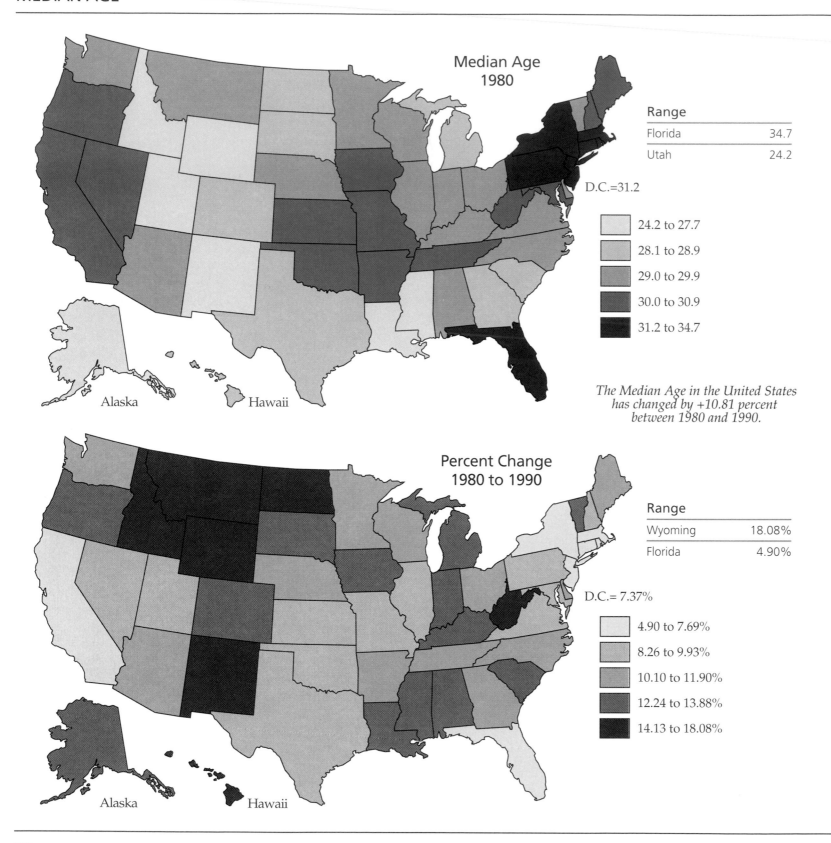

Median Age 1980

Range

Florida	34.7
Utah	24.2

D.C.=31.2

- 24.2 to 27.7
- 28.1 to 28.9
- 29.0 to 29.9
- 30.0 to 30.9
- 31.2 to 34.7

Alaska   Hawaii

The Median Age in the United States has changed by +10.81 percent between 1980 and 1990.

Percent Change 1980 to 1990

Range

Wyoming	18.08%
Florida	4.90%

D.C.= 7.37%

- 4.90 to 7.69%
- 8.26 to 9.93%
- 10.10 to 11.90%
- 12.24 to 13.88%
- 14.13 to 18.08%

Alaska   Hawaii

Median Age,1980

United States	29.6
Alabama	29.3
Alaska	26.1
Arizona	29.2
Arkansas	30.6
California	30.0
Colorado	28.6
Connecticut	32.0
Delaware	29.8
District of Columbia	31.2
Florida	34.7
Georgia	28.7
Hawaii	28.4
Idaho	27.6
Illinois	29.9
Indiana	29.2
Iowa	30.0
Kansas	30.1
Kentucky	29.2
Louisiana	27.4
Maine	30.4
Maryland	30.3
Massachusetts	31.2
Michigan	28.9
Minnesota	29.3
Mississippi	27.7
Missouri	30.9
Montana	29.0
Nebraska	29.8
Nevada	30.3
New Hampshire	30.2
New Jersey	32.2
New Mexico	27.4
New York	31.9
North Carolina	29.6
North Dakota	28.3
Ohio	29.9
Oklahoma	30.2
Oregon	30.3
Pennsylvania	32.1
Rhode Island	31.8
South Carolina	28.1
South Dakota	28.9
Tennessee	30.1
Texas	28.2
Utah	24.2
Vermont	29.4
Virginia	29.8
Washington	29.8
West Virginia	30.4
Wisconsin	29.4
Wyoming	27.1

Median Age, 1990

United States	32.8
Alabama	33.0
Alaska	29.4
Arizona	32.2
Arkansas	33.8
California	31.5
Colorado	32.5
Connecticut	34.4
Delaware	32.9
District of Columbia	33.5
Florida	36.4
Georgia	31.6
Hawaii	32.6
Idaho	31.5
Illinois	32.8
Indiana	32.8
Iowa	34.0
Kansas	32.9
Kentucky	33.0
Louisiana	31.0
Maine	33.9
Maryland	33.0
Massachusetts	33.6
Michigan	32.6
Minnesota	32.5
Mississippi	31.2
Missouri	33.5
Montana	33.8
Nebraska	33.0
Nevada	33.3
New Hampshire	32.8
New Jersey	34.5
New Mexico	31.3
New York	33.9
North Carolina	33.1
North Dakota	32.4
Ohio	33.3
Oklahoma	33.2
Oregon	34.5
Pennsylvania	35.0
Rhode Island	34.0
South Carolina	32.0
South Dakota	32.5
Tennessee	33.6
Texas	30.8
Utah	26.2
Vermont	33.0
Virginia	32.6
Washington	33.1
West Virginia	35.4
Wisconsin	32.9
Wyoming	32.0

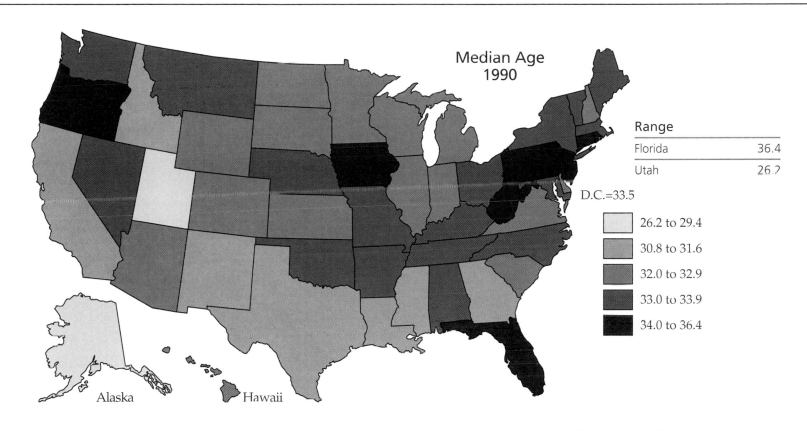

Median Age
1990

Range	
Florida	36.4
Utah	26.2

D.C.=33.5

- 26.2 to 29.4
- 30.8 to 31.6
- 32.0 to 32.9
- 33.0 to 33.9
- 34.0 to 36.4

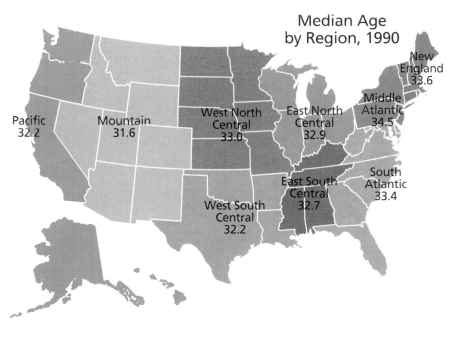

Median Age
by Region, 1990

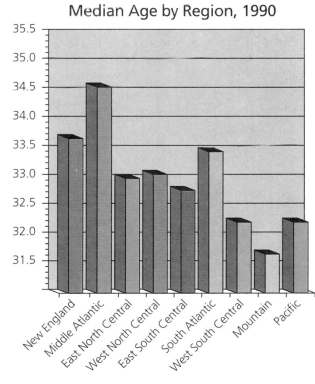

Median Age by Region, 1990

Major Cities

Boston, MA	26.3	Paterson, NJ	35.8
Bridgeport, CT	36.3	Philadelphia, PA	33.2
Buffalo, NY	35.6	Pittsburgh, PA	36.7
Burlington, VT	26.0	Portland, ME	29.4
Elizabeth, NJ	35.8	Providence, RI	29.4
Hartford, CT	35.3	Rochester, NY	28.8
Jersey City, NJ	33.1	Springfield, MA	29.3
Manchester, NH	27.9	Syracuse, NY	28.6
New Haven, CT	29.9	Waterbury, CT	36.3
New York, NY	36.4	Worcester, MA	28.8
Newark, NJ	33.4	Yonkers, NY	37.0

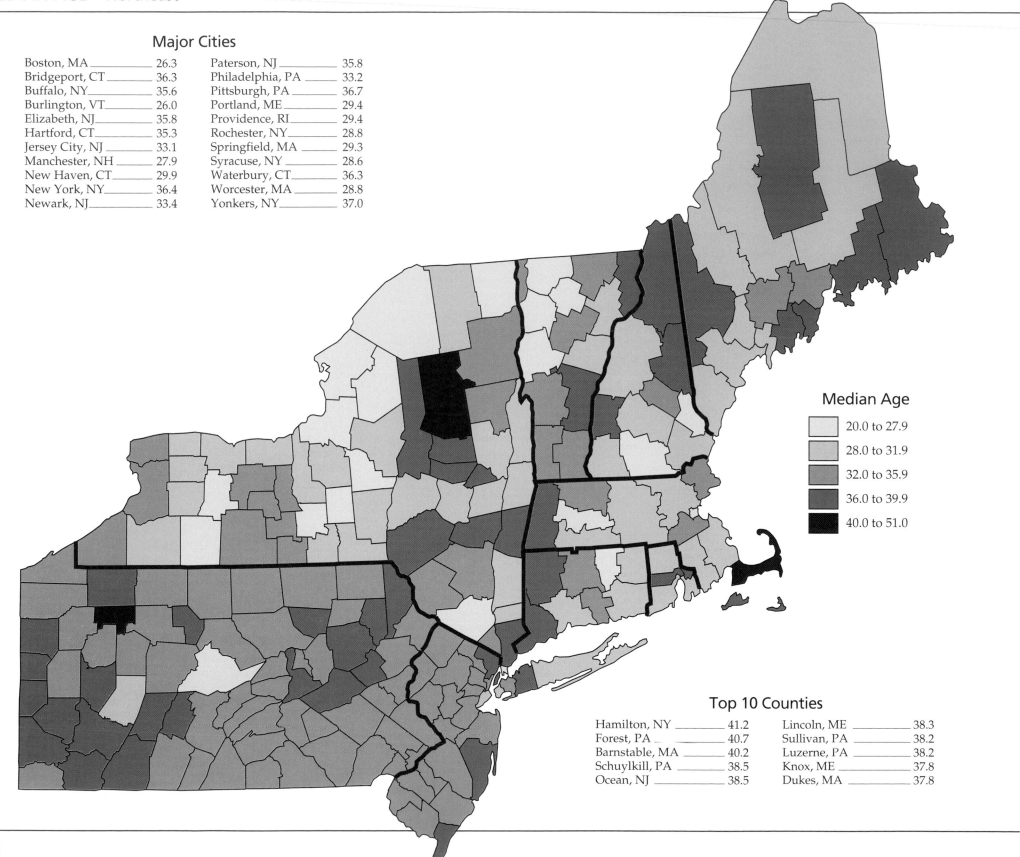

Median Age

- 20.0 to 27.9
- 28.0 to 31.9
- 32.0 to 35.9
- 36.0 to 39.9
- 40.0 to 51.0

Top 10 Counties

Hamilton, NY	41.2	Lincoln, ME	38.3
Forest, PA	40.7	Sullivan, PA	38.2
Barnstable, MA	40.2	Luzerne, PA	38.2
Schuylkill, PA	38.5	Knox, ME	37.8
Ocean, NJ	38.5	Dukes, MA	37.8

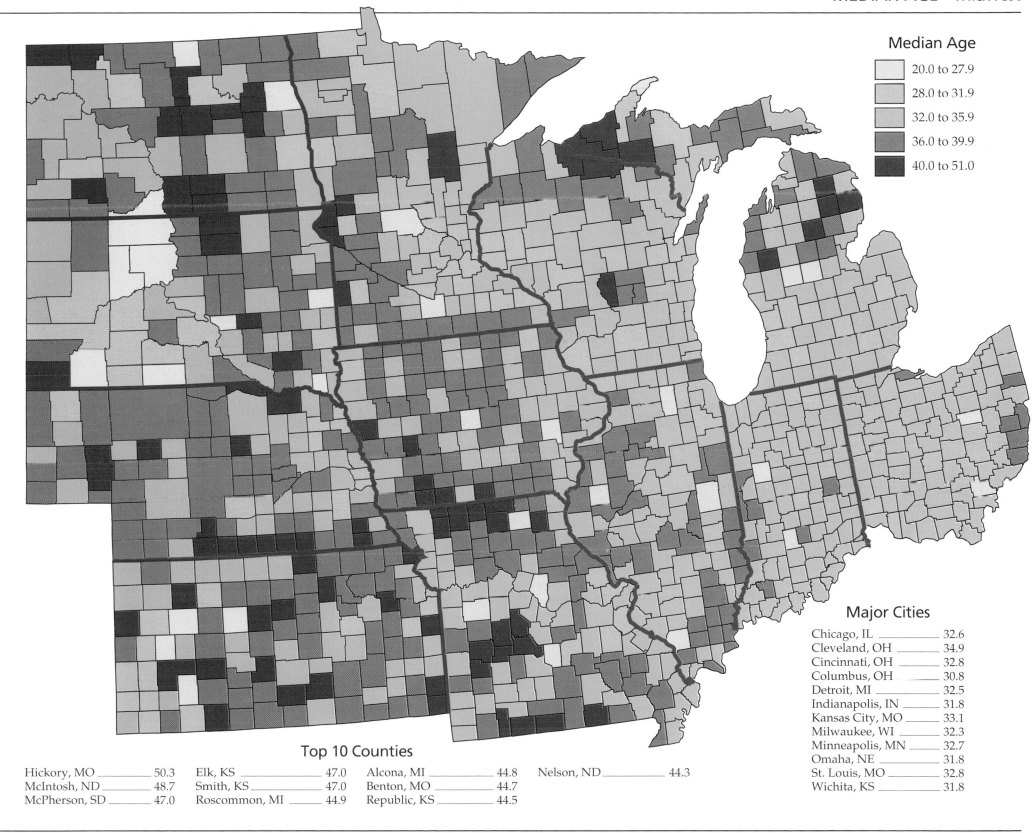

Median Age

- 20.0 to 27.9
- 28.0 to 31.9
- 32.0 to 35.9
- 36.0 to 39.9
- 40.0 to 51.0

Major Cities

Chicago, IL	32.6
Cleveland, OH	34.9
Cincinnati, OH	32.8
Columbus, OH	30.8
Detroit, MI	32.5
Indianapolis, IN	31.8
Kansas City, MO	33.1
Milwaukee, WI	32.3
Minneapolis, MN	32.7
Omaha, NE	31.8
St. Louis, MO	32.8
Wichita, KS	31.8

Top 10 Counties

Hickory, MO	50.3	Elk, KS	47.0	Alcona, MI	44.8	Nelson, ND	44.3
McIntosh, ND	48.7	Smith, KS	47.0	Benton, MO	44.7		
McPherson, SD	47.0	Roscommon, MI	44.9	Republic, KS	44.5		

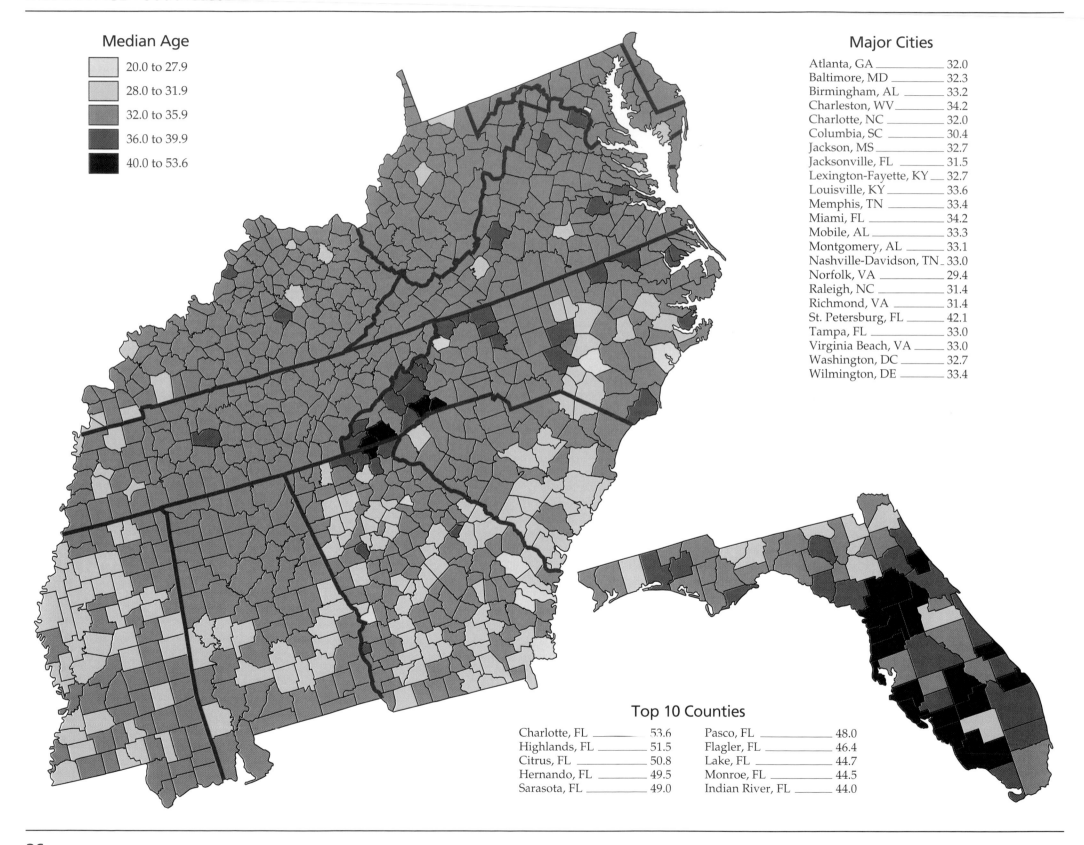

Median Age

- 20.0 to 27.9
- 28.0 to 31.9
- 32.0 to 35.9
- 36.0 to 39.9
- 40.0 to 53.6

Major Cities

Atlanta, GA	32.0
Baltimore, MD	32.3
Birmingham, AL	33.2
Charleston, WV	34.2
Charlotte, NC	32.0
Columbia, SC	30.4
Jackson, MS	32.7
Jacksonville, FL	31.5
Lexington-Fayette, KY	32.7
Louisville, KY	33.6
Memphis, TN	33.4
Miami, FL	34.2
Mobile, AL	33.3
Montgomery, AL	33.1
Nashville-Davidson, TN	33.0
Norfolk, VA	29.4
Raleigh, NC	31.4
Richmond, VA	31.4
St. Petersburg, FL	42.1
Tampa, FL	33.0
Virginia Beach, VA	33.0
Washington, DC	32.7
Wilmington, DE	33.4

Top 10 Counties

Charlotte, FL	53.6	Pasco, FL	48.0
Highlands, FL	51.5	Flagler, FL	46.4
Citrus, FL	50.8	Lake, FL	44.7
Hernando, FL	49.5	Monroe, FL	44.5
Sarasota, FL	49.0	Indian River, FL	44.0

Top 10 Counties

Llano, TX	50.1
Sabine, TX	45.2
Sevier, AR	44.8
Coke, TX	44.0
Izard, AR	43.9
Baxter, AR	43.6
Hamilton, TX	43.5
Motley, TX	43.4
Union, AR	43.2
Hall, TX	42.9

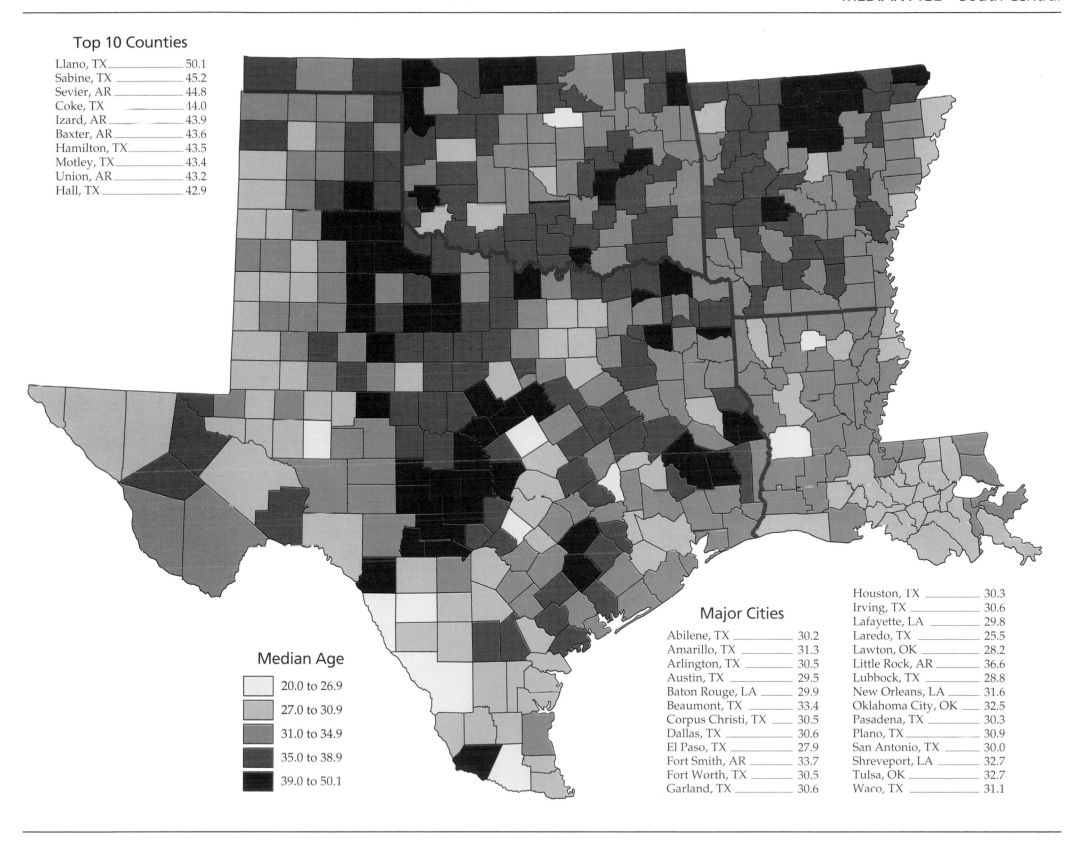

Median Age

	20.0 to 26.9
	27.0 to 30.9
	31.0 to 34.9
	35.0 to 38.9
	39.0 to 50.1

Major Cities

Abilene, TX	30.2	Houston, TX	30.3
Amarillo, TX	31.3	Irving, TX	30.6
Arlington, TX	30.5	Lafayette, LA	29.8
Austin, TX	29.5	Laredo, TX	25.5
Baton Rouge, LA	29.9	Lawton, OK	28.2
Beaumont, TX	33.4	Little Rock, AR	36.6
Corpus Christi, TX	30.5	Lubbock, TX	28.8
Dallas, TX	30.6	New Orleans, LA	31.6
El Paso, TX	27.9	Oklahoma City, OK	32.5
Fort Smith, AR	33.7	Pasadena, TX	30.3
Fort Worth, TX	30.5	Plano, TX	30.9
Garland, TX	30.6	San Antonio, TX	30.0
		Shreveport, LA	32.7
		Tulsa, OK	32.7
		Waco, TX	31.1

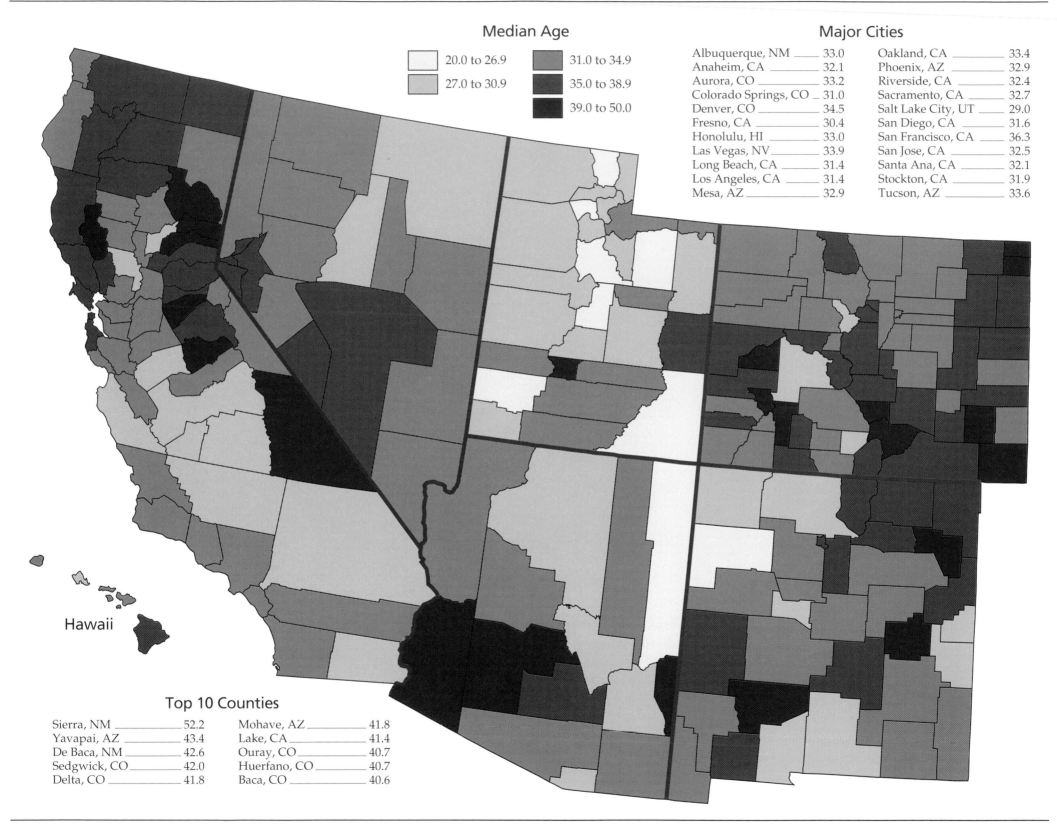

Median Age

20.0 to 26.9	31.0 to 34.9
27.0 to 30.9	35.0 to 38.9
	39.0 to 50.0

Major Cities

Albuquerque, NM	33.0	Oakland, CA	33.4
Anaheim, CA	32.1	Phoenix, AZ	32.9
Aurora, CO	33.2	Riverside, CA	32.4
Colorado Springs, CO	31.0	Sacramento, CA	32.7
Denver, CO	34.5	Salt Lake City, UT	29.0
Fresno, CA	30.4	San Diego, CA	31.6
Honolulu, HI	33.0	San Francisco, CA	36.3
Las Vegas, NV	33.9	San Jose, CA	32.5
Long Beach, CA	31.4	Santa Ana, CA	32.1
Los Angeles, CA	31.4	Stockton, CA	31.9
Mesa, AZ	32.9	Tucson, AZ	33.6

Hawaii

Top 10 Counties

Sierra, NM	52.2	Mohave, AZ	41.8
Yavapai, AZ	43.4	Lake, CA	41.4
De Baca, NM	42.6	Ouray, CO	40.7
Sedgwick, CO	42.0	Huerfano, CO	40.7
Delta, CO	41.8	Baca, CO	40.6

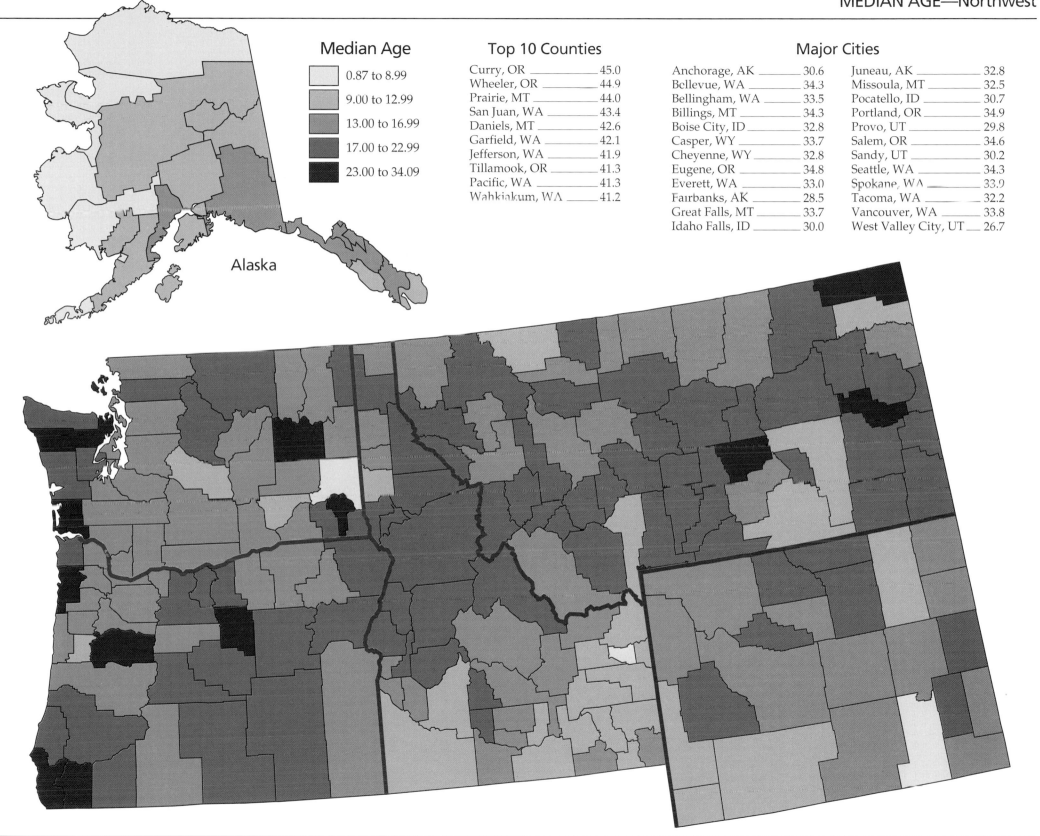

Median Age

	0.87 to 8.99
	9.00 to 12.99
	13.00 to 16.99
	17.00 to 22.99
	23.00 to 34.09

Alaska

Top 10 Counties

Curry, OR	45.0
Wheeler, OR	44.9
Prairie, MT	44.0
San Juan, WA	43.4
Daniels, MT	42.6
Garfield, WA	42.1
Jefferson, WA	41.9
Tillamook, OR	41.3
Pacific, WA	41.3
Wahkiakum, WA	41.2

Major Cities

Anchorage, AK	30.6	Juneau, AK	32.8
Bellevue, WA	34.3	Missoula, MT	32.5
Bellingham, WA	33.5	Pocatello, ID	30.7
Billings, MT	34.3	Portland, OR	34.9
Boise City, ID	32.8	Provo, UT	29.8
Casper, WY	33.7	Salem, OR	34.6
Cheyenne, WY	32.8	Sandy, UT	30.2
Eugene, OR	34.8	Seattle, WA	34.3
Everett, WA	33.0	Spokane, WA	33.9
Fairbanks, AK	28.5	Tacoma, WA	32.2
Great Falls, MT	33.7	Vancouver, WA	33.8
Idaho Falls, ID	30.0	West Valley City, UT	26.7

Total Population, by Sex, Race, and Age (in thousands), 1989

Age	Total	Male	Female	White	Black
Under 5 yrs old	18,752	9,598	9,155	15,050	2,890
Under 1 yr old	3,945	2,020	1,925	3,163	619
1 yr old	3,717	1,904	1,813	2,983	577
2 yrs old	3,660	1,872	1,788	2,931	567
3 yrs old	3,710	1,898	1,812	2,983	561
4 yrs old	3,721	1,904	1,816	2,989	565
5–9 yrs old	18,212	9,321	8,891	14,628	2,802
5 yrs old	3,605	1,844	1,761	2,895	550
6 yrs old	3,678	1,883	1,795	2,959	558
7 yrs old	3,733	1,910	1,822	3,000	573
8 yrs old	3,573	1,831	1,742	2,874	549
9 yrs old	3,624	1,853	1,770	2,900	573
10–14 yrs old	16,950	8,689	8,260	13,574	2,679
10 yrs old	3,563	1,826	1,737	2,846	571
11 yrs old	3,418	1,751	1,667	2,740	540
12 yrs old	3,384	1,735	1,649	2,712	534
13 yrs old	3,257	1,668	1,589	2,608	513
14 yrs old	3,327	1,708	1,619	2,668	522
15–19 yrs old	17,847	9,123	8,725	14,367	2,767
15 yrs old	3,278	1,681	1,598	2,619	520
16 yrs old	3,355	1,718	1,637	2,672	542
17 yrs old	3,536	1,815	1,720	2,832	561
18 yrs old	3,794	1,936	1,858	3,068	583
19 yrs old	3,884	1,973	1,911	3,177	561
20–24 yrs old	18,886	9,529	9,356	15,490	2,695
20 yrs old	3,772	1,913	1,859	3,078	549
21 yrs old	3,625	1,835	1,790	2,964	523
22 yrs old	3,671	1,851	1,820	3,014	521
23 yrs old	3,777	1,899	1,879	3,101	538
24 yrs old	4,040	2,031	2,008	3,332	563
25–29 yrs old	21,830	10,979	10,851	18,192	2,861
25 yrs old	4,242	2,136	2,106	3,519	571
26 yrs old	4,282	2,153	2,128	3,564	566
27 yrs old	4,400	2,210	2,191	3,666	578
28 yrs old	4,326	2,173	2,153	3,618	555
29 yrs old	4,580	2,307	2,273	3,825	591
30-34 yrs old	22,218	11,151	11,068	18,622	2,767
30 yrs old	4,575	2,299	2,276	3,812	590
31 yrs old	4,483	2,251	2,233	3,764	552
32 yrs old	4,507	2,263	2,244	3,778	561
33 yrs old	4,297	2,149	2,147	3,602	527
34 yrs old	4,357	2,189	2,168	3,666	536
35–39 yrs old	19,676	5,782	9,894	16,664	2,273
35 yrs old	4,204	2,101	2,103	3,545	504
36 yrs old	4,033	2,008	2,025	3,417	462
37 yrs old	3,934	1,954	1,980	3,332	456
3 yrs old	3,744	1,853	1,891	3,183	419
39 yrs old	3,762	1,866	1,896	3,187	431
40–44 yrs old	16,908	8,319	8,589	14,571	1,731
40 yrs old	3,761	1,856	1,905	3,200	419
41 yrs old	3,583	1,768	1,815	3,091	364
42 yrs oid	3,855	1,903	1,952	3,376	357
43 yrs old	2,825	1,381	1,444	2,430	287
44 yrs old	2,885	1,411	1,473	2,474	303
45–49 yrs old	13,528	6,608	6,921	11,678	1,396
45 yrs old	2,846	1,391	1,455	2,447	299
46 yrs old	3,068	1,499	1,569	2,676	296
47 yrs old	2,748	1,339	1,409	2,359	296
48 yrs old	2,440	1,193	1,247	2,112	246
49 yrs old	2,427	1,185	1,241	2,083	260
50–54 yrs old	11,377	5,511	5,866	9,790	1,223

Age	Total	Male	Female	White	Black
50 yrs old	2,411	1,165	1,247	2,063	267
51 yrs old	2,312	1,123	1,189	1,991	245
52 yrs old	2,209	1,070	1,139	1,896	240
53 yrs old	2,210	1,073	1,137	1,908	234
54 yrs old	2,235	1,079	1,155	1,931	237
55–59 yrs old	10,726	5,121	5,605	9,310	1,116
55 yrs old	2,102	1,010	1,092	1,809	228
56 yrs old	2,076	995	1,081	1,796	219
57 yrs old	2,176	1,039	1,137	1,886	230
58 yrs old	2,163	1,027	1,135	1,886	219
59 yrs old	2,209	1,049	1,160	1,933	219
60–64 yrs old	10,867	5,079	5,788	9,569	1,035
60 yrs old	2,229	1,053	1,176	1,937	234
61 yrs old	2,235	1,053	1,182	1,970	212
62 yrs old	2,114	984	1,129	1,858	203
63 yrs old	2,103	978	1,125	1,859	194
64 yrs old	2,187	1,010	1,176	1,945	192
65–69 yrs old	10,170	4,631	5,538	9,029	916
65 yrs old	2,175	1,001	1,174	1,921	204
66 yrs old	2,045	935	1,111	1,812	187
67 yrs old	2,089	954	1,135	1,857	186
68 yrs old	1,987	905	1,082	1,781	164
69 yrs old	1,874	837	1,037	1,657	176
70–74 yrs old	8,012	3,464	4,549	7,193	661
70 yrs old	1,741	772	969	1,552	154
71 yrs old	1,708	751	956	1,541	134
72 yrs old	1,619	700	918	1,457	131
73 yrs old	1,487	632	855	1,338	120
74 yrs old	1,458	608	850	1,306	123
75–79 yrs old	6,033	2,385	3,648	5,430	486
75 yrs old	1,376	566	811	1,237	113
76 yrs old	1,297	521	776	1,165	106
77 yrs old	1,212	476	735	1,089	98
78 yrs old	1,120	432	688	1,009	89
79 yrs old	1,028	391	637	930	79
80–84 yrs old	3,728	1,306	2,422	3,409	256
80 yrs old	921	338	583	832	72
81 yrs old	815	290	526	750	51
82 yrs old	720	253	467	661	47
83 yrs old	669	228	441	614	44
84 yrs old	603	198	405	552	42
85–89 yrs old	1,962	588	1,374	1,791	142
85 yrs old	515	164	351	470	37
86 yrs old	448	137	311	408	32
87 yrs old	387	114	272	353	28
88 yrs old	332	95	237	303	24
89 yrs old	281	78	203	257	20
90–94 yrs old	790	195	594	719	61
90 yrs old	234	62	171	213	17
91 yrs old	190	48	142	174	14
92 yrs old	151	36	115	138	12
93 yrs old	117	26	91	107	9
94 yrs old	97	23	74	87	9
95–99 yrs old	229	53	176	200	25
95 yrs old	77	19	59	69	8
96 yrs old	58	14	44	51	6
97 yrsold	42	10	32	37	5
98 yrs old	30	7	23	25	4
99 yrs old	22	5	17	19	3
100 yrs old and over	61	13	48	50	9

Source: U.S. Bureau of the Census, *Current Population Reports*, series P–25, Nos. 1045 and 1057.

Projections of the Hispanic Population, 1995 to 2010

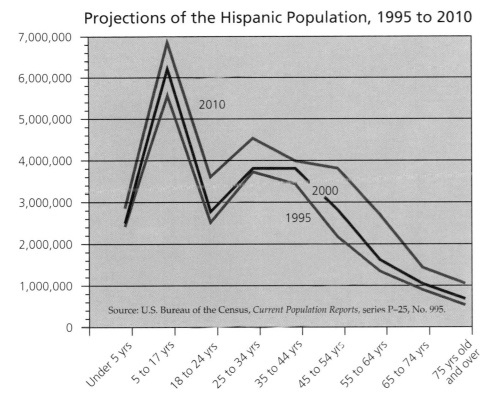

Source: U.S. Bureau of the Census, *Current Population Reports*, series P–25, No. 995.

Percent Change, Hispanic Population, 1990 to 2010

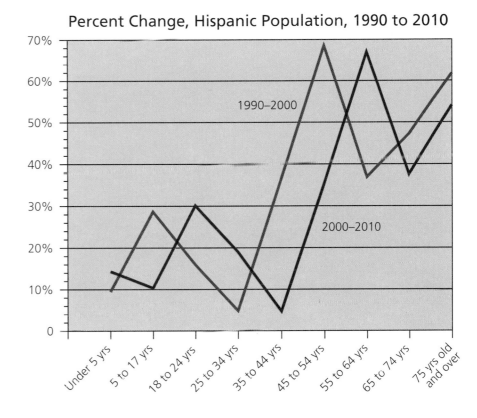

Total Population Under 5 and Over 65, 1960 to 1989

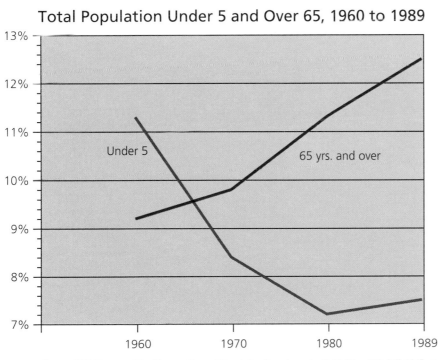

Source: U.S. Bureau of the Census, *Current Population Reports*, series P–25, Nos. 519, 917, 1045, and 1057.

Total Population 5 to 13 yrs. and 14 to 17 yrs., 1960 to 1989

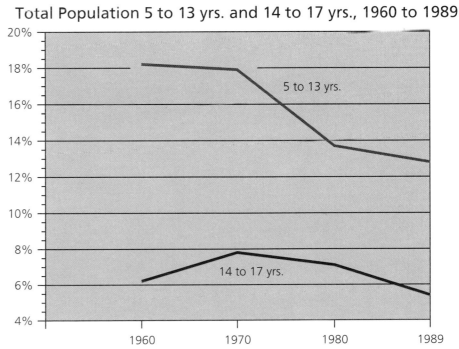

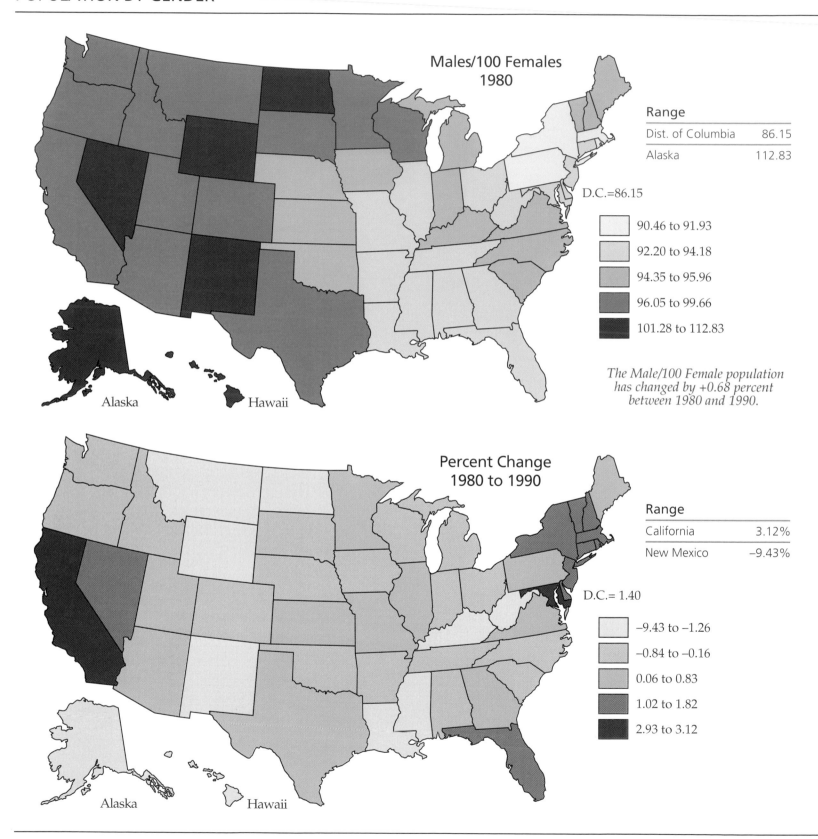

Males/100 Females 1980

Range

Dist. of Columbia	86.15
Alaska	112.83

D.C.=86.15

- 90.46 to 91.93
- 92.20 to 94.18
- 94.35 to 95.96
- 96.05 to 99.66
- 101.28 to 112.83

The Male/100 Female population has changed by +0.68 percent between 1980 and 1990.

Alaska   Hawaii

Percent Change 1980 to 1990

Range

California	3.12%
New Mexico	−9.43%

D.C.= 1.40

- −9.43 to −1.26
- −0.84 to −0.16
- 0.06 to 0.83
- 1.02 to 1.82
- 2.93 to 3.12

Alaska   Hawaii

Male Population, 1980

United States	110,053,161
Alabama	1,871,534
Alaska	213,041
Arizona	1,337,942
Arkansas	1,104,688
California	11,666,485
Colorado	1,434,293
Connecticut	1,498,005
Delaware	288,599
District of Columbia	295,417
Florida	4,675,626
Georgia	2,640,445
Hawaii	494,683
Idaho	471,155
Illinois	5,537,537
Indiana	2,665,825
Iowa	1,416,390
Kansas	1,156,941
Kentucky	1,789,039
Louisiana	2,039,894
Maine	546,235
Maryland	2,042,810
Massachusetts	2,730,893
Michigan	4,516,189
Minnesota	1,997,826
Mississippi	1,213,878
Missouri	2,365,487
Montana	392,625
Nebraska	765,894
Nevada	405,060
New Hampshire	448,462
New Jersey	3,533,012
New Mexico	642,157
New York	8,339,422
North Carolina	2,855,385
North Dakota	328,426
Ohio	5,217,137
Oklahoma	1,476,705
Oregon	1,296,566
Pennsylvania	5,682,590
Rhode Island	451,251
South Carolina	1,518,013
South Dakota	340,683
Tennessee	2,216,600
Texas	6,998,723
Utah	724,501
Vermont	249,080
Virginia	2,618,310
Washington	2,052,307
West Virginia	945,408
Wisconsin	2,305,427
Wyoming	240,560

Male Population, 1990

United States	121,302,418
Alabama	1,936,162
Alaska	289,867
Arizona	1,810,691
Arkansas	1,133,076
California	14,897,627
Colorado	1,631,295
Connecticut	1,592,873
Delaware	322,968
District of Columbia	282,970
Florida	6,261,719
Georgia	3,144,503
Hawaii	563,891
Idaho	500,956
Illinois	5,552,233
Indiana	2,688,281
Iowa	1,344,802
Kansas	1,214,645
Kentucky	1,785,235
Louisiana	2,031,386
Maine	597,850
Maryland	2,381,671
Massachusetts	2,888,745
Michigan	4,512,781
Minnesota	2,145,183
Mississippi	1,230,617
Missouri	2,464,315
Montana	395,769
Nebraska	769,439
Nevada	611,880
New Hampshire	543,544
New Jersey	3,735,685
New Mexico	745,253
New York	8,625,673
North Carolina	3,214,290
North Dakota	318,201
Ohio	5,226,340
Oklahoma	1,530,819
Oregon	1,397,073
Pennsylvania	5,694,265
Rhode Island	481,496
South Carolina	1,688,510
South Dakota	342,498
Tennessee	2,348,928
Texas	8,365,963
Utah	855,759
Vermont	275,492
Virginia	3,033,974
Washington	2,413,747
West Virginia	861,536
Wisconsin	2,392,935
Wyoming	227,007

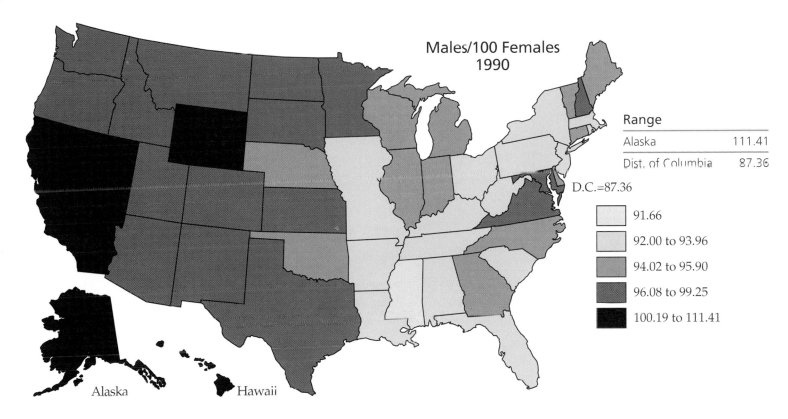

Males/100 Females
1990

Range

Alaska	111.41
Dist. of Columbia	87.36

D.C.=87.36

- 91.66
- 92.00 to 93.96
- 94.02 to 95.90
- 96.08 to 99.25
- 100.19 to 111.41

Alaska

Hawaii

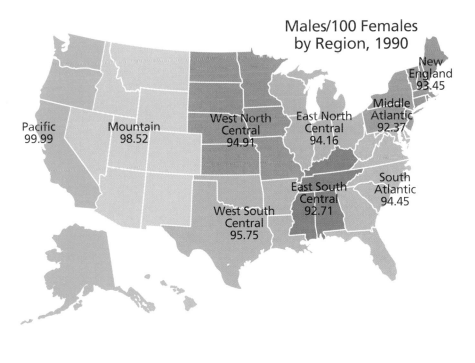

Males/100 Females
by Region, 1990

Pacific 99.99

Mountain 98.52

West North Central 94.91

East North Central 94.16

Middle Atlantic 92.37

New England 93.45

West South Central 95.75

East South Central 92.71

South Atlantic 94.45

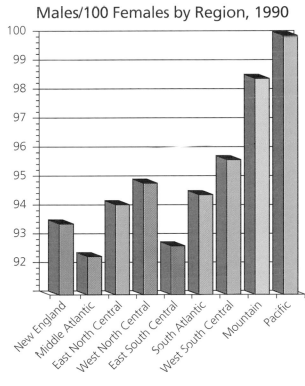

Males/100 Females by Region, 1990

New England, Middle Atlantic, East North Central, West North Central, East South Central, South Atlantic, West South Central, Mountain, Pacific

Resident Population by Age and Sex—1970

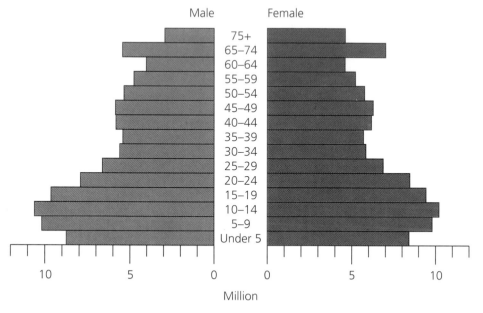

Source: U.S. Bureau of the Census, *Current Population Reports*, series P–25, Nos. 1045 and 1057.

Resident Population by Age and Sex—1980

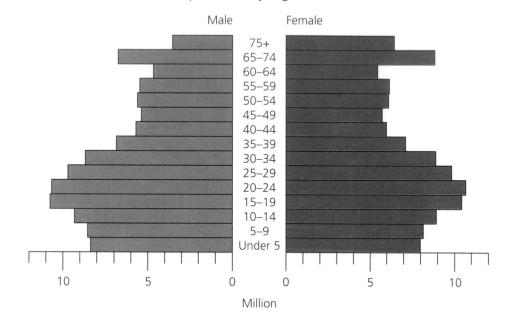

Resident Population by Age and Sex—1989

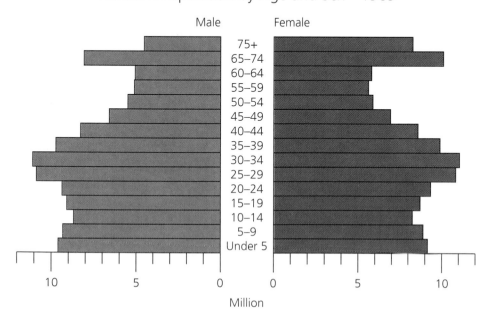

Total Population, 1910–1990

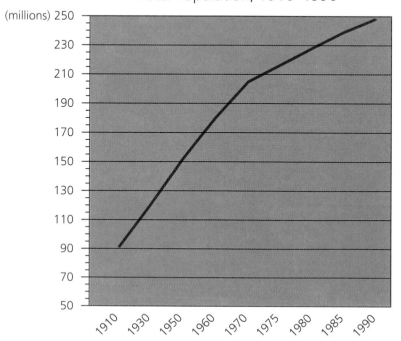

White Population by Age and Sex, 1989

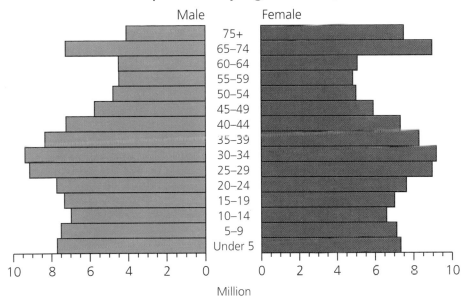

Male   Female

75+
65–74
60–64
55–59
50–54
45–49
40–44
35–39
30–34
25–29
20–24
15–19
10–14
5–9
Under 5

10 8 6 4 2 0   0 2 4 6 8 10

Million

African American Population by Age and Sex, 1989

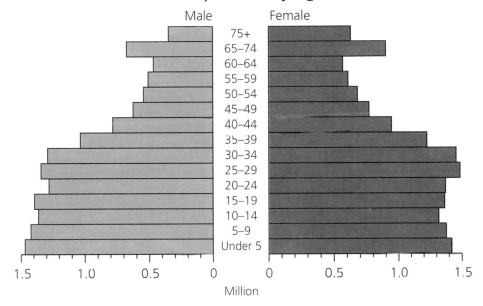

Male   Female

75+
65–74
60–64
55–59
50–54
45–49
40–44
35–39
30–34
25–29
20–24
15–19
10–14
5–9
Under 5

1.5 1.0 0.5 0   0 0.5 1.0 1.5

Million

Source: U.S. Bureau of the Census, *Current Population Reports*, series P–25, Nos. 917, 1045, and 1057.

Other Races Population by Age and Sex, 1989

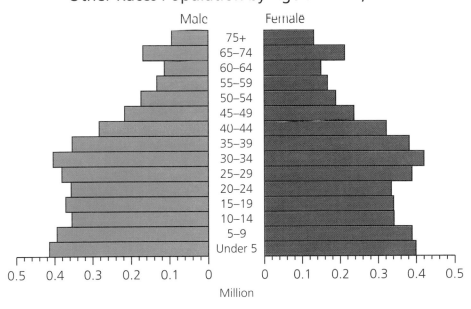

Male   Female

75+
65–74
60–64
55–59
50–54
45–49
40–44
35–39
30–34
25–29
20–24
15–19
10–14
5–9
Under 5

0.5 0.4 0.3 0.2 0.1 0   0 0.1 0.2 0.3 0.4 0.5

Million

Total Population, by Age (000's), 1970 to 1989

Age	1970	1980	1989
Under 5 Years	17,163	16,348	18,752
5 to 9 Years	19,969	16,700	18,212
10 to 14 Years	20,804	18,242	16,950
15 to 19 Years	19,084	21,168	17,812
20 to 24 Years	16,383	21,319	18,702
25 to 29 Years	13,486	19,521	21,699
30 to 34 Years	11,437	17,561	22,135
35 to 39 Years	11,113	13,965	19,621
40 to 44 Years	11,988	11,669	16,882
45 to 49 Years	12,124	11,090	13,521
50 to 54 Years	11,111	11,710	11,375
55 to 59 Years	9,979	11,615	10,726
60 to 64 Years	8,623	10,088	10,867
65 to 74 Years	12,443	15,581	18,182
75+ Years	7,530	9,969	12,802

Population Projections through Year 2025, by Race

	Projections			Population			
Year	Low	Middle	High	White	Black	Other	Hispanic
1991	250,178	252,502	254,570	211,993	31,571	8,938	N/A
1992	251,592	254,521	257,835	213,301	31,988	9,232	N/A
1993	252,906	256,466	259,888	214,542	32,398	9,527	N/A
1994	254,121	258,338	262,526	215,714	32,801	9,823	N/A
1995	255,239	260,138	265,151	216,820	33,199	10,119	22,550
1996	256,266	261,872	267,788	217,862	33,592	10,418	N/A
1997	257,207	263,543	270,376	218,845	33,981	10,717	N/A
1998	258,068	265,157	272,986	219,773	34,366	11,017	N/A
1999	258,856	266,730	275,602	220,661	34,749	11,320	N/A
2000	259,576	268,266	278,228	221,514	35,129	11,624	25,223
2005	262,363	275,604	291,710	225,424	37,003	13,177	27,959
2010	264,193	282,575	305,882	228,978	38,833	14,764	30,795
2015	265,072	288,997	320,494	232,081	40,564	16,352	N/A
2020	264,536	294,364	335,022	234,330	42,128	17,906	N/A
2025	262,218	298,252	348,985	235,369	43,473	19,410	N/A

Source: U.S. Bureau of the Census. Current Population Reports, series P–25, No. 1018.

Various Population Projections through Year 2025

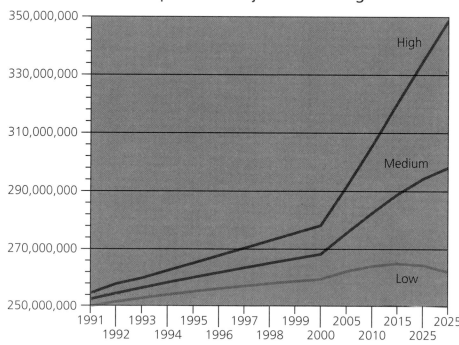

U.S. Population Projected through Year 2025, by Race
Middle Series

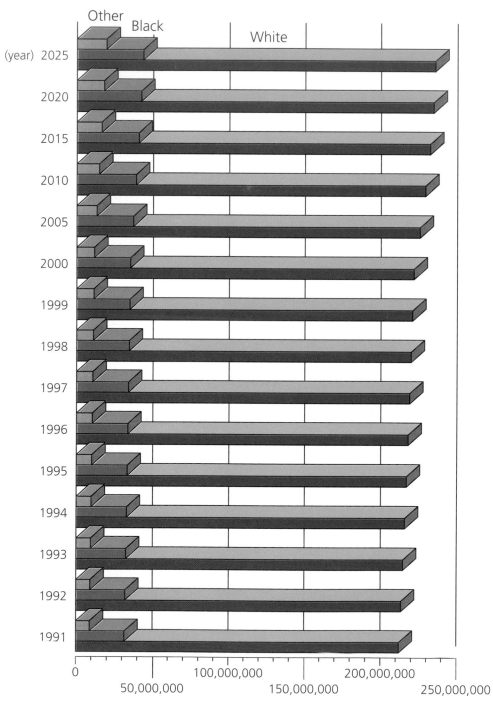

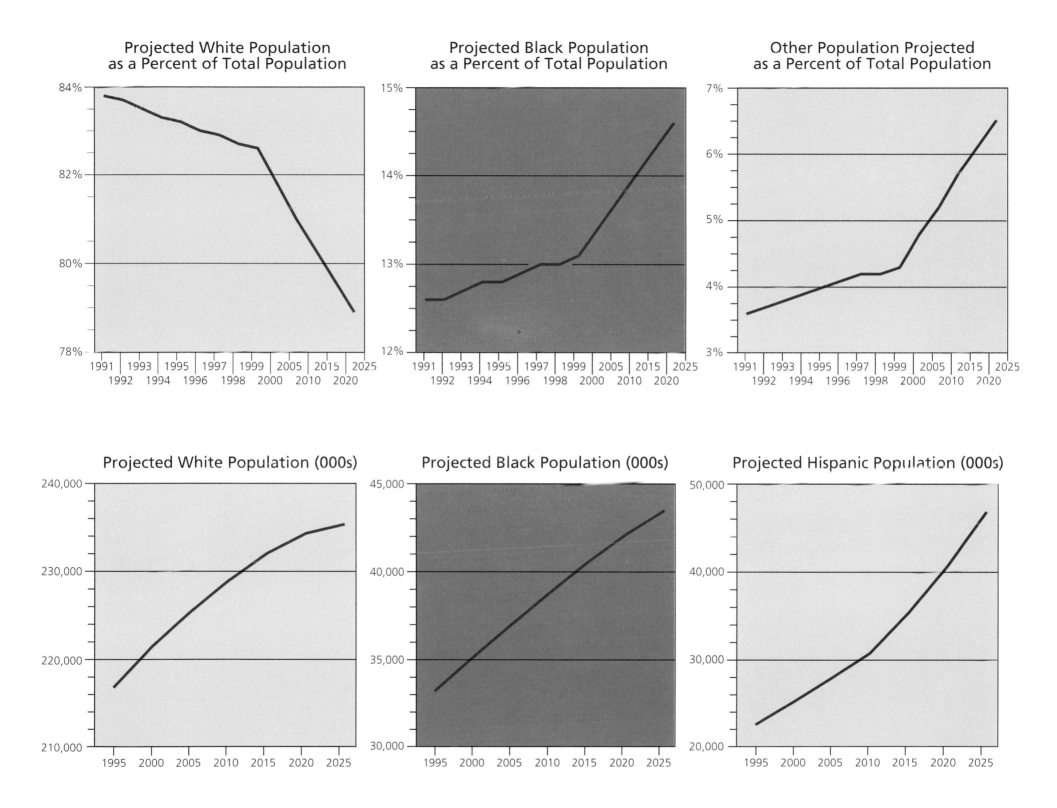

Projected White Population as a Percent of Total Population

Projected Black Population as a Percent of Total Population

Other Population Projected as a Percent of Total Population

Projected White Population (000s)

Projected Black Population (000s)

Projected Hispanic Population (000s)

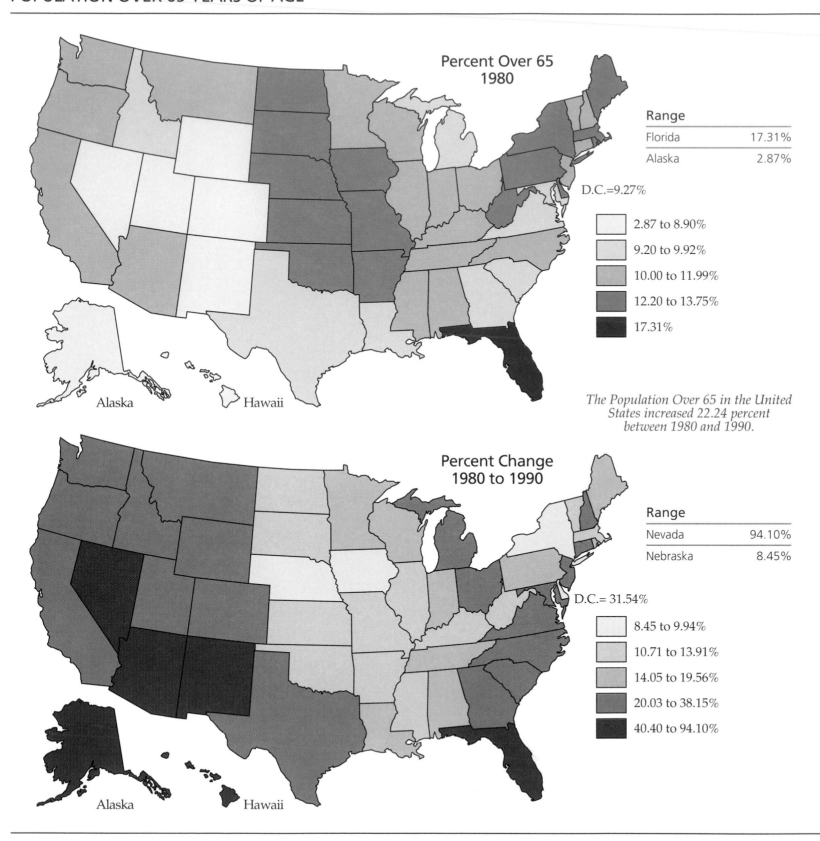

Percent Over 65
1980

Range

Florida	17.31%
Alaska	2.87%

D.C.=9.27%

- 2.87 to 8.90%
- 9.20 to 9.92%
- 10.00 to 11.99%
- 12.20 to 13.75%
- 17.31%

Alaska Hawaii

The Population Over 65 in the United States increased 22.24 percent between 1980 and 1990.

Percent Change
1980 to 1990

Range

Nevada	94.10%
Nebraska	8.45%

D.C.= 31.54%

- 8.45 to 9.94%
- 10.71 to 13.91%
- 14.05 to 19.56%
- 20.03 to 38.15%
- 40.40 to 94.10%

Alaska Hawaii

Population Over 65, 1980

United States	25,549,427
Alabama	440,015
Alaska	11,547
Arizona	307,362
Arkansas	312,477
California	2,414,250
Colorado	247,325
Connecticut	364,864
Delaware	74,287
District of Columbia	59,179
Florida	1,687,573
Georgia	516,731
Hawaii	76,150
Idaho	93,680
Illinois	1,261,885
Indiana	585,384
Iowa	387,584
Kansas	306,263
Kentucky	409,828
Louisiana	404,279
Maine	140,918
Maryland	395,609
Massachusetts	726,531
Michigan	912,258
Minnesota	479,564
Mississippi	289,357
Missouri	648,126
Montana	84,559
Nebraska	205,684
Nevada	65,756
New Hampshire	102,967
New Jersey	859,771
New Mexico	115,906
New York	2,160,767
North Carolina	603,181
North Dakota	80,445
Ohio	1,169,460
Oklahoma	376,126
Oregon	303,336
Pennsylvania	1,530,933
Rhode Island	126,992
South Carolina	287,328
South Dakota	91,019
Tennessee	517,588
Texas	1,371,161
Utah	109,220
Vermont	58,166
Virginia	505,304
Washington	431,562
West Virginia	237,868
Wisconsin	564,197
Wyoming	37,175

Population Over 65, 1990

United States	31,230,535
Alabama	522,989
Alaska	22,396
Arizona	478,774
Arkansas	350,058
California	3,135,552
Colorado	329,443
Connecticut	445,907
Delaware	80,735
District of Columbia	77,847
Florida	2,369,431
Georgia	654,270
Hawaii	125,005
Idaho	121,265
Illinois	1,436,545
Indiana	696,196
Iowa	426,106
Kansas	342,571
Kentucky	466,845
Louisiana	468,991
Maine	163,373
Maryland	517,482
Massachusetts	819,284
Michigan	1,108,461
Minnesota	546,934
Mississippi	321,284
Missouri	717,531
Montana	106,497
Nebraska	223,068
Nevada	127,631
New Hampshire	125,029
New Jersey	1,032,025
New Mexico	163,062
New York	2,363,722
North Carolina	804,341
North Dakota	91,055
Ohio	1,406,961
Oklahoma	424,231
Oregon	391,324
Pennsylvania	1,829,106
Rhode Island	150,547
South Carolina	396,935
South Dakota	102,331
Tennessee	618,818
Texas	1,716,576
Utah	149,958
Vermont	66,163
Virginia	664,470
Washington	564,115
West Virginia	268,897
Wisconsin	651,221
Wyoming	47,195

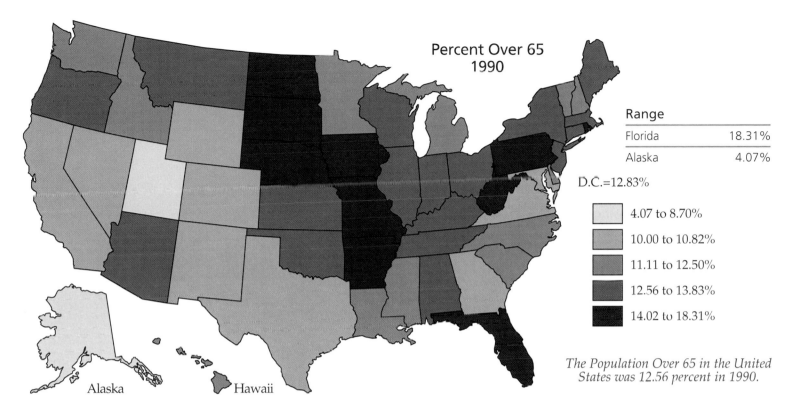

Percent Over 65 1990

Range

Florida	18.31%
Alaska	4.07%

D.C.=12.83%

- 4.07 to 8.70%
- 10.00 to 10.82%
- 11.11 to 12.50%
- 12.56 to 13.83%
- 14.02 to 18.31%

The Population Over 65 in the United States was 12.56 percent in 1990.

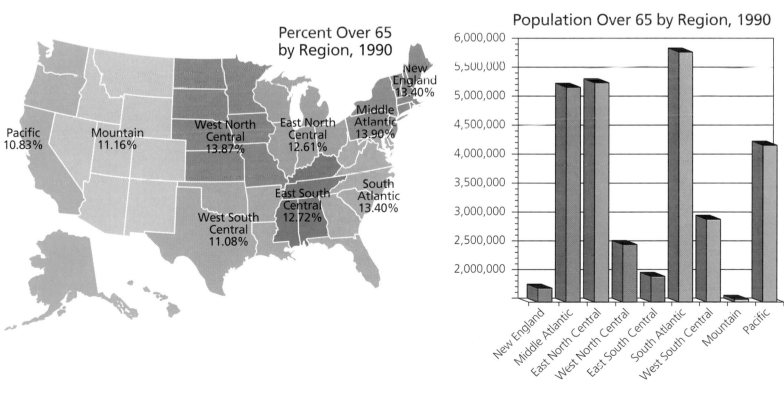

Percent Over 65 by Region, 1990

New England 13.40%
Middle Atlantic 13.90%
East North Central 12.61%
West North Central 13.87%
Pacific 10.83%
Mountain 11.16%
East South Central 12.72%
West South Central 11.08%
South Atlantic 13.40%

Population Over 65 by Region, 1990

Regions: New England, Middle Atlantic, East North Central, West North Central, East South Central, South Atlantic, West South Central, Mountain, Pacific

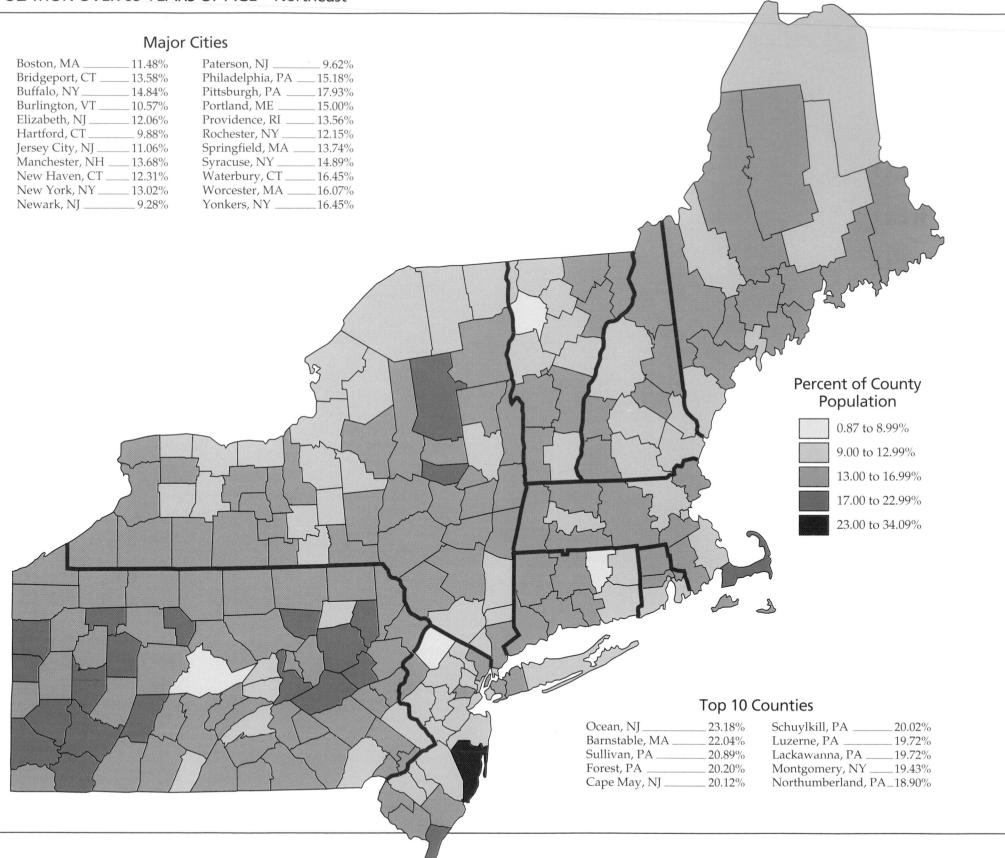

Major Cities

Boston, MA	11.48%	Paterson, NJ	9.62%
Bridgeport, CT	13.58%	Philadelphia, PA	15.18%
Buffalo, NY	14.84%	Pittsburgh, PA	17.93%
Burlington, VT	10.57%	Portland, ME	15.00%
Elizabeth, NJ	12.06%	Providence, RI	13.56%
Hartford, CT	9.88%	Rochester, NY	12.15%
Jersey City, NJ	11.06%	Springfield, MA	13.74%
Manchester, NH	13.68%	Syracuse, NY	14.89%
New Haven, CT	12.31%	Waterbury, CT	16.45%
New York, NY	13.02%	Worcester, MA	16.07%
Newark, NJ	9.28%	Yonkers, NY	16.45%

Percent of County Population

- 0.87 to 8.99%
- 9.00 to 12.99%
- 13.00 to 16.99%
- 17.00 to 22.99%
- 23.00 to 34.09%

Top 10 Counties

Ocean, NJ	23.18%	Schuylkill, PA	20.02%
Barnstable, MA	22.04%	Luzerne, PA	19.72%
Sullivan, PA	20.89%	Lackawanna, PA	19.72%
Forest, PA	20.20%	Montgomery, NY	19.43%
Cape May, NJ	20.12%	Northumberland, PA	18.90%

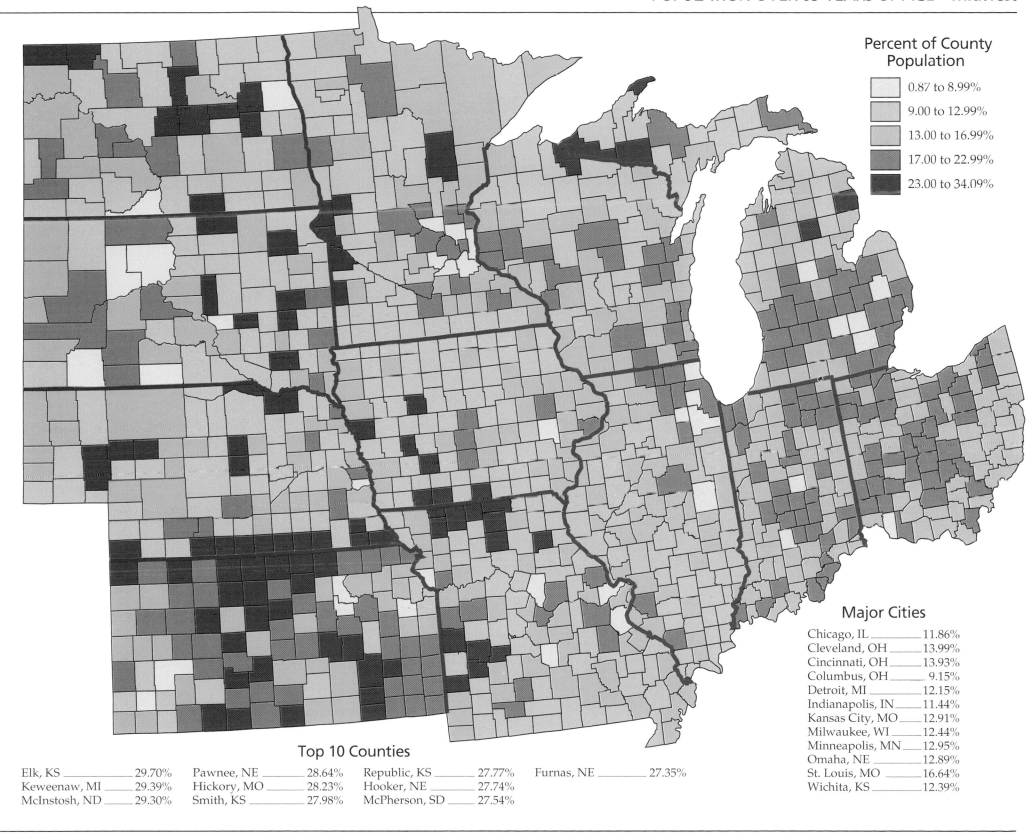

Percent of County Population

- 0.87 to 8.99%
- 9.00 to 12.99%
- 13.00 to 16.99%
- 17.00 to 22.99%
- 23.00 to 34.09%

Major Cities

City	Percent
Chicago, IL	11.86%
Cleveland, OH	13.99%
Cincinnati, OH	13.93%
Columbus, OH	9.15%
Detroit, MI	12.15%
Indianapolis, IN	11.44%
Kansas City, MO	12.91%
Milwaukee, WI	12.44%
Minneapolis, MN	12.95%
Omaha, NE	12.89%
St. Louis, MO	16.64%
Wichita, KS	12.39%

Top 10 Counties

County	Percent	County	Percent	County	Percent	County	Percent
Elk, KS	29.70%	Pawnee, NE	28.64%	Republic, KS	27.77%	Furnas, NE	27.35%
Keweenaw, MI	29.39%	Hickory, MO	28.23%	Hooker, NE	27.74%		
McInstosh, ND	29.30%	Smith, KS	27.98%	McPherson, SD	27.54%		

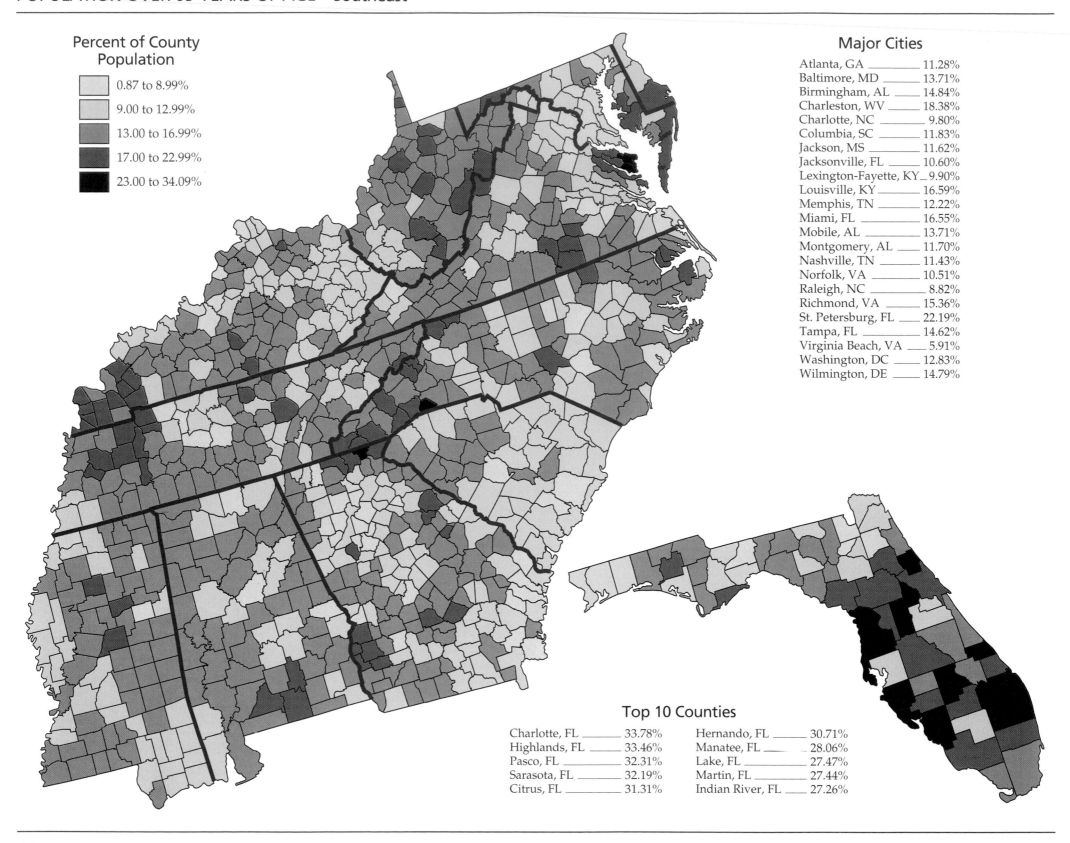

Percent of County Population

- 0.87 to 8.99%
- 9.00 to 12.99%
- 13.00 to 16.99%
- 17.00 to 22.99%
- 23.00 to 34.09%

Major Cities

City	Percent
Atlanta, GA	11.28%
Baltimore, MD	13.71%
Birmingham, AL	14.84%
Charleston, WV	18.38%
Charlotte, NC	9.80%
Columbia, SC	11.83%
Jackson, MS	11.62%
Jacksonville, FL	10.60%
Lexington-Fayette, KY	9.90%
Louisville, KY	16.59%
Memphis, TN	12.22%
Miami, FL	16.55%
Mobile, AL	13.71%
Montgomery, AL	11.70%
Nashville, TN	11.43%
Norfolk, VA	10.51%
Raleigh, NC	8.82%
Richmond, VA	15.36%
St. Petersburg, FL	22.19%
Tampa, FL	14.62%
Virginia Beach, VA	5.91%
Washington, DC	12.83%
Wilmington, DE	14.79%

Top 10 Counties

County	Percent	County	Percent
Charlotte, FL	33.78%	Hernando, FL	30.71%
Highlands, FL	33.46%	Manatee, FL	28.06%
Pasco, FL	32.31%	Lake, FL	27.47%
Sarasota, FL	32.19%	Martin, FL	27.44%
Citrus, FL	31.31%	Indian River, FL	27.26%

Top 10 Counties

County	Percent
Llano, TX	34.09%
Baxter, AR	29.20%
Hamilton, TX	27.22%
Sharp, AR	27.17%
Mills, TX	26.68%
Hall, TX	26.43%
Motley, TX	26.24%
Baylor, TX	26.07%
Izard, AR	25.87%
Coke, TX	25.58%

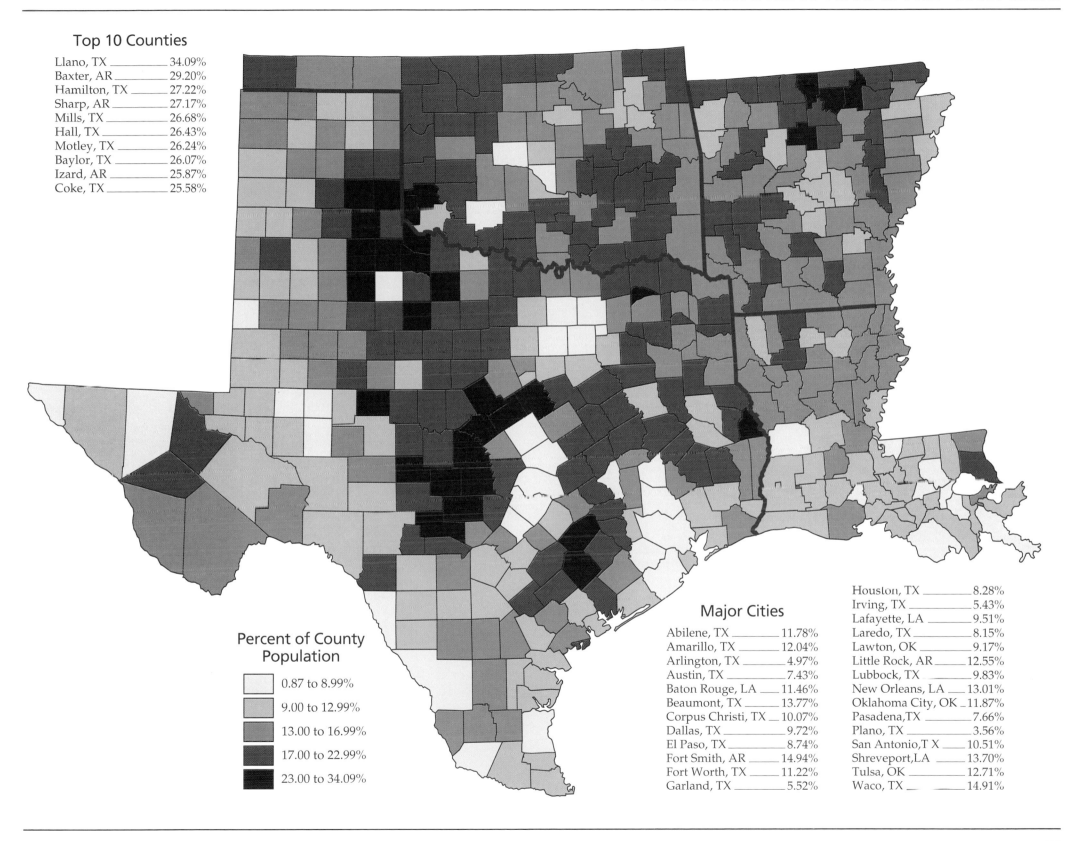

Percent of County Population

- 0.87 to 8.99%
- 9.00 to 12.99%
- 13.00 to 16.99%
- 17.00 to 22.99%
- 23.00 to 34.09%

Major Cities

City	Percent
Abilene, TX	11.78%
Amarillo, TX	12.04%
Arlington, TX	4.97%
Austin, TX	7.43%
Baton Rouge, LA	11.46%
Beaumont, TX	13.77%
Corpus Christi, TX	10.07%
Dallas, TX	9.72%
El Paso, TX	8.74%
Fort Smith, AR	14.94%
Fort Worth, TX	11.22%
Garland, TX	5.52%
Houston, TX	8.28%
Irving, TX	5.43%
Lafayette, LA	9.51%
Laredo, TX	8.15%
Lawton, OK	9.17%
Little Rock, AR	12.55%
Lubbock, TX	9.83%
New Orleans, LA	13.01%
Oklahoma City, OK	11.87%
Pasadena, TX	7.66%
Plano, TX	3.56%
San Antonio, TX	10.51%
Shreveport, LA	13.70%
Tulsa, OK	12.71%
Waco, TX	14.91%

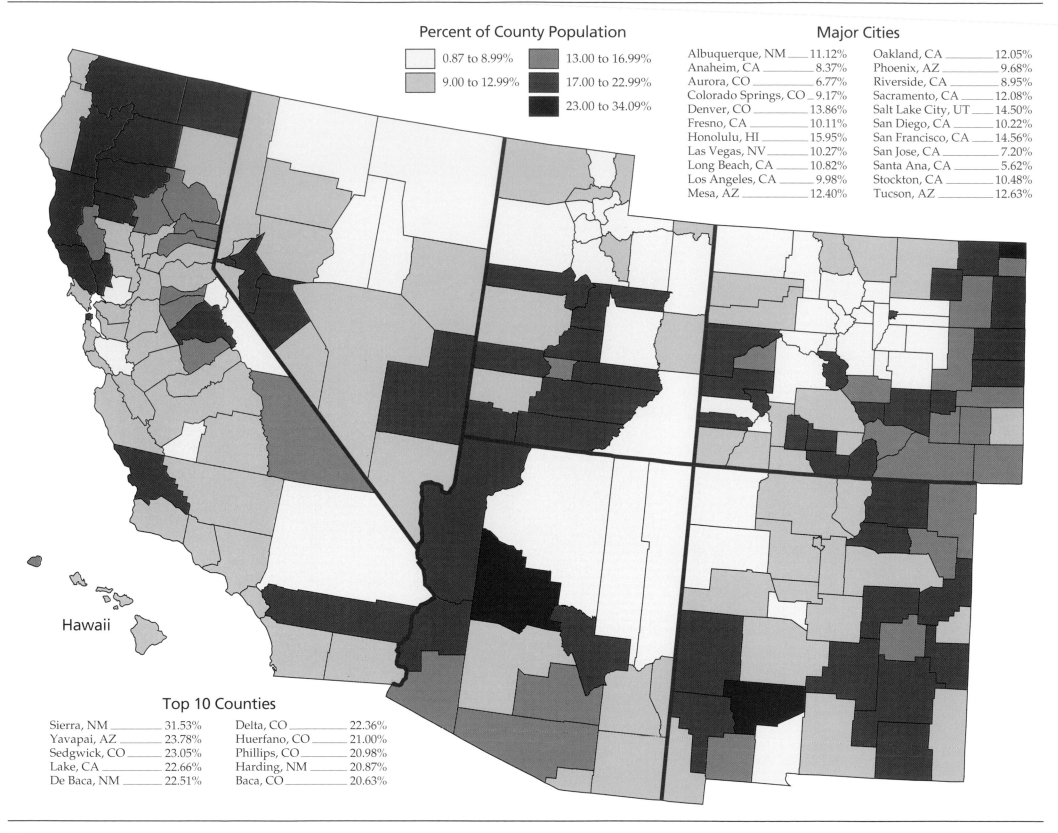

Percent of County Population

- 0.87 to 8.99%
- 9.00 to 12.99%
- 13.00 to 16.99%
- 17.00 to 22.99%
- 23.00 to 34.09%

Major Cities

City	Percent	City	Percent
Albuquerque, NM	11.12%	Oakland, CA	12.05%
Anaheim, CA	8.37%	Phoenix, AZ	9.68%
Aurora, CO	6.77%	Riverside, CA	8.95%
Colorado Springs, CO	9.17%	Sacramento, CA	12.08%
Denver, CO	13.86%	Salt Lake City, UT	14.50%
Fresno, CA	10.11%	San Diego, CA	10.22%
Honolulu, HI	15.95%	San Francisco, CA	14.56%
Las Vegas, NV	10.27%	San Jose, CA	7.20%
Long Beach, CA	10.82%	Santa Ana, CA	5.62%
Los Angeles, CA	9.98%	Stockton, CA	10.48%
Mesa, AZ	12.40%	Tucson, AZ	12.63%

Hawaii

Top 10 Counties

County	Percent	County	Percent
Sierra, NM	31.53%	Delta, CO	22.36%
Yavapai, AZ	23.78%	Huerfano, CO	21.00%
Sedgwick, CO	23.05%	Phillips, CO	20.98%
Lake, CA	22.66%	Harding, NM	20.87%
De Baca, NM	22.51%	Baca, CO	20.63%

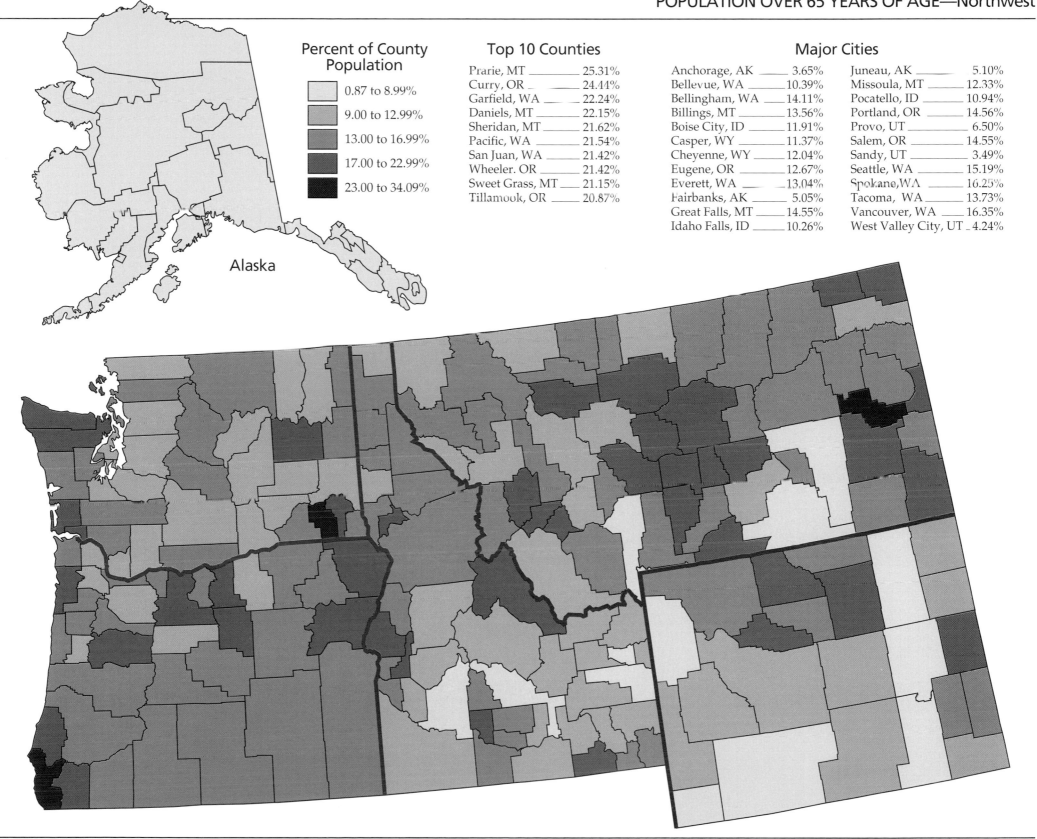

Percent of County Population

- 0.87 to 8.99%
- 9.00 to 12.99%
- 13.00 to 16.99%
- 17.00 to 22.99%
- 23.00 to 34.09%

Alaska

Top 10 Counties

County	Percent
Prarie, MT	25.31%
Curry, OR	24.44%
Garfield, WA	22.24%
Daniels, MT	22.15%
Sheridan, MT	21.62%
Pacific, WA	21.54%
San Juan, WA	21.42%
Wheeler. OR	21.42%
Sweet Grass, MT	21.15%
Tillamook, OR	20.87%

Major Cities

City	Percent	City	Percent
Anchorage, AK	3.65%	Juneau, AK	5.10%
Bellevue, WA	10.39%	Missoula, MT	12.33%
Bellingham, WA	14.11%	Pocatello, ID	10.94%
Billings, MT	13.56%	Portland, OR	14.56%
Boise City, ID	11.91%	Provo, UT	6.50%
Casper, WY	11.37%	Salem, OR	14.55%
Cheyenne, WY	12.04%	Sandy, UT	3.49%
Eugene, OR	12.67%	Seattle, WA	15.19%
Everett, WA	13.04%	Spokane, WA	16.25%
Fairbanks, AK	5.05%	Tacoma, WA	13.73%
Great Falls, MT	14.55%	Vancouver, WA	16.35%
Idaho Falls, ID	10.26%	West Valley City, UT	4.24%

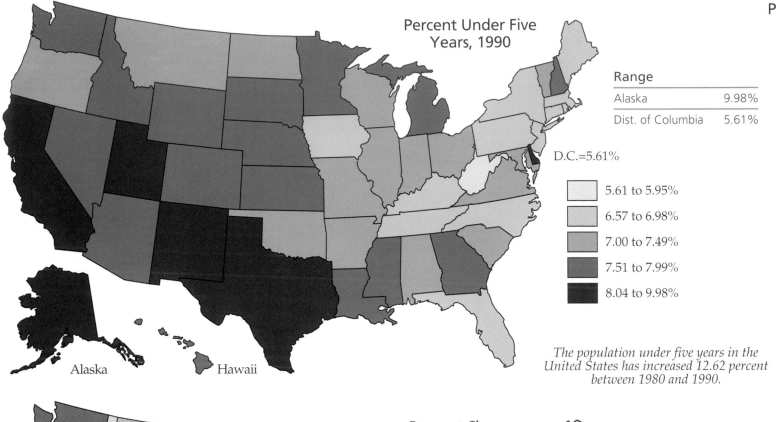

Percent Under Five Years, 1990

Range	
Alaska	9.98%
Dist. of Columbia	5.61%

D.C.=5.61%

- 5.61 to 5.95%
- 6.57 to 6.98%
- 7.00 to 7.49%
- 7.51 to 7.99%
- 8.04 to 9.98%

Alaska   Hawaii

The population under five years in the United States has increased 12.62 percent between 1980 and 1990.

Percent Change 1980 to 1990

Range	
Nevada	65.28%
West Virginia	−26.68%

D.C.= 9.71%

- −26.68 to −10.60%
- −9.04 to −0.11%
- 0.95 to 9.82%
- 11.22 to 23.59%
- 31.80 to 65.28%

Alaska   Hawaii

Population Under Five Years, 1990

United States	18,354,443
Alabama	283,295
Alaska	54,897
Arizona	292,859
Arkansas	164,667
California	2,397,715
Colorado	252,893
Connecticut	228,356
Delaware	48,824
District of Columbia	37,351
Florida	849,596
Georgia	495,535
Hawaii	83,223
Idaho	80,193
Illinois	848,141
Indiana	398,656
Iowa	193,203
Kansas	188,390
Kentucky	250,871
Louisiana	334,650
Maine	85,722
Maryland	357,818
Massachusetts	412,473
Michigan	702,554
Minnesota	336,800
Mississippi	195,365
Missouri	369,244
Montana	59,257
Nebraska	119,606
Nevada	92,217
New Hampshire	84,565
New Jersey	532,637
New Mexico	125,878
New York	1,255,764
North Carolina	458,955
North Dakota	47,845
Ohio	785,149
Oklahoma	226,523
Oregon	201,421
Pennsylvania	797,058
Rhode Island	66,969
South Carolina	256,337
South Dakota	54,504
Tennessee	333,415
Texas	1,390,054
Utah	169,633
Vermont	41,261
Virginia	443,155
Washington	366,780
West Virginia	106,659
Wisconsin	360,730
Wyoming	34,780

Population Under 18 Years, 1990

United States	63,656,241
Alabama	1,058,788
Alaska	172,344
Arizona	981,119
Arkansas	621,131
California	7,750,725
Colorado	861,266
Connecticut	749,581
Delaware	163,341
District of Columbia	117,092
Florida	2,866,237
Georgia	1,727,303
Hawaii	280,126
Idaho	308,405
Illinois	2,946,366
Indiana	1,455,964
Iowa	718,880
Kansas	661,614
Kentucky	954,094
Louisiana	1,227,269
Maine	309,002
Maryland	1,162,241
Massachusetts	1,353,075
Michigan	2,458,765
Minnesota	1,166,783
Mississippi	746,761
Missouri	1,389,043
Montana	222,104
Nebraska	429,012
Nevada	296,948
New Hampshire	278,755
New Jersey	1,799,462
New Mexico	446,741
New York	4,259,549
North Carolina	1,606,149
North Dakota	175,385
Ohio	2,799,744
Oklahoma	837,007
Oregon	724,130
Pennsylvania	2,794,810
Rhode Island	225,690
South Carolina	920,207
South Dakota	198,462
Tennessee	1,216,604
Texas	4,835,839
Utah	627,444
Vermont	143,083
Virginia	1,504,738
Washington	1,238,979
West Virginia	443,577
Wisconsin	1,288,982
Wyoming	135,525

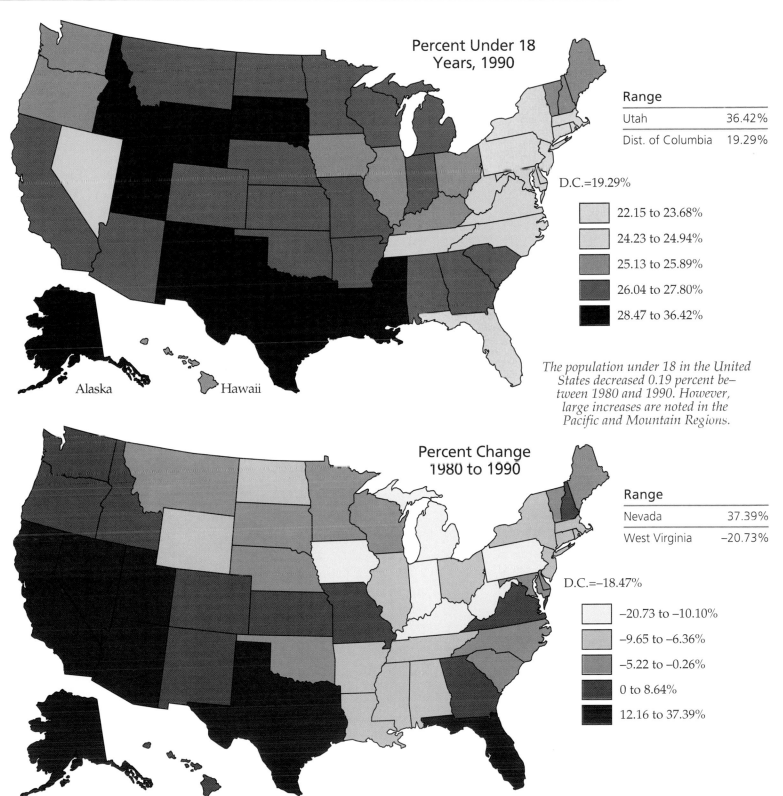

Percent Under 18 Years, 1990

Range

Utah	36.42%
Dist. of Columbia	19.29%

D.C.=19.29%

- 22.15 to 23.68%
- 24.23 to 24.94%
- 25.13 to 25.89%
- 26.04 to 27.80%
- 28.47 to 36.42%

The population under 18 in the United States decreased 0.19 percent between 1980 and 1990. However, large increases are noted in the Pacific and Mountain Regions.

Alaska

Hawaii

Percent Change 1980 to 1990

Range

Nevada	37.39%
West Virginia	−20.73%

D.C.=−18.47%

- −20.73 to −10.10%
- −9.65 to −6.36%
- −5.22 to −0.26%
- 0 to 8.64%
- 12.16 to 37.39%

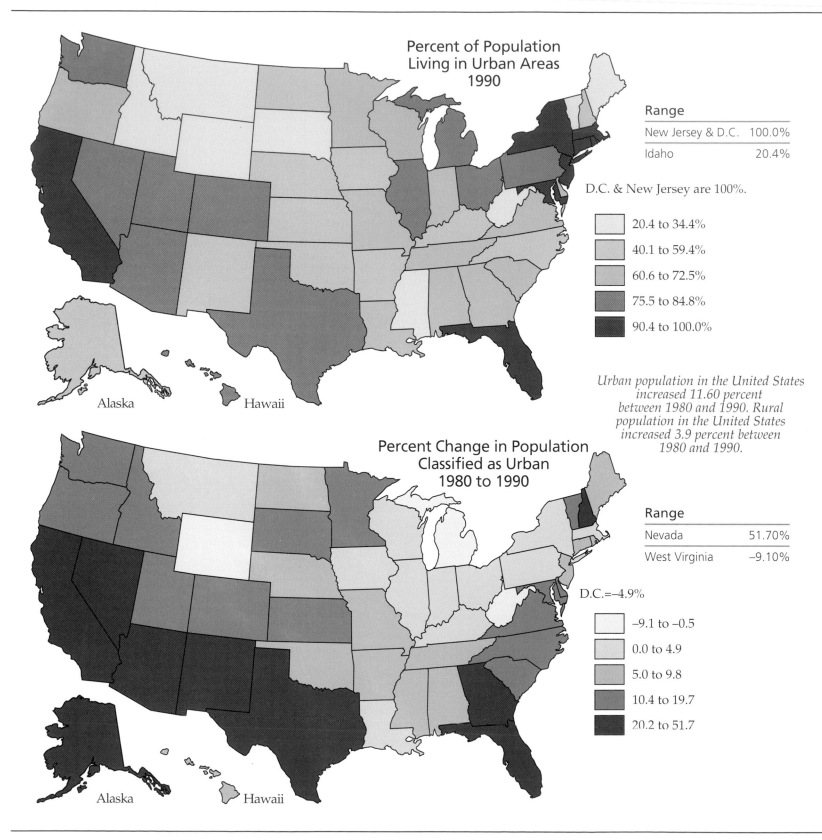

Percent of Population Living in Urban Areas 1990

Range

New Jersey & D.C.	100.0%
Idaho	20.4%

D.C. & New Jersey are 100%.

- ☐ 20.4 to 34.4%
- ☐ 40.1 to 59.4%
- ☐ 60.6 to 72.5%
- ☐ 75.5 to 84.8%
- ☐ 90.4 to 100.0%

Urban population in the United States increased 11.60 percent between 1980 and 1990. Rural population in the United States increased 3.9 percent between 1980 and 1990.

Alaska   Hawaii

Percent Change in Population Classified as Urban 1980 to 1990

Range

Nevada	51.70%
West Virginia	−9.10%

D.C.=−4.9%

- ☐ −9.1 to −0.5
- ☐ 0.0 to 4.9
- ☐ 5.0 to 9.8
- ☐ 10.4 to 19.7
- ☐ 20.2 to 51.7

Alaska   Hawaii

Percent of Population Living in Urban Areas, 1990

United States	77.5
Alabama	67.4
Alaska	41.1
Arizona	79.0
Arkansas	40.1
California	95.7
Colorado	81.5
Connecticut	92.4
Delaware	66.3
District of Columbia	100.0
Florida	90.8
Georgia	65.0
Hawaii	75.5
Idaho	20.4
Illinois	82.7
Indiana	68.5
Iowa	44.0
Kansas	53.8
Kentucky	46.5
Louisiana	69.5
Maine	35.9
Maryland	92.8
Massachusetts	90.4
Michigan	80.1
Minnesota	67.7
Mississippi	30.1
Missouri	66.2
Montana	23.9
Nebraska	48.5
Nevada	82.9
New Hampshire	56.1
New Jersey	100.0
New Mexico	48.4
New York	91.1
North Carolina	56.7
North Dakota	40.3
Ohio	79.0
Oklahoma	59.4
Oregon	68.5
Pennsylvania	84.8
Rhode Island	92.5
South Carolina	60.6
South Dakota	29.5
Tennessee	67.7
Texas	81.6
Utah	77.5
Vermont	23.4
Virginia	72.5
Washington	81.7
West Virginia	36.4
Wisconsin	67.4
Wyoming	29.6

Population and Population Change Within the Largest United States Metropolitan Areas, by Race, 1990

Metropolitan Area	Total Population (000's)	Percent of Total Metropolitan Population				Percent Change in Pop. 1980 to 1990
		African American	American Indian, Eskimo, Aleut	Asian and Pacific Islander	Hispanic	
United States Metropolitan Population	192,726					11.6
N.Y.–No. New Jersey–Long Island, NY–NJ–CT CMSA	18,087	18.2	0.3	4.8	15.4	3.1
Los Angeles–Anaheim–Riverside, CA CMSA	14,532	8.5	0.6	9.2	32.9	26.4
Chicago–Gary–Lake County (IL), IL–IN–WI CMSA	8,066	19.2	0.2	3.2	11.1	1.6
San Francisco–Oakland–San Jose, CA CMSA	6,253	8.6	0.7	14.8	15.5	16.5
Philadelphia–Wilmington–Trenton,PA–NJ–DE–MD CMSA	5,899	10.7	0.2	2.1	3.8	3.9
Detroit–Ann Arbor, MI CMSA	4,665	20.9	0.4	1.5	1.9	-1.8
Boston–Lawrence–Salem–Lowell–Brockton, MA NECMA	4,172	5.7	0.2	2.9	4.6	5.0
Washington, DC–MD–VA MSA	3,924	26.6	0.3	5.2	5.7	20.7
Dallas–Fort Worth , TX CMSA	3,885	14.3	0.5	2.5	13.4	32.6
Houston–Galveston–Brazoria, TX CMSA	3,711	17.9	0.3	3.6	20.8	19.7
Miami–Fort Lauderdale, FL CMSA	3,193	18.5	0.2	1.4	33.3	20.8
Atlanta, GA MSA	2,834	26.0	0.2	1.8	2.0	32.5
Cleveland–Akron–Lorain, OH CMSA	2,760	16.0	0.2	1.0	1.9	-2.6
Seattle–Tacoma, WA CMSA	2,559	4.8	1.3	6.4	3.0	22.3
San Diego, CA MSA	2,498	6.4	0.8	7.9	20.4	34.2
Minneapolis–St. Paul, MN WI MSA	2,464	3.6	1.0	2.6	1.5	15.3
St. Louis, MO–Il MSA	2,444	17.3	0.2	1.0	1.1	2.8
Baltimore, MD MSA	2,382	25.9	0.3	1.8	1.3	8.3
Pittsburgh–Beaver Valley, PA CMSA	2,243	8.0	0.1	0.7	0.6	-7.4
Phoenix, AZ MSA	2,122	3.5	1.8	1.7	16.3	40.6
Tampa–St. Petersburg Clearwater, FL MSA	2,068	9.0	0.3	1.1	6.7	28.2
Denver–Boulder, CO CMSA	1,848	5.3	0.8	2.3	12.2	14.2
Cincinnati–Hamilton, OH–KY–IN CMSA	1,744	11.7	0.1	0.8	0.5	5.1
Milwaukee–Racine, WI CMSA	1,607	13.3	0.5	1.2	3.8	2.4
Kansas City, MO–KS MSA	1,566	12.8	0.5	1.1	2.9	9.3
Sacramento, CA MSA	1,481	6.9	1.1	7.7	11.0	34.7
Portland–Vancouver, OR–WA CMSA	1,478	2.8	0.9	3.5	3.4	13.9
Norfolk–Virginia Beach–Newport News, VA MSA	1,396	28.5	0.3	2.5	2.3	20.3
Columbus, OH MSA	1,377	12.0	0.2	1.5	0.8	10.7
San Antonio, TX MSA	1,302	6.8	0.4	1.2	47.6	21.5
Indianapolis, IN MSA	1,250	13.8	0.2	0.8	0.9	7.1
New Orleans, LA MSA	1,239	34.7	0.3	1.7	4.3	-1.4
Buffalo–Niagara Falls, NY CMSA	1,189	10.3	0.6	0.9	2.0	-4.3
Charlotte–Gastonia–Rock Hill, NC–SC MSA	1,162	19.9	0.4	1.0	0.9	19.6
Providence–Pawtucket–Fall River, RI–MA CMSA	1,142	3.3	0.3	1.8	4.2	5.4
Hartford–New Britain–Middletown, CT CMSA	1,086	8.7	0.2	1.5	7.0	7.1
Orlando, FL MSA	1,073	12.4	0.3	1.9	9.0	53.3
Salt Lake City–Ogden, UT MSA	1,072	1.0	0.8	2.4	5.8	17.8
Rochester, NY MSA	1,002	9.4	0.3	1.4	3.1	3.2
Nashville, TN MSA	985	15.5	0.2	1.0	0.8	15.8
Memphis, TN–AR–MS MSA	982	40.6	0.2	0.8	0.8	7.5
Oklahoma City, OK MSA	959	10.5	4.8	1.9	3.6	11.4
Louisville, KY–IN MSA	953	13.1	0.2	0.6	0.6	-0.4
Dayton–Springfield, OH MSA	951	13.3	0.2	1.0	0.8	1.0
Greensboro–Winston-Salem–High Point, NC MSA	942	19.3	0.3	0.7	0.8	10.6
Birmingham, AL MSA	908	27.1	0.2	0.4	0.4	2.7
Jacksonville, FL MSA	907	20.0	0.3	1.7	2.5	25.5
Albany–Schenectady–Troy, NY MSA	874	4.7	0.2	1.2	1.8	4.6

Note: CMSA—Consolidated Metropolitan Statistical Area; MSA—Metropolitan Statistical Area. Persons of Hispanic origin may be of any race.
Source: U.S. Bureau of the Census, press release CB91–66 and unpublished data.

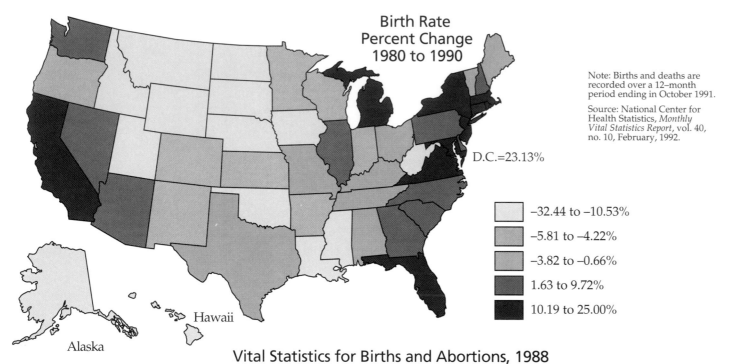

Birth Rate Percent Change 1980 to 1990

Note: Births and deaths are recorded over a 12–month period ending in October 1991.

Source: National Center for Health Statistics, *Monthly Vital Statistics Report*, vol. 40, no. 10, February, 1992.

D.C.=23.13%

- −32.44 to −10.53%
- −5.81 to −4.22%
- −3.82 to −0.66%
- 1.63 to 9.72%
- 10.19 to 25.00%

Hawaii

Alaska

Live Births, 1990

	Births	Rate
United States	4,185,989	14.9
Alabama	65,060	16.1
Alaska	11,389	20.7
Arizona	68,665	18.7
Arkansas	36,148	15.4
California	608,278	20.4
Colorado	53,217	16.2
Connecticut	51,185	15.6
Delaware	11,287	16.9
Dist. of Col.	10,989	18.1
Florida	200,195	15.5
Georgia	113,897	17.6
Hawaii	20,391	18.4
Idaho	16,819	16.7
Illinois	193,985	17.0
Indiana	85,375	15.4
Iowa	38,461	13.9
Kansas	40,450	16.3
Kentucky	58,735	15.9
Louisiana	73,572	17.4
Maine	17,456	14.2
Maryland	81,814	17.1
Massachusetts	94,894	15.8
Michigan	160,665	17.3
Minnesota	69,376	15.9
Mississippi	43,783	17.0
Missouri	80,838	15.8
Montana	11,709	14.7
Nebraska	24,014	15.2
Nevada	20,698	17.2
New Hampshire	17,547	15.8
New Jersey	118,284	15.3
New Mexico	28,962	19.1
New York	306,061	17.0
North Carolina	105,022	15.8
North Dakota	9,592	15.0
Ohio	164,103	15.1
Oklahoma	47,151	15.0
Oregon	44,576	15.7
Pennsylvania	172,977	14.6
Rhode Island	14,978	14.9
South Carolina	58,907	17.0
South Dakota	11,145	16.0
Tennessee	73,270	15.0
Texas	320,214	18.9
Utah	36,561	21.2
Vermont	8,377	14.9
Virginia	100,858	16.3
Washington	81,140	16.7
West Virginia	22,702	12.7
Wisconsin	73,309	15.0
Wyoming	6,906	15.2

Vital Statistics for Births and Abortions, 1988

State	% of Births with Low Birth Weight	Births to (% of Total) Teenage Mothers	Births to (% of Total) Unmarried Women	# of Abortions (000's)	Ratio: Abortions/1,000 Live Births	State	% of Births with Low Birth Weight	Births to (% of Total) Teenage Mothers	Births to (% of Total) Unmarried Women	# of Abortions (000's)	Ratio: Abortions/1,000 Live Births
United States	6.9	12.5	25.7	1,590.8	404	Missouri	6.8	13.7	25.0	19.5	264
Alabama	8.0	17.4	27.9	18.2	284	Montana	6.0	9.9	20.8	3.1	265
Alaska	5.0	9.3	23.4	2.4	215	Nebraska	5.5	9.3	18.1	6.5	263
Arizona	6.2	13.8	28.7	23.1	350	Nevada	7.5	12.5	19.1	10.2	558
Arkansas	8.2	18.9	26.5	6.3	182	New Hampshire	4.8	7.5	14.4	4.7	261
California	6.0	11.1	28.6	311.7	598	New Jersey	7.0	8.9	24.3	63.9	557
Colorado	7.8	10.7	19.5	18.7	335	New Mexico	7.2	15.7	32.2	6.8	251
Connecticut	6.7	8.6	23.8	23.6	510	New York	7.8	9.4	30.1	184.0	634
Delaware	7.4	12.8	27.1	5.7	502	North Carolina	8.0	16.0	26.3	39.7	392
D.C.	14.3	17.6	61.7	26.1	1,257	North Dakota	4.8	7.6	15.6	2.2	198
Florida	7.7	13.7	28.7	82.9	437	Ohio	6.9	13.5	26.4	53.4	326
Georgia	8.4	16.5	29.6	36.7	333	Oklahoma	6.5	16.0	22.4	12.1	257
Hawaii	6.9	9.4	22.2	11.2	579	Oregon	5.2	11.4	23.6	16.0	393
Idaho	5.1	11.6	14.1	1.9	125	Pennsylvania	6.9	10.9	26.5	51.8	302
Illinois	7.5	12.5	29.5	72.6	395	Rhode Island	6.0	10.3	22.9	7.2	481
Indiana	6.6	14.1	22.7	15.8	185	South Carolina	9.0	16.8	30.3	14.2	259
Iowa	5.4	9.3	17.7	9.4	254	South Dakota	4.7	10.6	20.9	0.9	82
Kansas	6.1	11.4	18.1	11.4	308	Tennessee	7.9	17.2	27.6	22.1	292
Kentucky	6.7	17.3	21.9	11.5	215	Texas	6.8	15.2	19.7	100.7	333
Louisiana	8.8	16.8	33.5	17.3	243	Utah	5.7	9.3	11.7	5.0	139
Maine	4.8	10.9	20.3	4.6	283	Vermont	5.0	8.9	18.6	3.6	454
Maryland	8.1	11.2	32.6	32.7	466	Virginia	7.0	11.2	23.8	35.4	385
Massachusetts	6.0	8.2	22.2	43.7	452	Washington	5.2	10.6	22.3	31.2	475
Michigan	7.3	12.5	21.6	63.4	446	West Virginia	6.4	16.9	22.6	3.3	141
Minnesota	5.0	7.3	18.3	18.6	281	Wisconsin	5.4	9.8	21.9	18.0	251
Mississippi	8.7	20.7	37.6	5.1	123	Wyoming	7.0	12.0	17.2	0.6	90

Source: U.S. National Center for Health Statistics, *Vital Statistics of the United States*, annual; and *Monthly Vital Statistics Report*. S.K. Henshaw and J. Van Vort, "*Abortion Services in the United States, 1987 and 1988*," *Family Planning Perspectives*, Vol. 22, 1990.

Deaths, 1990

	Deaths	Rate/ 1,000 Pop.
United States	2,158,809	8.7
Alabama	39,961	9.9
Alaska	2,182	4.0
Arizona	28,651	7.8
Arkansas	24,874	10.6
California	219,629	7.4
Colorado	21,186	6.4
Connecticut	26,706	8.1
Delaware	5,728	8.6
Dist. of Columbia	7,492	12.3
Florida	133,327	10.3
Georgia	52,964	8.2
Hawaii	6,757	6.1
Idaho	7,628	7.6
Illinois	102,931	9.0
Indiana	49,690	9.0
Iowa	27,561	9.9
Kansas	22,671	9.2
Kentucky	35,719	9.7
Louisiana	37,786	9.0
Maine	11,032	9.0
Maryland	37,945	7.9
Massachusetts	54,678	9.1
Michigan	78,943	8.5
Minnesota	34,550	7.9
Mississippi	25,231	9.8
Missouri	51,366	10.0
Montana	6,922	8.7
Nebraska	14,338	9.1
Nevada	8,916	7.4
New Hampshire	8,461	7.6
New Jersey	69,902	9.0
New Mexico	10,751	7.1
New York	169,662	9.4
North Carolina	57,164	8.6
North Dakota	5,698	8.9
Ohio	98,443	9.1
Oklahoma	30,390	9.7
Oregon	25,484	9.0
Pennsylvania	122,396	10.3
Rhode Island	9,417	9.4
South Carolina	29,578	8.5
South Dakota	6,509	9.4
Tennessee	45,733	9.4
Texas	128,032	7.5
Utah	9,362	5.4
Vermont	4,636	8.2
Virginia	48,124	7.8
Washington	36,990	7.6
West Virginia	19,861	11.1
Wisconsin	41,622	8.5
Wyoming	3,230	7.1

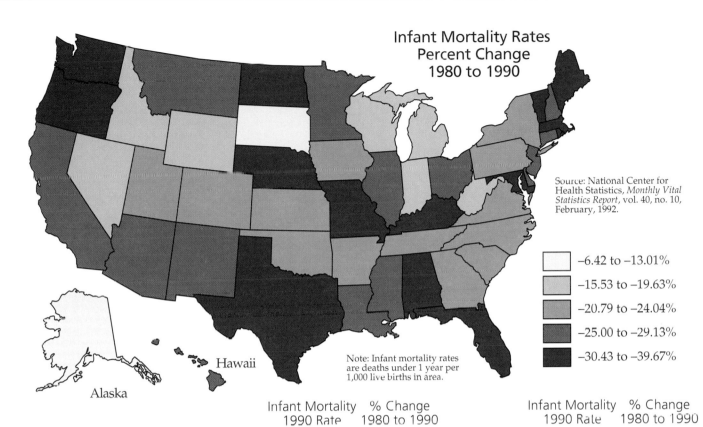

Infant Mortality Rates Percent Change 1980 to 1990

Source: National Center for Health Statistics, *Monthly Vital Statistics Report*, vol. 40, no. 10, February, 1992.

	−6.42 to −13.01%
	−15.53 to −19.63%
	−20.79 to −24.04%
	−25.00 to −29.13%
	−30.43 to −39.67%

Note: Infant mortality rates are deaths under 1 year per 1,000 live births in area.

Deaths, 1990

New England	114,931
Middle Atlantic	361,960
East North Central	371,630
West North Central	162,692
South Atlantic	392,182
East South Central	146,645
West South Central	221,082
Mountain	96,647
Pacific	291,042

Infant Mortality Rate, 1990

New England	7.4
Middle Atlantic	9.7
East North Central	10.0
West North Central	8.2
South Atlantic	10.5
East South Central	10.2
West South Central	8.7
Mountain	8.5
Pacific	8.0

	Infant Mortality 1990 Rate	% Change 1980 to 1990		Infant Mortality 1990 Rate	% Change 1980 to 1990
United States	9.4	−27.1	Missouri	8.5	−29.2
Alabama	10.0	−33.3	Montana	9.0	−25.0
Alaska	11.0	−8.3	Nebraska	7.2	−40.0
Arizona	9.2	−23.3	Nevada	8.9	−19.1
Arkansas	10.0	−23.1	New Hampshire	7.3	−26.3
California	8.0	−27.3	New Jersey	9.1	−30.0
Colorado	8.0	−20.0	New Mexico	8.4	−30.0
Connecticut	8.1	−26.4	New York	9.6	−26.2
Delaware	10.0	−28.6	North Carolina	11.0	−26.7
Dist. of Columbia	18.0	−28.0	North Dakota	7.3	−39.2
Florida	9.5	−36.7	Ohio	9.5	−26.9
Georgia	11.0	−26.7	Oklahoma	10.0	−23.1
Hawaii	7.3	−27.0	Oregon	7.4	−38.3
Idaho	8.6	−21.8	Pennsylvania	10.0	−23.1
Illinois	11.0	−26.7	Rhode Island	7.3	−33.6
Indiana	10.0	−16.7	South Carolina	12.0	−25.0
Iowa	9.2	−23.3	South Dakota	10.0	−9.1
Kansas	8.0	−20.0	Tennessee	10.0	−28.6
Kentucky	8.5	−34.6	Texas	8.0	−33.3
Louisiana	10.0	−28.6	Utah	7.9	−21.0
Maine	6.4	−30.4	Vermont	6.6	−40.0
Maryland	9.2	−34.3	Virginia	10.0	−28.6
Massachusetts	7.3	−33.6	Washington	7.7	−35.8
Michigan	11.0	−15.4	West Virginia	9.5	−20.8
Minnesota	7.5	−25.0	Wisconsin	8.7	−13.0
Mississippi	12.0	−29.4	Wyoming	8.2	−16.3

Part Two

HOUSEHOLDS

HOUSEHOLDS

According to the Census of Population and Housing of 1990, there were 91,947,410 households in the United States. Of this number, 63,642,253 were classified as family households and 28,305,157 were designated as nonfamily households. The following table shows the distribution of various household types. (Totals do not add to the numbers stated above as these data were transcribed from the *1990 Current Population Reports.*)

	1970	1980	1990
Total households (000s)	63,401	80,776	93,347
Average Size	2.94	2.76	2.63
Family households	51,456	59,550	66,090
Married couples	44,728	49,112	52,317
Male householder	1,228	1,733	2,884
Female householder	5,500	8,705	10,890
Nonfamily households	11,945	21,226	27,257
Male householder	4,063	8,807	11,606
Female householder	7,882	12,419	15,651
Married couples	45,373	49,714	53,256
With own household	44,728	49,112	52,317
Without own household	645	602	939

The number of family households has increased 11.0 percent in the years between 1980 and 1990. This is compared to a figure of 15.7 percent between 1970 and 1980. Male householders are the fastest growing component of the household universe. In the ten years between the 1980 and 1990 censuses, male householders in family households increased 66.4 percent. In nonfamily households, male householders increased 31.8 percent as a group. These figures compare to 25.1 and 26.0 for women householders respectively.

African American households and Hispanic households varied from White households. Both groups had a greater percentage of households that were classified as families (71.2 and 81.6 percent as compared to 70.6 percent for Whites). Blacks had less married couples heading households than both Whites and Hispanics (35.8 percent as opposed to 58.6 for Whites and 57.2 for Hispanics respectively).

HOUSEHOLD SIZE

The average number of persons per household was 2.63 in 1990. The table below shows that household size has decreased in all but the Pacific region. In fact, household size has increased in only one state since 1980—California.

	1980	1990	Change
Northeast	2.74	2.61	–4.7%
New England	2.74	2.58	–5.8%
Middle Atlantic	2.74	2.62	–4.4%
Midwest	2.75	2.60	–5.5%
East North Central	2.78	2.63	–5.4%
West North Central	2.68	2.55	–4.9%
South	2.77	2.61	–5.8%
South Atlantic	2.73	2.56	–6.2%
East South Central	2.83	2.62	–7.4%
West South Central	2.80	2.69	–3.9%
West	2.71	2.72	0.4%
Mountain	2.79	2.65	–5.0%
Pacific	2.68	2.74	2.2%

If we look at the next table, several interesting facts can be seen. Single–person households are increasing rapidly since 1970. Their increase seems to come at the expense of larger household sizes. Other data confirms that smaller, nonfamily household units are growing 250 percent faster than larger family household units. The data is confirmed when one considers that 22.2 percent of the American population over the age of 18 was single in 1989 as opposed to 16.2 percent in 1970, and 8.5 percent were divorced as opposed to 3.2 percent for the same dates.

	Percent Distribution		
Size of Household	1970	1980	1990
1 person	17.1	22.7	24.6
2 persons	28.9	31.4	32.3
3 persons	17.3	17.5	17.3
4 persons	15.8	15.7	15.5
5 persons	10.3	7.5	6.7
6 persons	5.6	3.1	2.3
7 persons or more	5.0	2.2	1.4

CHARACTERISTICS OF HOUSEHOLDERS

America's basic household and family unit is changing as we have seen briefly in earlier paragraphs. The idea of what constitutes a household family is being redefined through current statistical observations. In many cases, the household with one father, one mother, and two children no longer exists and is being replaced by single parent families, persons living alone, and householders 65 years of age and older.

The United States had 10,891,646 females who were heads of family households in 1990 representing a national increase of 25.1 percent since 1980. Of this number, 9.1 percent of all White households were run by female heads. Figures for Blacks and Hispanics were 31.2 and 18.8 percent respectively.

The country has also seen an increase in households occupied by single individuals and persons over the age of 65 years.

The age of householders is also changing. People between the ages of 14 and 24 are declining the opportunity to accept household management responsibilities and, as a result, are living with their parents into their mid– to late twenties. The table below confirms this notion.

	Percent Distribution		
Age of Householder	1970	1980	1990
15 to 24 years	6.8	8.1	5.5
25 to 29 years	9.6	11.5	10.1
30 to 34 years	8.8	11.5	11.8
35 to 44 years	18.6	17.3	22.0
45 to 54 years	19.5	15.7	15.5
55 to 64 years	17.1	15.5	13.4
65 to 74 years	12.1	12.5	12.6
75 years and above	7.6	7.9	9.0

FAMILIES AND FAMILY SIZE

Like household size, family size has also decreased since 1960. In 1960, the average family was comprised of 3.67 people. By 1990, that figure changed to 3.17. Families constitute a smaller percent of total households. In 1990, 70.8 percent of all households were families. In 1960, such description was applied to 85.4 percent of the nation's household units. We can see, from the table below, that the number of households operated by married couples has increased for the past three decades. These numbers are misleading, however, when one looks at the percent distribution of households managed by married couples and the total household units for these same years. In 1970, 70.5 percent of all households had married householders. By 1980, this figure dropped to 60.8 and further to 56.0 by 1990.

	1970	1980	1990
Families	51,586	59,550	66,090
Average size	3.58	3.29	3.17
Married couple	44,755	49,112	52,317
Male householder	1,239	1,733	2,884
Female householder	5,591	8,705	10,890

Single male and female householders have actually increased in size relative to total household units. In 1970, these two groups were 10.6 percent of all householders. In 1990, this figure increased to 14.7 percent.

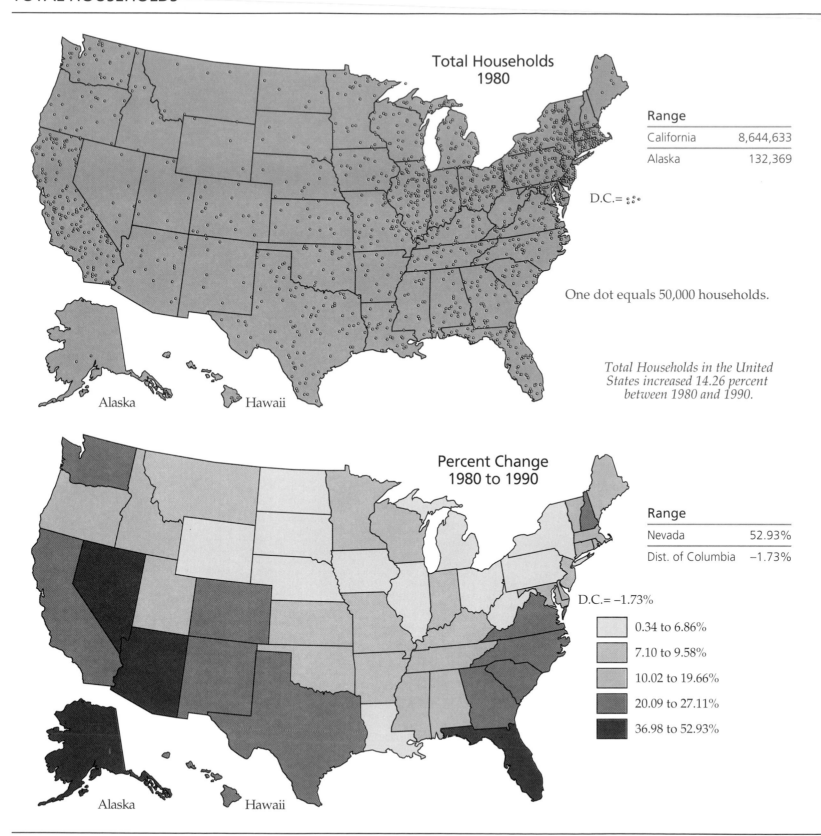

Total Households 1980

Range

California	8,644,633
Alaska	132,369

D.C.=

One dot equals 50,000 households.

Total Households in the United States increased 14.26 percent between 1980 and 1990.

Alaska   Hawaii

Percent Change 1980 to 1990

Range

Nevada	52.93%
Dist. of Columbia	−1.73%

D.C.= −1.73%

- 0.34 to 6.86%
- 7.10 to 9.58%
- 10.02 to 19.66%
- 20.09 to 27.11%
- 36.98 to 52.93%

Alaska   Hawaii

Total Households, 1980

United States	80,467,697
Alabama	1,342,371
Alaska	132,369
Arizona	959,554
Arkansas	816,706
California	8,644,633
Colorado	1,062,879
Connecticut	1,094,281
Delaware	206,960
District of Columbia	254,032
Florida	3,748,542
Georgia	1,872,564
Hawaii	294,934
Idaho	324,889
Illinois	4,046,638
Indiana	1,928,375
Iowa	1,053,107
Kansas	873,336
Kentucky	1,263,102
Louisiana	1,413,394
Maine	395,474
Maryland	1,461,680
Massachusetts	2,032,576
Michigan	3,199,830
Minnesota	1,447,310
Mississippi	828,389
Missouri	1,794,872
Montana	285,034
Nebraska	572,615
Nevada	304,900
New Hampshire	323,482
New Jersey	2,550,290
New Mexico	443,069
New York	6,345,951
North Carolina	2,045,714
North Dakota	228,565
Ohio	3,834,529
Oklahoma	1,118,191
Oregon	992,750
Pennsylvania	4,220,660
Rhode Island	338,340
South Carolina	1,030,722
South Dakota	243,448
Tennessee	1,618,434
Texas	4,934,936
Utah	449,524
Vermont	178,394
Virginia	1,864,922
Washington	1,542,685
West Virginia	686,210
Wisconsin	1,654,777
Wyoming	166,758

Total Households, 1990

United States	91,947,410
Alabama	1,506,790
Alaska	188,915
Arizona	1,368,843
Arkansas	891,179
California	10,381,206
Colorado	1,282,489
Connecticut	1,230,479
Delaware	247,497
District of Columbia	249,634
Florida	5,134,869
Georgia	2,366,615
Hawaii	356,267
Idaho	360,723
Illinois	4,202,240
Indiana	2,065,355
Iowa	1,064,325
Kansas	944,726
Kentucky	1,379,782
Louisiana	1,499,269
Maine	465,312
Maryland	1,748,991
Massachusetts	2,247,110
Michigan	3,419,331
Minnesota	1,647,853
Mississippi	911,374
Missouri	1,961,206
Montana	306,163
Nebraska	602,363
Nevada	466,297
New Hampshire	411,189
New Jersey	2,794,711
New Mexico	542,709
New York	6,639,322
North Carolina	2,517,026
North Dakota	240,878
Ohio	4,087,546
Oklahoma	1,206,135
Oregon	1,103,313
Pennsylvania	4,495,966
Rhode Island	377,977
South Carolina	1,258,044
South Dakota	259,034
Tennessee	1,853,725
Texas	6,070,937
Utah	537,273
Vermont	210,650
Virginia	2,291,830
Washington	1,872,431
West Virginia	688,557
Wisconsin	1,822,118
Wyoming	168,839

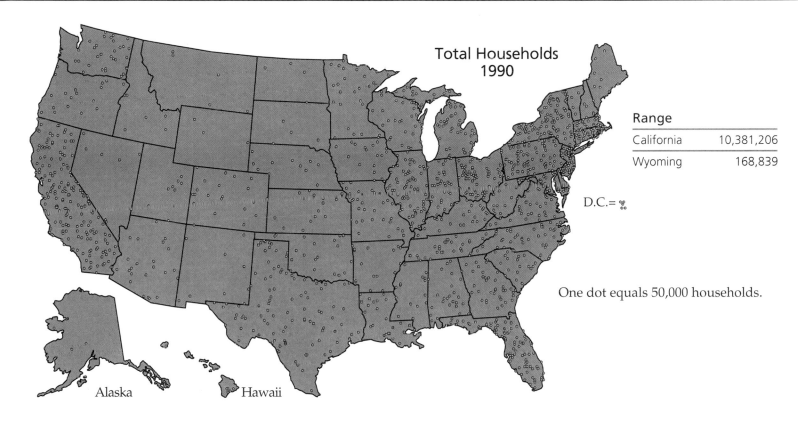

Total Households
1990

Range

California	10,381,206
Wyoming	168,839

D.C.= ⁏

One dot equals 50,000 households.

Alaska   Hawaii

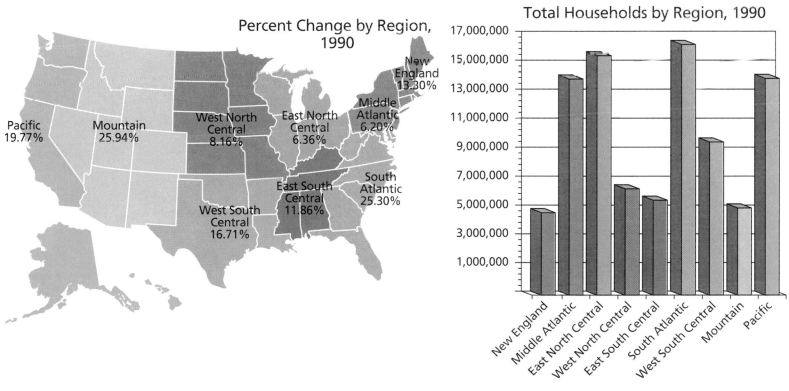

Percent Change by Region, 1990

New England 13.30%
Middle Atlantic 6.20%
Pacific 19.77%
Mountain 25.94%
West North Central 8.16%
East North Central 6.36%
East South Central 11.86%
South Atlantic 25.30%
West South Central 16.71%

Total Households by Region, 1990

New England
Middle Atlantic
East North Central
West North Central
East South Central
South Atlantic
West South Central
Mountain
Pacific

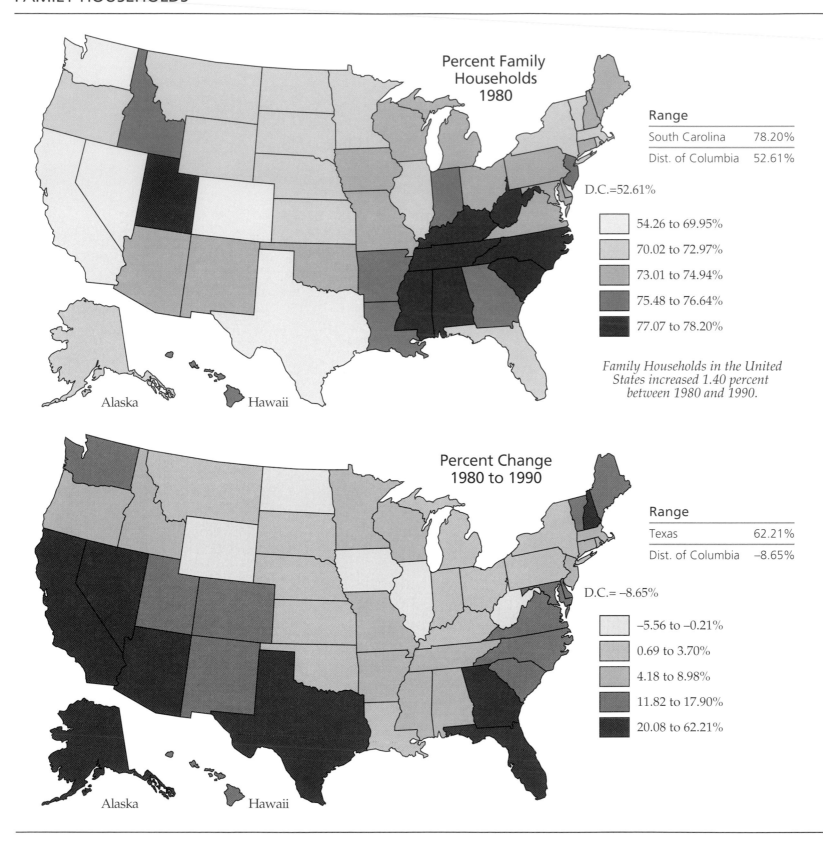

Percent Family Households 1980

Range

South Carolina	78.20%
Dist. of Columbia	52.61%

D.C.=52.61%

- 54.26 to 69.95%
- 70.02 to 72.97%
- 73.01 to 74.94%
- 75.48 to 76.64%
- 77.07 to 78.20%

Family Households in the United States increased 1.40 percent between 1980 and 1990.

Alaska   Hawaii

Percent Change 1980 to 1990

Range

Texas	62.21%
Dist. of Columbia	−8.65%

D.C.= −8.65%

- −5.56 to −0.21%
- 0.69 to 3.70%
- 4.18 to 8.98%
- 11.82 to 17.90%
- 20.08 to 62.21%

Alaska   Hawaii

Family Households, 1980

United States	63,642,253
Alabama	1,038,881
Alaska	95,564
Arizona	705,048
Arkansas	625,390
California	5,936,810
Colorado	739,446
Connecticut	814,080
Delaware	154,900
District of Columbia	133,643
Florida	2,690,122
Georgia	1,426,645
Hawaii	226,035
Idaho	246,550
Illinois	2,931,117
Indiana	1,455,556
Iowa	770,283
Kansas	635,123
Kentucky	983,353
Louisiana	1,068,835
Maine	293,936
Maryland	1,089,559
Massachusetts	1,438,602
Michigan	2,392,504
Minnesota	1,037,522
Mississippi	642,704
Missouri	1,311,652
Montana	205,290
Nebraska	411,708
Nevada	207,424
New Hampshire	238,667
New Jersey	1,931,578
New Mexico	332,058
New York	4,443,248
North Carolina	1,576,622
North Dakota	166,702
Ohio	2,854,191
Oklahoma	827,078
Oregon	698,930
Pennsylvania	3,134,328
Rhode Island	245,128
South Carolina	806,037
South Dakota	177,071
Tennessee	1,248,433
Texas	2,677,865
Utah	351,508
Vermont	128,460
Virginia	1,397,516
Washington	1,079,038
West Virginia	529,734
Wisconsin	1,208,094
Wyoming	121,685

Family Households, 1990

United States	64,535,947
Alabama	1,103,835
Alaska	132,837
Arizona	940,106
Arkansas	651,555
California	7,139,394
Colorado	854,214
Connecticut	864,493
Delaware	175,867
District of Columbia	122,087
Florida	3,511,825
Georgia	1,713,072
Hawaii	263,456
Idaho	263,194
Illinois	2,924,880
Indiana	1,480,351
Iowa	740,819
Kansas	658,600
Kentucky	1,015,998
Louisiana	1,089,882
Maine	328,685
Maryland	1,245,814
Massachusetts	1,514,746
Michigan	2,439,171
Minnesota	1,130,683
Mississippi	674,378
Missouri	1,386,334
Montana	211,666
Nebraska	415,427
Nevada	307,400
New Hampshire	292,601
New Jersey	2,021,346
New Mexico	391,487
New York	4,489,312
North Carolina	1,812,053
North Dakota	166,270
Ohio	2,895,223
Oklahoma	855,321
Oregon	750,844
Pennsylvania	3,155,989
Rhode Island	258,886
South Carolina	928,206
South Dakota	180,306
Tennessee	1,348,019
Texas	4,343,878
Utah	410,862
Vermont	144,895
Virginia	1,629,490
Washington	1,264,934
West Virginia	500,259
Wisconsin	1,275,172
Wyoming	119,825

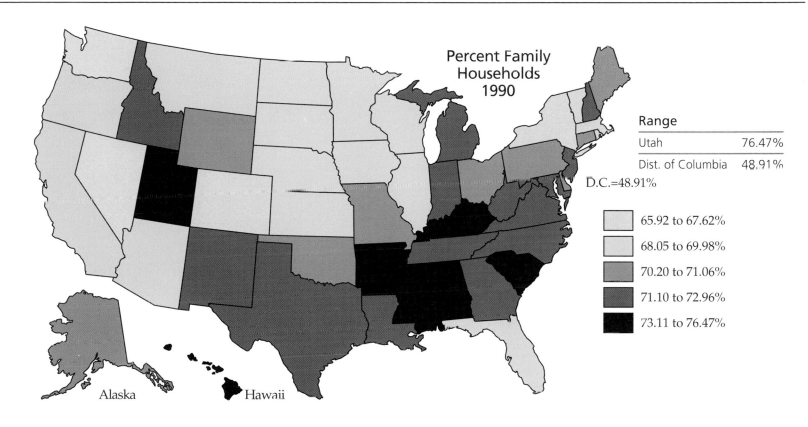

Percent Family Households 1990

Range

Utah	76.47%
Dist. of Columbia	48.91%

D.C.=48.91%

- 65.92 to 67.62%
- 68.05 to 69.98%
- 70.20 to 71.06%
- 71.10 to 72.96%
- 73.11 to 76.47%

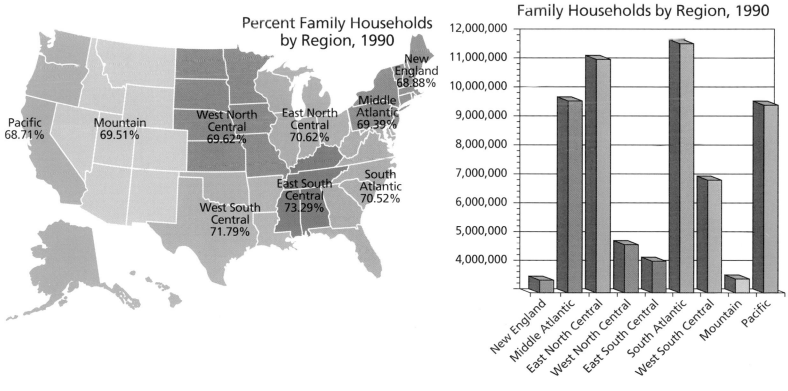

Percent Family Households by Region, 1990

New England 68.88%
Middle Atlantic 69.39%
East North Central 70.62%
West North Central 69.62%
Pacific 68.71%
Mountain 69.51%
South Atlantic 70.52%
East South Central 73.29%
West South Central 71.79%

Family Households by Region, 1990

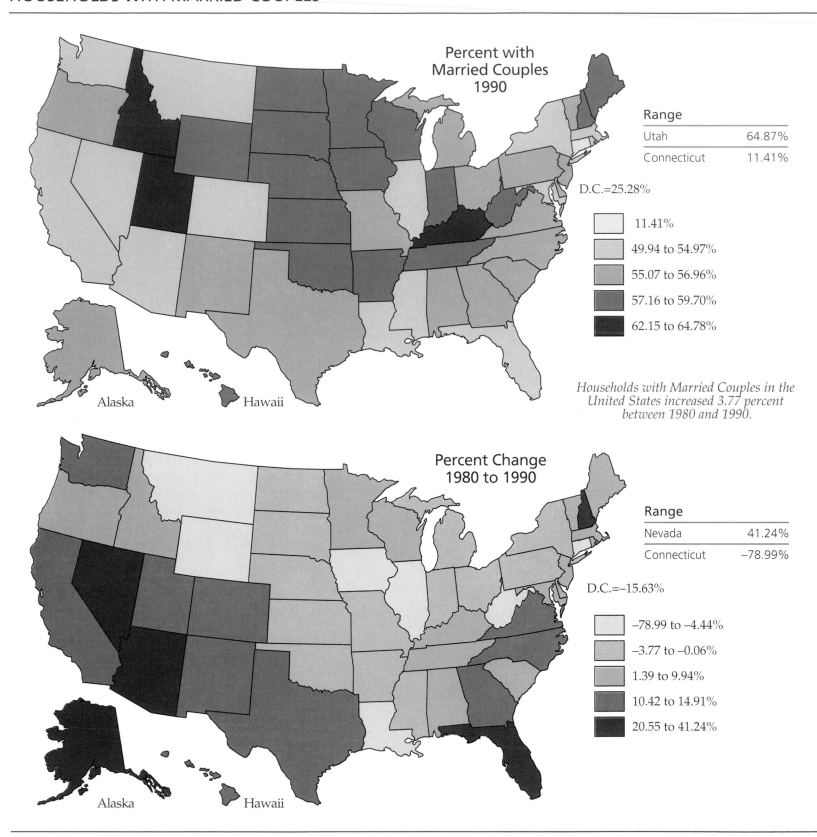

Percent with Married Couples 1990

Range

Utah	64.87%
Connecticut	11.41%

D.C.=25.28%

- 11.41%
- 49.94 to 54.97%
- 55.07 to 56.96%
- 57.16 to 59.70%
- 62.15 to 64.78%

Alaska   Hawaii

Households with Married Couples in the United States increased 3.77 percent between 1980 and 1990.

Percent Change 1980 to 1990

Range

Nevada	41.24%
Connecticut	−78.99%

D.C.=−15.63%

- −78.99 to −4.44%
- −3.77 to −0.06%
- 1.39 to 9.94%
- 10.42 to 14.91%
- 20.55 to 41.24%

Alaska   Hawaii

Households with Married Couples, 1990

United States	50,199,555
Alabama	858,327
Alaska	106,079
Arizona	747,806
Arkansas	527,358
California	5,469,522
Colorado	690,292
Connecticut	140,385
Delaware	137,983
District of Columbia	63,110
Florida	2,791,734
Georgia	1,306,756
Hawaii	210,468
Idaho	224,198
Illinois	2,271,962
Indiana	1,202,020
Iowa	629,893
Kansas	552,495
Kentucky	861,732
Louisiana	803,282
Maine	270,565
Maryland	948,563
Massachusetts	1,170,275
Michigan	1,883,143
Minnesota	942,524
Mississippi	498,248
Missouri	1,104,223
Montana	167,526
Nebraska	350,514
Nevada	239,573
New Hampshire	245,307
New Jersey	1,578,702
New Mexico	303,789
New York	3,315,845
North Carolina	1,424,206
North Dakota	142,374
Ohio	2,294,111
Oklahoma	695,691
Oregon	613,297
Pennsylvania	2,502,072
Rhode Island	202,283
South Carolina	710,089
South Dakota	152,519
Tennessee	1,059,569
Texas	3,435,540
Utah	348,029
Vermont	118,905
Virginia	1,302,219
Washington	1,029,267
West Virginia	406,105
Wisconsin	1,048,010
Wyoming	100,800

Households with Female Heads, 1990

United States	10,891,646
Alabama	201,220
Alaska	18,229
Arizona	142,320
Arkansas	98,924
California	1,192,180
Colorado	124,569
Connecticut	365,986
Delaware	29,319
District of Columbia	48,575
Florida	548,556
Georgia	329,641
Hawaii	37,409
Idaho	28,883
Illinois	505,745
Indiana	217,628
Iowa	85,141
Kansas	81,433
Kentucky	159,660
Louisiana	234,129
Maine	44,360
Maryland	231,889
Massachusetts	270,925
Michigan	442,239
Minnesota	141,554
Mississippi	145,221
Missouri	208,175
Montana	26,397
Nebraska	50,175
Nevada	47,509
New Hampshire	34,777
New Jersey	338,455
New Mexico	64,555
New York	919,266
North Carolina	309,876
North Dakota	17,523
Ohio	478,070
Oklahoma	125,469
Oregon	101,762
Pennsylvania	507,008
Rhode Island	44,342
South Carolina	176,204
South Dakota	20,711
Tennessee	232,699
Texas	701,826
Utah	49,077
Vermont	19,360
Virginia	255,106
Washington	175,522
West Virginia	73,527
Wisconsin	174,530
Wyoming	13,990

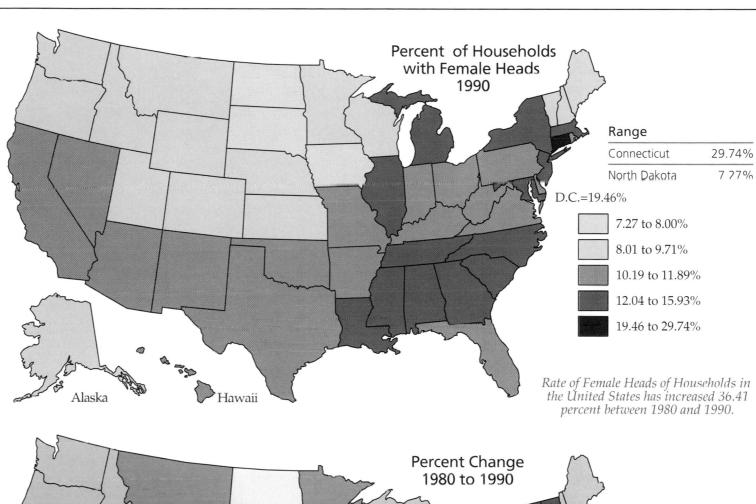

Percent of Households with Female Heads 1990

Range

Connecticut	29.74%
North Dakota	7.27%

D.C.=19.46%

- 7.27 to 8.00%
- 8.01 to 9.71%
- 10.19 to 11.89%
- 12.04 to 15.93%
- 19.46 to 29.74%

Alaska Hawaii

Rate of Female Heads of Households in the United States has increased 36.41 percent between 1980 and 1990.

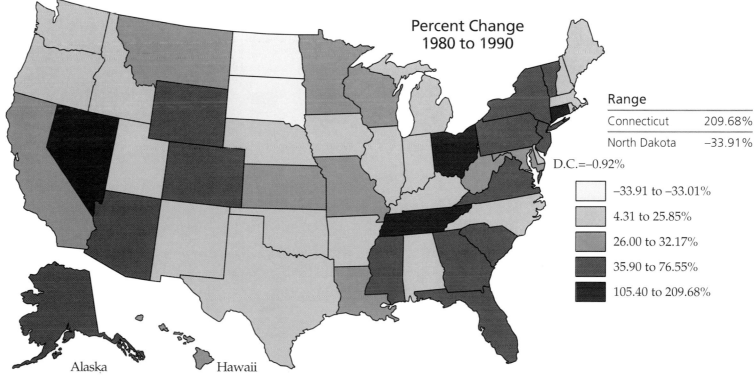

Percent Change 1980 to 1990

Range

Connecticut	209.68%
North Dakota	−33.91%

D.C.=−0.92%

- −33.91 to −33.01%
- 4.31 to 25.85%
- 26.00 to 32.17%
- 35.90 to 76.55%
- 105.40 to 209.68%

Alaska Hawaii

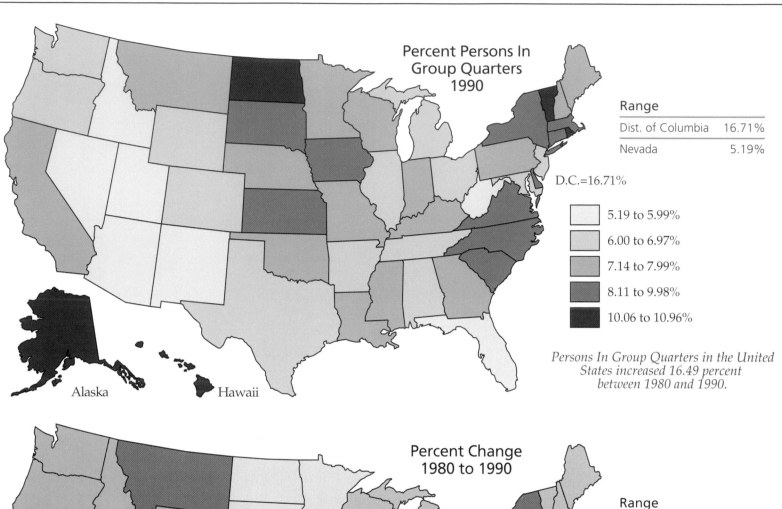

Percent Persons In Group Quarters 1990

Range

Dist. of Columbia	16.71%
Nevada	5.19%

D.C.=16.71%

- 5.19 to 5.99%
- 6.00 to 6.97%
- 7.14 to 7.99%
- 8.11 to 9.98%
- 10.06 to 10.96%

Alaska   Hawaii

Persons In Group Quarters in the United States increased 16.49 percent between 1980 and 1990.

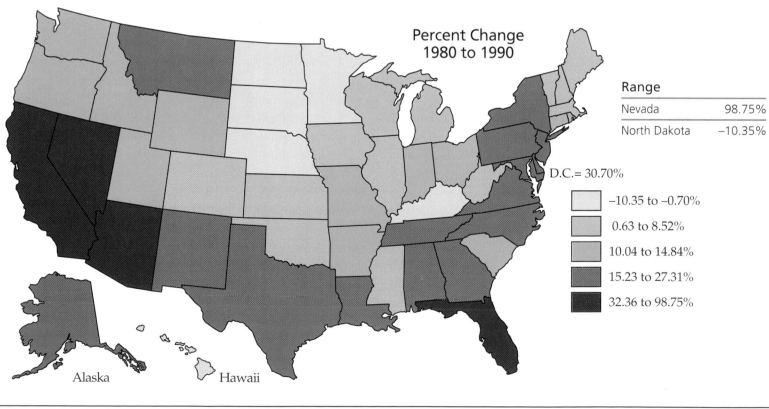

Percent Change 1980 to 1990

Range

Nevada	98.75%
North Dakota	−10.35%

D.C.= 30.70%

- −10.35 to −0.70%
- 0.63 to 8.52%
- 10.04 to 14.84%
- 15.23 to 27.31%
- 32.36 to 98.75%

Alaska   Hawaii

Persons In Group Quarters, 1990

United States	6,697,744
Alabama	92,402
Alaska	20,701
Arizona	80,683
Arkansas	58,332
California	751,860
Colorado	79,472
Connecticut	101,167
Delaware	20,071
District of Columbia	41,717
Florida	307,461
Georgia	173,633
Hawaii	37,632
Idaho	21,490
Illinois	286,956
Indiana	161,992
Iowa	99,520
Kansas	82,765
Kentucky	101,176
Louisiana	112,578
Maine	37,169
Maryland	113,856
Massachusetts	214,307
Michigan	211,692
Minnesota	117,621
Mississippi	69,717
Missouri	145,397
Montana	23,747
Nebraska	47,553
Nevada	24,200
New Hampshire	32,151
New Jersey	171,368
New Mexico	28,807
New York	545,265
North Carolina	224,470
North Dakota	24,234
Ohio	261,451
Oklahoma	93,677
Oregon	66,205
Pennsylvania	348,424
Rhode Island	38,595
South Carolina	116,543
South Dakota	25,841
Tennessee	129,129
Texas	393,447
Utah	29,048
Vermont	21,642
Virginia	209,300
Washington	120,531
West Virginia	36,911
Wisconsin	133,598
Wyoming	10,240

Householders 65 and Over, 1990

United States	8,824,845
Alabama	154,191
Alaska	5,737
Arizona	119,287
Arkansas	103,386
California	818,520
Colorado	95,849
Connecticut	121,918
Delaware	21,566
District of Columbia	27,237
Florida	591,468
Georgia	185,027
Hawaii	20,933
Idaho	32,939
Illinois	423,740
Indiana	208,437
Iowa	130,964
Kansas	104,297
Kentucky	142,045
Louisiana	137,596
Maine	48,257
Maryland	135,318
Massachusetts	243,334
Michigan	317,659
Minnesota	167,001
Mississippi	98,180
Missouri	221,516
Montana	32,208
Nebraska	69,640
Nevada	33,244
New Hampshire	34,522
New Jersey	273,736
New Mexico	42,964
New York	700,016
North Carolina	226,384
North Dakota	28,021
Ohio	416,352
Oklahoma	131,237
Oregon	108,579
Pennsylvania	526,264
Rhode Island	44,627
South Carolina	109,012
South Dakota	31,560
Tennessee	178,077
Texas	472,029
Utah	38,320
Vermont	19,648
Virginia	178,575
Washington	162,520
West Virginia	84,405
Wisconsin	192,072
Wyoming	14,431

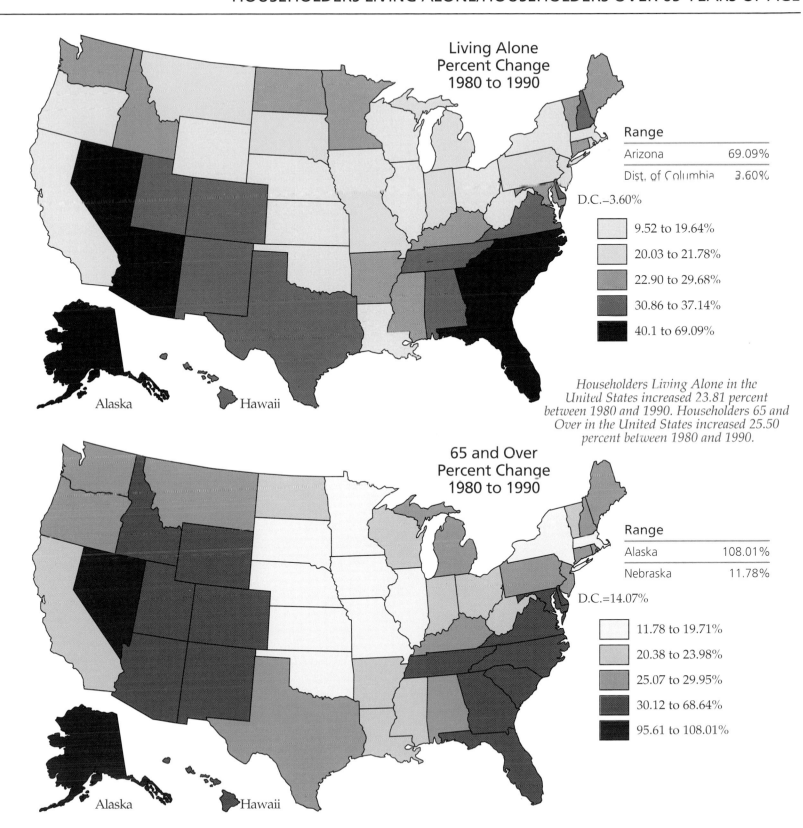

Living Alone Percent Change 1980 to 1990

Range

Arizona	69.09%
Dist. of Columbia	3.60%

D.C. −3.60%

- 9.52 to 19.64%
- 20.03 to 21.78%
- 22.90 to 29.68%
- 30.86 to 37.14%
- 40.1 to 69.09%

Householders Living Alone in the United States increased 23.81 percent between 1980 and 1990. Householders 65 and Over in the United States increased 25.50 percent between 1980 and 1990.

65 and Over Percent Change 1980 to 1990

Range

Alaska	108.01%
Nebraska	11.78%

D.C. = 14.07%

- 11.78 to 19.71%
- 20.38 to 23.98%
- 25.07 to 29.95%
- 30.12 to 68.64%
- 95.61 to 108.01%

Alaska   Hawaii

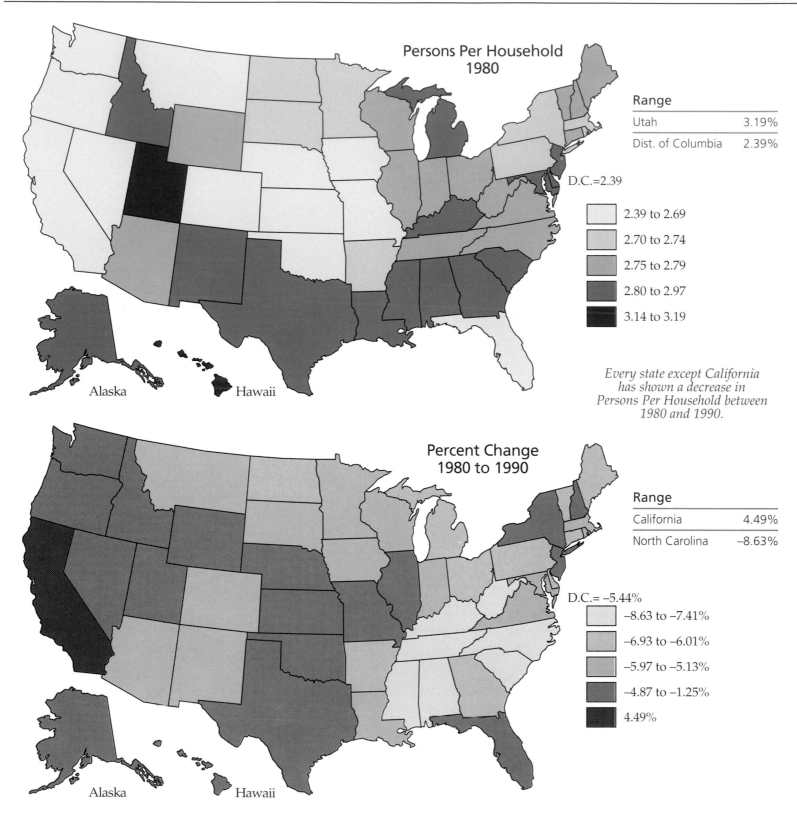

Persons Per Household 1980

Range

| Utah | 3.19% |
| Dist. of Columbia | 2.39% |

D.C.=2.39

- 2.39 to 2.69
- 2.70 to 2.74
- 2.75 to 2.79
- 2.80 to 2.97
- 3.14 to 3.19

Alaska   Hawaii

Every state except California has shown a decrease in Persons Per Household between 1980 and 1990.

Percent Change 1980 to 1990

Range

| California | 4.49% |
| North Carolina | −8.63% |

D.C.= −5.44%

- −8.63 to −7.41%
- −6.93 to −6.01%
- −5.97 to −5.13%
- −4.87 to −1.25%
- 4.49%

Alaska   Hawaii

Persons Per Household, 1980

United States	2.77
Alabama	2.84
Alaska	2.91
Arizona	2.78
Arkansas	2.74
California	2.67
Colorado	2.65
Connecticut	2.76
Delaware	2.80
District of Columbia	2.39
Florida	2.55
Georgia	2.84
Hawaii	3.14
Idaho	2.85
Illinois	2.76
Indiana	2.77
Iowa	2.68
Kansas	2.61
Kentucky	2.82
Louisiana	2.91
Maine	2.75
Maryland	2.82
Massachusetts	2.73
Michigan	2.83
Minnesota	2.73
Mississippi	2.97
Missouri	2.67
Montana	2.69
Nebraska	2.66
Nevada	2.59
New Hampshire	2.75
New Jersey	2.83
New Mexico	2.89
New York	2.70
North Carolina	2.78
North Dakota	2.74
Ohio	2.76
Oklahoma	2.62
Oregon	2.59
Pennsylvania	2.74
Rhode Island	2.70
South Carolina	2.93
South Dakota	2.73
Tennessee	2.77
Texas	2.81
Utah	3.19
Vermont	2.75
Virginia	2.77
Washington	2.61
West Virginia	2.79
Wisconsin	2.77
Wyoming	2.76

Persons Per Household, 1990

United States	2.62
Alabama	2.62
Alaska	2.80
Arizona	2.62
Arkansas	2.57
California	2.79
Colorado	2.51
Connecticut	2.59
Delaware	2.61
District of Columbia	2.26
Florida	2.46
Georgia	2.66
Hawaii	3.01
Idaho	2.73
Illinois	2.65
Indiana	2.61
Iowa	2.52
Kansas	2.53
Kentucky	2.60
Louisiana	2.74
Maine	2.56
Maryland	2.67
Massachusetts	2.58
Michigan	2.66
Minnesota	2.58
Mississippi	2.75
Missouri	2.54
Montana	2.53
Nebraska	2.54
Nevada	2.53
New Hampshire	2.62
New Jersey	2.70
New Mexico	2.74
New York	2.63
North Carolina	2.54
North Dakota	2.55
Ohio	2.59
Oklahoma	2.53
Oregon	2.52
Pennsylvania	2.57
Rhode Island	2.55
South Carolina	2.68
South Dakota	2.59
Tennessee	2.56
Texas	2.73
Utah	3.15
Vermont	2.57
Virginia	2.61
Washington	2.53
West Virginia	2.55
Wisconsin	2.61
Wyoming	2.63

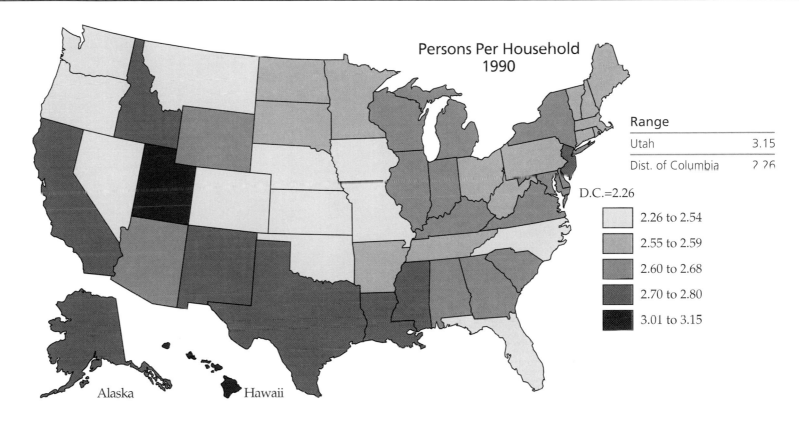

Persons Per Household 1990

Range

Utah	3.15
Dist. of Columbia	2.26

D.C.=2.26

	2.26 to 2.54
	2.55 to 2.59
	2.60 to 2.68
	2.70 to 2.80
	3.01 to 3.15

Alaska   Hawaii

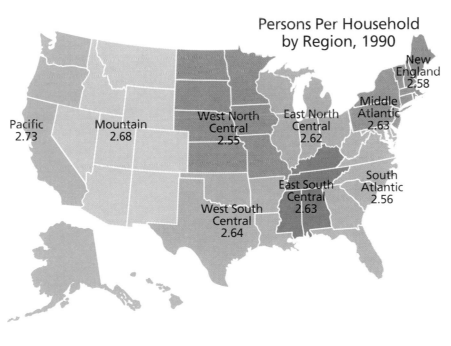

Persons Per Household by Region, 1990

- New England 2.58
- Middle Atlantic 2.63
- West North Central 2.55
- East North Central 2.62
- Pacific 2.73
- Mountain 2.68
- West South Central 2.64
- East South Central 2.63
- South Atlantic 2.56

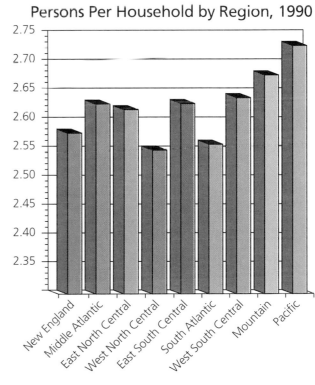

Persons Per Household by Region, 1990

(Bar chart, x-axis regions: New England, Middle Atlantic, East North Central, West North Central, East South Central, South Atlantic, West South Central, Mountain, Pacific; y-axis 2.35 to 2.75)

Major Cities

Boston, MA	2.37	Paterson, NJ	3.14
Bridgeport, CT	2.63	Philadelphia, PA	2.56
Buffalo, NY	2.33	Pittsburgh, PA	2.27
Burlington, VT	2.29	Portland, ME	2.21
Elizabeth, NJ	2.76	Providence, RI	2.52
Hartford, CT	2.55	Rochester, NY	2.37
Jersey City, NJ	2.73	Springfield, MA	2.60
Manchester, NH	2.40	Syracuse, NY	2.33
New Haven, CT	2.41	Waterbury, CT	2.48
New York, NY	2.54	Worcester, MA	2.46
Newark, NJ	2.91	Yonkers, NY	2.57

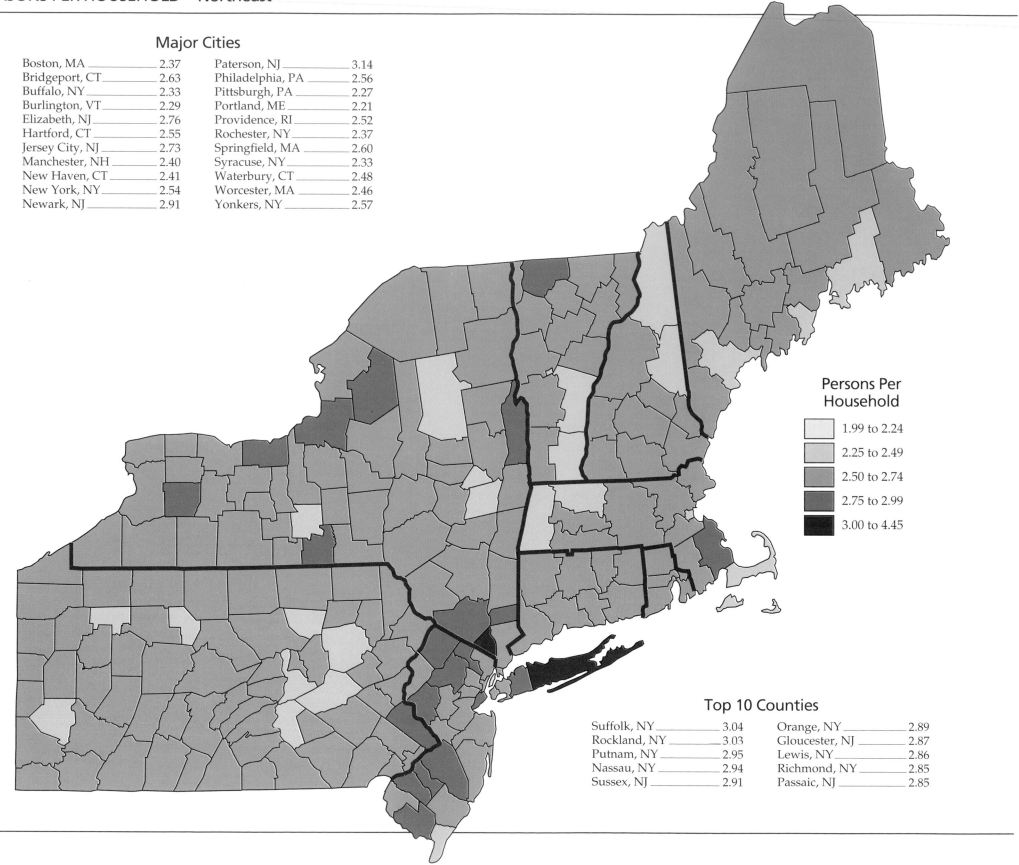

Persons Per Household

- 1.99 to 2.24
- 2.25 to 2.49
- 2.50 to 2.74
- 2.75 to 2.99
- 3.00 to 4.45

Top 10 Counties

Suffolk, NY	3.04	Orange, NY	2.89
Rockland, NY	3.03	Gloucester, NJ	2.87
Putnam, NY	2.95	Lewis, NY	2.86
Nassau, NY	2.94	Richmond, NY	2.85
Sussex, NJ	2.91	Passaic, NJ	2.85

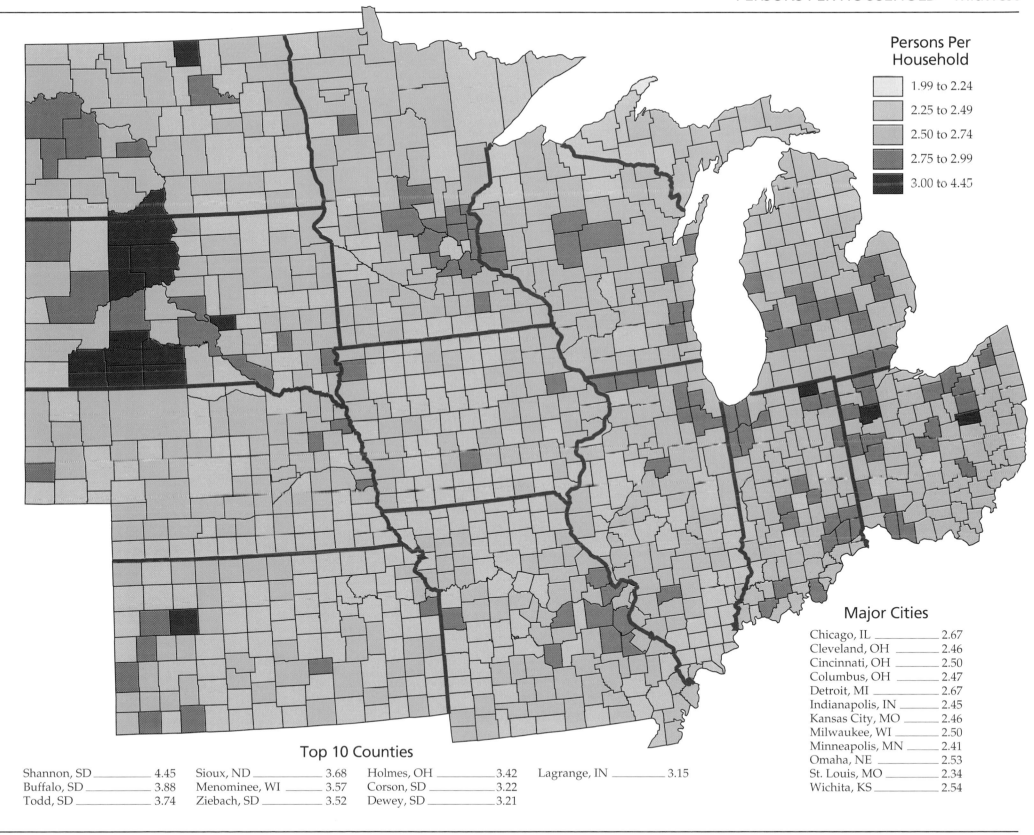

Persons Per Household

	1.99 to 2.24
	2.25 to 2.49
	2.50 to 2.74
	2.75 to 2.99
	3.00 to 4.45

Major Cities

Chicago, IL _____ 2.67
Cleveland, OH _____ 2.46
Cincinnati, OH _____ 2.50
Columbus, OH _____ 2.47
Detroit, MI _____ 2.67
Indianapolis, IN _____ 2.45
Kansas City, MO _____ 2.46
Milwaukee, WI _____ 2.50
Minneapolis, MN _____ 2.41
Omaha, NE _____ 2.53
St. Louis, MO _____ 2.34
Wichita, KS _____ 2.54

Top 10 Counties

Shannon, SD _____ 4.45	Sioux, ND _____ 3.68	Holmes, OH _____ 3.42	Lagrange, IN _____ 3.15
Buffalo, SD _____ 3.88	Menominee, WI _____ 3.57	Corson, SD _____ 3.22	
Todd, SD _____ 3.74	Ziebach, SD _____ 3.52	Dewey, SD _____ 3.21	

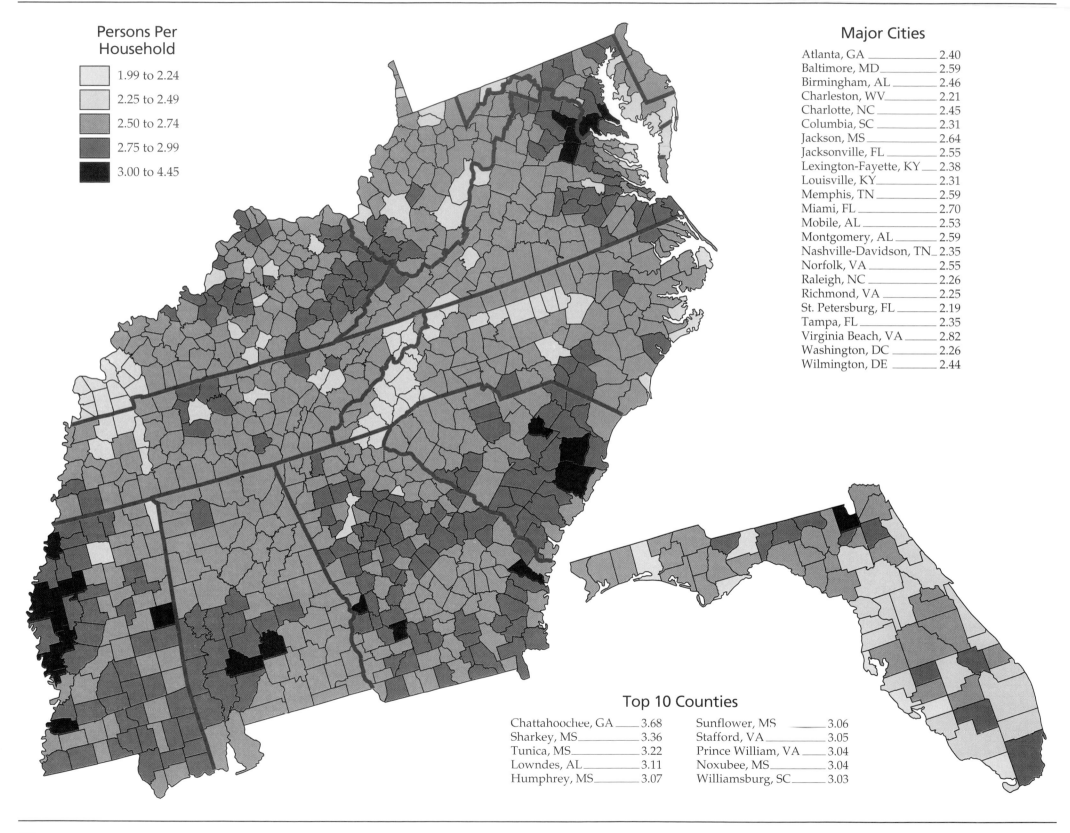

Persons Per Household

- 1.99 to 2.24
- 2.25 to 2.49
- 2.50 to 2.74
- 2.75 to 2.99
- 3.00 to 4.45

Major Cities

Atlanta, GA	2.40
Baltimore, MD	2.59
Birmingham, AL	2.46
Charleston, WV	2.21
Charlotte, NC	2.45
Columbia, SC	2.31
Jackson, MS	2.64
Jacksonville, FL	2.55
Lexington-Fayette, KY	2.38
Louisville, KY	2.31
Memphis, TN	2.59
Miami, FL	2.70
Mobile, AL	2.53
Montgomery, AL	2.59
Nashville-Davidson, TN	2.35
Norfolk, VA	2.55
Raleigh, NC	2.26
Richmond, VA	2.25
St. Petersburg, FL	2.19
Tampa, FL	2.35
Virginia Beach, VA	2.82
Washington, DC	2.26
Wilmington, DE	2.44

Top 10 Counties

Chattahoochee, GA	3.68	Sunflower, MS	3.06
Sharkey, MS	3.36	Stafford, VA	3.05
Tunica, MS	3.22	Prince William, VA	3.04
Lowndes, AL	3.11	Noxubee, MS	3.04
Humphrey, MS	3.07	Williamsburg, SC	3.03

Top 10 Counties

Starr, TX	3.90
Webb, TX	3.81
Maverick, TX	3.70
Hidalgo, TX	3.67
Zavala, TX	3.54
Willacy, TX	3.48
Cameron, TX	3.48
Dimmit, TX	3.38
Reagan, TX	3.29
El Paso, TX	3.25

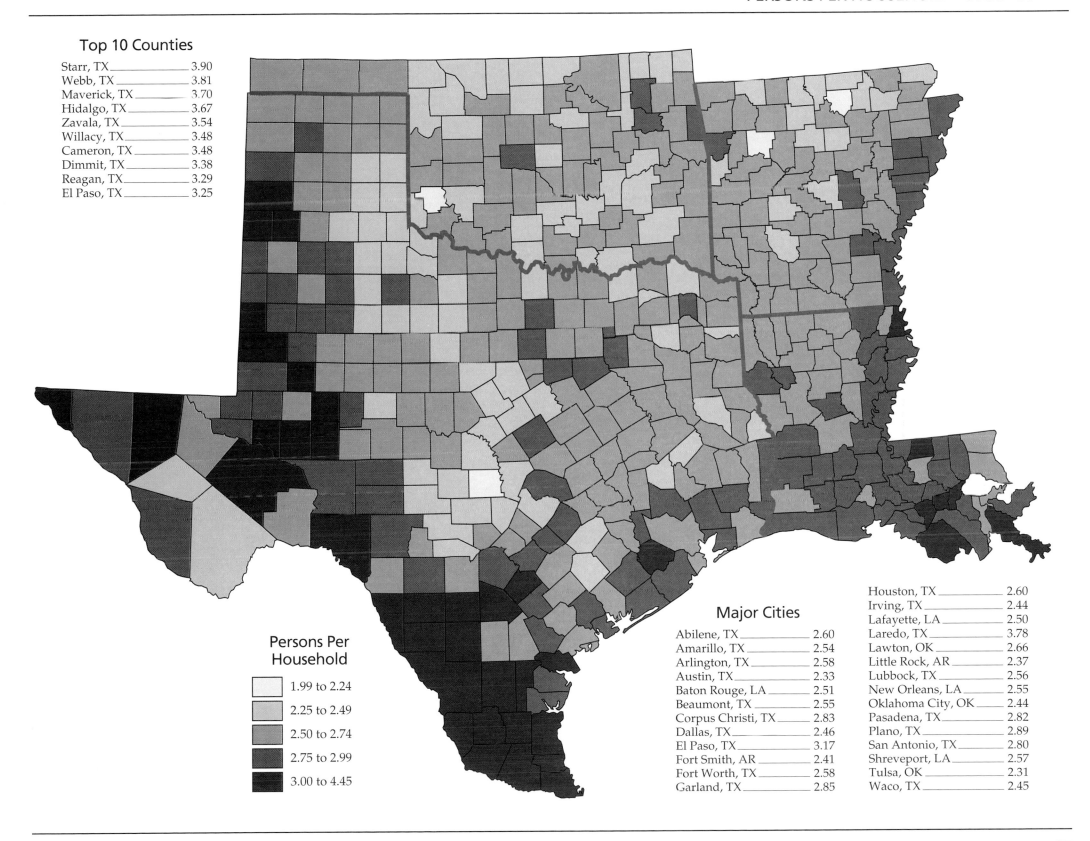

Persons Per Household

☐	1.99 to 2.24
☐	2.25 to 2.49
☐	2.50 to 2.74
☐	2.75 to 2.99
☐	3.00 to 4.45

Major Cities

Abilene, TX	2.60		Houston, TX	2.60
Amarillo, TX	2.54		Irving, TX	2.44
Arlington, TX	2.58		Lafayette, LA	2.50
Austin, TX	2.33		Laredo, TX	3.78
Baton Rouge, LA	2.51		Lawton, OK	2.66
Beaumont, TX	2.55		Little Rock, AR	2.37
Corpus Christi, TX	2.83		Lubbock, TX	2.56
Dallas, TX	2.46		New Orleans, LA	2.55
El Paso, TX	3.17		Oklahoma City, OK	2.44
Fort Smith, AR	2.41		Pasadena, TX	2.82
Fort Worth, TX	2.58		Plano, TX	2.89
Garland, TX	2.85		San Antonio, TX	2.80
			Shreveport, LA	2.57
			Tulsa, OK	2.31
			Waco, TX	2.45

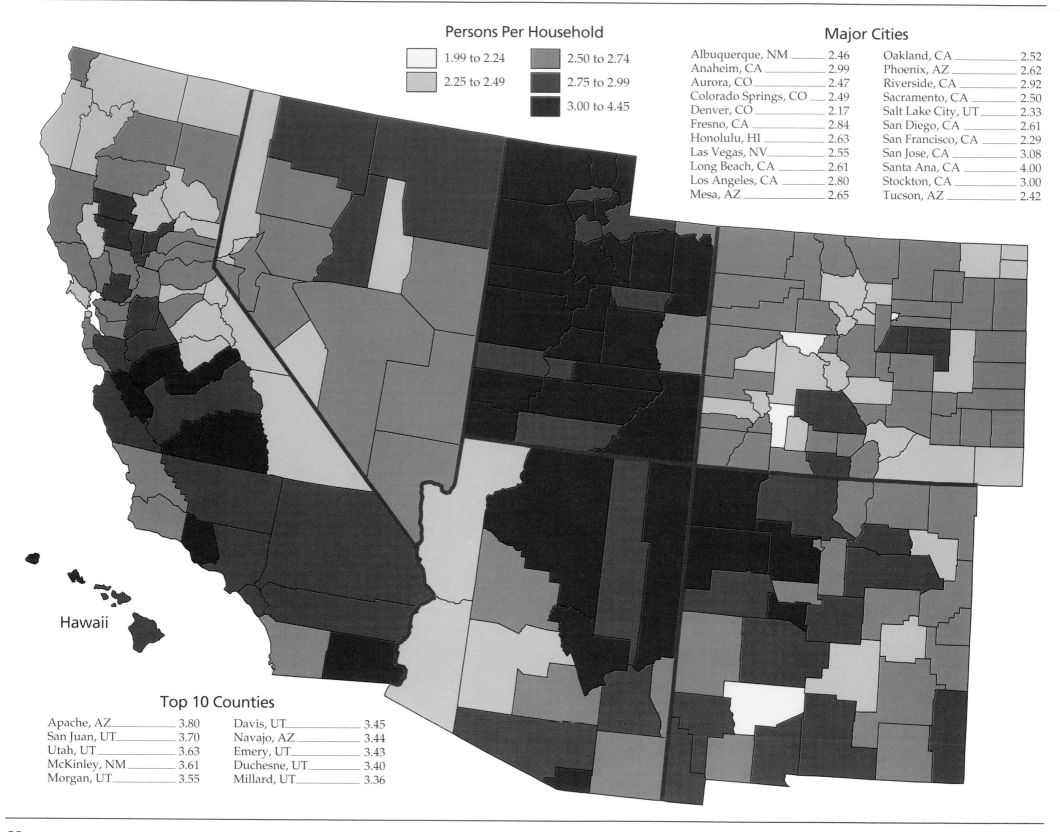

Persons Per Household

1.99 to 2.24	2.50 to 2.74
2.25 to 2.49	2.75 to 2.99
	3.00 to 4.45

Major Cities

Albuquerque, NM	2.46	Oakland, CA	2.52
Anaheim, CA	2.99	Phoenix, AZ	2.62
Aurora, CO	2.47	Riverside, CA	2.92
Colorado Springs, CO	2.49	Sacramento, CA	2.50
Denver, CO	2.17	Salt Lake City, UT	2.33
Fresno, CA	2.84	San Diego, CA	2.61
Honolulu, HI	2.63	San Francisco, CA	2.29
Las Vegas, NV	2.55	San Jose, CA	3.08
Long Beach, CA	2.61	Santa Ana, CA	4.00
Los Angeles, CA	2.80	Stockton, CA	3.00
Mesa, AZ	2.65	Tucson, AZ	2.42

Hawaii

Top 10 Counties

Apache, AZ	3.80	Davis, UT	3.45
San Juan, UT	3.70	Navajo, AZ	3.44
Utah, UT	3.63	Emery, UT	3.43
McKinley, NM	3.61	Duchesne, UT	3.40
Morgan, UT	3.55	Millard, UT	3.36

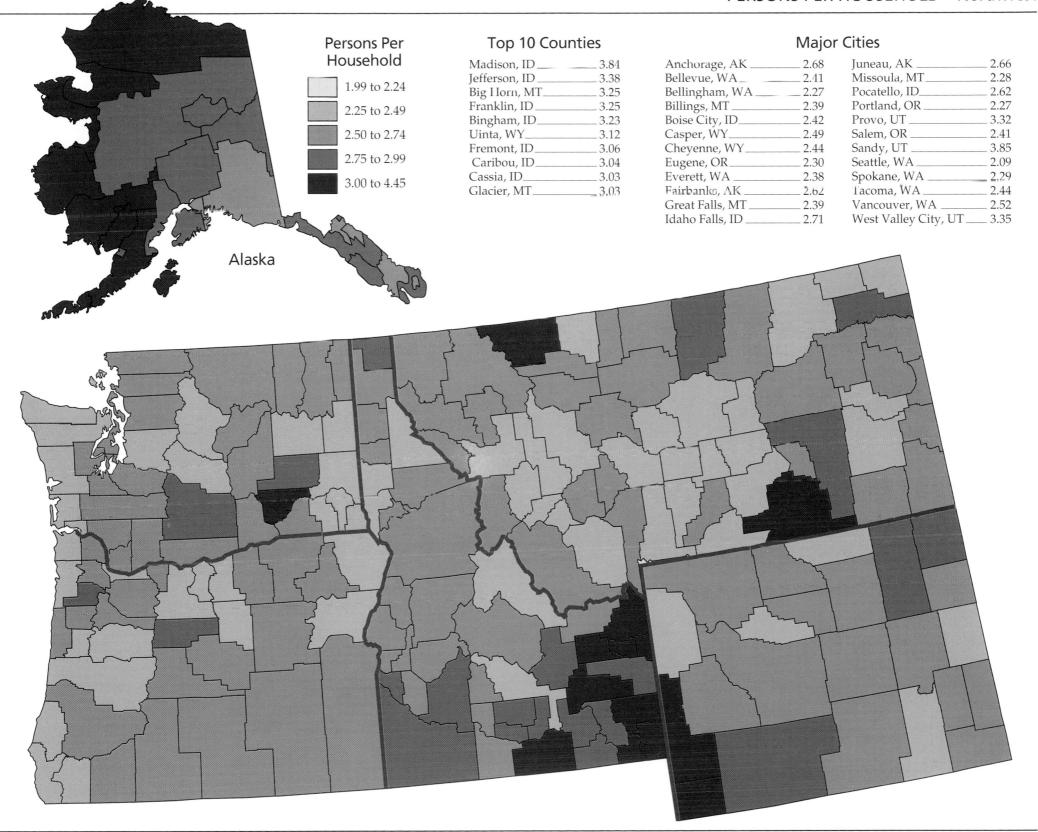

Persons Per Household

- ☐ 1.99 to 2.24
- ☐ 2.25 to 2.49
- ☐ 2.50 to 2.74
- ☐ 2.75 to 2.99
- ☐ 3.00 to 4.45

Alaska

Top 10 Counties

Madison, ID	3.84
Jefferson, ID	3.38
Big Horn, MT	3.25
Franklin, ID	3.25
Bingham, ID	3.23
Uinta, WY	3.12
Fremont, ID	3.06
Caribou, ID	3.04
Cassia, ID	3.03
Glacier, MT	3.03

Major Cities

City	Value	City	Value
Anchorage, AK	2.68	Juneau, AK	2.66
Bellevue, WA	2.41	Missoula, MT	2.28
Bellingham, WA	2.27	Pocatello, ID	2.62
Billings, MT	2.39	Portland, OR	2.27
Boise City, ID	2.42	Provo, UT	3.32
Casper, WY	2.49	Salem, OR	2.41
Cheyenne, WY	2.44	Sandy, UT	3.85
Eugene, OR	2.30	Seattle, WA	2.09
Everett, WA	2.38	Spokane, WA	2.29
Fairbanks, AK	2.62	Tacoma, WA	2.44
Great Falls, MT	2.39	Vancouver, WA	2.52
Idaho Falls, ID	2.71	West Valley City, UT	3.35

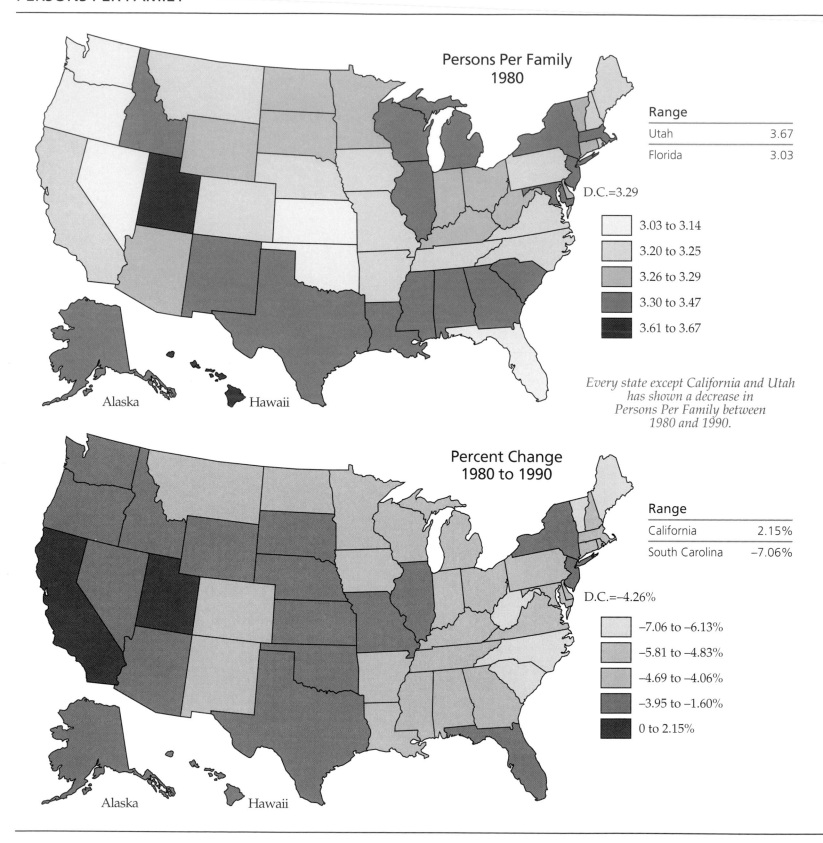

Persons Per Family 1980

Range

| Utah | 3.67 |
| Florida | 3.03 |

D.C.=3.29

	3.03 to 3.14
	3.20 to 3.25
	3.26 to 3.29
	3.30 to 3.47
	3.61 to 3.67

Every state except California and Utah has shown a decrease in Persons Per Family between 1980 and 1990.

Percent Change 1980 to 1990

Range

| California | 2.15% |
| South Carolina | −7.06% |

D.C.=−4.26%

	−7.06 to −6.13%
	−5.81 to −4.83%
	−4.69 to −4.06%
	−3.95 to −1.60%
	0 to 2.15%

Alaska

Hawaii

Persons Per Family, 1980

United States	3.28
Alabama	3.32
Alaska	3.46
Arizona	3.28
Arkansas	3.21
California	3.25
Colorado	3.20
Connecticut	3.26
Delaware	3.27
District of Columbia	3.29
Florida	3.03
Georgia	3.33
Hawaii	3.61
Idaho	3.33
Illinois	3.33
Indiana	3.26
Iowa	3.20
Kansas	3.13
Kentucky	3.27
Louisiana	3.44
Maine	3.23
Maryland	3.30
Massachusetts	3.31
Michigan	3.34
Minnesota	3.29
Mississippi	3.47
Missouri	3.20
Montana	3.24
Nebraska	3.22
Nevada	3.13
New Hampshire	3.24
New Jersey	3.33
New Mexico	3.42
New York	3.31
North Carolina	3.24
North Dakota	3.29
Ohio	3.28
Oklahoma	3.13
Oregon	3.10
Pennsylvania	3.25
Rhode Island	3.25
South Carolina	3.40
South Dakota	3.29
Tennessee	3.22
Texas	3.34
Utah	3.67
Vermont	3.26
Virginia	3.25
Washington	3.14
West Virginia	3.26
Wisconsin	3.31
Wyoming	3.29

Persons Per Family, 1990

United States	3.16
Alabama	3.13
Alaska	3.33
Arizona	3.16
Arkansas	3.06
California	3.32
Colorado	3.07
Connecticut	3.10
Delaware	3.09
District of Columbia	3.15
Florida	2.95
Georgia	3.16
Hawaii	3.48
Idaho	3.23
Illinois	3.23
Indiana	3.11
Iowa	3.05
Kansas	3.08
Kentucky	3.08
Louisiana	3.28
Maine	3.03
Maryland	3.14
Massachusetts	3.15
Michigan	3.16
Minnesota	3.13
Mississippi	3.27
Missouri	3.08
Montana	3.08
Nebraska	3.11
Nevada	3.06
New Hampshire	3.09
New Jersey	3.21
New Mexico	3.26
New York	3.22
North Carolina	3.03
North Dakota	3.13
Ohio	3.12
Oklahoma	3.06
Oregon	3.02
Pennsylvania	3.10
Rhode Island	3.11
South Carolina	3.16
South Dakota	3.16
Tennessee	3.05
Texas	3.28
Utah	3.67
Vermont	3.06
Virginia	3.09
Washington	3.06
West Virginia	3.05
Wisconsin	3.14
Wyoming	3.16

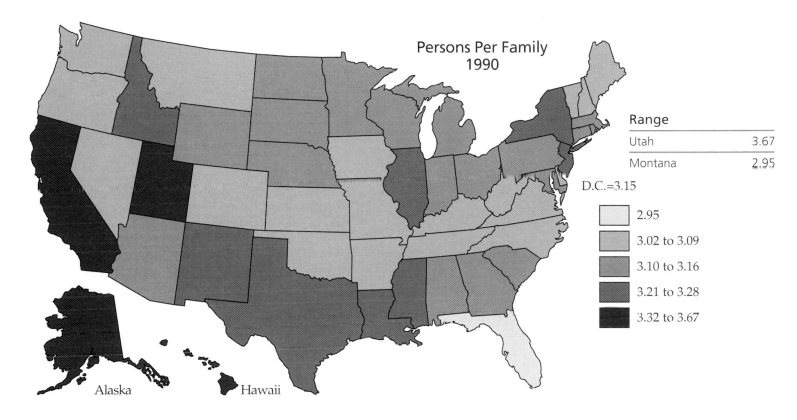

Persons Per Family
1990

Range

Utah	3.67
Montana	2.95

D.C.=3.15

- 2.95
- 3.02 to 3.09
- 3.10 to 3.16
- 3.21 to 3.28
- 3.32 to 3.67

Alaska   Hawaii

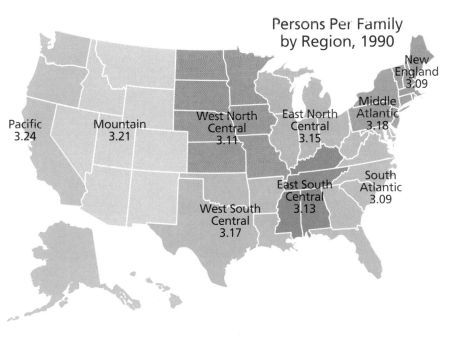

Persons Per Family
by Region, 1990

New England 3.09
Middle Atlantic 3.18
West North Central 3.11
East North Central 3.15
East South Central 3.13
South Atlantic 3.09
West South Central 3.17
Pacific 3.24
Mountain 3.21

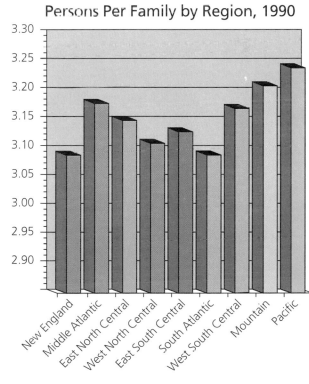

Persons Per Family by Region, 1990

(Bar chart regions, left to right: New England, Middle Atlantic, East North Central, West North Central, East South Central, South Atlantic, West South Central, Mountain, Pacific)

Part Three

HOUSING

MEDIAN HOUSING VALUE AND SALES PRICE

The value of the average home in the United States rose 73.6 percent in the decade between 1980 and 1990. Median housing value for 1980 was $48,500, and $84,200 for 1990. Median sales prices also rose. During the same period, values were $64,600 and $123,000.

Housing values showed distinct regional differences and profound variations among metropolitan areas. The table below exhibits how median sales price varied from region to region from 1970 to 1990. It also shows the rate of increase from 1980 to 1990.

	1970	1980	1990	Change
U. S.	$23,400	$64,600	$123,000	90.4%
Northeast	$30,300	$69,500	$157,500	126.6%
Midwest	$24,400	$63,400	$108,000	70.3%
South	$20,300	$59,600	$99,000	66.1%
West	$24,000	$72,300	$148,000	104.7%

The Northeastern *megalopolis* has some of the highest housing values in the 1990s. Page 76 shows a corridor of homes between $100,000 and $488,000 that runs in a belt along the Atlantic Ocean about two hundred miles inland from southern Maine to the Northern portions of Virginia. New York County has the most expensive homes in this area averaging just under $500,000 apiece.

Housing values are generally high in California and the portions of the Mountain Region shown on page 80.

CHANGES IN HOUSING VALUES

Median housing values have increased 73.7 percent across the country between 1980 and 1990. The map on page 74 demonstrates that the largest increases in median housing values have occurred in the Northeast and in California and Hawaii. A relative stability in housing values can be noted through the Dakotas and the northern Mountain states.

On pages 84 through 89, we can see changes in housing values by county between 1980 to 1990. The spatial distribution of change in the Northeast and the Middle Atlantic states show significant positive changes in urbanized areas. Such positive changes are almost unnoticeable in the Midwest where housing price stagnation and devaluation have become the norm. Southeastern counties, as portrayed in this volume, have experienced slow to modest appreciation in housing values. The same can be said of the South

Central portion of the United States. Much of the Southwest has appreciated in housing value unlike the Northwest which has experienced massive devaluation and stagnation.

HOMES SALES

In 1990, 3.83 million single–family houses were sold. Of this number, the majority were existing structures. Regional variation can be seen below.

	Existing Units	New Units	Total Units Sold
United States	3,296,000	535,000	3,831,000
Northeast	522,000	72,000	594,000
Midwest	892,000	89,000	981,000
South	1,325,000	225,000	1,550,000
West	557,000	149,000	706,000

OCCUPANCY AND VACANCY

There were 102 million housing units in the United States in 1990, representing an increase of 15.7 percent from 1980. Of these units, 89.9 percent or 91.9 million were occupied. The remaining 10.3 million units were vacant and by definition were awaiting sale, up for rent, seasonally occupied, or awaiting occupation by a new tenant or owner. The following table shows vacancy rates for housing stock in U.S. regions. Simple subtraction reveals rates of occupancy using the numbers presented below.

	Total Units (000s)	Vacant Units (000s)	Vacancy Rate 1990
Northeast	20,811	1,938	9.3%
New England	5,570	628	11.3%
Middle Atlantic	15,240	1,310	8.6%
Midwest	24,493	2,176	8.9%
East North Central	17,028	1,431	8.4%
West North Central	7,465	744	10.0%
South	36,065	4,243	11.8%
South Atlantic	18,719	2,216	11.8%
East South Central	6,214	562	9.0%
West South Central	11,132	1,465	13.2%
West	20,895	1,960	9.4%
Mountain	5,864	831	14.2%
Pacific	15,031	1,129	7.5%

Vacancy rates for houses inside and outside metropolitan areas show a remarkable similarity for both homeowner and renter–occupied units. Inside MSAs, 7.1 percent of renter–occupied units were vacant, together with 1.7 percent of homeowner–occupied

stock. Outside MSAs, rental units were uninhabited in 7.7 percent of all cases as were 1.6 percent of owner–occupied stock. Regional variations in 1990 follow.

	Homeowner Units	Rental Units
Northeast		
Vacancy Rates 1985	1.0%	3.5%
Vacancy Rates 1990	1.5%	6.2%
Midwest		
Vacancy Rates 1985	1.6%	5.9%
Vacancy Rates 1990	1.4%	6.6%
South		
Vacancy Rates 1985	2.1%	9.1%
Vacancy Rates 1990	2.0%	8.9%
West		
Vacancy Rates 1985	2.1%	6.2%
Vacancy Rates 1990	1.8%	6.4%

CHARACTERISTICS OF RECENT HOME BUYERS

The median price paid for first homes was $105,200 in 1989. Repeat buyers spent $144,700. The average monthly mortgage in the United States was $1,054. That figure was 31.8 percent of a typical household income. 21.8 percent of recent home buyers purchased new homes. 78.2 percent bought existing homes. Single–family home sales accounted for 84.8 percent of recent sales. 13.5 percent of individuals purchased condominiums. The average age of first–time buyers was 29.6 years. This figure was up from 28.1 in 1976. The average age for repeat buyers was 39.4. This figure was also up from 35.9 years in 1976. First–time buyers placed downpayments of 15.8 percent of the sales prices of their homes. Repeat buyers made larger downpayments (30.3 percent).

CHARACTERISTICS OF NEW HOMES

The average new home, sold in 1990, had 2,080 square feet of floor area, 3 bedrooms, 2.5 bathrooms, and was heated with gas, had central air–conditioning, 1 fireplace, warm air heat, and a garage. Since 1970, buyers insist on more space, more bathrooms, and more air–conditioning in their new home purchases. In 1990, 29 percent of all new home sold had more than 2,400 square feet. This is compared to 15 percent in 1980. Median floor space available in new homes sold was 1,905 square feet.

A greater percentage of buyers are opting for conventional financing and for cash sales. Federal Housing Authority (FHA) insured financing is becoming less popular in the last two decades.

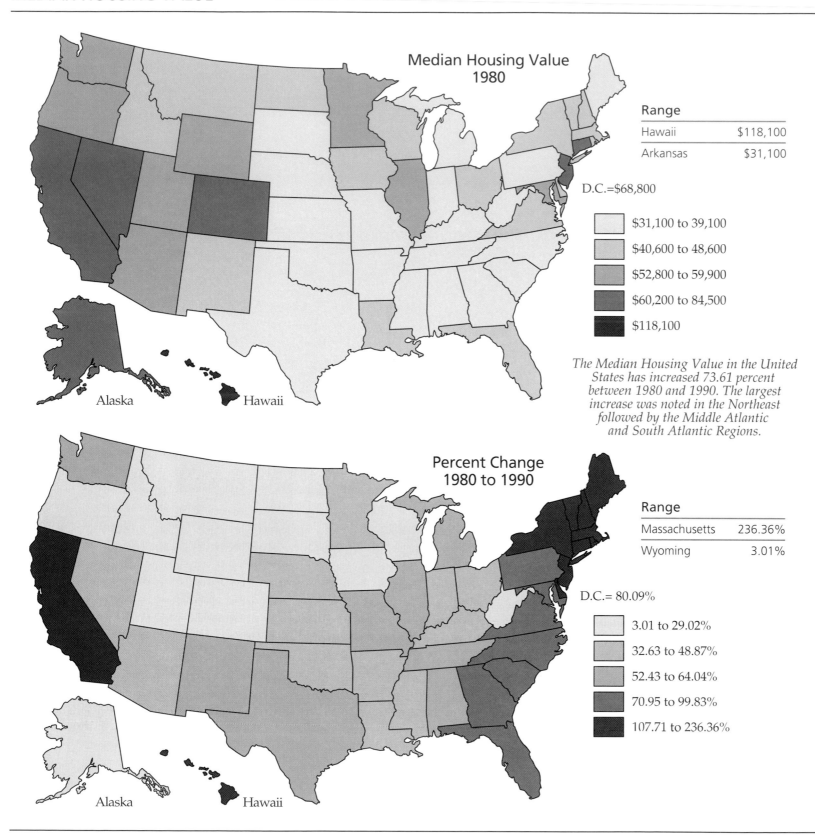

Median Housing Value 1980

Range

Hawaii	$118,100
Arkansas	$31,100

D.C.=$68,800

- $31,100 to 39,100
- $40,600 to 48,600
- $52,800 to 59,900
- $60,200 to 84,500
- $118,100

Alaska   Hawaii

The Median Housing Value in the United States has increased 73.61 percent between 1980 and 1990. The largest increase was noted in the Northeast followed by the Middle Atlantic and South Atlantic Regions.

Percent Change 1980 to 1990

Range

Massachusetts	236.36%
Wyoming	3.01%

D.C.= 80.09%

- 3.01 to 29.02%
- 32.63 to 48.87%
- 52.43 to 64.04%
- 70.95 to 99.83%
- 107.71 to 236.36%

Alaska   Hawaii

Median Housing Value, 1980

United States	$48,500
Alabama	33,900
Alaska	76,300
Arizona	54,800
Arkansas	31,100
California	84,500
Colorado	64,100
Connecticut	65,600
Delaware	44,400
District of Columbia	68,800
Florida	45,100
Georgia	36,900
Hawaii	118,100
Idaho	45,600
Illinois	52,800
Indiana	37,200
Iowa	40,600
Kansas	37,800
Kentucky	34,200
Louisiana	43,000
Maine	37,900
Maryland	58,300
Massachusetts	48,400
Michigan	39,000
Minnesota	53,100
Mississippi	31,400
Missouri	36,700
Montana	46,500
Nebraska	38,000
Nevada	68,700
New Hampshire	48,000
New Jersey	60,200
New Mexico	45,300
New York	45,600
North Carolina	36,000
North Dakota	43,900
Ohio	44,900
Oklahoma	35,600
Oregon	56,900
Pennsylvania	39,100
Rhode Island	46,800
South Carolina	35,100
South Dakota	36,600
Tennessee	35,600
Texas	39,100
Utah	57,300
Vermont	42,200
Virginia	48,000
Washington	59,900
West Virginia	38,500
Wisconsin	48,600
Wyoming	59,800

Median Housing Value, 1990

United States	$84,200
Alabama	53,700
Alaska	94,400
Arizona	80,100
Arkansas	46,300
California	195,500
Colorado	82,700
Connecticut	177,800
Delaware	100,100
District of Columbia	123,900
Florida	77,100
Georgia	71,300
Hawaii	245,300
Idaho	58,200
Illinois	80,900
Indiana	53,900
Iowa	45,900
Kansas	52,200
Kentucky	50,500
Louisiana	58,500
Maine	87,400
Maryland	116,500
Massachusetts	162,800
Michigan	60,900
Minnesota	74,000
Mississippi	45,600
Missouri	59,800
Montana	56,600
Nebraska	50,400
Nevada	95,700
New Hampshire	129,400
New Jersey	162,300
New Mexico	70,100
New York	131,600
North Carolina	65,800
North Dakota	50,800
Ohio	63,500
Oklahoma	48,100
Oregon	67,100
Pennsylvania	69,700
Rhode Island	133,500
South Carolina	61,100
South Dakota	45,200
Tennessee	58,400
Texas	59,600
Utah	68,900
Vermont	95,500
Virginia	91,000
Washington	93,400
West Virginia	47,900
Wisconsin	62,500
Wyoming	61,600

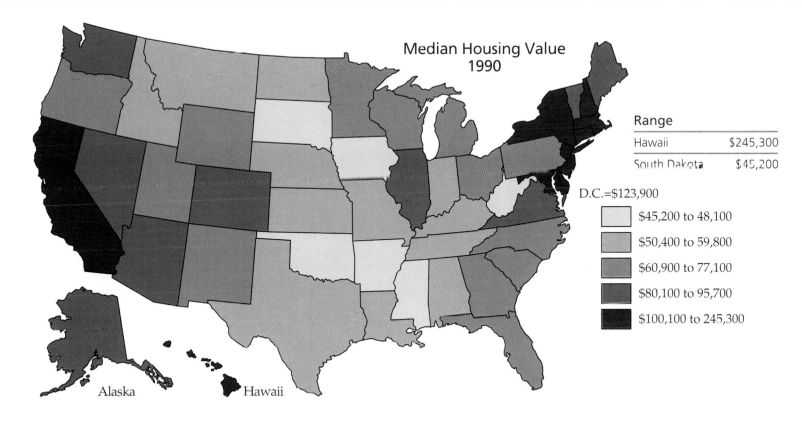

Median Housing Value
1990

Range

Hawaii	$245,300
South Dakota	$45,200

D.C.=$123,900

- $45,200 to 48,100
- $50,400 to 59,800
- $60,900 to 77,100
- $80,100 to 95,700
- $100,100 to 245,300

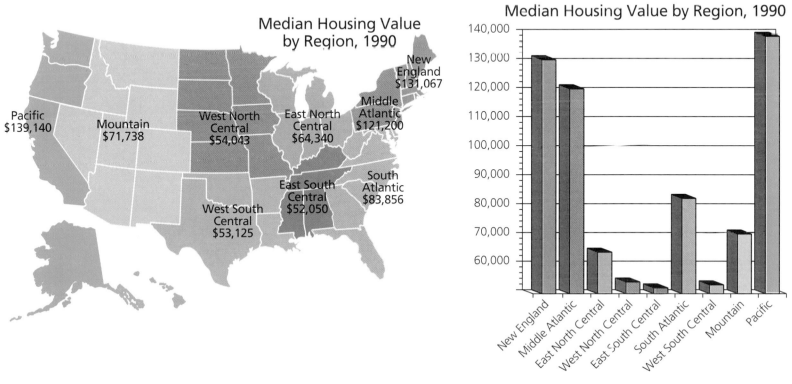

Median Housing Value
by Region, 1990

New England $131,067
Middle Atlantic $121,200
Pacific $139,140
Mountain $71,738
West North Central $54,043
East North Central $64,340
South Atlantic $83,856
East South Central $52,050
West South Central $53,125

Median Housing Value by Region, 1990

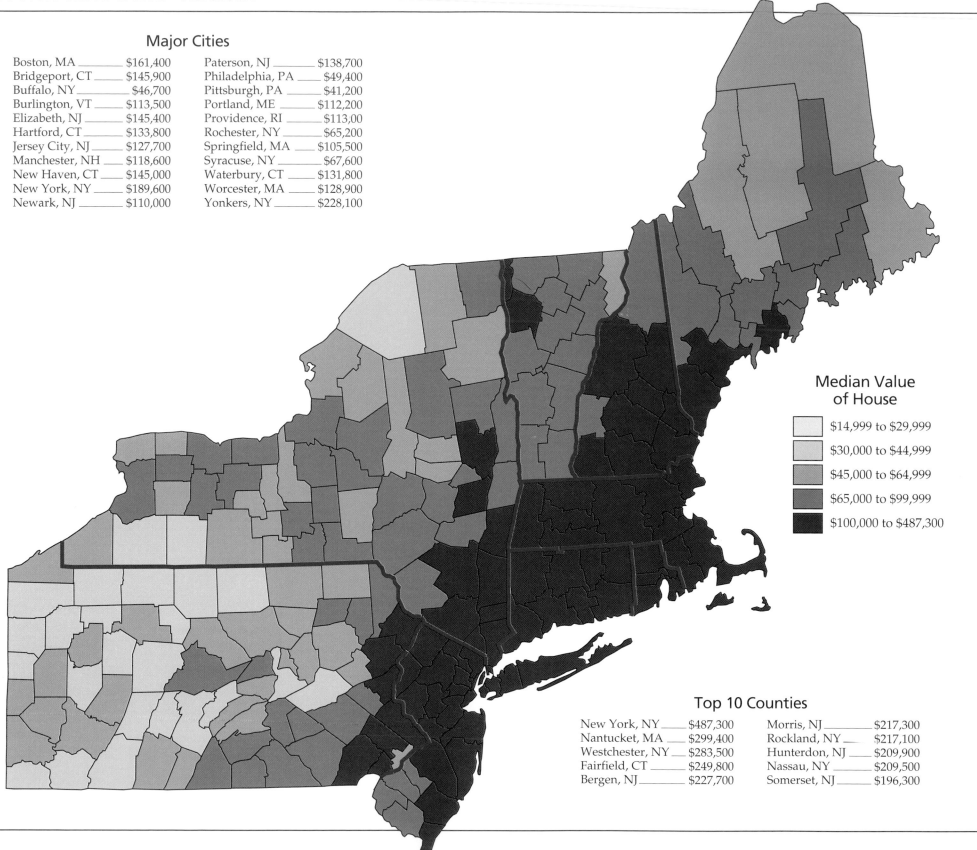

Major Cities

Boston, MA	$161,400	Paterson, NJ	$138,700
Bridgeport, CT	$145,900	Philadelphia, PA	$49,400
Buffalo, NY	$46,700	Pittsburgh, PA	$41,200
Burlington, VT	$113,500	Portland, ME	$112,200
Elizabeth, NJ	$145,400	Providence, RI	$113,00
Hartford, CT	$133,800	Rochester, NY	$65,200
Jersey City, NJ	$127,700	Springfield, MA	$105,500
Manchester, NH	$118,600	Syracuse, NY	$67,600
New Haven, CT	$145,000	Waterbury, CT	$131,800
New York, NY	$189,600	Worcester, MA	$128,900
Newark, NJ	$110,000	Yonkers, NY	$228,100

Median Value of House

- $14,999 to $29,999
- $30,000 to $44,999
- $45,000 to $64,999
- $65,000 to $99,999
- $100,000 to $487,300

Top 10 Counties

New York, NY	$487,300	Morris, NJ	$217,300
Nantucket, MA	$299,400	Rockland, NY	$217,100
Westchester, NY	$283,500	Hunterdon, NJ	$209,900
Fairfield, CT	$249,800	Nassau, NY	$209,500
Bergen, NJ	$227,700	Somerset, NJ	$196,300

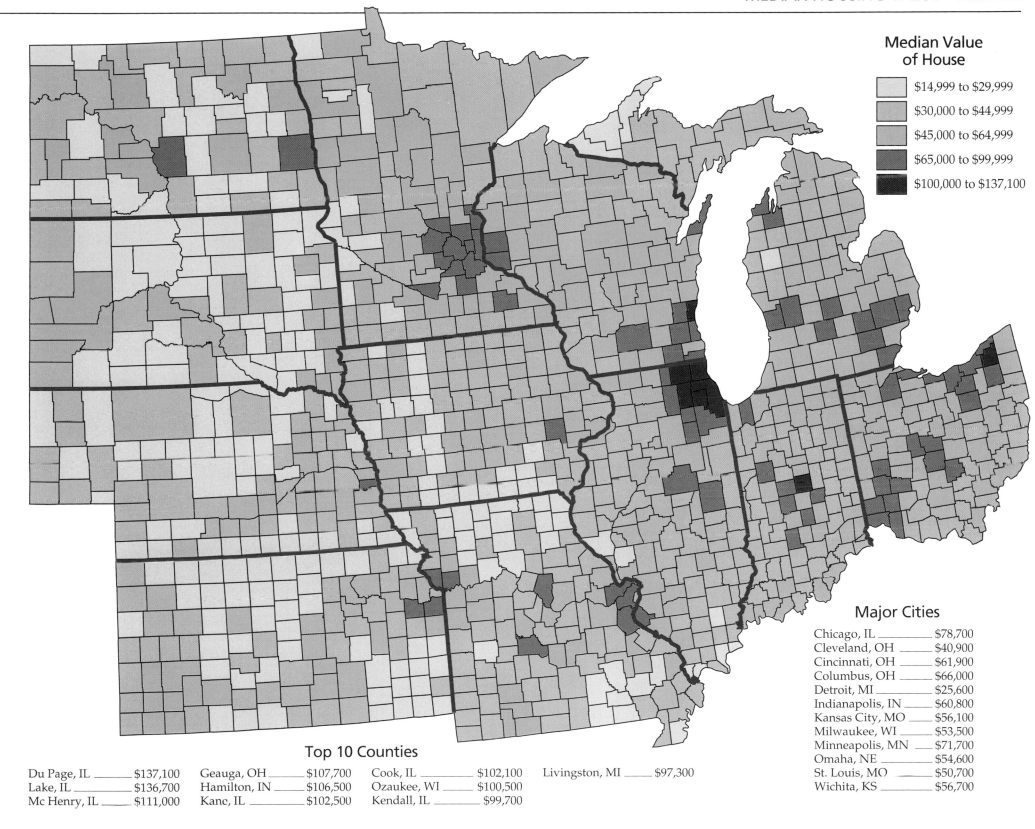

Median Value of House

- $14,999 to $29,999
- $30,000 to $44,999
- $45,000 to $64,999
- $65,000 to $99,999
- $100,000 to $137,100

Major Cities

Chicago, IL	$78,700
Cleveland, OH	$40,900
Cincinnati, OH	$61,900
Columbus, OH	$66,000
Detroit, MI	$25,600
Indianapolis, IN	$60,800
Kansas City, MO	$56,100
Milwaukee, WI	$53,500
Minneapolis, MN	$71,700
Omaha, NE	$54,600
St. Louis, MO	$50,700
Wichita, KS	$56,700

Top 10 Counties

Du Page, IL	$137,100	Geauga, OH	$107,700	Cook, IL	$102,100	Livingston, MI	$97,300
Lake, IL	$136,700	Hamilton, IN	$106,500	Ozaukee, WI	$100,500		
Mc Henry, IL	$111,000	Kane, IL	$102,500	Kendall, IL	$99,700		

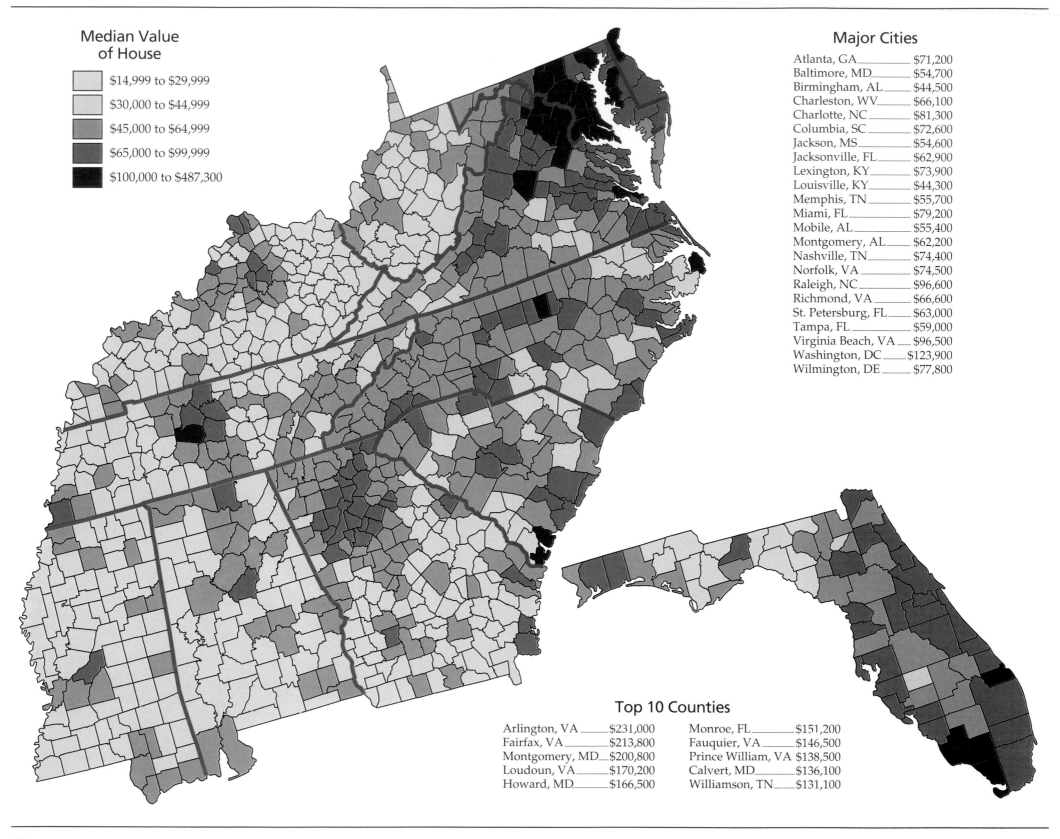

Median Value of House

- $14,999 to $29,999
- $30,000 to $44,999
- $45,000 to $64,999
- $65,000 to $99,999
- $100,000 to $487,300

Major Cities

Atlanta, GA	$71,200
Baltimore, MD	$54,700
Birmingham, AL	$44,500
Charleston, WV	$66,100
Charlotte, NC	$81,300
Columbia, SC	$72,600
Jackson, MS	$54,600
Jacksonville, FL	$62,900
Lexington, KY	$73,900
Louisville, KY	$44,300
Memphis, TN	$55,700
Miami, FL	$79,200
Mobile, AL	$55,400
Montgomery, AL	$62,200
Nashville, TN	$74,400
Norfolk, VA	$74,500
Raleigh, NC	$96,600
Richmond, VA	$66,600
St. Petersburg, FL	$63,000
Tampa, FL	$59,000
Virginia Beach, VA	$96,500
Washington, DC	$123,900
Wilmington, DE	$77,800

Top 10 Counties

Arlington, VA	$231,000	Monroe, FL	$151,200
Fairfax, VA	$213,800	Fauquier, VA	$146,500
Montgomery, MD	$200,800	Prince William, VA	$138,500
Loudoun, VA	$170,200	Calvert, MD	$136,100
Howard, MD	$166,500	Williamson, TN	$131,100

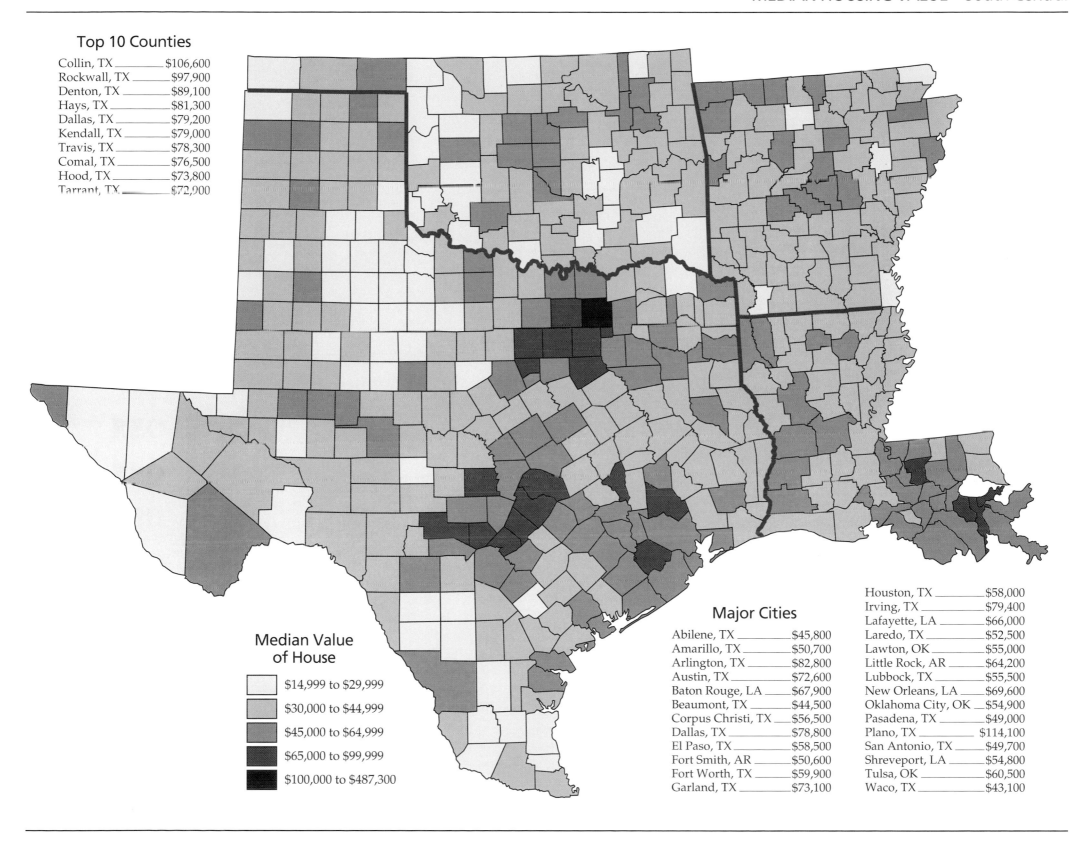

Top 10 Counties

Collin, TX ——————— $106,600
Rockwall, TX ——————— $97,900
Denton, TX ——————— $89,100
Hays, TX ——————— $81,300
Dallas, TX ——————— $79,200
Kendall, TX ——————— $79,000
Travis, TX ——————— $78,300
Comal, TX ——————— $76,500
Hood, TX ——————— $73,800
Tarrant, TX ——————— $72,900

Median Value of House

	$14,999 to $29,999
	$30,000 to $44,999
	$45,000 to $64,999
	$65,000 to $99,999
	$100,000 to $487,300

Major Cities

Abilene, TX ——————— $45,800
Amarillo, TX ——————— $50,700
Arlington, TX ——————— $82,800
Austin, TX ——————— $72,600
Baton Rouge, LA ——————— $67,900
Beaumont, TX ——————— $44,500
Corpus Christi, TX ——————— $56,500
Dallas, TX ——————— $78,800
El Paso, TX ——————— $58,500
Fort Smith, AR ——————— $50,600
Fort Worth, TX ——————— $59,900
Garland, TX ——————— $73,100

Houston, TX ——————— $58,000
Irving, TX ——————— $79,400
Lafayette, LA ——————— $66,000
Laredo, TX ——————— $52,500
Lawton, OK ——————— $55,000
Little Rock, AR ——————— $64,200
Lubbock, TX ——————— $55,500
New Orleans, LA ——————— $69,600
Oklahoma City, OK ——————— $54,900
Pasadena, TX ——————— $49,000
Plano, TX ——————— $114,100
San Antonio, TX ——————— $49,700
Shreveport, LA ——————— $54,800
Tulsa, OK ——————— $60,500
Waco, TX ——————— $43,100

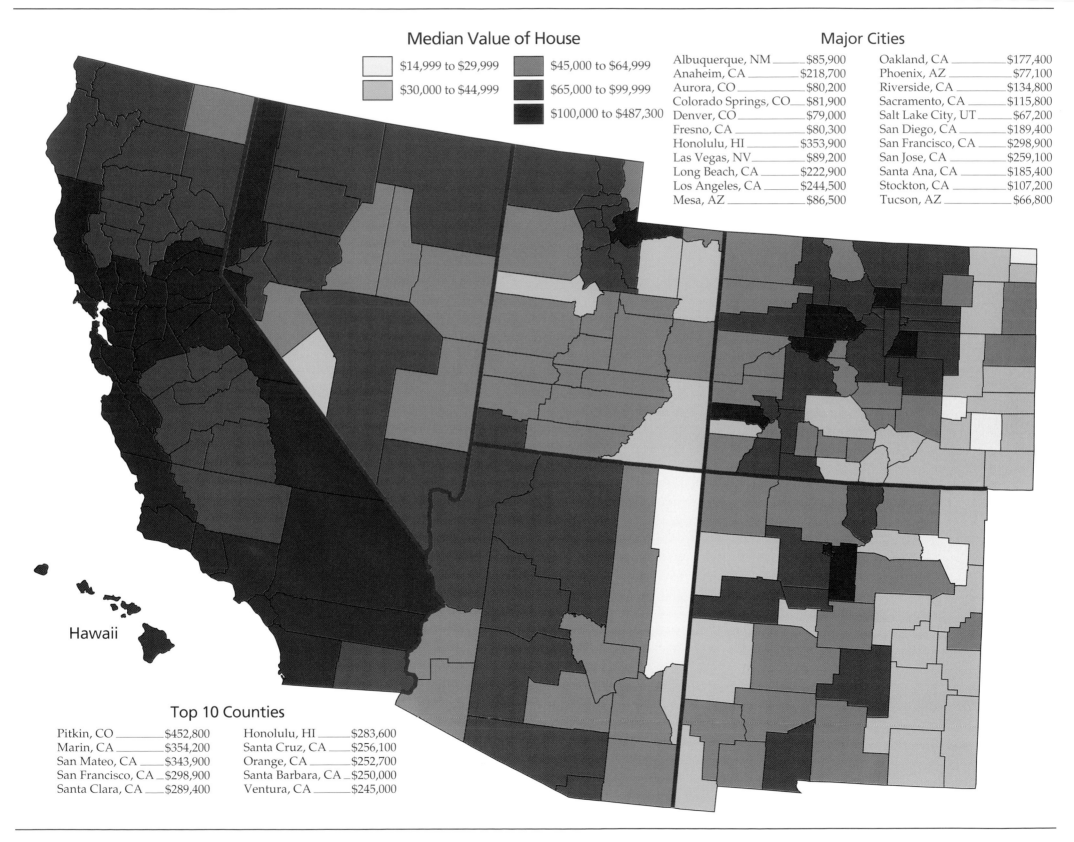

Median Value of House

- $14,999 to $29,999
- $30,000 to $44,999
- $45,000 to $64,999
- $65,000 to $99,999
- $100,000 to $487,300

Major Cities

Albuquerque, NM	$85,900
Anaheim, CA	$218,700
Aurora, CO	$80,200
Colorado Springs, CO	$81,900
Denver, CO	$79,000
Fresno, CA	$80,300
Honolulu, HI	$353,900
Las Vegas, NV	$89,200
Long Beach, CA	$222,900
Los Angeles, CA	$244,500
Mesa, AZ	$86,500
Oakland, CA	$177,400
Phoenix, AZ	$77,100
Riverside, CA	$134,800
Sacramento, CA	$115,800
Salt Lake City, UT	$67,200
San Diego, CA	$189,400
San Francisco, CA	$298,900
San Jose, CA	$259,100
Santa Ana, CA	$185,400
Stockton, CA	$107,200
Tucson, AZ	$66,800

Hawaii

Top 10 Counties

Pitkin, CO	$452,800	Honolulu, HI	$283,600
Marin, CA	$354,200	Santa Cruz, CA	$256,100
San Mateo, CA	$343,900	Orange, CA	$252,700
San Francisco, CA	$298,900	Santa Barbara, CA	$250,000
Santa Clara, CA	$289,400	Ventura, CA	$245,000

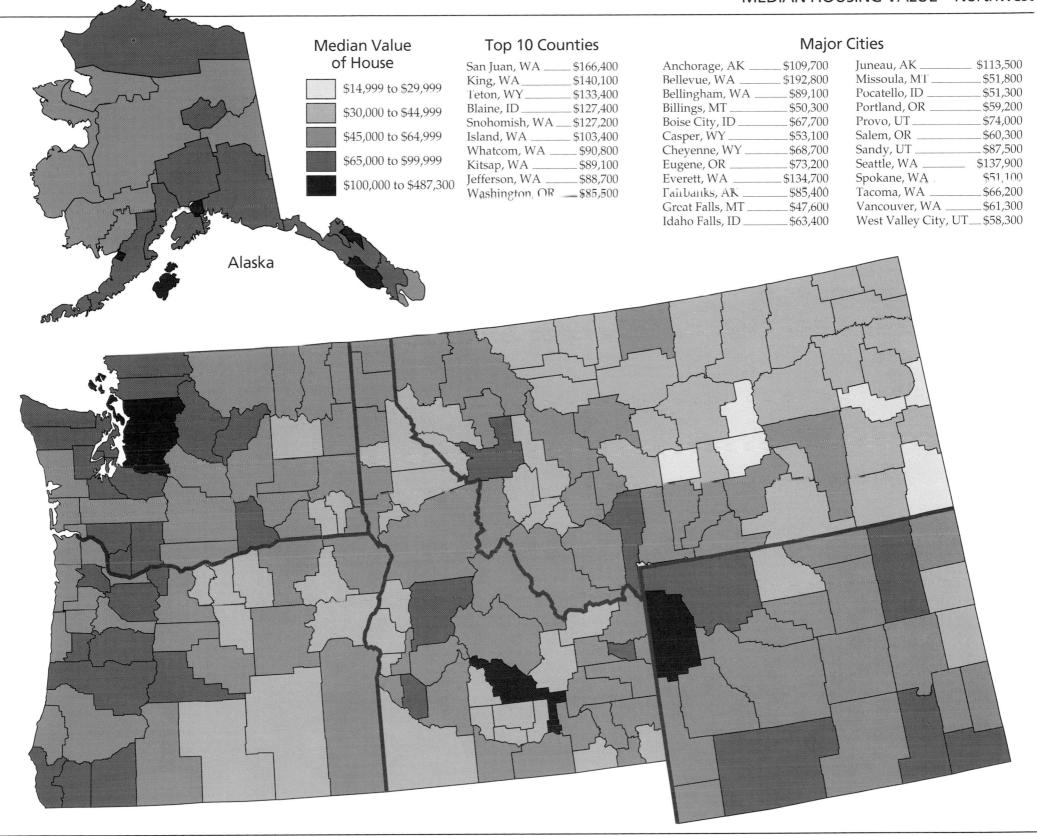

Median Value of House

- $14,999 to $29,999
- $30,000 to $44,999
- $45,000 to $64,999
- $65,000 to $99,999
- $100,000 to $487,300

Alaska

Top 10 Counties

San Juan, WA	$166,400
King, WA	$140,100
Teton, WY	$133,400
Blaine, ID	$127,400
Snohomish, WA	$127,200
Island, WA	$103,400
Whatcom, WA	$90,800
Kitsap, WA	$89,100
Jefferson, WA	$88,700
Washington, OR	$85,500

Major Cities

Anchorage, AK	$109,700	Juneau, AK	$113,500
Bellevue, WA	$192,800	Missoula, MT	$51,800
Bellingham, WA	$89,100	Pocatello, ID	$51,300
Billings, MT	$50,300	Portland, OR	$59,200
Boise City, ID	$67,700	Provo, UT	$74,000
Casper, WY	$53,100	Salem, OR	$60,300
Cheyenne, WY	$68,700	Sandy, UT	$87,500
Eugene, OR	$73,200	Seattle, WA	$137,900
Everett, WA	$134,700	Spokane, WA	$51,100
Fairbanks, AK	$85,400	Tacoma, WA	$66,200
Great Falls, MT	$47,600	Vancouver, WA	$61,300
Idaho Falls, ID	$63,400	West Valley City, UT	$58,300

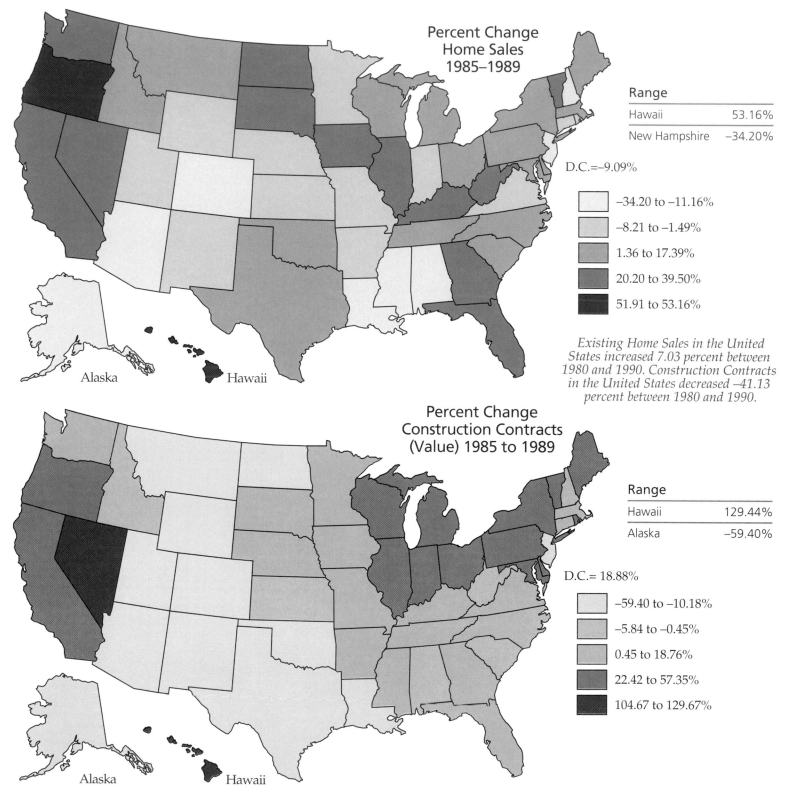

Percent Change Home Sales 1985–1989

Range

Hawaii	53.16%
New Hampshire	−34.20%

D.C.=−9.09%

	−34.20 to −11.16%
	−8.21 to −1.49%
	1.36 to 17.39%
	20.20 to 39.50%
	51.91 to 53.16%

Existing Home Sales in the United States increased 7.03 percent between 1980 and 1990. Construction Contracts in the United States decreased −41.13 percent between 1980 and 1990.

Percent Change Construction Contracts (Value) 1985 to 1989

Range

Hawaii	129.44%
Alaska	−59.40%

D.C.= 18.88%

	−59.40 to −10.18%
	−5.84 to −0.45%
	0.45 to 18.76%
	22.42 to 57.35%
	104.67 to 129.67%

Alaska

Hawaii

Existing Home Sales (000's), 1989

United States	3,440.0
Alabama	51.1
Alaska	7.1
Arizona	63.4
Arkansas	47.5
California	538.8
Colorado	43.8
Connecticut	51.4
Delaware	12.8
District of Columbia	9.0
Florida	185.9
Georgia	82.0
Hawaii	12.1
Idaho	13.5
Illinois	187.9
Indiana	87.7
Iowa	52.9
Kansas	45.1
Kentucky	70.7
Louisiana	35.4
Maine	30.4
Maryland	82.0
Massachusetts	86.5
Michigan	178.6
Minnesota	72.8
Mississippi	31.5
Missouri	83.8
Montana	12.7
Nebraska	24.0
Nevada	12.9
New Hampshire	12.7
New Jersey	128.0
New Mexico	19.1
New York	198.3
North Carolina	132.8
North Dakota	11.7
Ohio	189.1
Oklahoma	53.6
Oregon	59.7
Pennsylvania	242.9
Rhode Island	12.9
South Carolina	60.2
South Dakota	14.4
Tennessee	105.4
Texas	229.3
Utah	14.4
Vermont	11.9
Virginia	100.3
Washington	61.6
West Virginia	45.9
Wisconsin	70.3
Wyoming	6.0

Median Sales Price of New Privately Owned One-Family Houses Sold, by Region, 1970 to 1990

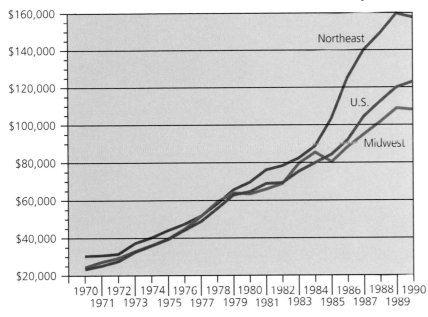

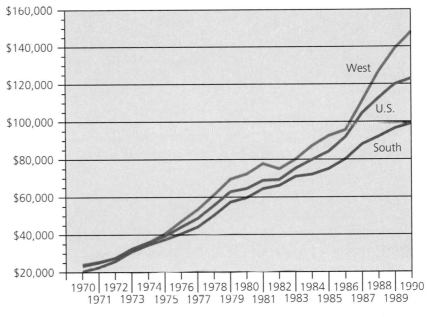

Source: U.S. Bureau of the Census and U.S. Dept. of Housing and Urban Development, *Construction Reports*, series C25, *Characteristics of New Housing*, annual; and *New One-Family Houses Sold and For Sale*, monthly.

Value of New Construction Put in Place, 1970 to 1990

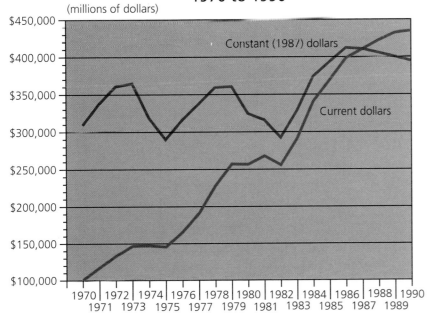

Source: U.S. Bureau of the Census, *Current Construction Reports*, series C30, and press release, CB-91-14.

Median Sales Price of Existing One-Family Homes by MSA, 1989

U.S., all areas	$96,900
Akron, OH PMSA	67,000
Albany-Schenectady-Troy, NY	106,900
Albuquerque, NM	86,100
Anaheim-Santa Ana, CA PMSA	248,900
Baltimore, MD	100,900
Baton Rouge, LA	66,500
Birmingham, AL	82,600
Boston, MA PMSA	176,200
Buffalo-Niagara Falls, NY CMSA	77,300
Chicago, IL PMSA	116,600
Cincinnati, OH-KY-IN PMSA	81,400
Cleveland, OH PMSA	81,500
Columbus, OH	82,400
Dallas, TX PMSA	92,000
Denver, CO PMSA	87,000
Des Moines, IA	58,100
Detroit, MI PMSA	77,900
Ft. Lauderdale-Hollywood-Pompano Beach, FL PMSA	92,200
Ft. Worth, TX PMSA	74,600
Hartford, CT PMSA	159,300
Honolulu, HI	345,000
Houston, TX PMSA	71,400
Indianapolis, IN	82,300
Jacksonville, FL	73,000
Kansas City, MO-KS	73,200
Las Vegas, NV	93,300
Los Angeles-Long Beach, CA PMSA	216,900
Louisville, KY-IN	$59,700
Memphis, TN-AR-MS	78,100
Miami-Hialeah, FL PMSA	89,000
Milwaukee, WI PMSA	86,600
Minneapolis-St. Paul, MN-WI	90,300
Nashville, TN	82,400
New York-No. New Jersey-Long Island, NY-NJ-CT CMSA	175,000
Oklahoma City, OK	54,100
Omaha, NE-IA	61,400
Orlando, FL	83,300
Philadelphia, PA-NJ PMSA	110,800
Phoenix, AZ	84,000
Portland, OR PMSA	79,700
Providence, RI PMSA	130,500
Riverside/San Bernardino, CA PMSA	133,200
Rochester, NY	79,900
St. Louis, MO-IL	82,000
Salt Lake City-Ogden, UT	69,200
San Antonio, TX	62,800
San Diego, CA	183,700
San Francisco-Oakland-San Jose, CA CMSA	263,600
Seattle/Tacoma, WA CMSA	147,600
Syracuse, NY	80,500
Tampa-St. Petersburg-Clearwater, FL	70,400
Tulsa, OK	64,400
Washington, DC-MD-VA	150,900
West Palm Beach-Boca Raton-Delray Beach, FL	108,200

MSA: Metropolitan Statistical Area. CMSA: Consolidated Metropolitan Statistical Area. PMSA: Primary Metropolitan Statistical Area. Source: National Association of Realtors, Washington, DC, *Existing Home Sales*, monthly. (Copyright).

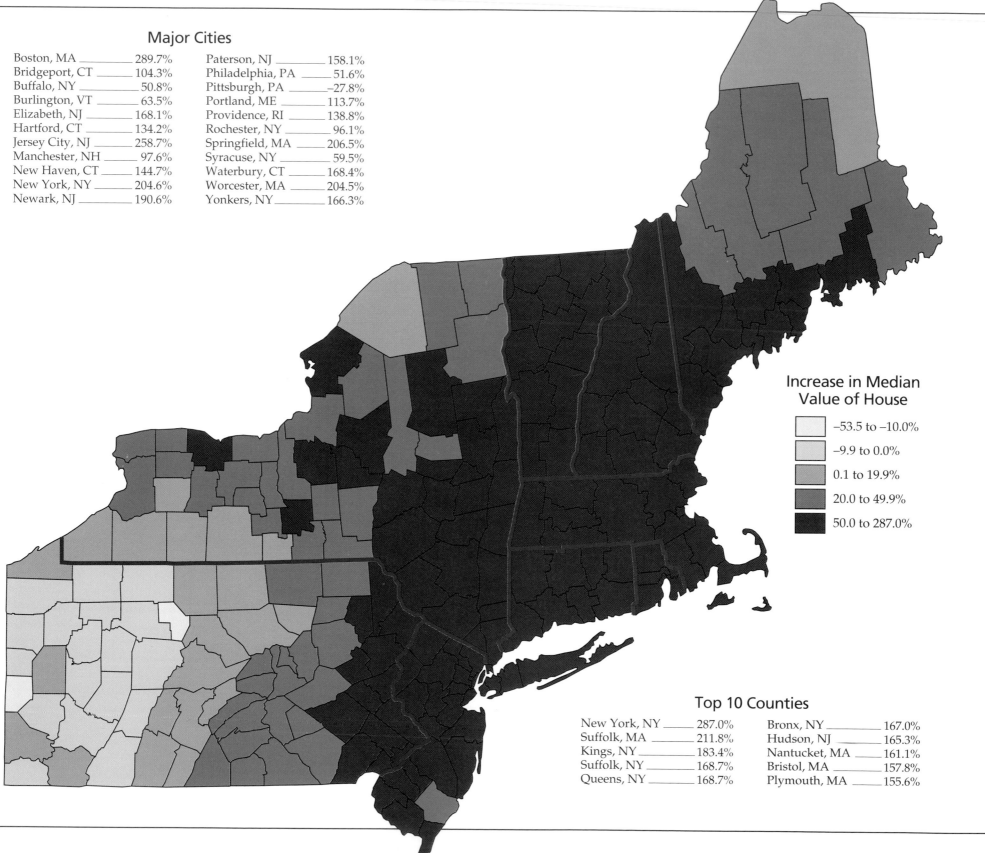

Major Cities

Boston, MA	289.7%	Paterson, NJ	158.1%
Bridgeport, CT	104.3%	Philadelphia, PA	51.6%
Buffalo, NY	50.8%	Pittsburgh, PA	−27.8%
Burlington, VT	63.5%	Portland, ME	113.7%
Elizabeth, NJ	168.1%	Providence, RI	138.8%
Hartford, CT	134.2%	Rochester, NY	96.1%
Jersey City, NJ	258.7%	Springfield, MA	206.5%
Manchester, NH	97.6%	Syracuse, NY	59.5%
New Haven, CT	144.7%	Waterbury, CT	168.4%
New York, NY	204.6%	Worcester, MA	204.5%
Newark, NJ	190.6%	Yonkers, NY	166.3%

Increase in Median Value of House

- −53.5 to −10.0%
- −9.9 to 0.0%
- 0.1 to 19.9%
- 20.0 to 49.9%
- 50.0 to 287.0%

Top 10 Counties

New York, NY	287.0%	Bronx, NY	167.0%
Suffolk, MA	211.8%	Hudson, NJ	165.3%
Kings, NY	183.4%	Nantucket, MA	161.1%
Suffolk, NY	168.7%	Bristol, MA	157.8%
Queens, NY	168.7%	Plymouth, MA	155.6%

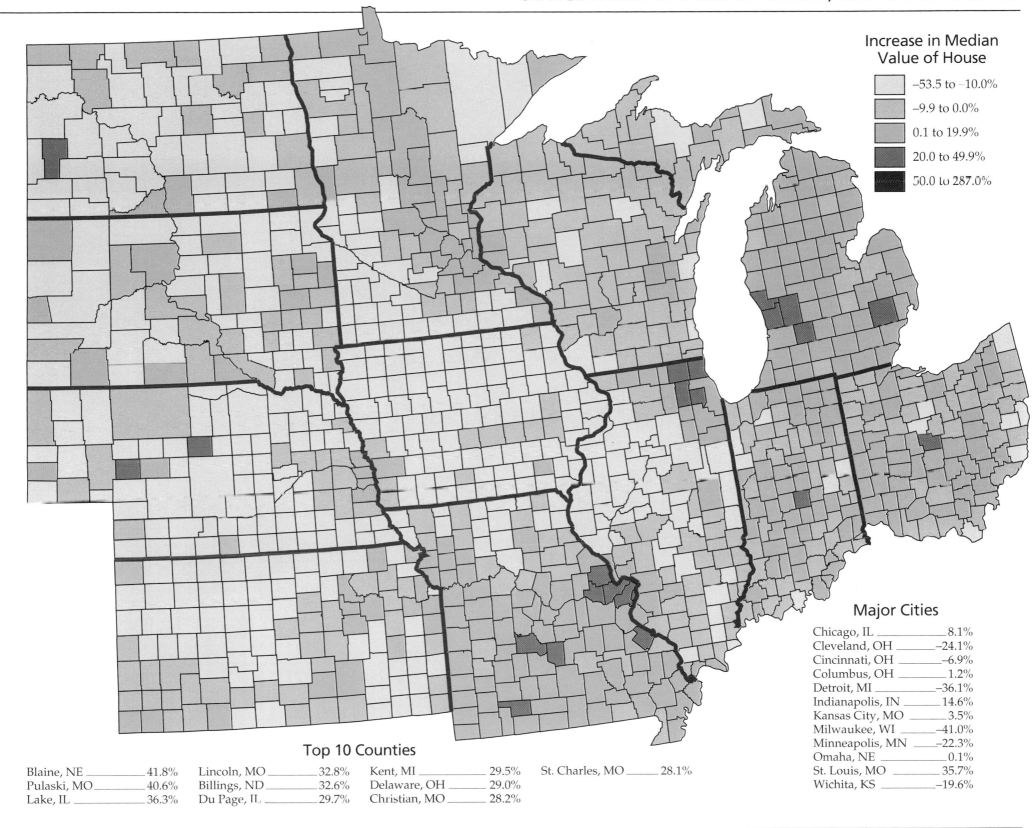

Increase in Median Value of House

- −53.5 to −10.0%
- −9.9 to 0.0%
- 0.1 to 19.9%
- 20.0 to 49.9%
- 50.0 to 287.0%

Major Cities

Chicago, IL	8.1%
Cleveland, OH	−24.1%
Cincinnati, OH	−6.9%
Columbus, OH	1.2%
Detroit, MI	−36.1%
Indianapolis, IN	14.6%
Kansas City, MO	3.5%
Milwaukee, WI	−41.0%
Minneapolis, MN	−22.3%
Omaha, NE	0.1%
St. Louis, MO	35.7%
Wichita, KS	−19.6%

Top 10 Counties

Blaine, NE	41.8%	Lincoln, MO	32.8%	Kent, MI	29.5%	St. Charles, MO	28.1%
Pulaski, MO	40.6%	Billings, ND	32.6%	Delaware, OH	29.0%		
Lake, IL	36.3%	Du Page, IL	29.7%	Christian, MO	28.2%		

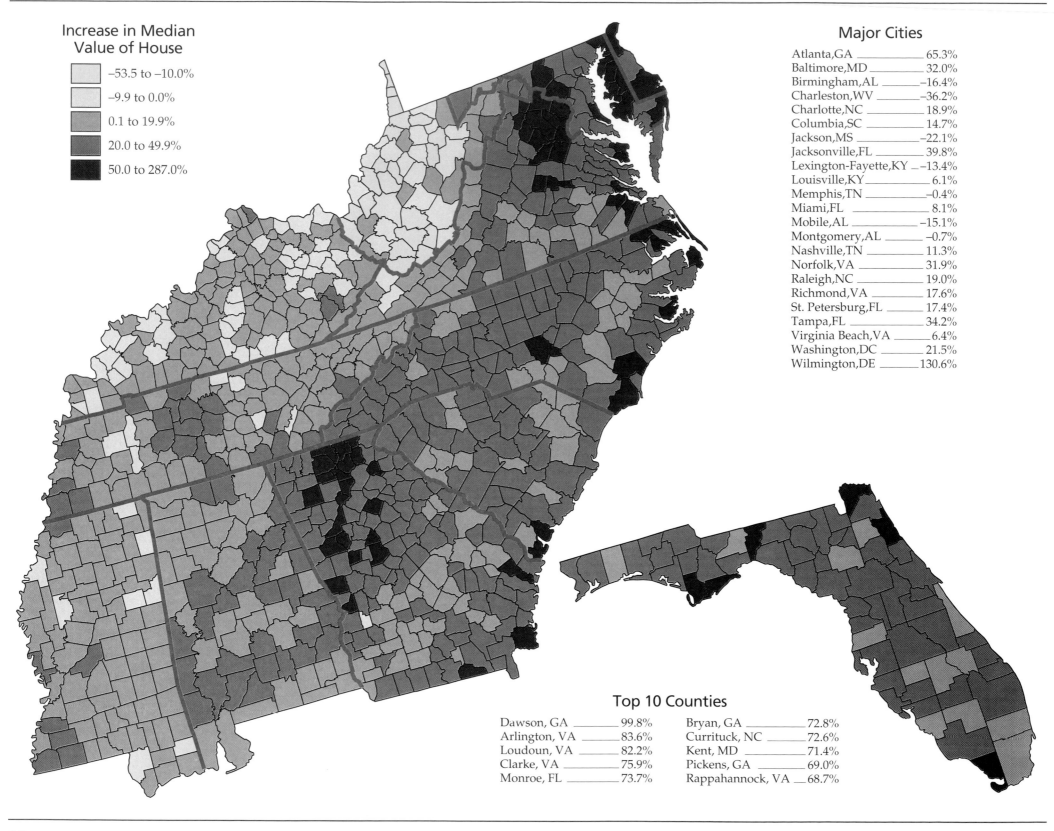

Increase in Median Value of House

- −53.5 to −10.0%
- −9.9 to 0.0%
- 0.1 to 19.9%
- 20.0 to 49.9%
- 50.0 to 287.0%

Major Cities

Atlanta, GA	65.3%
Baltimore, MD	32.0%
Birmingham, AL	−16.4%
Charleston, WV	−36.2%
Charlotte, NC	18.9%
Columbia, SC	14.7%
Jackson, MS	−22.1%
Jacksonville, FL	39.8%
Lexington-Fayette, KY	−13.4%
Louisville, KY	6.1%
Memphis, TN	−0.4%
Miami, FL	8.1%
Mobile, AL	−15.1%
Montgomery, AL	−0.7%
Nashville, TN	11.3%
Norfolk, VA	31.9%
Raleigh, NC	19.0%
Richmond, VA	17.6%
St. Petersburg, FL	17.4%
Tampa, FL	34.2%
Virginia Beach, VA	6.4%
Washington, DC	21.5%
Wilmington, DE	130.6%

Top 10 Counties

Dawson, GA	99.8%	Bryan, GA	72.8%
Arlington, VA	83.6%	Currituck, NC	72.6%
Loudoun, VA	82.2%	Kent, MD	71.4%
Clarke, VA	75.9%	Pickens, GA	69.0%
Monroe, FL	73.7%	Rappahannock, VA	68.7%

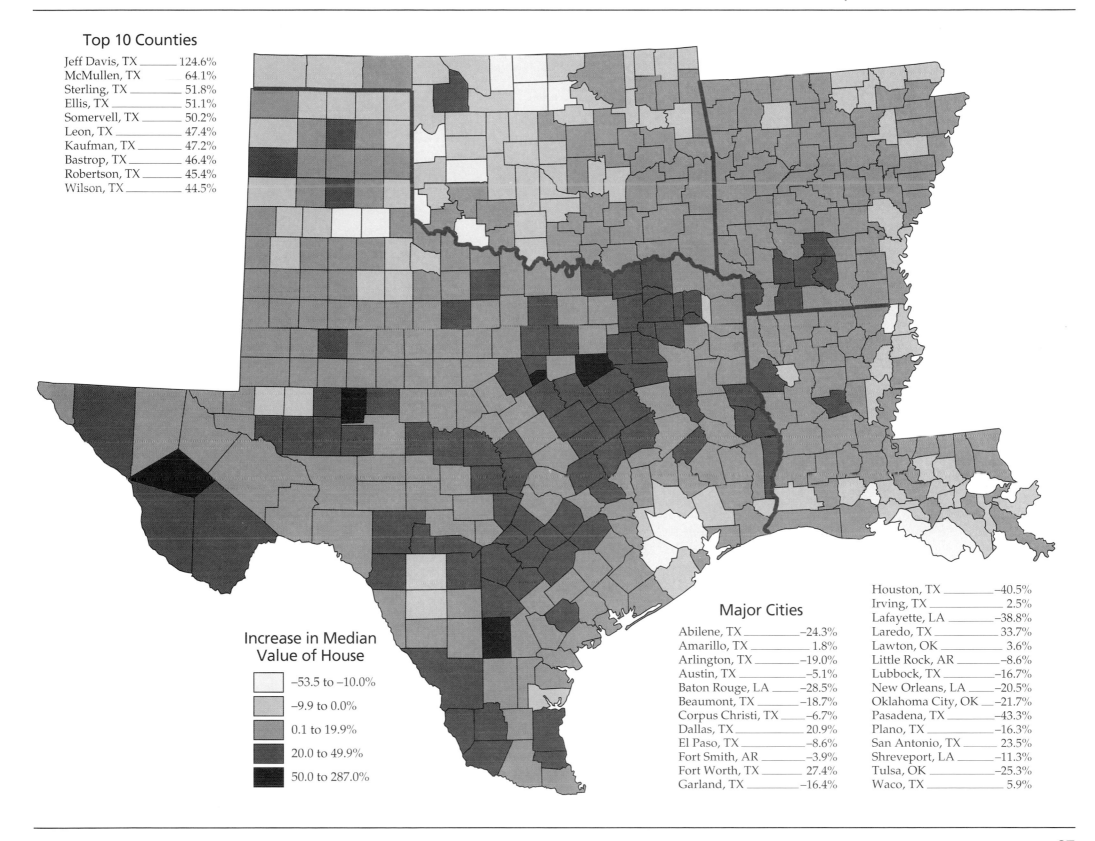

Top 10 Counties

Jeff Davis, TX ———— 124.6%
McMullen, TX   64.1%
Sterling, TX ———————— 51.8%
Ellis, TX ——————————— 51.1%
Somervell, TX ——————— 50.2%
Leon, TX ——————————— 47.4%
Kaufman, TX ———————— 47.2%
Bastrop, TX———————— 46.4%
Robertson, TX ———————— 45.4%
Wilson, TX ——————————— 44.5%

Increase in Median Value of House

- −53.5 to −10.0%
- −9.9 to 0.0%
- 0.1 to 19.9%
- 20.0 to 49.9%
- 50.0 to 287.0%

Major Cities

City	%	City	%
Abilene, TX	−24.3%	Houston, TX	−40.5%
Amarillo, TX	1.8%	Irving, TX	2.5%
Arlington, TX	−19.0%	Lafayette, LA	−38.8%
Austin, TX	−5.1%	Laredo, TX	33.7%
Baton Rouge, LA	−28.5%	Lawton, OK	3.6%
Beaumont, TX	−18.7%	Little Rock, AR	−8.6%
Corpus Christi, TX	−6.7%	Lubbock, TX	−16.7%
Dallas, TX	20.9%	New Orleans, LA	−20.5%
El Paso, TX	−8.6%	Oklahoma City, OK	−21.7%
Fort Smith, AR	−3.9%	Pasadena, TX	−43.3%
Fort Worth, TX	27.4%	Plano, TX	−16.3%
Garland, TX	−16.4%	San Antonio, TX	23.5%
		Shreveport, LA	−11.3%
		Tulsa, OK	−25.3%
		Waco, TX	5.9%

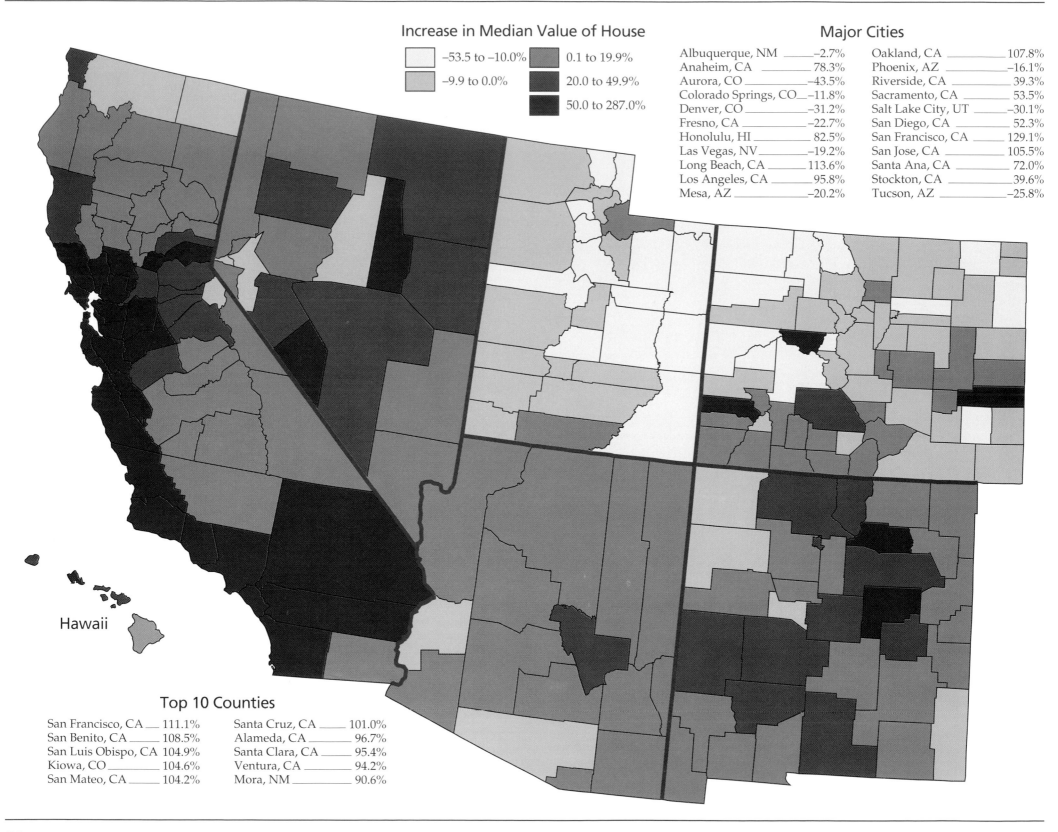

Increase in Median Value of House

- −53.5 to −10.0%
- −9.9 to 0.0%
- 0.1 to 19.9%
- 20.0 to 49.9%
- 50.0 to 287.0%

Major Cities

Albuquerque, NM	−2.7%	Oakland, CA	107.8%
Anaheim, CA	78.3%	Phoenix, AZ	−16.1%
Aurora, CO	−43.5%	Riverside, CA	39.3%
Colorado Springs, CO	−11.8%	Sacramento, CA	53.5%
Denver, CO	−31.2%	Salt Lake City, UT	−30.1%
Fresno, CA	−22.7%	San Diego, CA	52.3%
Honolulu, HI	82.5%	San Francisco, CA	129.1%
Las Vegas, NV	−19.2%	San Jose, CA	105.5%
Long Beach, CA	113.6%	Santa Ana, CA	72.0%
Los Angeles, CA	95.8%	Stockton, CA	39.6%
Mesa, AZ	−20.2%	Tucson, AZ	−25.8%

Hawaii

Top 10 Counties

San Francisco, CA	111.1%	Santa Cruz, CA	101.0%
San Benito, CA	108.5%	Alameda, CA	96.7%
San Luis Obispo, CA	104.9%	Santa Clara, CA	95.4%
Kiowa, CO	104.6%	Ventura, CA	94.2%
San Mateo, CA	104.2%	Mora, NM	90.6%

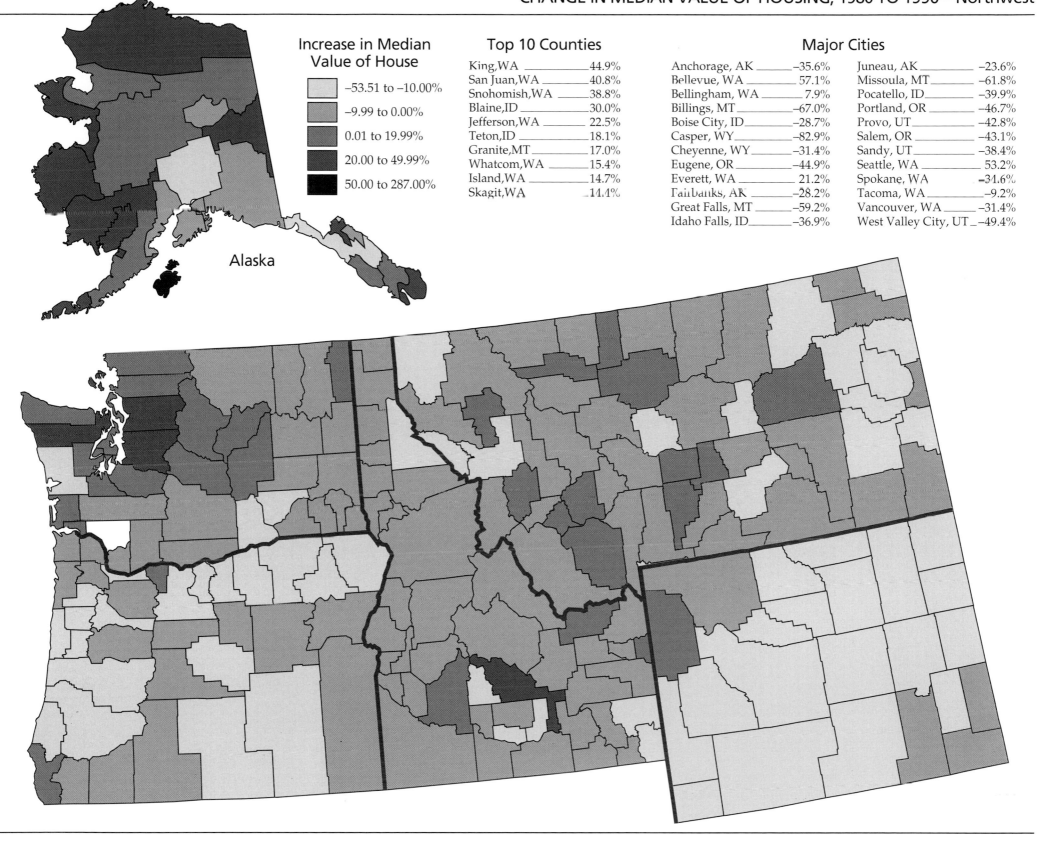

Increase in Median Value of House

- −53.51 to −10.00%
- −9.99 to 0.00%
- 0.01 to 19.99%
- 20.00 to 49.99%
- 50.00 to 287.00%

Alaska

Top 10 Counties

County	%
King, WA	44.9%
San Juan, WA	40.8%
Snohomish, WA	38.8%
Blaine, ID	30.0%
Jefferson, WA	22.5%
Teton, ID	18.1%
Granite, MT	17.0%
Whatcom, WA	15.4%
Island, WA	14.7%
Skagit, WA	14.4%

Major Cities

City	%	City	%
Anchorage, AK	−35.6%	Juneau, AK	−23.6%
Bellevue, WA	57.1%	Missoula, MT	−61.8%
Bellingham, WA	7.9%	Pocatello, ID	−39.9%
Billings, MT	−67.0%	Portland, OR	−46.7%
Boise City, ID	−28.7%	Provo, UT	−42.8%
Casper, WY	−82.9%	Salem, OR	−43.1%
Cheyenne, WY	−31.4%	Sandy, UT	−38.4%
Eugene, OR	−44.9%	Seattle, WA	53.2%
Everett, WA	21.2%	Spokane, WA	−34.6%
Fairbanks, AK	−28.2%	Tacoma, WA	−9.2%
Great Falls, MT	−59.2%	Vancouver, WA	−31.4%
Idaho Falls, ID	−36.9%	West Valley City, UT	−49.4%

Percent Households Owner–Occupied 1990

Range

West Virginia	74.08%
Dist. of Columbia	38.90%

D.C.=38.90%

- 52.18 to 56.10%
- 59.25 to 65.89%
- 66.08 to 68.77%
- 69.01 to 70.64%
- 71.00 to 74.08%

Alaska   Hawaii

Owner–Occupied Households in the United States increased 13.96 percent between 1980 and 1990.

Percent Change 1980 to 1990

Range

Nevada	40.89%
Iowa	−1.47%

D.C.= 8.08%

- −1.47 to −0.10%
- 0.93 to 8.00%
- 8.08 to 19.66%
- 21.49 to 34.37%
- 35.00 to 40.89%

Alaska   Hawaii

Households Owner–Occupied, 1990

United States	59,024,811
Alabama	1,061,897
Alaska	105,989
Arizona	878,561
Arkansas	619,938
California	5,773,943
Colorado	798,277
Connecticut	807,481
Delaware	173,813
District of Columbia	97,108
Florida	3,452,160
Georgia	1,536,759
Hawaii	191,911
Idaho	252,734
Illinois	2,699,182
Indiana	1,450,898
Iowa	745,377
Kansas	641,762
Kentucky	960,469
Louisiana	987,919
Maine	327,888
Maryland	1,137,296
Massachusetts	1,331,493
Michigan	2,427,643
Minnesota	1,183,673
Mississippi	651,587
Missouri	1,348,746
Montana	205,899
Nebraska	400,394
Nevada	255,388
New Hampshire	280,372
New Jersey	1,813,381
New Mexico	365,965
New York	3,464,436
North Carolina	1,711,817
North Dakota	157,950
Ohio	2,758,149
Oklahoma	821,188
Oregon	695,957
Pennsylvania	3,176,121
Rhode Island	224,792
South Carolina	878,704
South Dakota	171,161
Tennessee	1,261,118
Texas	3,695,115
Utah	365,979
Vermont	145,368
Virginia	1,519,521
Washington	1,171,580
West Virginia	510,058
Wisconsin	1,215,350
Wyoming	114,544

Renter–Occupied Households, 1990

United States	32,922,599
Alabama	444,893
Alaska	82,926
Arizona	490,282
Arkansas	271,241
California	4,607,263
Colorado	484,212
Connecticut	422,998
Delaware	73,684
District of Columbia	152,526
Florida	1,682,709
Georgia	829,856
Hawaii	164,356
Idaho	107,989
Illinois	1,503,058
Indiana	614,457
Iowa	318,948
Kansas	302,964
Kentucky	419,313
Louisiana	511,350
Maine	137,424
Maryland	611,695
Massachusetts	915,617
Michigan	991,688
Minnesota	464,180
Mississippi	259,787
Missouri	621,460
Montana	100,264
Nebraska	201,969
Nevada	210,909
New Hampshire	130,814
New Jersey	981,330
New Mexico	176,744
New York	3,174,886
North Carolina	805,209
North Dakota	82,928
Ohio	1,329,397
Oklahoma	384,947
Oregon	407,356
Pennsylvania	1,319,845
Rhode Island	153,185
South Carolina	379,340
South Dakota	87,873
Tennessee	592,607
Texas	2,375,822
Utah	171,294
Vermont	65,282
Virginia	772,309
Washington	700,851
West Virginia	178,499
Wisconsin	606,768
Wyoming	54,295

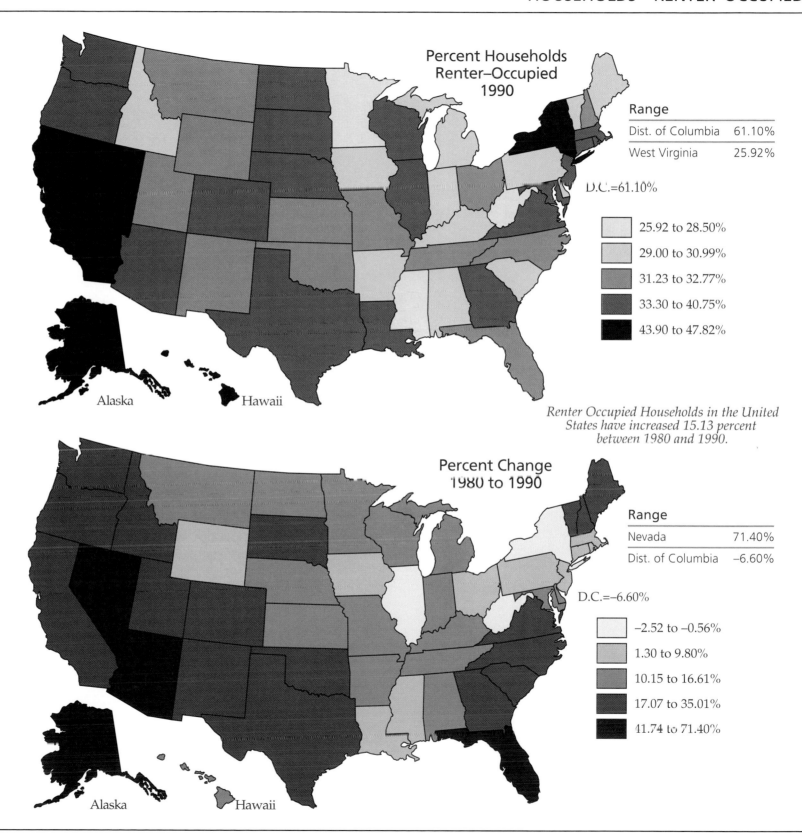

Percent Households Renter–Occupied 1990

Range

Dist. of Columbia	61.10%
West Virginia	25.92%

D.C.=61.10%

- 25.92 to 28.50%
- 29.00 to 30.99%
- 31.23 to 32.77%
- 33.30 to 40.75%
- 43.90 to 47.82%

Renter Occupied Households in the United States have increased 15.13 percent between 1980 and 1990.

Percent Change 1980 to 1990

Range

Nevada	71.40%
Dist. of Columbia	−6.60%

D.C.=−6.60%

- −2.52 to −0.56%
- 1.30 to 9.80%
- 10.15 to 16.61%
- 17.07 to 35.01%
- 41.74 to 71.40%

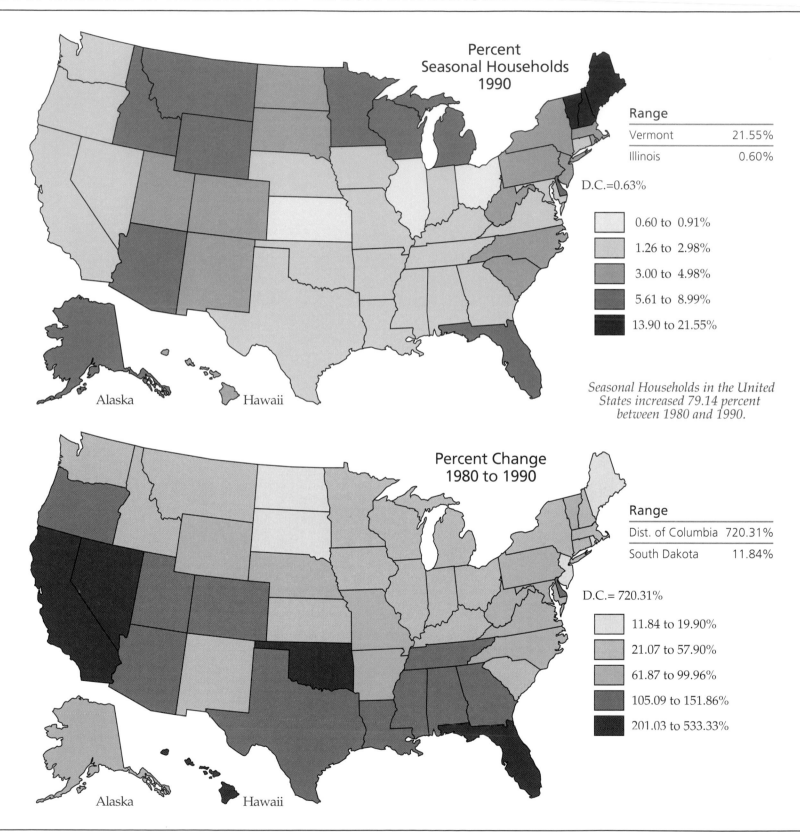

Percent
Seasonal Households
1990

Range

Vermont	21.55%
Illinois	0.60%

D.C.=0.63%

- 0.60 to 0.91%
- 1.26 to 2.98%
- 3.00 to 4.98%
- 5.61 to 8.99%
- 13.90 to 21.55%

Alaska   Hawaii

Seasonal Households in the United States increased 79.14 percent between 1980 and 1990.

Percent Change
1980 to 1990

Range

Dist. of Columbia	720.31%
South Dakota	11.84%

D.C.= 720.31%

- 11.84 to 19.90%
- 21.07 to 57.90%
- 61.87 to 99.96%
- 105.09 to 151.86%
- 201.03 to 533.33%

Alaska   Hawaii

Seasonal Households 1990

United States	3,081,923
Alabama	35,609
Alaska	16,991
Arizona	96,104
Arkansas	18,224
California	195,385
Colorado	63,814
Connecticut	20,428
Delaware	19,328
District of Columbia	1,575
Florida	417,670
Georgia	33,637
Hawaii	12,806
Idaho	24,252
Illinois	25,056
Indiana	36,945
Iowa	14,644
Kansas	7,336
Kentucky	20,962
Louisiana	30,333
Maine	88,039
Maryland	42,268
Massachusetts	90,367
Michigan	223,549
Minnesota	105,122
Mississippi	16,002
Missouri	55,492
Montana	20,481
Nebraska	10,978
Nevada	11,258
New Hampshire	57,135
New Jersey	100,591
New Mexico	21,862
New York	212,625
North Carolina	98,714
North Dakota	7,236
Ohio	37,324
Oklahoma	25,169
Oregon	30,200
Pennsylvania	144,359
Rhode Island	12,037
South Carolina	49,843
South Dakota	8,391
Tennessee	23,389
Texas	151,919
Utah	21,023
Vermont	45,405
Virginia	41,742
Washington	55,832
West Virginia	22,403
Wisconsin	150,601
Wyoming	9,468

Rental Vacancy Rates, 1990

United States	8.9
Alabama	9.4
Alaska	8.5
Arizona	15.3
Arkansas	10.4
California	5.9
Colorado	11.4
Connecticut	6.9
Delaware	7.8
District of Columbia	7.9
Florida	12.4
Georgia	12.2
Hawaii	5.4
Idaho	7.3
Illinois	8.0
Indiana	8.3
Iowa	6.4
Kansas	11.1
Kentucky	8.2
Louisiana	12.5
Maine	8.4
Maryland	6.8
Massachusetts	6.9
Michigan	7.2
Minnesota	7.9
Mississippi	9.5
Missouri	10.7
Montana	9.6
Nebraska	7.7
Nevada	9.1
New Hampshire	11.8
New Jersey	7.4
New Mexico	11.4
New York	4.9
North Carolina	9.2
North Dakota	9.0
Ohio	7.5
Oklahoma	14.7
Oregon	5.3
Pennsylvania	7.2
Rhode Island	7.9
South Carolina	11.5
South Dakota	7.3
Tennessee	9.6
Texas	13.0
Utah	8.6
Vermont	7.5
Virginia	8.1
Washington	5.8
West Virginia	10.1
Wisconsin	4.7
Wyoming	14.4

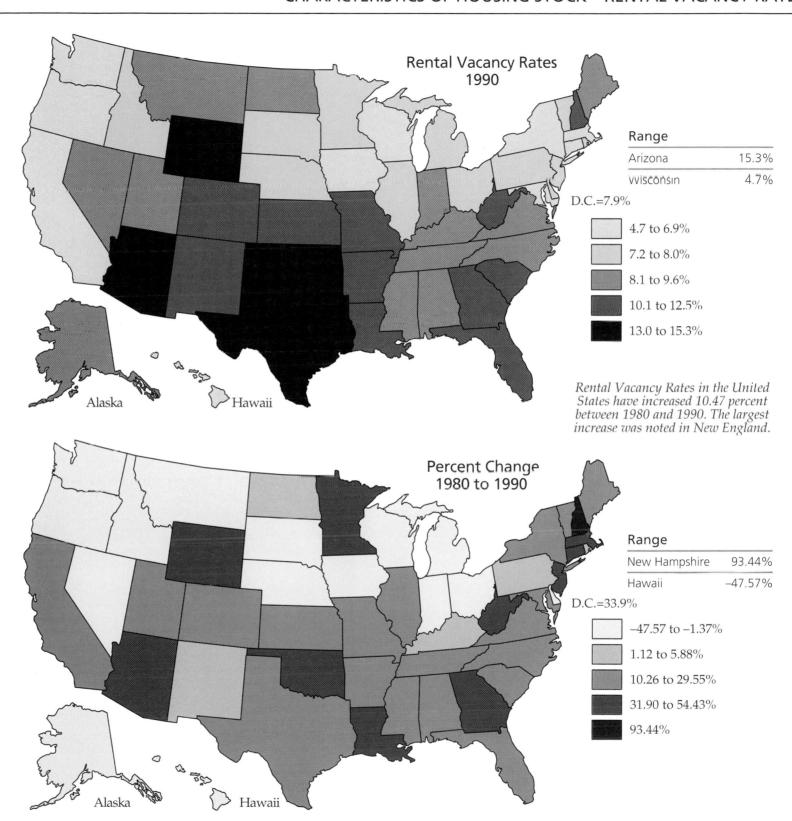

Rental Vacancy Rates 1990

Range

Arizona	15.3%
Wisconsin	4.7%

D.C.=7.9%

- 4.7 to 6.9%
- 7.2 to 8.0%
- 8.1 to 9.6%
- 10.1 to 12.5%
- 13.0 to 15.3%

Rental Vacancy Rates in the United States have increased 10.47 percent between 1980 and 1990. The largest increase was noted in New England.

Percent Change 1980 to 1990

Range

New Hampshire	93.44%
Hawaii	−47.57%

D.C.=33.9%

- −47.57 to −1.37%
- 1.12 to 5.88%
- 10.26 to 29.55%
- 31.90 to 54.43%
- 93.44%

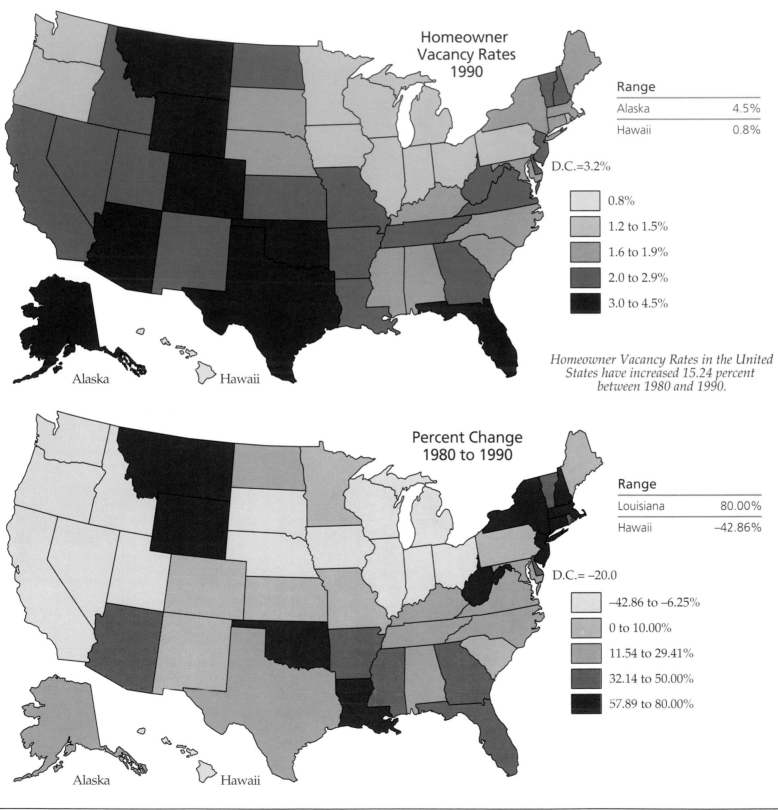

Homeowner Vacancy Rates 1990

Range
Alaska	4.5%
Hawaii	0.8%

D.C.=3.2%

	0.8%
	1.2 to 1.5%
	1.6 to 1.9%
	2.0 to 2.9%
	3.0 to 4.5%

Alaska   Hawaii

Homeowner Vacancy Rates in the United States have increased 15.24 percent between 1980 and 1990.

Percent Change 1980 to 1990

Range
Louisiana	80.00%
Hawaii	−42.86%

D.C.= −20.0

	−42.86 to −6.25%
	0 to 10.00%
	11.54 to 29.41%
	32.14 to 50.00%
	57.89 to 80.00%

Alaska   Hawaii

Homeowner Vacancy Rates, 1990

United States	2.2
Alabama	1.8
Alaska	4.5
Arizona	3.7
Arkansas	2.4
California	2.0
Colorado	3.3
Connecticut	1.9
Delaware	2.3
District of Columbia	3.2
Florida	3.5
Georgia	2.5
Hawaii	0.8
Idaho	2.0
Illinois	1.5
Indiana	1.5
Iowa	1.5
Kansas	2.3
Kentucky	1.6
Louisiana	2.7
Maine	1.8
Maryland	1.7
Massachusetts	1.7
Michigan	1.3
Minnesota	1.5
Mississippi	1.9
Missouri	2.2
Montana	3.0
Nebraska	1.7
Nevada	2.4
New Hampshire	2.7
New Jersey	2.5
New Mexico	2.3
New York	1.9
North Carolina	1.8
North Dakota	2.9
Ohio	1.4
Oklahoma	3.7
Oregon	1.4
Pennsylvania	1.5
Rhode Island	1.5
South Carolina	1.7
South Dakota	1.8
Tennessee	2.1
Texas	3.2
Utah	2.4
Vermont	2.1
Virginia	2.2
Washington	1.3
West Virginia	2.2
Wisconsin	1.2
Wyoming	3.9

Median Contract Rent, 1990

United States	$389
Alabama	229
Alaska	503
Arizona	370
Arkansas	230
California	561
Colorado	362
Connecticut	510
Delaware	425
District of Columbia	441
Florida	402
Georgia	344
Hawaii	599
Idaho	261
Illinois	369
Indiana	291
Iowa	261
Kansas	285
Kentucky	250
Louisiana	260
Maine	358
Maryland	473
Massachusetts	506
Michigan	343
Minnesota	384
Mississippi	215
Missouri	282
Montana	251
Nebraska	282
Nevada	445
New Hampshire	479
New Jersey	521
New Mexico	312
New York	428
North Carolina	284
North Dakota	266
Ohio	296
Oklahoma	259
Oregon	344
Pennsylvania	322
Rhode Island	416
South Carolina	276
South Dakota	242
Tennessee	273
Texas	328
Utah	300
Vermont	378
Virginia	411
Washington	383
West Virginia	221
Wisconsin	331
Wyoming	270

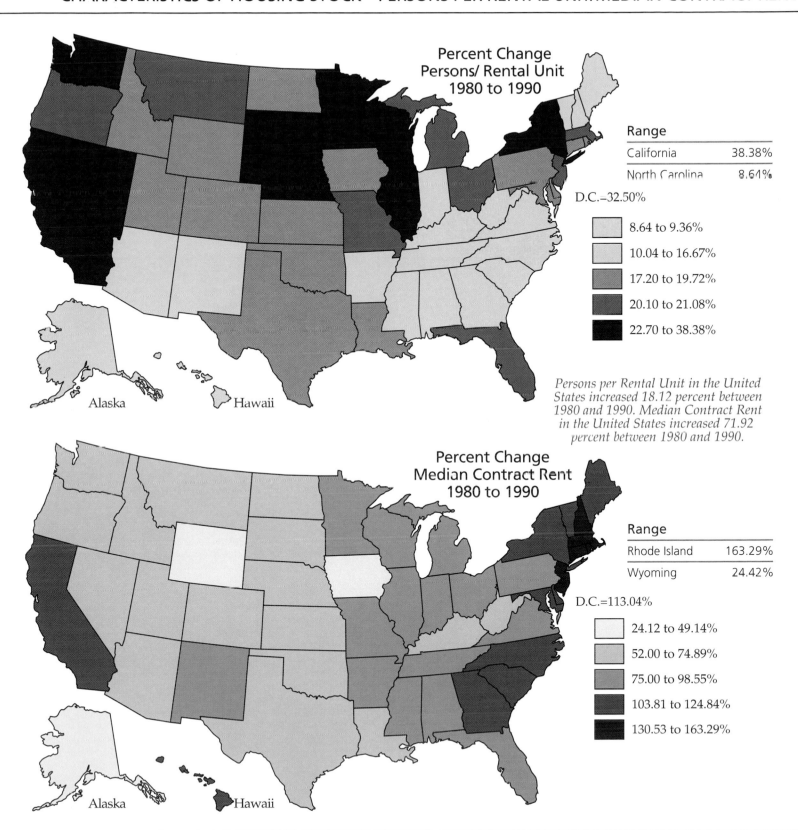

Percent Change Persons/ Rental Unit 1980 to 1990

Range

California	38.38%
North Carolina	8.64%

D.C.–32.50%

- 8.64 to 9.36%
- 10.04 to 16.67%
- 17.20 to 19.72%
- 20.10 to 21.08%
- 22.70 to 38.38%

Alaska Hawaii

Persons per Rental Unit in the United States increased 18.12 percent between 1980 and 1990. Median Contract Rent in the United States increased 71.92 percent between 1980 and 1990.

Percent Change Median Contract Rent 1980 to 1990

Range

Rhode Island	163.29%
Wyoming	24.42%

D.C.=113.04%

- 24.12 to 49.14%
- 52.00 to 74.89%
- 75.00 to 98.55%
- 103.81 to 124.84%
- 130.53 to 163.29%

Alaska Hawaii

Part Four

RACE AND ETHNICITY

IMMIGRATION AND COUNTRY OF ORIGIN

Most Americans acknowledge an ethnic heritage. Many have parents, grandparents, or direct knowledge of relatives that left foreign lands to become citizens of the United States. This migration has happened over the entire history of the United States. It has happened steadily and sometimes in great waves due to economic and political circumstances.

The uneven flow of immigrants into the United States can be studied quickly by looking at the following graph.

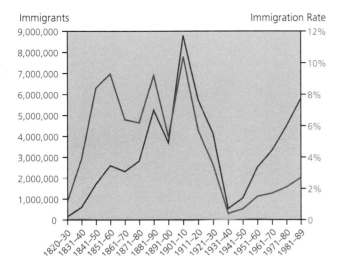

The graph above shows a wave of immigration that started in 1840 and continued to 1920. Not only do the absolute numbers of immigrants appear to be quite large during this period, but the rate of immigration—the percent of immigrants to the existing population—was the largest in U.S. history. This period of unprecedented growth was followed by a significant decline during the Depression and through the Second World War. Not until the Refugee Acts of the last 25 years did immigration numbers increase.

Maps on pages 98 and 99 show countries of origin for immigrants since 1971. The lower sections of the bars situated in each country show the proportion of total immigration during the period between 1971 and 1980. The upper sections of the bars show immigration between the years of 1981 and 1989. It is interesting to note that number of immigrants from Central America, Mexico, South America, and many Asian countries is greater in more recent years. Throughout the eighties, 86.5 percent of all new arrivals came from these areas as compared to European immigration, which has dropped significantly.

AFRICAN AMERICANS

African Americans are the largest ethnic minority in the United States. In 1990, 12.1 percent of the American population or 29,986,000 citizens were of African descent. The African American population is also one of the fastest growing. By the year 2025, it is predicted that 14.6 percent of the population in the United States will be Black (43.5 million). By the year 2050, the Black population is expected to grow to 150 percent of its present size.

America's Black population is spread across the country in a very distinct pattern. Reflecting the early days of slavery and emancipation, the largest concentrations of Blacks are located in a belt starting in North Carolina and winding south and west through Louisiana. The maps on pages 100 and 101 demonstrate this pattern well, showing regional Black populations of 20.5 percent in the South Atlantic and 19.6 percent in the East South Central. The state with the largest African American population is New York with 2,859,055. It is followed closely by California (2,208,801) and Texas (2,021,632). The states with the greatest percent of the population that are Black are Mississippi with 35.6 percent and Louisiana with 30.8. The District of Columbia had 65.8 percent of its citizens declaring African heritage.

By the year 2000, ten states have been projected to emerge with the highest Black concentrations. These are the District of Columbia (67.8 percent), Mississippi (36.1 percent), Louisiana (32.1 percent), South Carolina (30.0 percent), Maryland (27.9 percent), Georgia (27.0 percent), Alabama (25.8 percent), North Carolina (21.9 percent), Delaware (21.1 percent), and Virginia (19.4 percent).

The African American population has been moving in two directions from its southern roots in recent decades. The first movement is northward and easterly. Blacks from Mississippi and Alabama have migrated to Michigan, Ohio, and New York in significant numbers. Blacks from Georgia, South Carolina, and North Carolina have move directly north to Maryland, New Jersey, and New York.

The second major movement is westward. African Americans from Louisiana, Mississippi, and Texas have chosen to migrate to southern California.

HISPANIC AMERICANS

Latinos, as many Hispanic Americans prefer to be called, are America's second largest ethnic minority (9.0 percent of the population). They are also the fastest growing component. In the decade of the nineties, America's Hispanic population is predicted to grow 26.8 percent. A further increase of 22.1 percent is expected between 2000 and 2010.

The Hispanic population of the United States also has a distinct spatial distribution. The southwest corner of the United States, parts of the Middle Atlantic region, Florida, and Illinois have significant proportions of Hispanic citizens. Of America's 22,354,059 Latinos, 59.5 percent live in California, Arizona, New Mexico, and Texas. Most of these citizens have a Mexican or South American cultural heritage. Puerto Rican Americans have settled mainly in New York, New Jersey, and northward in Connecticut and Massachusetts. Smaller pockets of Puerto Rican Americans can be found in Dade County, Florida; and Chicago, Illinois. Cuban Americans are found primarily in Dade County, Florida (Miami). Many Haitian Americans live in Miami, Boston, and Chicago. New York City has the largest Haitian population.

The distribution of Jamaican Americans follows that of Haitians. Cuban Americans are predominantly located in Dade County, Florida, with smaller concentrations in Chicago and New York City.

The migration of Puerto Rican Americans from their heaviest concentration in New York City has been primarily westward to southern California and southward to Florida. Many Puerto Ricans have moved to New Jersey and to western Pennsylvania.

Americans of Mexican blood have moved into the Midwestern and Western states from their origins along the Rio Grande and New Mexico. The vast majority have moved to southern California. Very few have moved anywhere east of the Mississippi River.

ASIAN AMERICANS

With the Refugee Acts of the past three decades, America's Asian population has grown rapidly. Currently, 2.9 percent of the U.S. population is of Asian or Pacific decent. Most Asian Americans live on the coasts in three large cities—Los Angeles, San Francisco, and New York. Chicago also has a large Asian American community. Most migration of Asian Americans is westward from New York to northern California. A large number of migrants have also moved from southern to northern California and many have continued beyond into Washington State and Oregon. The Pacific Northwest will become a growth area for Asian Americans with Chinese from Hong Kong moving southward from western Canada.

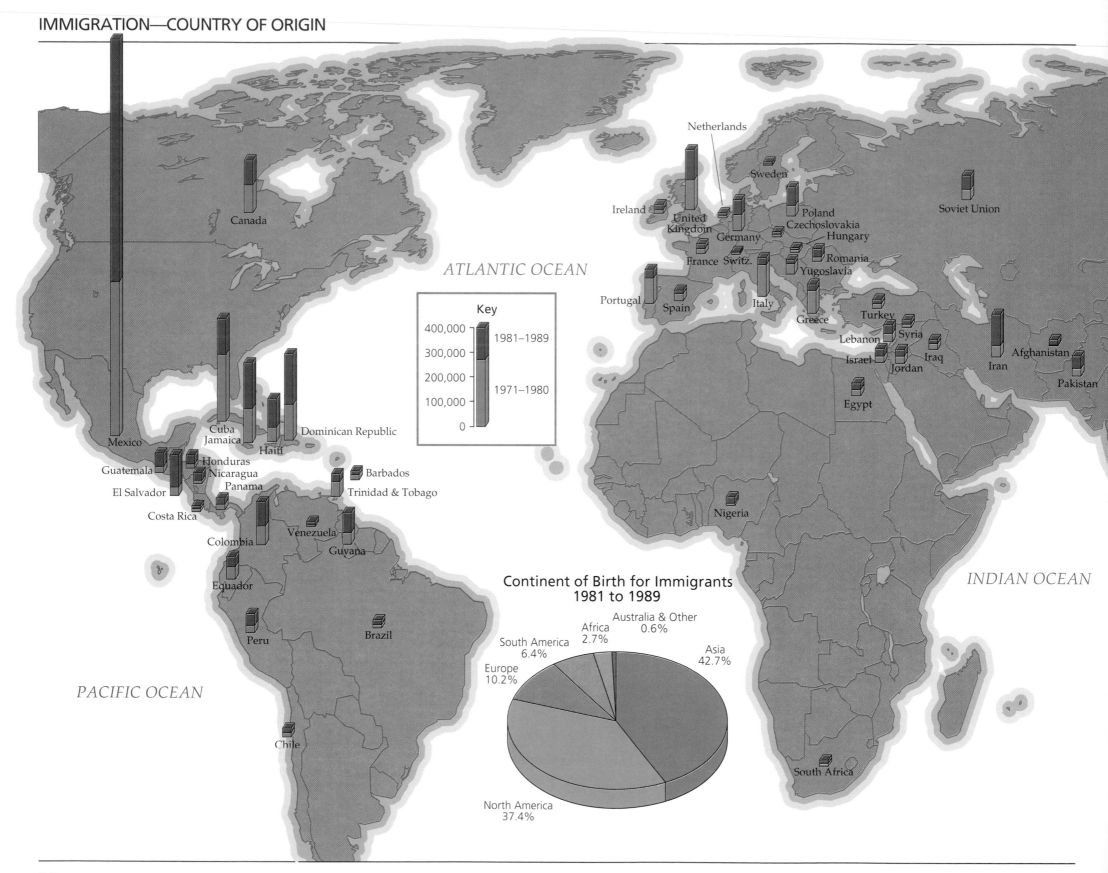

Key

400,000	1981–1989
300,000	
200,000	
100,000	1971–1980
0	

ATLANTIC OCEAN

PACIFIC OCEAN

INDIAN OCEAN

Canada

Mexico

Guatemala
Honduras
El Salvador
Nicaragua
Panama
Costa Rica

Cuba
Jamaica
Haiti
Dominican Republic

Barbados
Trinidad & Tobago

Colombia
Venezuela
Guyana

Equador

Peru

Brazil

Chile

Netherlands
Sweden
Ireland
United Kingdom
Germany
Poland
Czechoslovakia
Hungary
France   Switz.
Romania
Yugoslavia
Portugal
Spain
Italy
Greece
Turkey
Lebanon
Syria
Israel
Jordan
Iraq
Egypt
Soviet Union
Afghanistan
Iran
Pakistan

Nigeria

South Africa

**Continent of Birth for Immigrants
1981 to 1989**

Australia & Other
0.6%

Africa
2.7%

South America
6.4%

Europe
10.2%

Asia
42.7%

North America
37.4%

Immigrants' Countries of Origin, 1971 to 1989

	Total 1971–80	Total 1981–89	Percent of Total 1981–89		Total 1971–80	Total 1981–89	Percent of Total 1981–89
Total (000s)	4,493	5,802		Iraq	23	18	0.31
				Israel	27	32	0.54
EUROPE	801	593	10.22	Japan	48	38	0.65
Czechoslovakia	10	10	0.17	Jordan	30	28	0.49
France	18	20	0.35	Korea	272	307	5.28
Germany	66	63	1.08	Laos	23	135	2.33
Greece	94	26	0.46	Lebanon	34	36	0.62
Hungary	12	8	0.14	Pakistan	31	52	0.89
Ireland	14	23	0.39	Philippines	360	432	7.44
Italy	130	30	0.51	Syria	13	18	0.30
Netherlands	11	11	0.18	Thailand	44	56	0.96
Poland	44	77	1.33	Turkey	19	18	0.32
Portugal	105	36	0.62	Vietnam	180	353	6.08
Romania	18	34	0.59				
Soviet Union	43	59	1.01	NORTH AMERICA	1,645	2,167	37.36
Spain	30	14	0.24	Canada	115	102	1.76
Sweden	6	9	0.16	Mexico	637	974	16.79
Swizerland	7	6	0.11	Caribbean	760	777	13.40
United Kingdom	124	126	2.18	Barbados	21	16	0.27
Yugoslavia	42	16	0.28	Cuba	277	149	2.56
				Dominican Republic	148	210	3.61
ASIA	1,634	2,479	42.72	Haiti	59	120	2.07
Afghanistan	2	23	0.40	Jamaica	142	189	3.25
Cambodia	8	111	1.92	Trinidad and Tobago	62	33	0.57
China: Total	203	296	5.09	Central America	132	313	5.39
Mainland		32	0.56	Costa Rica	12	13	0.22
Taiwan		14	0.24	El Salvador	34	134	2.32
Hong Kong	48	54	0.92	Guatemala	26	56	0.96
India	177	231	3.98	Honduras	17	38	0.65
Iran	46	130	2.24	Nicaragua	13	33	0.56
				Panama	23	26	0.44
				SOUTH AMERICA	284	370	6.38
				Argentina	25	20	0.35
				Brazil	14	20	0.34
				Chile	18	19	0.33
				Colombia	78	100	1.73
				Ecuador	50	44	0.75
				Guyana	48	84	1.45
				Peru	29	49	0.84
				Venezuela	7	15	0.26
				AFRICA	92	156	2.70
				Egypt	26	27	0.47
				Nigeria	9	27	0.46
				South Africa	12	14	0.24
				AUSTRALIA	14	12	0.21
				OTHER COUNTRIES	23	24	0.41

Source: U.S. Immigration and Naturalization Service, *Statistical Yearbook*, annual.

Korea
Japan
Mainland China
Hong Kong
India
Laos
Thailand
Cambodia
Vietnam
Philippines
Australia

INDIAN OCEAN

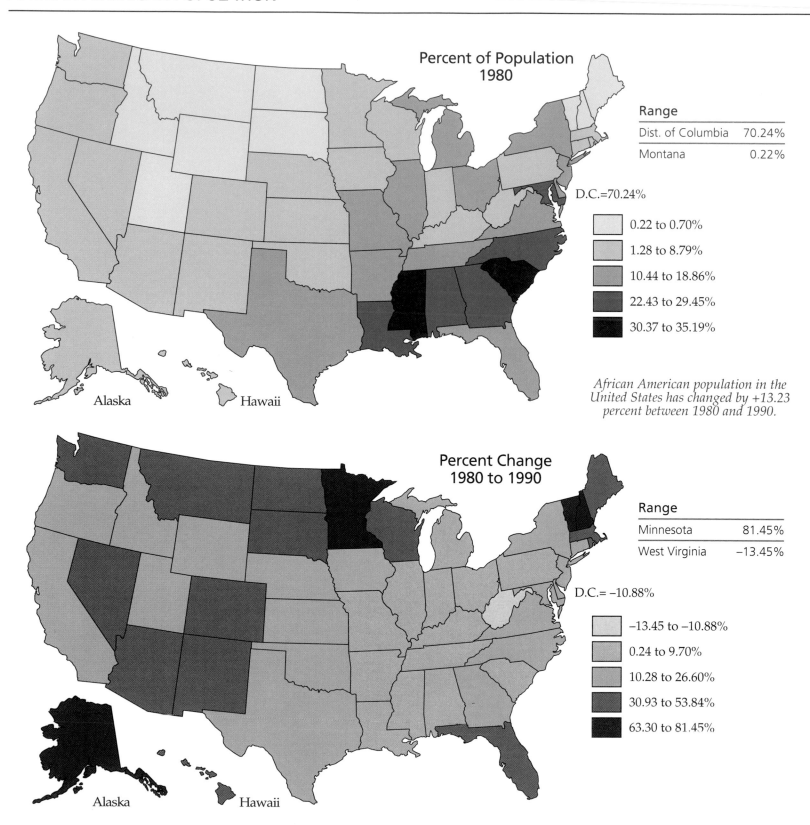

Percent of Population 1980

Range

Dist. of Columbia	70.24%
Montana	0.22%

D.C.=70.24%

- 0.22 to 0.70%
- 1.28 to 8.79%
- 10.44 to 18.86%
- 22.43 to 29.45%
- 30.37 to 35.19%

Alaska   Hawaii

African American population in the United States has changed by +13.23 percent between 1980 and 1990.

Percent Change 1980 to 1990

Range

Minnesota	81.45%
West Virginia	−13.45%

D.C.= −10.88%

- −13.45 to −10.88%
- 0.24 to 9.70%
- 10.28 to 26.60%
- 30.93 to 53.84%
- 63.30 to 81.45%

Alaska   Hawaii

African Americans, 1980

United States	26,482,349
Alabama	996,283
Alaska	13,748
Arizona	74,159
Arkansas	373,025
California	1,818,660
Colorado	101,695
Connecticut	216,641
Delaware	96,157
District of Columbia	448,370
Florida	1,343,134
Georgia	1,464,435
Hawaii	17,687
Idaho	2,711
Illinois	1,674,467
Indiana	414,489
Iowa	42,228
Kansas	126,356
Kentucky	259,289
Louisiana	1,238,472
Maine	3,381
Maryland	957,418
Massachusetts	221,029
Michigan	1,197,177
Minnesota	52,325
Mississippi	887,111
Missouri	513,385
Montana	1,738
Nebraska	47,946
Nevada	51,203
New Hampshire	4,324
New Jersey	924,909
New Mexico	23,071
New York	2,405,818
North Carolina	1,319,054
North Dakota	2,471
Ohio	1,076,742
Oklahoma	204,810
Oregon	37,454
Pennsylvania	1,045,318
Rhode Island	27,361
South Carolina	947,969
South Dakota	2,152
Tennessee	724,808
Texas	1,704,741
Utah	9,691
Vermont	1,188
Virginia	1,008,665
Washington	105,604
West Virginia	65,041
Wisconsin	183,169
Wyoming	3,270

African Americans, 1990

United States	29,986,161
Alabama	1,020,705
Alaska	22,451
Arizona	110,524
Arkansas	373,912
California	2,208,801
Colorado	133,146
Connecticut	274,269
Delaware	112,460
District of Columbia	399,604
Florida	1,759,534
Georgia	1,746,565
Hawaii	27,195
Idaho	3,370
Illinois	1,694,273
Indiana	432,092
Iowa	48,090
Kansas	143,076
Kentucky	262,907
Louisiana	1,299,281
Maine	5,138
Maryland	1,190,000
Massachusetts	300,130
Michigan	1,291,706
Minnesota	94,944
Mississippi	915,057
Missouri	548,208
Montana	2,381
Nebraska	57,404
Nevada	78,771
New Hampshire	7,198
New Jersey	1,036,825
New Mexico	30,210
New York	2,859,055
North Carolina	1,456,323
North Dakota	3,524
Ohio	1,154,826
Oklahoma	233,801
Oregon	46,178
Pennsylvania	1,089,795
Rhode Island	38,861
South Carolina	1,039,884
South Dakota	3,258
Tennessee	778,035
Texas	2,021,632
Utah	11,576
Vermont	1,951
Virginia	1,162,994
Washington	149,801
West Virginia	56,295
Wisconsin	244,539
Wyoming	3,606

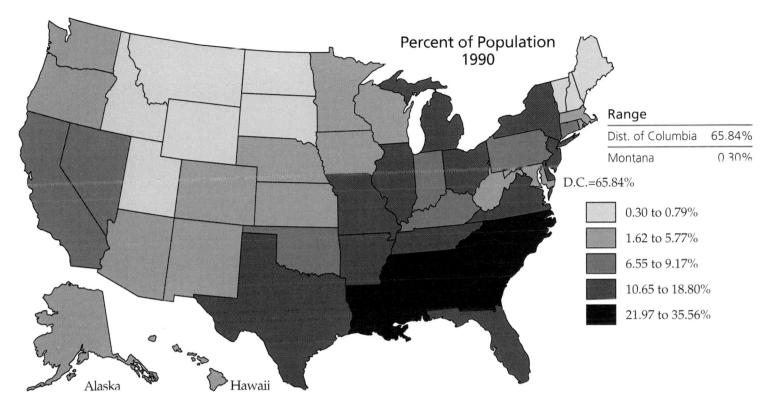

Percent of Population 1990

Range

Dist. of Columbia	65.84%
Montana	0.30%

D.C.=65.84%

- 0.30 to 0.79%
- 1.62 to 5.77%
- 6.55 to 9.17%
- 10.65 to 18.80%
- 21.97 to 35.56%

Alaska Hawaii

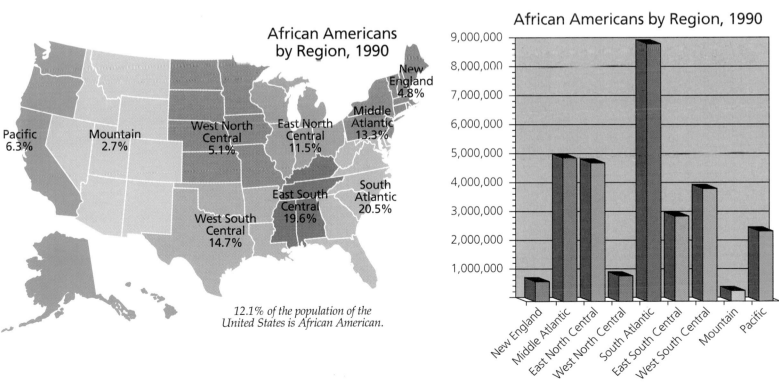

African Americans by Region, 1990

New England 4.8%
Middle Atlantic 13.3%
West North Central 5.1%
East North Central 11.5%
Pacific 6.3%
Mountain 2.7%
East South Central 19.6%
South Atlantic 20.5%
West South Central 14.7%

12.1% of the population of the United States is African American.

African Americans by Region, 1990

Bar chart with y-axis from 1,000,000 to 9,000,000. Categories: New England, Middle Atlantic, East North Central, West North Central, South Atlantic, East South Central, West South Central, Mountain, Pacific.

Major Cities

City	%	City	%
Boston, MA	5.29%	Paterson, NJ	36.01%
Bridgeport, CT	26.60%	Philadelphia, PA	39.86%
Buffalo, NY	30.65%	Pittsburgh, PA	25.78%
Burlington, VT	1.00%	Portland, ME	1.12%
Elizabeth, NJ	19.85%	Providence, RI	14.83%
Hartford, CT	38.89%	Rochester, NY	34.53%
Jersey City, NJ	29.69%	Springfield, MA	19.15%
Manchester, NH	0.97%	Syracuse, NY	20.33%
New Haven, CT	36.14%	Waterbury, CT	12.97%
New York, NY	28.71%	Worcester, MA	4.52%
Newark, NJ	58.46%	Yonkers, NY	14.11%

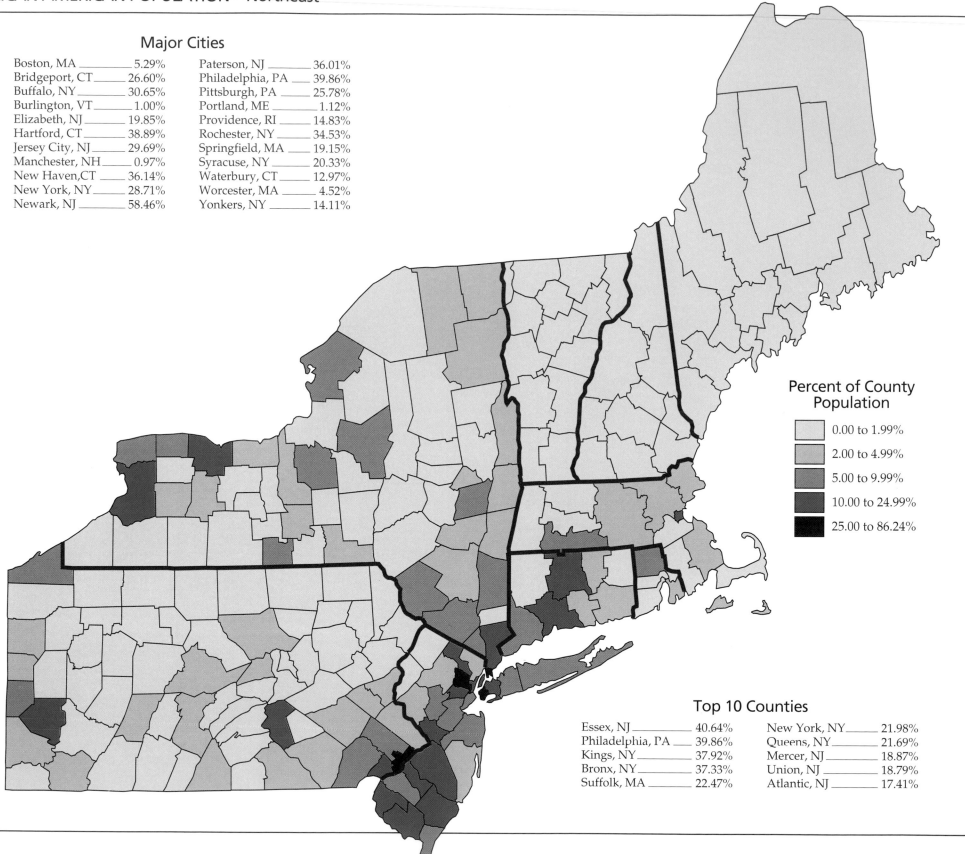

Percent of County Population

- 0.00 to 1.99%
- 2.00 to 4.99%
- 5.00 to 9.99%
- 10.00 to 24.99%
- 25.00 to 86.24%

Top 10 Counties

County	%	County	%
Essex, NJ	40.64%	New York, NY	21.98%
Philadelphia, PA	39.86%	Queens, NY	21.69%
Kings, NY	37.92%	Mercer, NJ	18.87%
Bronx, NY	37.33%	Union, NJ	18.79%
Suffolk, MA	22.47%	Atlantic, NJ	17.41%

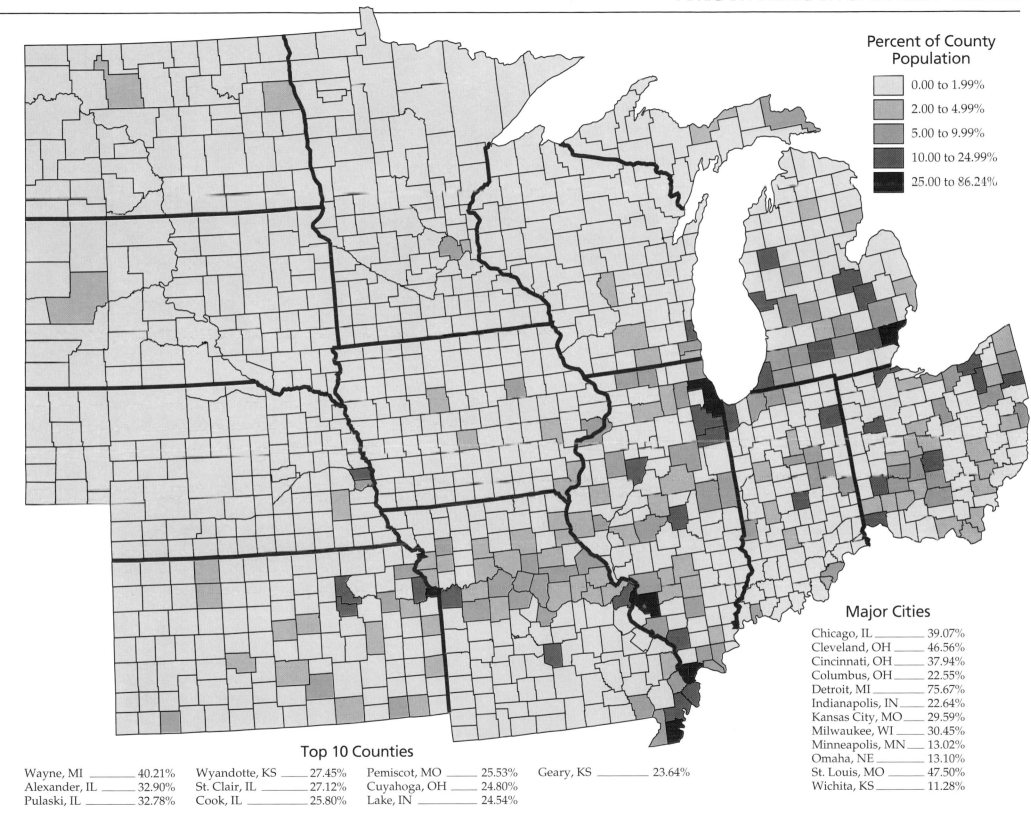

Percent of County
Population

0.00 to 1.99%
2.00 to 4.99%
5.00 to 9.99%
10.00 to 24.99%
25.00 to 86.24%

Major Cities

Chicago, IL _____ 39.07%
Cleveland, OH _____ 46.56%
Cincinnati, OH _____ 37.94%
Columbus, OH _____ 22.55%
Detroit, MI _____ 75.67%
Indianapolis, IN ___ 22.64%
Kansas City, MO ___ 29.59%
Milwaukee, WI _____ 30.45%
Minneapolis, MN ___ 13.02%
Omaha, NE _____ 13.10%
St. Louis, MO _____ 47.50%
Wichita, KS _____ 11.28%

Top 10 Counties

Wayne, MI _____ 40.21%   Wyandotte, KS _____ 27.45%   Pemiscot, MO _____ 25.53%   Geary, KS _____ 23.64%
Alexander, IL _____ 32.90%   St. Clair, IL _____ 27.12%   Cuyahoga, OH _____ 24.80%
Pulaski, IL _____ 32.78%   Cook, IL _____ 25.80%   Lake, IN _____ 24.54%

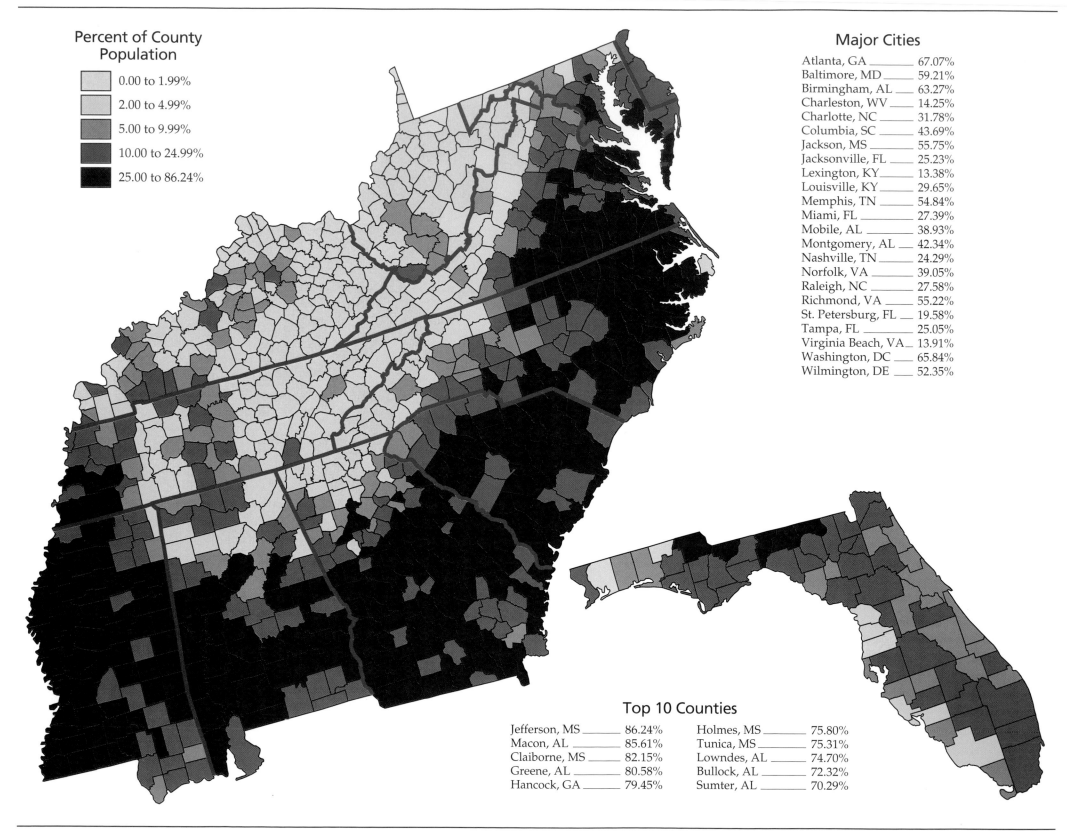

Percent of County Population

- 0.00 to 1.99%
- 2.00 to 4.99%
- 5.00 to 9.99%
- 10.00 to 24.99%
- 25.00 to 86.24%

Major Cities

Atlanta, GA	67.07%
Baltimore, MD	59.21%
Birmingham, AL	63.27%
Charleston, WV	14.25%
Charlotte, NC	31.78%
Columbia, SC	43.69%
Jackson, MS	55.75%
Jacksonville, FL	25.23%
Lexington, KY	13.38%
Louisville, KY	29.65%
Memphis, TN	54.84%
Miami, FL	27.39%
Mobile, AL	38.93%
Montgomery, AL	42.34%
Nashville, TN	24.29%
Norfolk, VA	39.05%
Raleigh, NC	27.58%
Richmond, VA	55.22%
St. Petersburg, FL	19.58%
Tampa, FL	25.05%
Virginia Beach, VA	13.91%
Washington, DC	65.84%
Wilmington, DE	52.35%

Top 10 Counties

Jefferson, MS	86.24%	Holmes, MS	75.80%
Macon, AL	85.61%	Tunica, MS	75.31%
Claiborne, MS	82.15%	Lowndes, AL	74.70%
Greene, AL	80.58%	Bullock, AL	72.32%
Hancock, GA	79.45%	Sumter, AL	70.29%

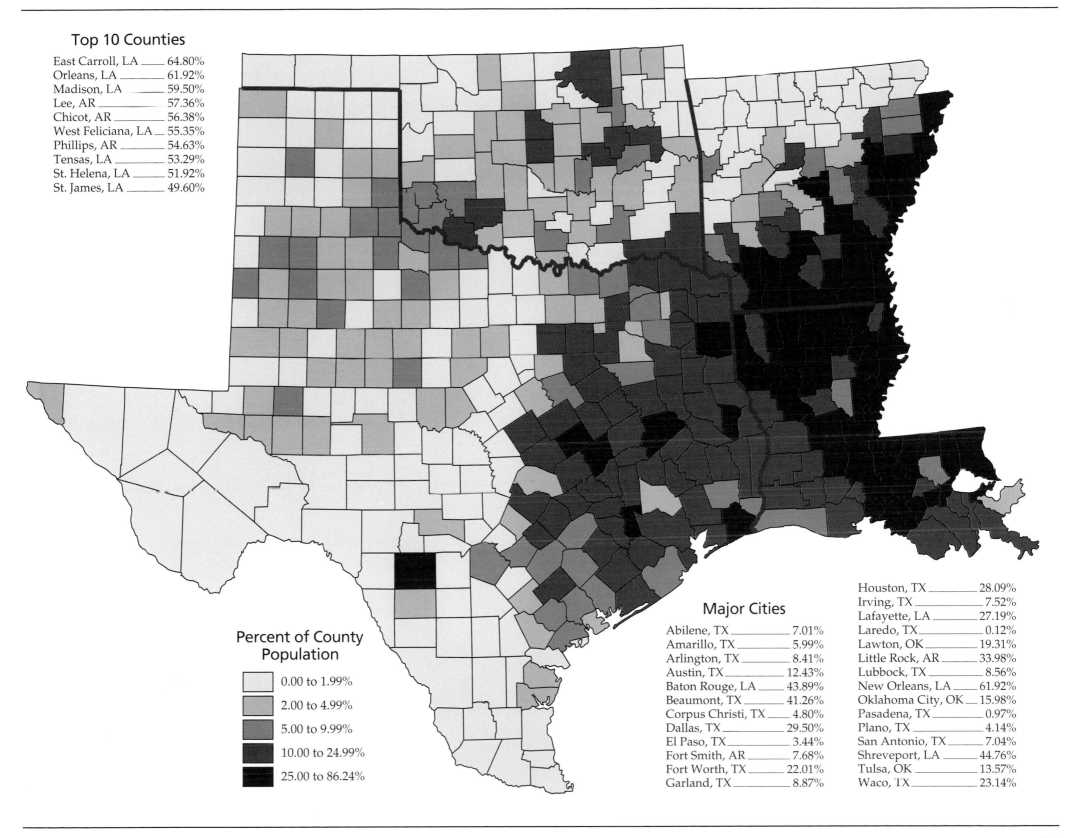

Top 10 Counties

East Carroll, LA —— 64.80%
Orleans, LA —— 61.92%
Madison, LA —— 59.50%
Lee, AR —— 57.36%
Chicot, AR —— 56.38%
West Feliciana, LA — 55.35%
Phillips, AR —— 54.63%
Tensas, LA —— 53.29%
St. Helena, LA —— 51.92%
St. James, LA —— 49.60%

Percent of County Population

- 0.00 to 1.99%
- 2.00 to 4.99%
- 5.00 to 9.99%
- 10.00 to 24.99%
- 25.00 to 86.24%

Major Cities

Abilene, TX —— 7.01%
Amarillo, TX —— 5.99%
Arlington, TX —— 8.41%
Austin, TX —— 12.43%
Baton Rouge, LA —— 43.89%
Beaumont, TX —— 41.26%
Corpus Christi, TX —— 4.80%
Dallas, TX —— 29.50%
El Paso, TX —— 3.44%
Fort Smith, AR —— 7.68%
Fort Worth, TX —— 22.01%
Garland, TX —— 8.87%
Houston, TX —— 28.09%
Irving, TX —— 7.52%
Lafayette, LA —— 27.19%
Laredo, TX —— 0.12%
Lawton, OK —— 19.31%
Little Rock, AR —— 33.98%
Lubbock, TX —— 8.56%
New Orleans, LA —— 61.92%
Oklahoma City, OK — 15.98%
Pasadena, TX —— 0.97%
Plano, TX —— 4.14%
San Antonio, TX —— 7.04%
Shreveport, LA —— 44.76%
Tulsa, OK —— 13.57%
Waco, TX —— 23.14%

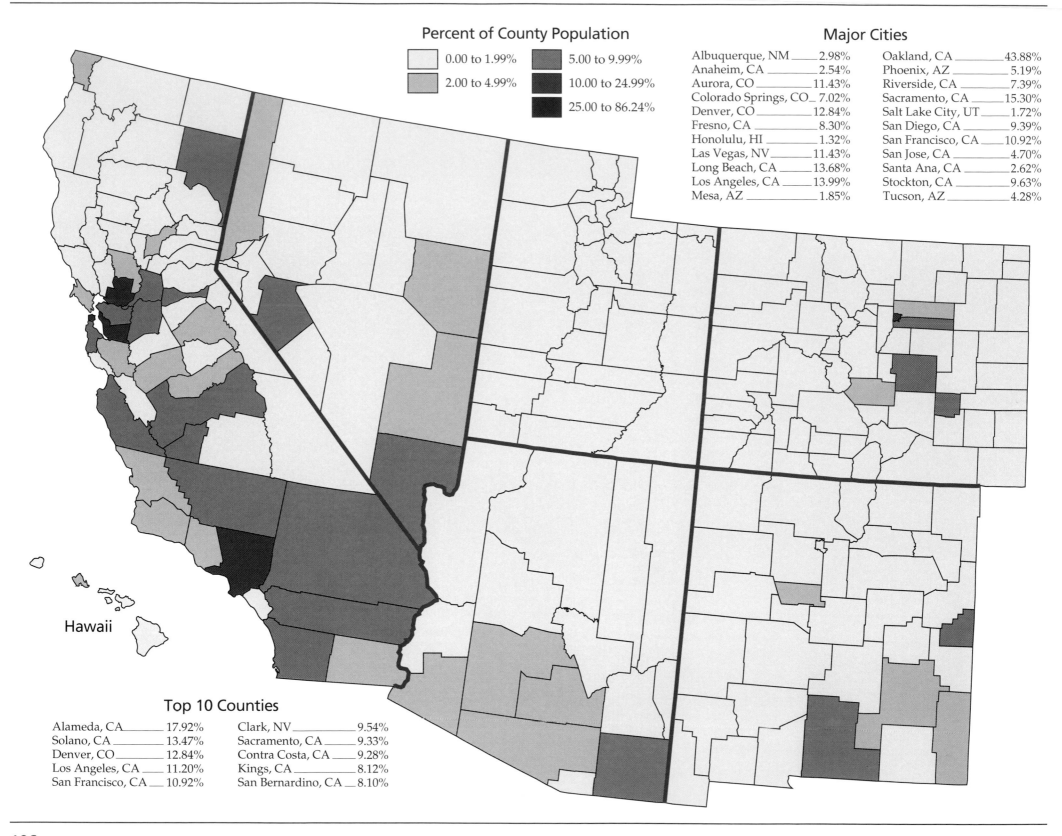

Percent of County Population

- 0.00 to 1.99%
- 2.00 to 4.99%
- 5.00 to 9.99%
- 10.00 to 24.99%
- 25.00 to 86.24%

Major Cities

City	Percent	City	Percent
Albuquerque, NM	2.98%	Oakland, CA	43.88%
Anaheim, CA	2.54%	Phoenix, AZ	5.19%
Aurora, CO	11.43%	Riverside, CA	7.39%
Colorado Springs, CO	7.02%	Sacramento, CA	15.30%
Denver, CO	12.84%	Salt Lake City, UT	1.72%
Fresno, CA	8.30%	San Diego, CA	9.39%
Honolulu, HI	1.32%	San Francisco, CA	10.92%
Las Vegas, NV	11.43%	San Jose, CA	4.70%
Long Beach, CA	13.68%	Santa Ana, CA	2.62%
Los Angeles, CA	13.99%	Stockton, CA	9.63%
Mesa, AZ	1.85%	Tucson, AZ	4.28%

Hawaii

Top 10 Counties

County	Percent	County	Percent
Alameda, CA	17.92%	Clark, NV	9.54%
Solano, CA	13.47%	Sacramento, CA	9.33%
Denver, CO	12.84%	Contra Costa, CA	9.28%
Los Angeles, CA	11.20%	Kings, CA	8.12%
San Francisco, CA	10.92%	San Bernardino, CA	8.10%

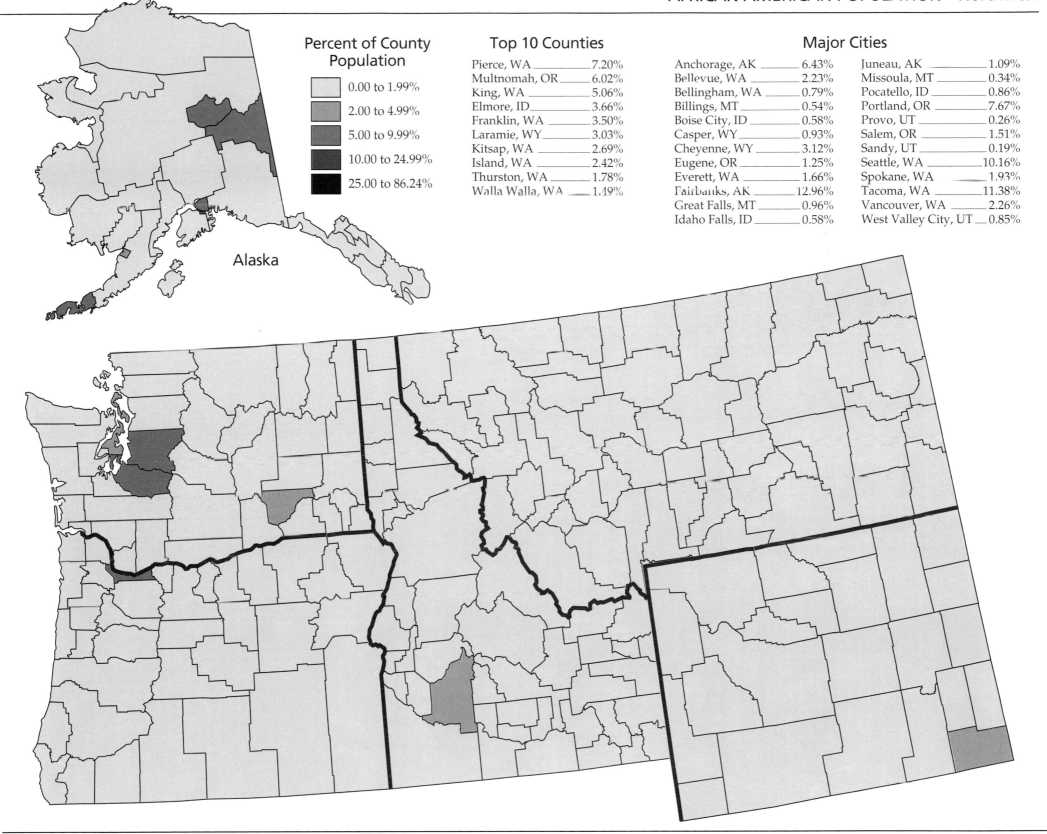

Percent of County Population

- 0.00 to 1.99%
- 2.00 to 4.99%
- 5.00 to 9.99%
- 10.00 to 24.99%
- 25.00 to 86.24%

Alaska

Top 10 Counties

County	%
Pierce, WA	7.20%
Multnomah, OR	6.02%
King, WA	5.06%
Elmore, ID	3.66%
Franklin, WA	3.50%
Laramie, WY	3.03%
Kitsap, WA	2.69%
Island, WA	2.42%
Thurston, WA	1.78%
Walla Walla, WA	1.49%

Major Cities

City	%	City	%
Anchorage, AK	6.43%	Juneau, AK	1.09%
Bellevue, WA	2.23%	Missoula, MT	0.34%
Bellingham, WA	0.79%	Pocatello, ID	0.86%
Billings, MT	0.54%	Portland, OR	7.67%
Boise City, ID	0.58%	Provo, UT	0.26%
Casper, WY	0.93%	Salem, OR	1.51%
Cheyenne, WY	3.12%	Sandy, UT	0.19%
Eugene, OR	1.25%	Seattle, WA	10.16%
Everett, WA	1.66%	Spokane, WA	1.93%
Fairbanks, AK	12.96%	Tacoma, WA	11.38%
Great Falls, MT	0.96%	Vancouver, WA	2.26%
Idaho Falls, ID	0.58%	West Valley City, UT	0.85%

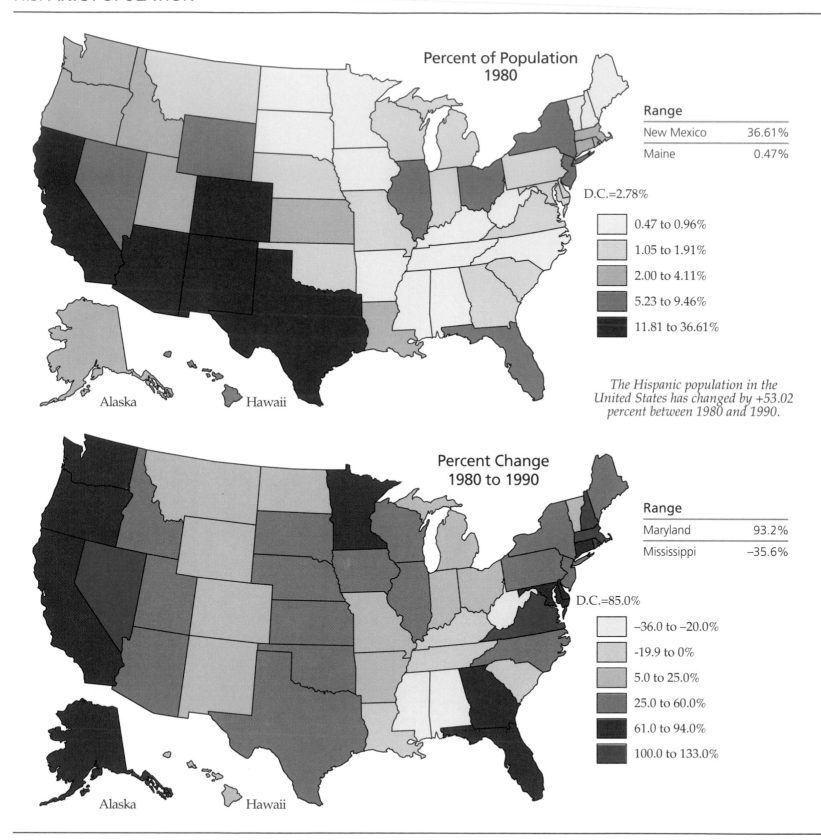

Percent of Population 1980

Range	
New Mexico	36.61%
Maine	0.47%

D.C.=2.78%

- 0.47 to 0.96%
- 1.05 to 1.91%
- 2.00 to 4.11%
- 5.23 to 9.46%
- 11.81 to 36.61%

Alaska   Hawaii

The Hispanic population in the United States has changed by +53.02 percent between 1980 and 1990.

Percent Change 1980 to 1990

Range	
Maryland	93.2%
Mississippi	−35.6%

D.C.=85.0%

- −36.0 to −20.0%
- -19.9 to 0%
- 5.0 to 25.0%
- 25.0 to 60.0%
- 61.0 to 94.0%
- 100.0 to 133.0%

Alaska   Hawaii

Hispanic Population, 1980

United States	14,608,673
Alabama	33,299
Alaska	9,507
Arizona	440,701
Arkansas	17,904
California	4,544,331
Colorado	339,717
Connecticut	124,499
Delaware	9,661
District of Columbia	17,679
Florida	858,158
Georgia	61,260
Hawaii	71,263
Idaho	36,615
Illinois	635,602
Indiana	87,047
Iowa	25,536
Kansas	63,339
Kentucky	27,406
Louisiana	99,134
Maine	5,005
Maryland	64,746
Massachusetts	141,043
Michigan	162,440
Minnesota	32,123
Mississippi	24,731
Missouri	51,653
Montana	9,974
Nebraska	28,025
Nevada	53,879
New Hampshire	5,587
New Jersey	491,883
New Mexico	477,222
New York	1,659,300
North Carolina	56,667
North Dakota	3,902
Ohio	119,883
Oklahoma	57,419
Oregon	65,847
Pennsylvania	153,961
Rhode Island	19,707
South Carolina	33,426
South Dakota	4,023
Tennessee	34,077
Texas	2,985,824
Utah	60,302
Vermont	3,304
Virginia	79,868
Washington	120,016
West Virginia	12,707
Wisconsin	62,972
Wyoming	24,499

Hispanic Population, 1990

United States	22,354,059
Alabama	24,629
Alaska	17,803
Arizona	688,338
Arkansas	19,876
California	7,687,938
Colorado	424,302
Connecticut	213,116
Delaware	15,820
District of Columbia	32,710
Florida	1,574,143
Georgia	108,922
Hawaii	81,390
Idaho	52,927
Illinois	904,446
Indiana	98,788
Iowa	32,647
Kansas	93,670
Kentucky	21,984
Louisiana	93,044
Maine	6,829
Maryland	125,102
Massachusetts	287,549
Michigan	201,596
Minnesota	53,884
Mississippi	15,931
Missouri	61,702
Montana	12,174
Nebraska	36,969
Nevada	124,419
New Hampshire	11,333
New Jersey	739,861
New Mexico	579,224
New York	2,214,026
North Carolina	76,726
North Dakota	4,665
Ohio	139,696
Oklahoma	86,160
Oregon	112,707
Pennsylvania	232,262
Rhode Island	45,752
South Carolina	30,551
South Dakota	5,252
Tennessee	32,741
Texas	4,339,905
Utah	84,597
Vermont	3,661
Virginia	160,288
Washington	214,570
West Virginia	8,489
Wisconsin	93,194
Wyoming	25,751

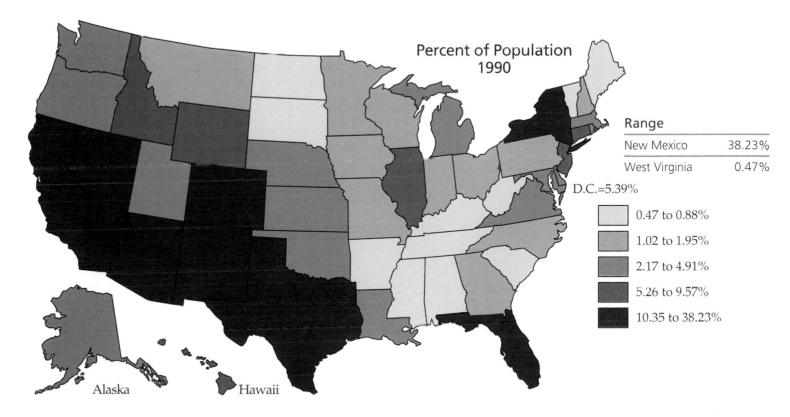

Percent of Population 1990

Range

New Mexico	38.23%
West Virginia	0.47%

D.C.=5.39%

- 0.47 to 0.88%
- 1.02 to 1.95%
- 2.17 to 4.91%
- 5.26 to 9.57%
- 10.35 to 38.23%

Alaska   Hawaii

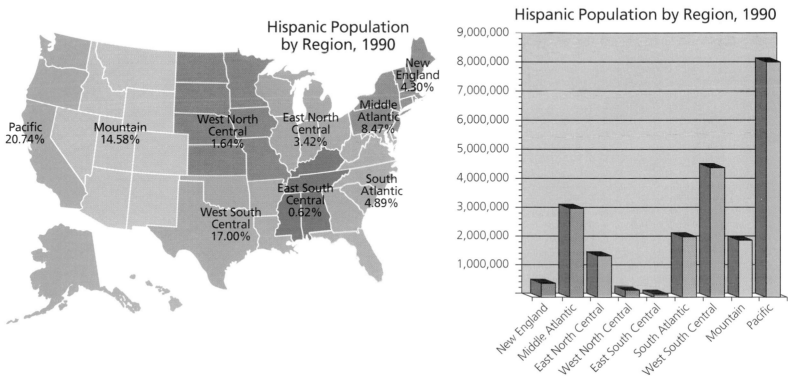

Hispanic Population by Region, 1990

Pacific 20.74%
Mountain 14.58%
West North Central 1.64%
East North Central 3.42%
Middle Atlantic 8.47%
New England 4.30%
West South Central 17.00%
East South Central 0.62%
South Atlantic 4.89%

Hispanic Population by Region, 1990

(Bar chart, y-axis: 1,000,000 to 9,000,000; x-axis regions: New England, Middle Atlantic, East North Central, West North Central, East South Central, South Atlantic, West South Central, Mountain, Pacific)

Major Cities

Boston, MA	10.79%	Paterson, NJ	40.96%
Bridgeport, CT	26.50%	Philadelphia, PA	5.63%
Buffalo, NY	4.92%	Pittsburgh, PA	0.94%
Burlington, VT	1.23%	Portland, ME	0.80%
Elizabeth, NJ	39.14%	Providence, RI	15.54%
Hartford, CT	31.59%	Rochester, NY	8.66%
Jersey City, NJ	24.24%	Springfield, MA	16.90%
Manchester, NH	2.13%	Syracuse, NY	2.89%
New Haven, CT	13.22%	Waterbury, CT	13.38%
New York, NY	24.36%	Worcester, MA	9.58%
Newark, NJ	26.07%	Yonkers, NY	16.74%

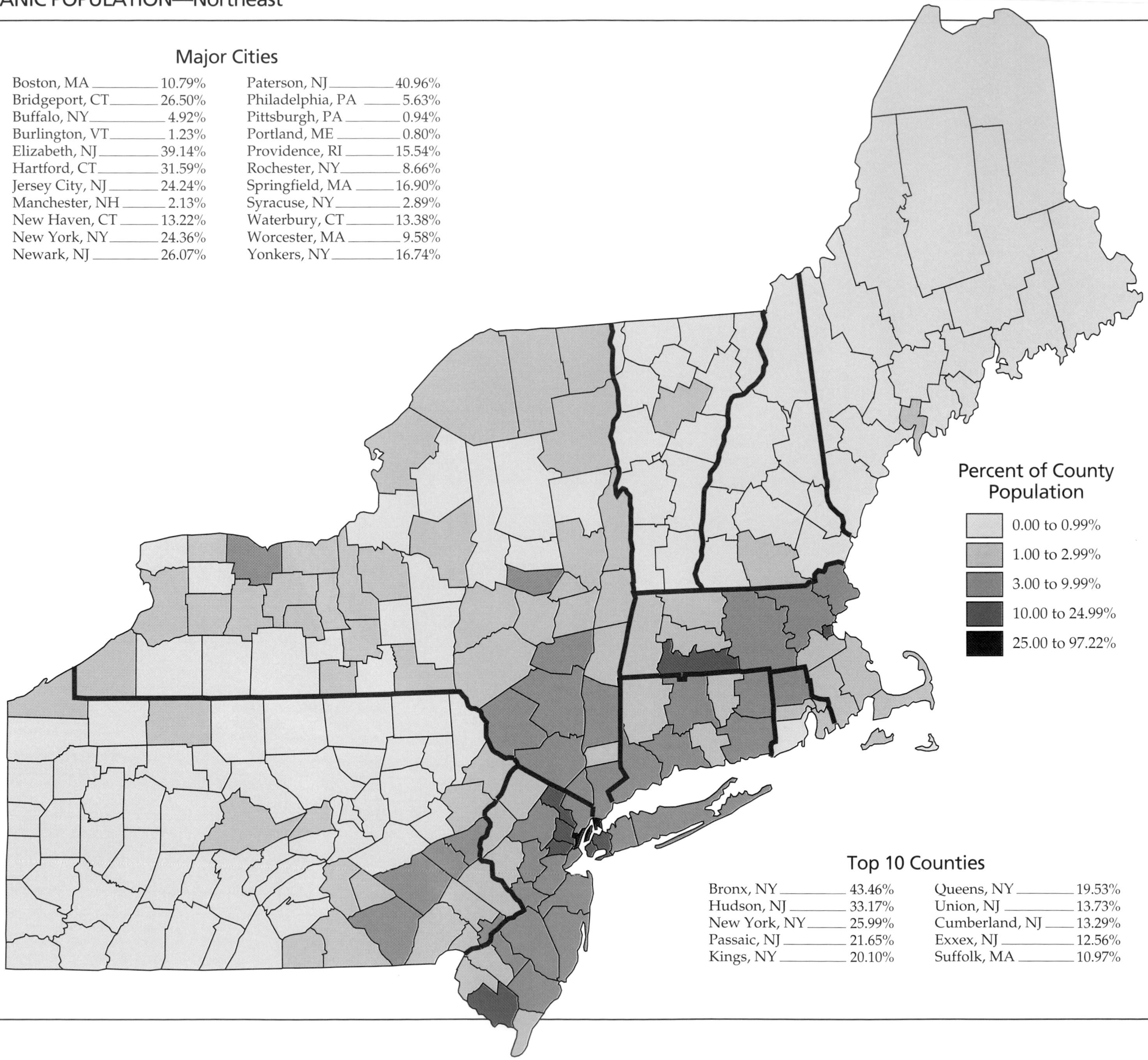

Percent of County Population

- 0.00 to 0.99%
- 1.00 to 2.99%
- 3.00 to 9.99%
- 10.00 to 24.99%
- 25.00 to 97.22%

Top 10 Counties

Bronx, NY	43.46%	Queens, NY	19.53%
Hudson, NJ	33.17%	Union, NJ	13.73%
New York, NY	25.99%	Cumberland, NJ	13.29%
Passaic, NJ	21.65%	Exxex, NJ	12.56%
Kings, NY	20.10%	Suffolk, MA	10.97%

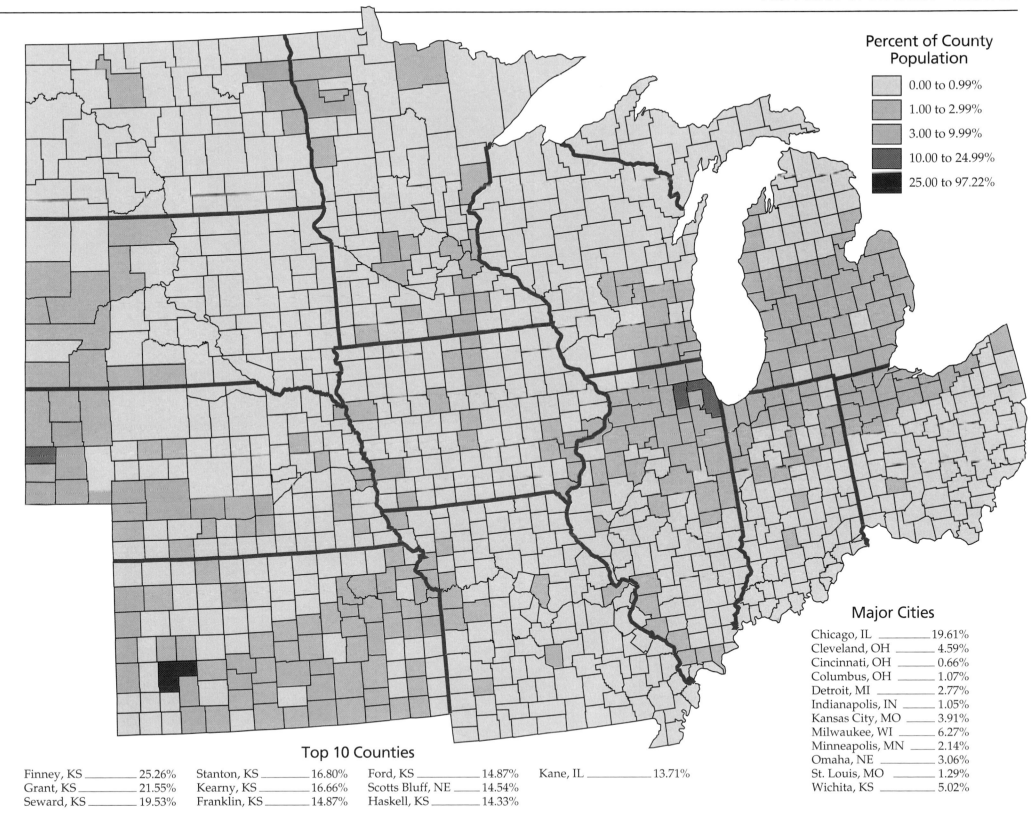

Percent of County Population

- 0.00 to 0.99%
- 1.00 to 2.99%
- 3.00 to 9.99%
- 10.00 to 24.99%
- 25.00 to 97.22%

Major Cities

City	Percent
Chicago, IL	19.61%
Cleveland, OH	4.59%
Cincinnati, OH	0.66%
Columbus, OH	1.07%
Detroit, MI	2.77%
Indianapolis, IN	1.05%
Kansas City, MO	3.91%
Milwaukee, WI	6.27%
Minneapolis, MN	2.14%
Omaha, NE	3.06%
St. Louis, MO	1.29%
Wichita, KS	5.02%

Top 10 Counties

County	Percent	County	Percent
Finney, KS	25.26%	Ford, KS	14.87%
Grant, KS	21.55%	Scotts Bluff, NE	14.54%
Seward, KS	19.53%	Haskell, KS	14.33%
Stanton, KS	16.80%	Kane, IL	13.71%
Kearny, KS	16.66%		
Franklin, KS	14.87%		

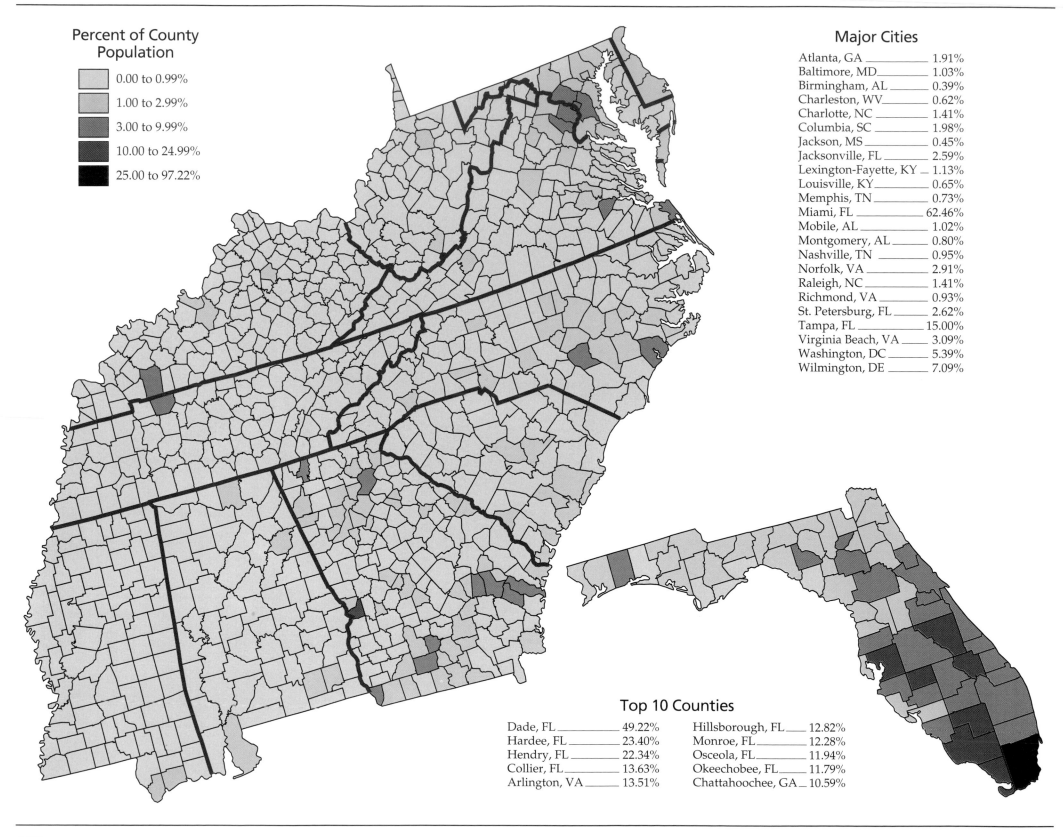

Percent of County Population

- 0.00 to 0.99%
- 1.00 to 2.99%
- 3.00 to 9.99%
- 10.00 to 24.99%
- 25.00 to 97.22%

Major Cities

City	Percent
Atlanta, GA	1.91%
Baltimore, MD	1.03%
Birmingham, AL	0.39%
Charleston, WV	0.62%
Charlotte, NC	1.41%
Columbia, SC	1.98%
Jackson, MS	0.45%
Jacksonville, FL	2.59%
Lexington-Fayette, KY	1.13%
Louisville, KY	0.65%
Memphis, TN	0.73%
Miami, FL	62.46%
Mobile, AL	1.02%
Montgomery, AL	0.80%
Nashville, TN	0.95%
Norfolk, VA	2.91%
Raleigh, NC	1.41%
Richmond, VA	0.93%
St. Petersburg, FL	2.62%
Tampa, FL	15.00%
Virginia Beach, VA	3.09%
Washington, DC	5.39%
Wilmington, DE	7.09%

Top 10 Counties

County	Percent	County	Percent
Dade, FL	49.22%	Hillsborough, FL	12.82%
Hardee, FL	23.40%	Monroe, FL	12.28%
Hendry, FL	22.34%	Osceola, FL	11.94%
Collier, FL	13.63%	Okeechobee, FL	11.79%
Arlington, VA	13.51%	Chattahoochee, GA	10.59%

Top 10 Counties

Starr, TX _____ 97.22%
Webb, TX _____ 93.87%
Maverick, TX _____ 93.53%
Jim Hogg, TX _____ 91.19%
Brooks, TX _____ 89.44%
Zavala, TX _____ 89.42%
Duval, TX _____ 87.22%
Hidalgo, TX _____ 85.25%
Willacy, TX _____ 84.37%
Dimmit, TX _____ 83.27%

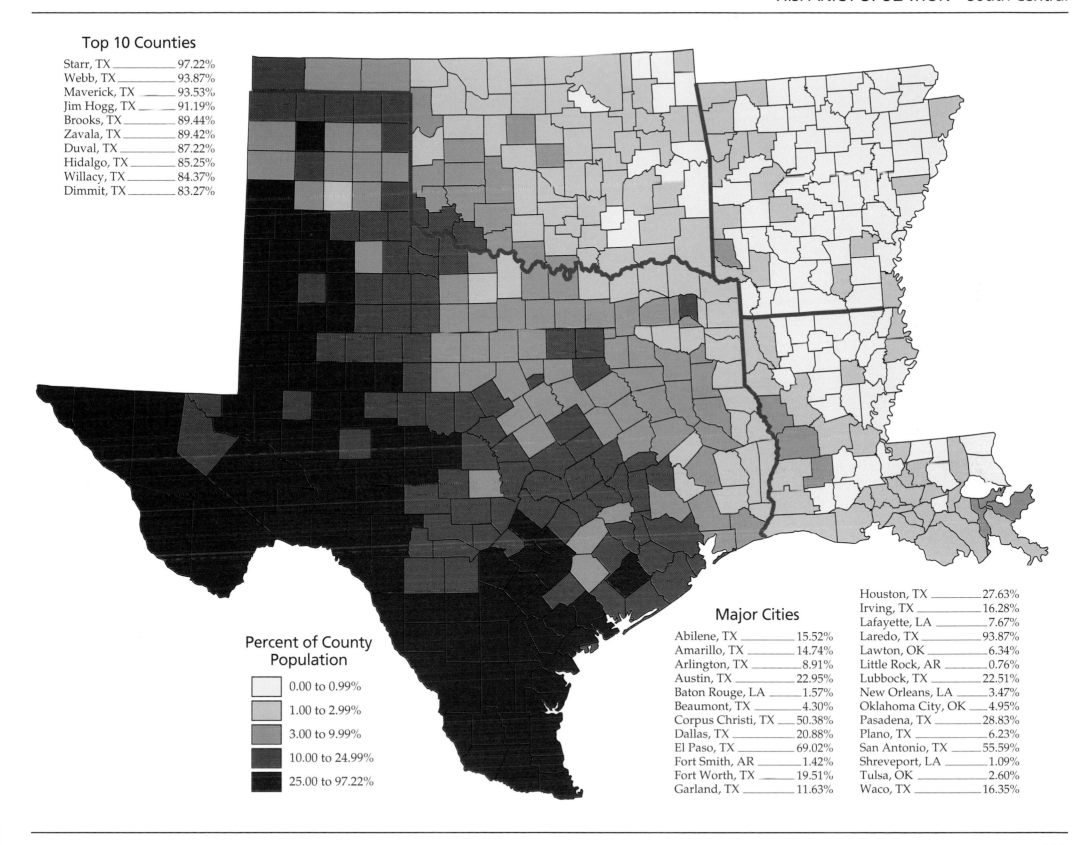

Percent of County Population

- 0.00 to 0.99%
- 1.00 to 2.99%
- 3.00 to 9.99%
- 10.00 to 24.99%
- 25.00 to 97.22%

Major Cities

Abilene, TX _____ 15.52%
Amarillo, TX _____ 14.74%
Arlington, TX _____ 8.91%
Austin, TX _____ 22.95%
Baton Rouge, LA _____ 1.57%
Beaumont, TX _____ 4.30%
Corpus Christi, TX ___ 50.38%
Dallas, TX _____ 20.88%
El Paso, TX _____ 69.02%
Fort Smith, AR _____ 1.42%
Fort Worth, TX _____ 19.51%
Garland, TX _____ 11.63%
Houston, TX _____ 27.63%
Irving, TX _____ 16.28%
Lafayette, LA _____ 7.67%
Laredo, TX _____ 93.87%
Lawton, OK _____ 6.34%
Little Rock, AR _____ 0.76%
Lubbock, TX _____ 22.51%
New Orleans, LA _____ 3.47%
Oklahoma City, OK ___ 4.95%
Pasadena, TX _____ 28.83%
Plano, TX _____ 6.23%
San Antonio, TX ____ 55.59%
Shreveport, LA _____ 1.09%
Tulsa, OK _____ 2.60%
Waco, TX _____ 16.35%

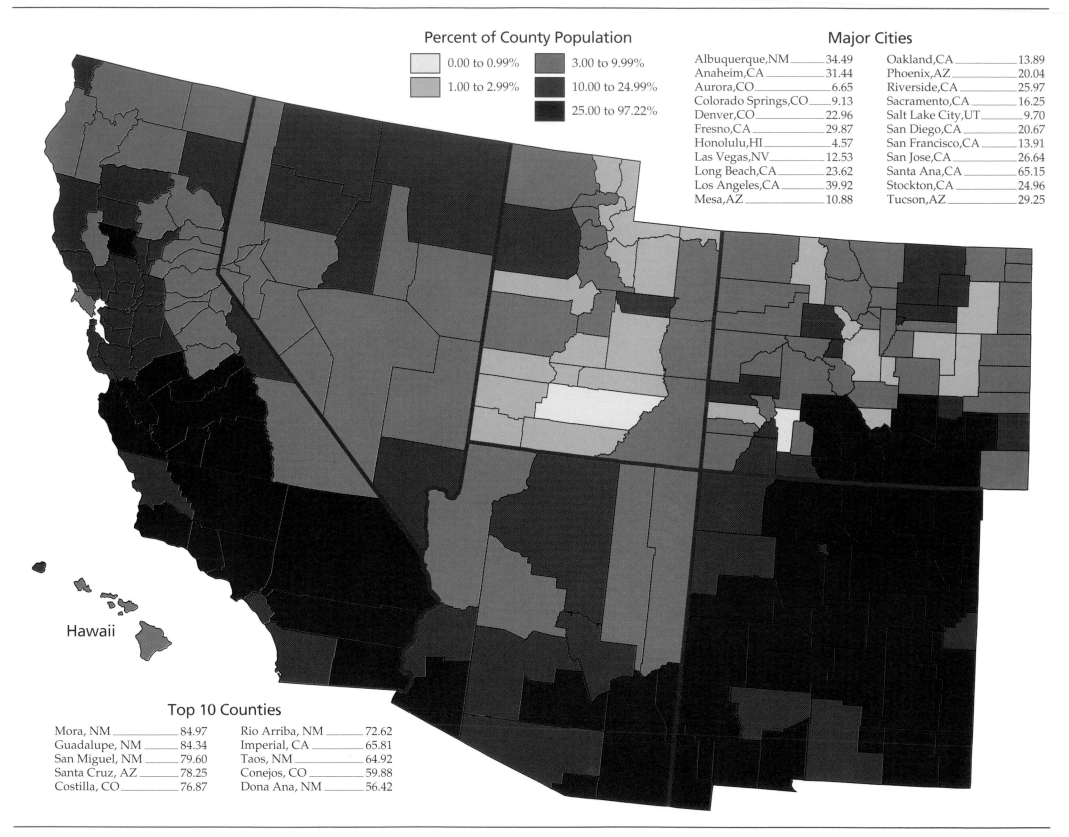

Percent of County Population

- 0.00 to 0.99%
- 1.00 to 2.99%
- 3.00 to 9.99%
- 10.00 to 24.99%
- 25.00 to 97.22%

Major Cities

City	Percent	City	Percent
Albuquerque,NM	34.49	Oakland,CA	13.89
Anaheim,CA	31.44	Phoenix,AZ	20.04
Aurora,CO	6.65	Riverside,CA	25.97
Colorado Springs,CO	9.13	Sacramento,CA	16.25
Denver,CO	22.96	Salt Lake City,UT	9.70
Fresno,CA	29.87	San Diego,CA	20.67
Honolulu,HI	4.57	San Francisco,CA	13.91
Las Vegas,NV	12.53	San Jose,CA	26.64
Long Beach,CA	23.62	Santa Ana,CA	65.15
Los Angeles,CA	39.92	Stockton,CA	24.96
Mesa,AZ	10.88	Tucson,AZ	29.25

Hawaii

Top 10 Counties

County	Percent	County	Percent
Mora, NM	84.97	Rio Arriba, NM	72.62
Guadalupe, NM	84.34	Imperial, CA	65.81
San Miguel, NM	79.60	Taos, NM	64.92
Santa Cruz, AZ	78.25	Conejos, CO	59.88
Costilla, CO	76.87	Dona Ana, NM	56.42

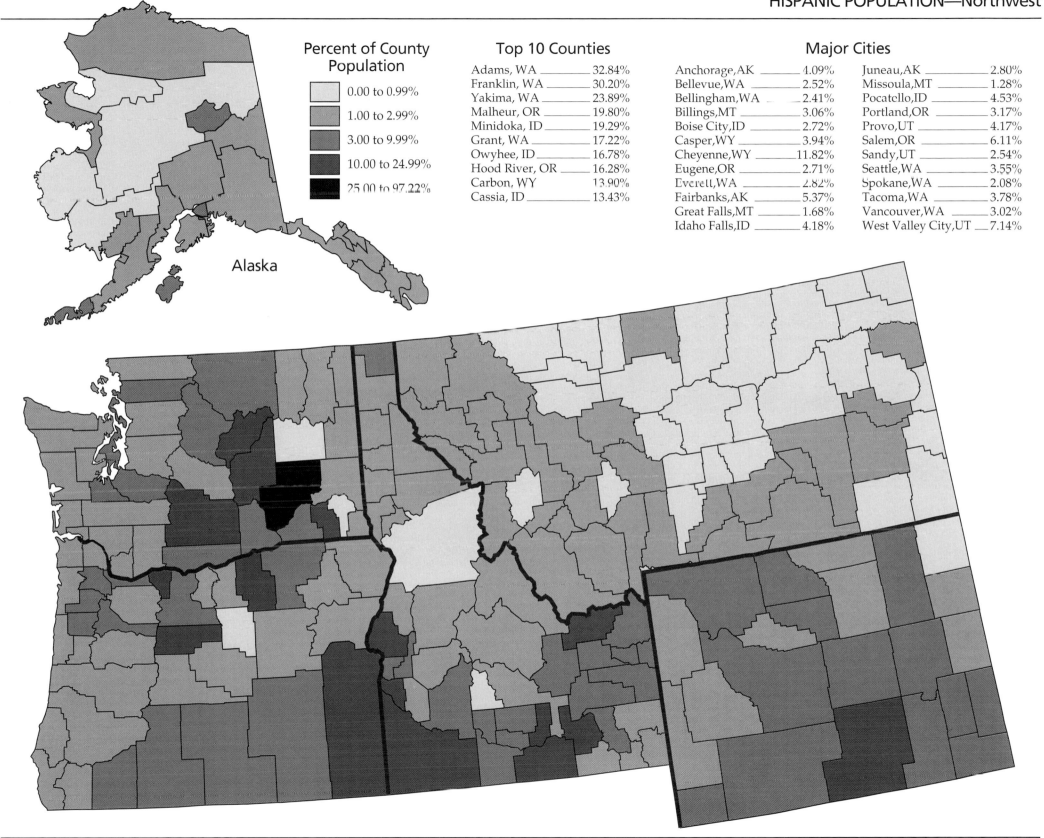

Percent of County Population

- 0.00 to 0.99%
- 1.00 to 2.99%
- 3.00 to 9.99%
- 10.00 to 24.99%
- 25.00 to 97.22%

Alaska

Top 10 Counties

County	%
Adams, WA	32.84%
Franklin, WA	30.20%
Yakima, WA	23.89%
Malheur, OR	19.80%
Minidoka, ID	19.29%
Grant, WA	17.22%
Owyhee, ID	16.78%
Hood River, OR	16.28%
Carbon, WY	13.90%
Cassia, ID	13.43%

Major Cities

City	%	City	%
Anchorage, AK	4.09%	Juneau, AK	2.80%
Bellevue, WA	2.52%	Missoula, MT	1.28%
Bellingham, WA	2.41%	Pocatello, ID	4.53%
Billings, MT	3.06%	Portland, OR	3.17%
Boise City, ID	2.72%	Provo, UT	4.17%
Casper, WY	3.94%	Salem, OR	6.11%
Cheyenne, WY	11.82%	Sandy, UT	2.54%
Eugene, OR	2.71%	Seattle, WA	3.55%
Everett, WA	2.82%	Spokane, WA	2.08%
Fairbanks, AK	5.37%	Tacoma, WA	3.78%
Great Falls, MT	1.68%	Vancouver, WA	3.02%
Idaho Falls, ID	4.18%	West Valley City, UT	7.14%

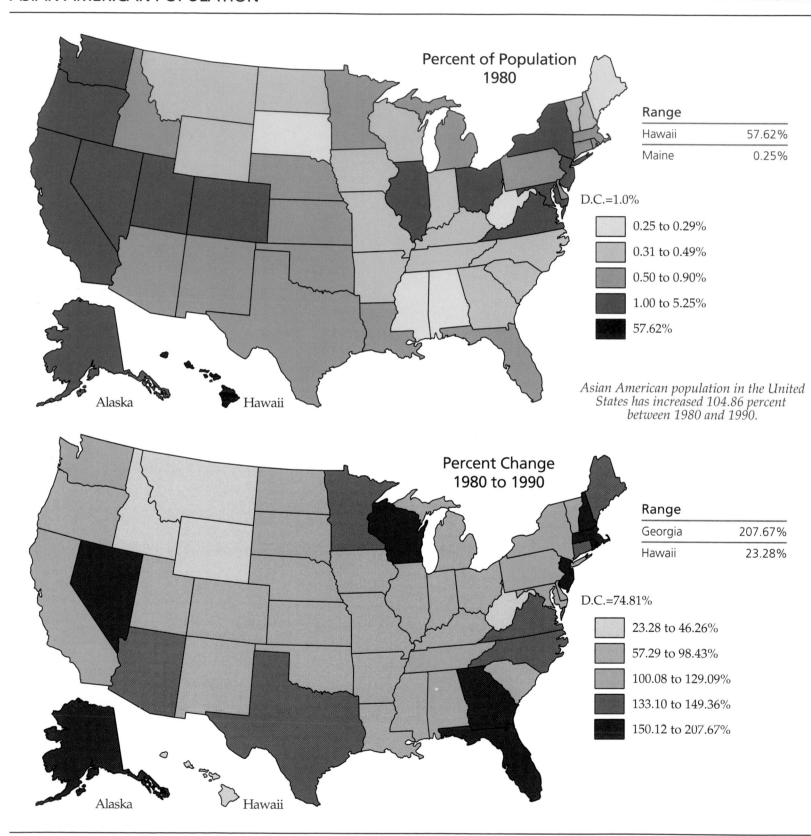

Percent of Population 1980

Range	
Hawaii	57.62%
Maine	0.25%

D.C.=1.0%

- 0.25 to 0.29%
- 0.31 to 0.49%
- 0.50 to 0.90%
- 1.00 to 5.25%
- 57.62%

Alaska   Hawaii

Asian American population in the United States has increased 104.86 percent between 1980 and 1990.

Percent Change 1980 to 1990

Range	
Georgia	207.67%
Hawaii	23.28%

D.C.=74.81%

- 23.28 to 46.26%
- 57.29 to 98.43%
- 100.08 to 129.09%
- 133.10 to 149.36%
- 150.12 to 207.67%

Alaska   Hawaii

Asian Americans, 1980

United States	3,550,635
Alabama	10,229
Alaska	7,696
Arizona	22,888
Arkansas	6,992
California	1,242,157
Colorado	32,747
Connecticut	20,403
Delaware	4,433
District of Columbia	6,415
Florida	57,660
Georgia	24,631
Hawaii	555,845
Idaho	6,403
Illinois	166,401
Indiana	23,407
Iowa	13,487
Kansas	16,897
Kentucky	11,241
Louisiana	24,183
Maine	2,867
Maryland	65,058
Massachusetts	51,723
Michigan	60,888
Minnesota	31,409
Mississippi	7,371
Missouri	23,979
Montana	2,937
Nebraska	7,840
Nevada	14,561
New Hampshire	3,300
New Jersey	106,498
New Mexico	7,118
New York	322,751
North Carolina	22,010
North Dakota	2,201
Ohio	51,100
Oklahoma	19,299
Oregon	39,303
Pennsylvania	68,625
Rhode Island	6,323
South Carolina	12,568
South Dakota	1,823
Tennessee	14,823
Texas	128,109
Utah	19,602
Vermont	1,591
Virginia	66,482
Washington	105,438
West Virginia	5,547
Wisconsin	21,423
Wyoming	1,953

Asian Americans, 1990

United States	7,273,662
Alabama	21,797
Alaska	19,728
Arizona	55,206
Arkansas	12,530
California	2,845,659
Colorado	59,862
Connecticut	50,698
Delaware	9,057
District of Columbia	11,214
Florida	154,302
Georgia	75,781
Hawaii	685,236
Idaho	9,365
Illinois	285,311
Indiana	37,617
Iowa	25,476
Kansas	31,750
Kentucky	17,812
Louisiana	41,099
Maine	6,683
Maryland	139,719
Massachusetts	143,392
Michigan	104,983
Minnesota	77,886
Mississippi	13,016
Missouri	41,277
Montana	4,259
Nebraska	12,422
Nevada	38,127
New Hampshire	9,343
New Jersey	272,521
New Mexico	14,124
New York	693,760
North Carolina	52,166
North Dakota	3,462
Ohio	91,179
Oklahoma	33,563
Oregon	69,269
Pennsylvania	137,438
Rhode Island	18,325
South Carolina	22,382
South Dakota	3,123
Tennessee	31,839
Texas	319,459
Utah	33,371
Vermont	3,215
Virginia	159,053
Washington	210,958
West Virginia	7,459
Wisconsin	53,583
Wyoming	2,806

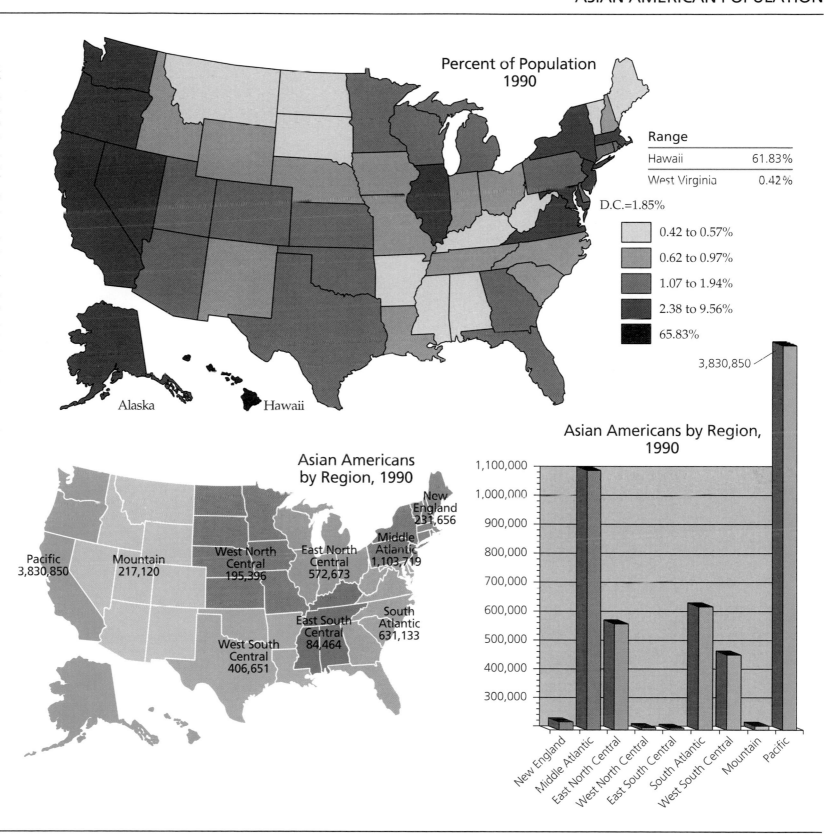

Percent of Population
1990

Range

| Hawaii | 61.83% |
| West Virginia | 0.42% |

D.C.=1.85%

- 0.42 to 0.57%
- 0.62 to 0.97%
- 1.07 to 1.94%
- 2.38 to 9.56%
- 65.83%

Alaska   Hawaii

Asian Americans
by Region, 1990

New England 231,656
Middle Atlantic 1,103,719
East North Central 572,673
West North Central 195,396
South Atlantic 631,133
East South Central 84,464
West South Central 406,651
Mountain 217,120
Pacific 3,830,850

Asian Americans by Region, 1990

3,830,850

Major Cities

Boston, MA	5.29%	Paterson, NJ	1.44%
Bridgeport, CT	2.32%	Philadelphia, PA	2.74%
Buffalo, NY	0.99%	Pittsburgh, PA	1.61%
Burlington, VT	1.49%	Portland, ME	1.66%
Elizabeth, NJ	2.73%	Providence, RI	5.94%
Hartford, CT	1.45%	Rochester, NY	1.76%
Jersey City, NJ	11.36%	Springfield, MA	1.04%
Manchester, NH	1.10%	Syracuse, NY	2.17%
New Haven, CT	2.41%	Waterbury, CT	0.72%
New York, NY	7.00%	Worcester, MA	2.81%
Newark, NJ	1.19%	Yonkers, NY	3.00%

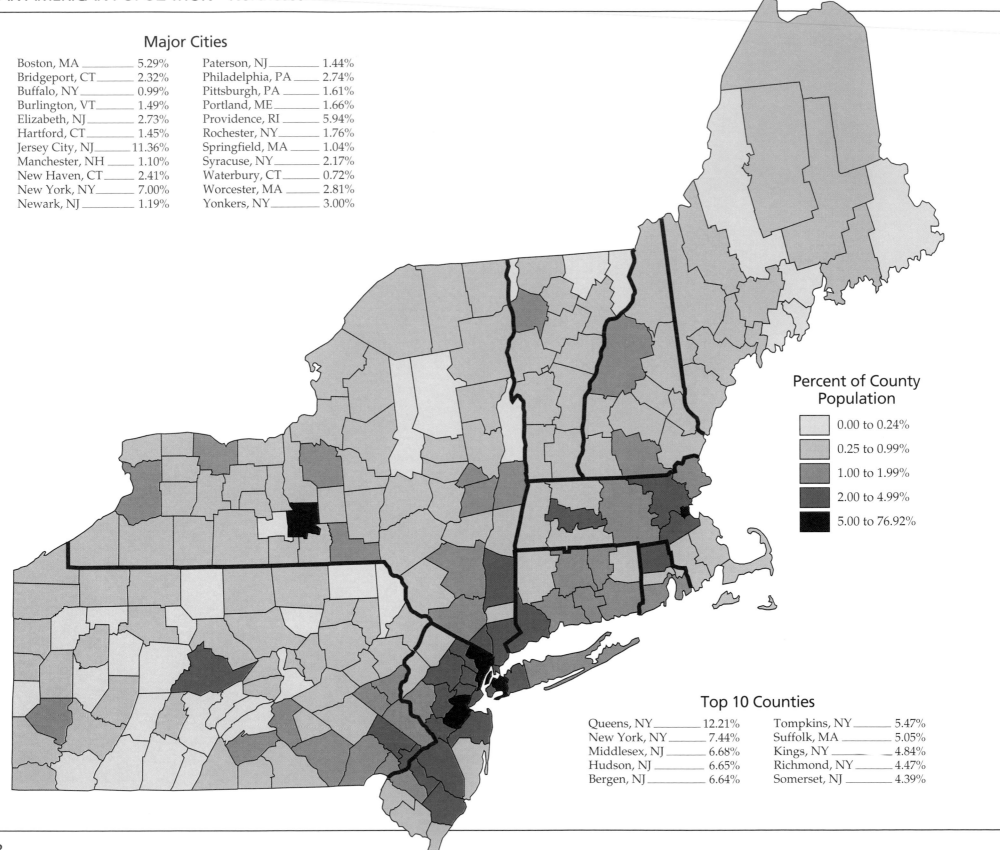

Percent of County Population

- 0.00 to 0.24%
- 0.25 to 0.99%
- 1.00 to 1.99%
- 2.00 to 4.99%
- 5.00 to 76.92%

Top 10 Counties

Queens, NY	12.21%	Tompkins, NY	5.47%
New York, NY	7.44%	Suffolk, MA	5.05%
Middlesex, NJ	6.68%	Kings, NY	4.84%
Hudson, NJ	6.65%	Richmond, NY	4.47%
Bergen, NJ	6.64%	Somerset, NJ	4.39%

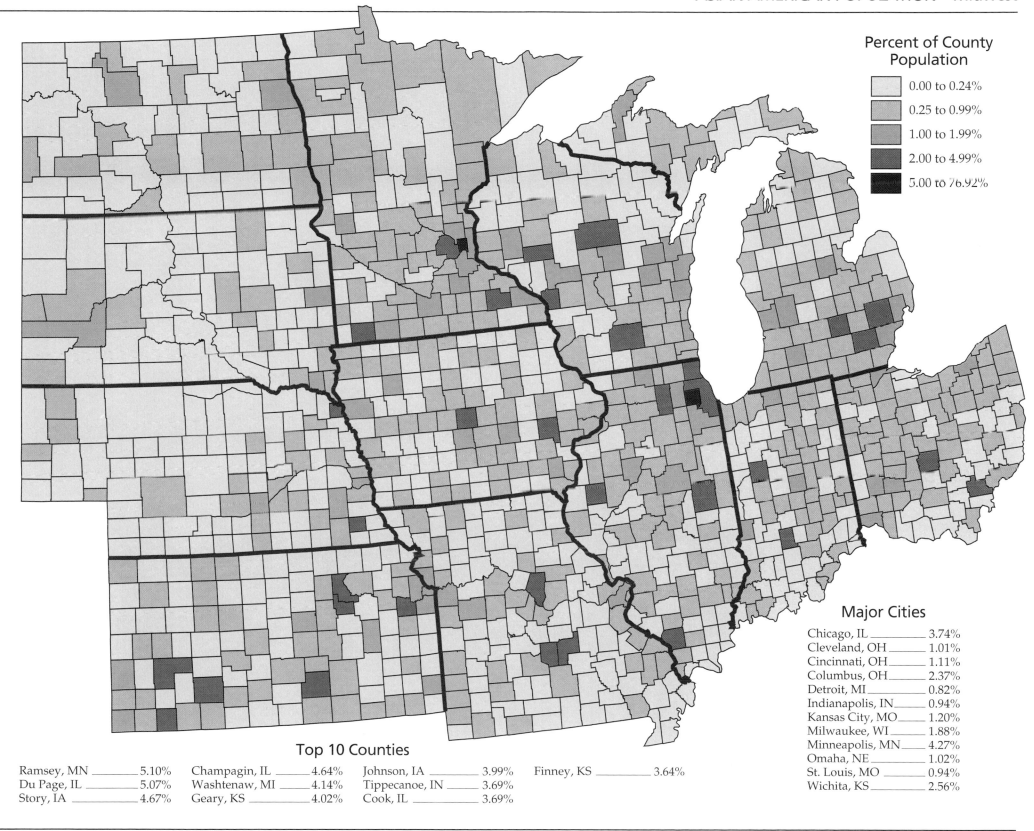

Percent of County Population

- 0.00 to 0.24%
- 0.25 to 0.99%
- 1.00 to 1.99%
- 2.00 to 4.99%
- 5.00 to 76.92%

Major Cities

Chicago, IL	3.74%
Cleveland, OH	1.01%
Cincinnati, OH	1.11%
Columbus, OH	2.37%
Detroit, MI	0.82%
Indianapolis, IN	0.94%
Kansas City, MO	1.20%
Milwaukee, WI	1.88%
Minneapolis, MN	4.27%
Omaha, NE	1.02%
St. Louis, MO	0.94%
Wichita, KS	2.56%

Top 10 Counties

Ramsey, MN — 5.10%	Champagin, IL — 4.64%	Johnson, IA — 3.99%	Finney, KS — 3.64%
Du Page, IL — 5.07%	Washtenaw, MI — 4.14%	Tippecanoe, IN — 3.69%	
Story, IA — 4.67%	Geary, KS — 4.02%	Cook, IL — 3.69%	

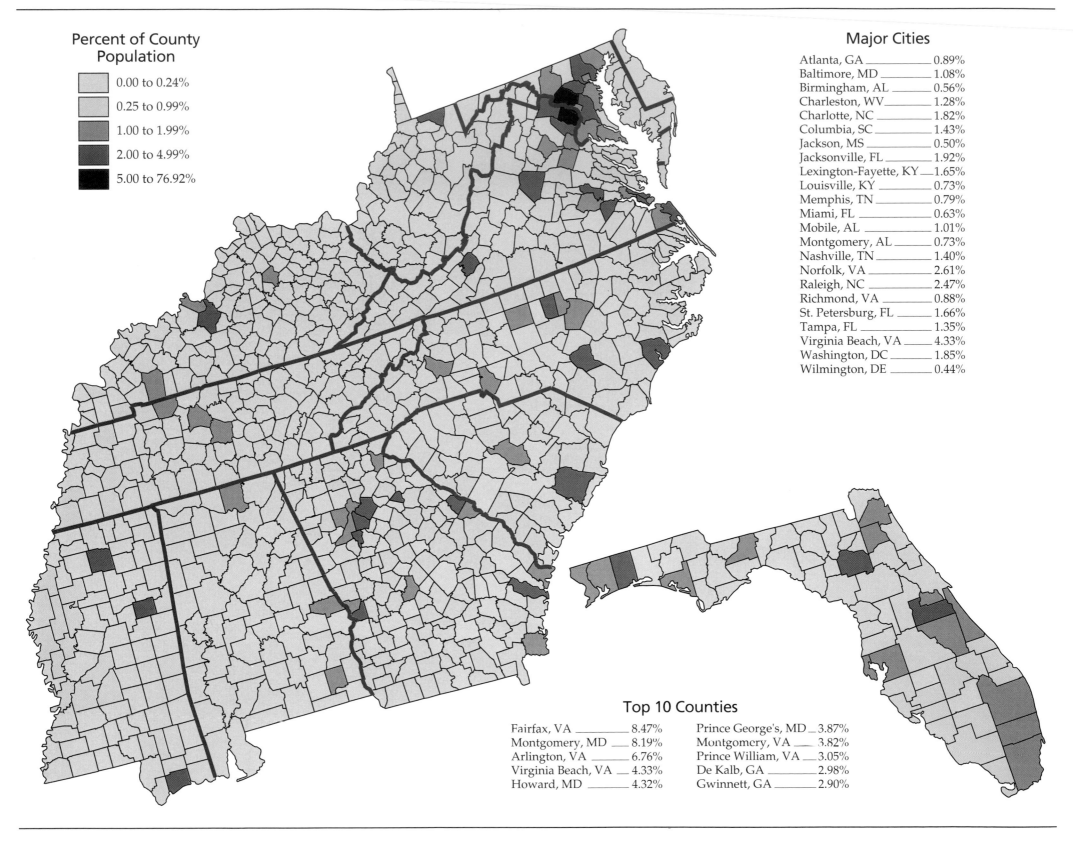

Percent of County Population

- 0.00 to 0.24%
- 0.25 to 0.99%
- 1.00 to 1.99%
- 2.00 to 4.99%
- 5.00 to 76.92%

Major Cities

Atlanta, GA	0.89%
Baltimore, MD	1.08%
Birmingham, AL	0.56%
Charleston, WV	1.28%
Charlotte, NC	1.82%
Columbia, SC	1.43%
Jackson, MS	0.50%
Jacksonville, FL	1.92%
Lexington-Fayette, KY	1.65%
Louisville, KY	0.73%
Memphis, TN	0.79%
Miami, FL	0.63%
Mobile, AL	1.01%
Montgomery, AL	0.73%
Nashville, TN	1.40%
Norfolk, VA	2.61%
Raleigh, NC	2.47%
Richmond, VA	0.88%
St. Petersburg, FL	1.66%
Tampa, FL	1.35%
Virginia Beach, VA	4.33%
Washington, DC	1.85%
Wilmington, DE	0.44%

Top 10 Counties

Fairfax, VA	8.47%	Prince George's, MD	3.87%
Montgomery, MD	8.19%	Montgomery, VA	3.82%
Arlington, VA	6.76%	Prince William, VA	3.05%
Virginia Beach, VA	4.33%	De Kalb, GA	2.98%
Howard, MD	4.32%	Gwinnett, GA	2.90%

Top 10 Counties

Fort Bend, TX ———— 6.36%
Harris, TX ———— 3.93%
Brazos, TX ———— 3.54%
Sebastian, AR ———— 3.30%
Aransas, TX ———— 3.29%
Calhoun, TX ———— 2.92%
Bell, TX ———— 2.89%
Travis, TX ———— 2.86%
Payne, OK ———— 2.85%
Collin, TX ———— 2.83%

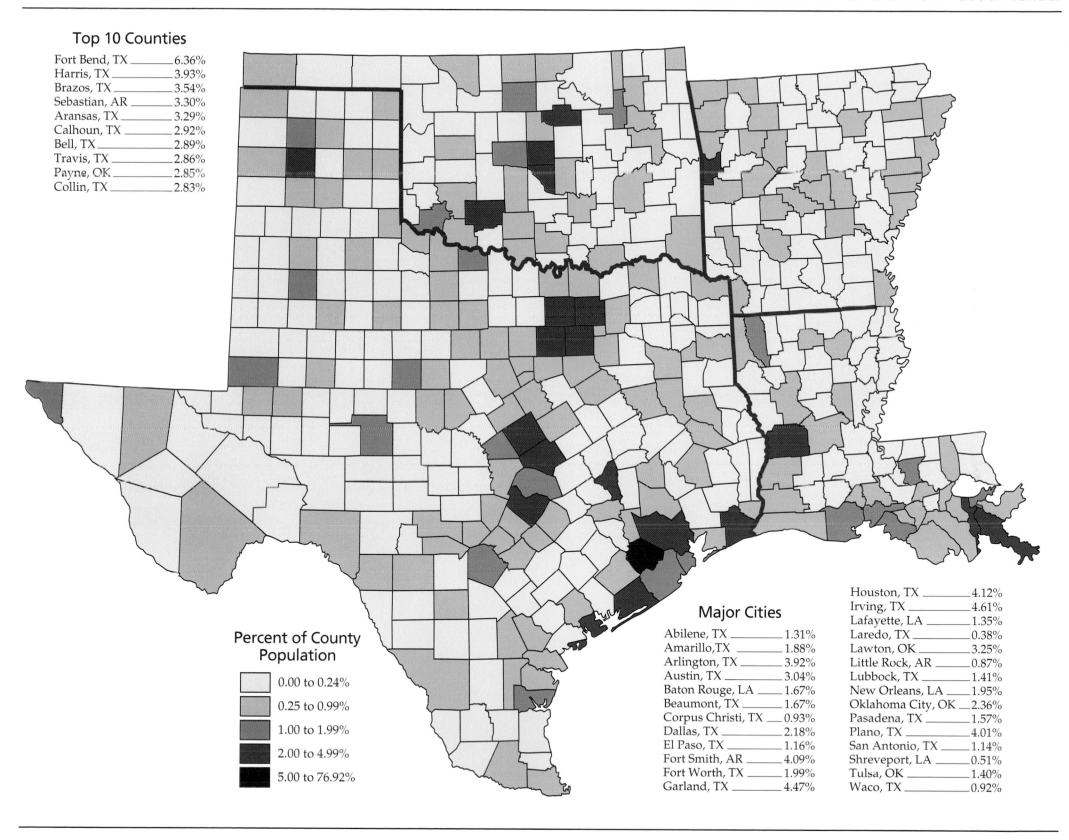

Percent of County Population

0.00 to 0.24%
0.25 to 0.99%
1.00 to 1.99%
2.00 to 4.99%
5.00 to 76.92%

Major Cities

Abilene, TX ———— 1.31%
Amarillo,TX ———— 1.88%
Arlington, TX ———— 3.92%
Austin, TX ———— 3.04%
Baton Rouge, LA ——— 1.67%
Beaumont, TX ———— 1.67%
Corpus Christi, TX ——— 0.93%
Dallas, TX ———— 2.18%
El Paso, TX ———— 1.16%
Fort Smith, AR ———— 4.09%
Fort Worth, TX ———— 1.99%
Garland, TX ———— 4.47%

Houston, TX ———— 4.12%
Irving, TX ———— 4.61%
Lafayette, LA ———— 1.35%
Laredo, TX ———— 0.38%
Lawton, OK ———— 3.25%
Little Rock, AR ———— 0.87%
Lubbock, TX ———— 1.41%
New Orleans, LA ——— 1.95%
Oklahoma City, OK —2.36%
Pasadena, TX ———— 1.57%
Plano, TX ———— 4.01%
San Antonio, TX ———— 1.14%
Shreveport, LA ———— 0.51%
Tulsa, OK ———— 1.40%
Waco, TX ———— 0.92%

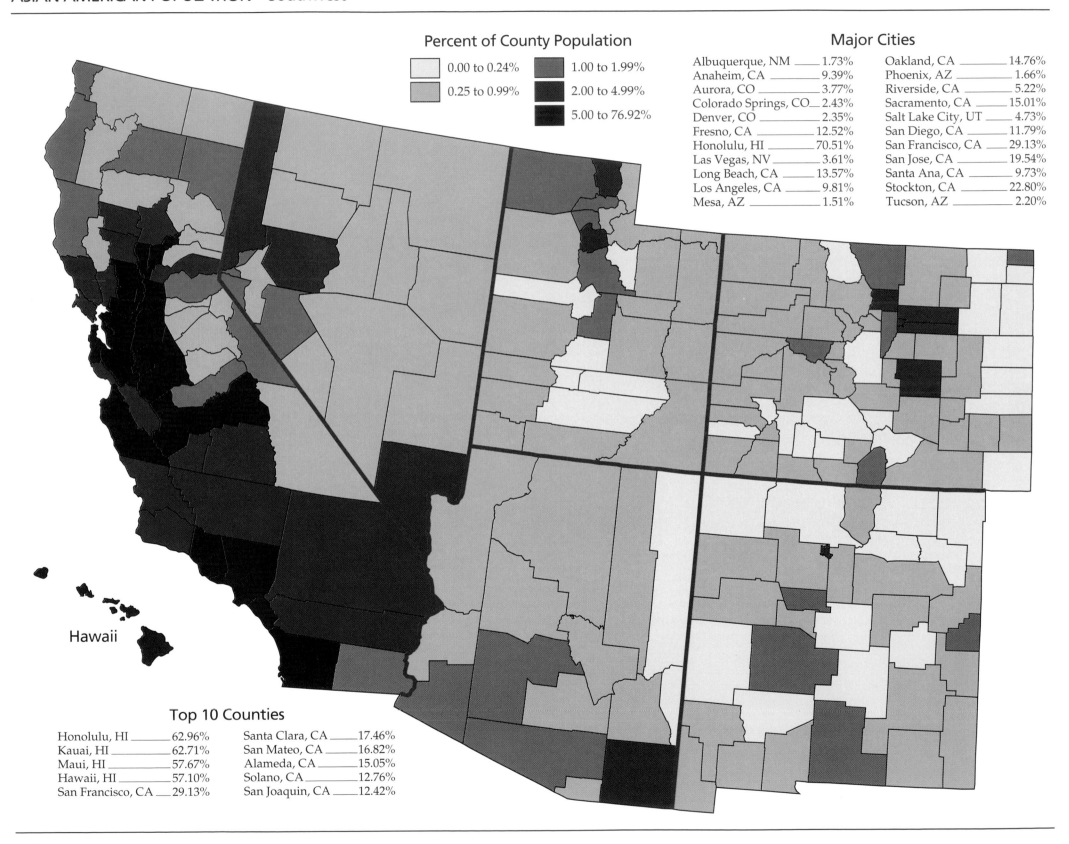

Percent of County Population

- 0.00 to 0.24%
- 0.25 to 0.99%
- 1.00 to 1.99%
- 2.00 to 4.99%
- 5.00 to 76.92%

Major Cities

Albuquerque, NM — 1.73%	Oakland, CA — 14.76%
Anaheim, CA — 9.39%	Phoenix, AZ — 1.66%
Aurora, CO — 3.77%	Riverside, CA — 5.22%
Colorado Springs, CO — 2.43%	Sacramento, CA — 15.01%
Denver, CO — 2.35%	Salt Lake City, UT — 4.73%
Fresno, CA — 12.52%	San Diego, CA — 11.79%
Honolulu, HI — 70.51%	San Francisco, CA — 29.13%
Las Vegas, NV — 3.61%	San Jose, CA — 19.54%
Long Beach, CA — 13.57%	Santa Ana, CA — 9.73%
Los Angeles, CA — 9.81%	Stockton, CA — 22.80%
Mesa, AZ — 1.51%	Tucson, AZ — 2.20%

Hawaii

Top 10 Counties

Honolulu, HI — 62.96%	Santa Clara, CA — 17.46%
Kauai, HI — 62.71%	San Mateo, CA — 16.82%
Maui, HI — 57.67%	Alameda, CA — 15.05%
Hawaii, HI — 57.10%	Solano, CA — 12.76%
San Francisco, CA — 29.13%	San Joaquin, CA — 12.42%

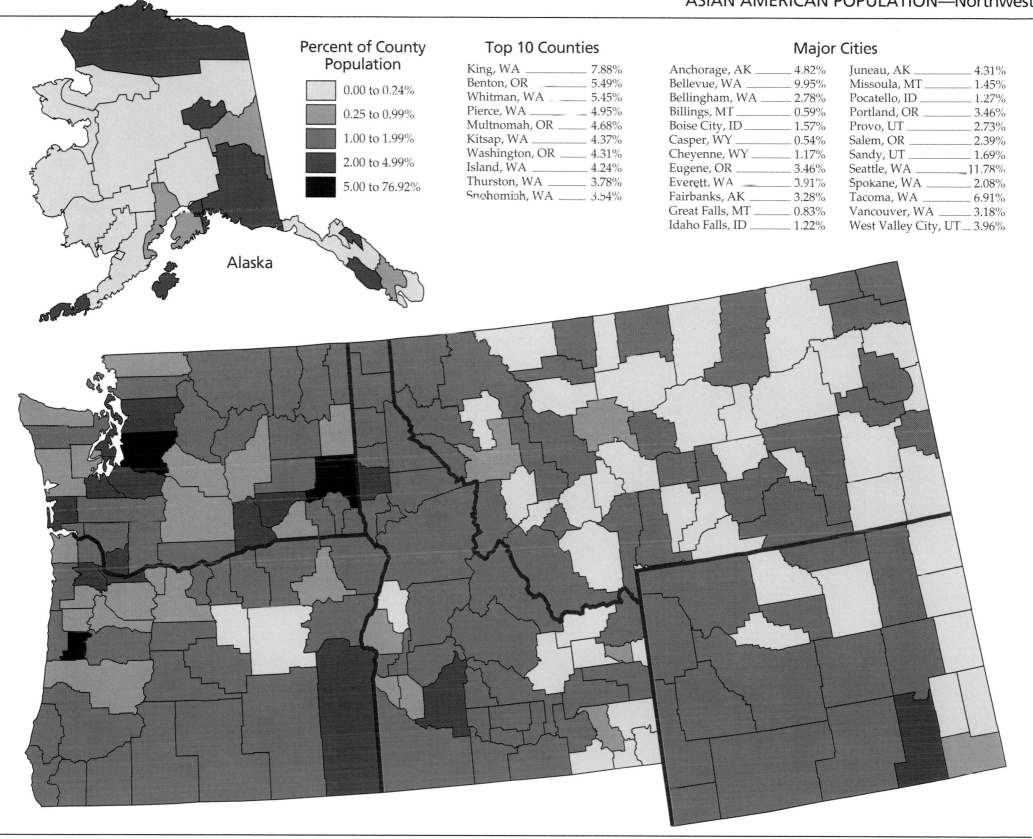

Percent of County Population

- 0.00 to 0.24%
- 0.25 to 0.99%
- 1.00 to 1.99%
- 2.00 to 4.99%
- 5.00 to 76.92%

Alaska

Top 10 Counties

County	Percent
King, WA	7.88%
Benton, OR	5.49%
Whitman, WA	5.45%
Pierce, WA	4.95%
Multnomah, OR	4.68%
Kitsap, WA	4.37%
Washington, OR	4.31%
Island, WA	4.24%
Thurston, WA	3.78%
Snohomish, WA	3.54%

Major Cities

City	Percent	City	Percent
Anchorage, AK	4.82%	Juneau, AK	4.31%
Bellevue, WA	9.95%	Missoula, MT	1.45%
Bellingham, WA	2.78%	Pocatello, ID	1.27%
Billings, MT	0.59%	Portland, OR	3.46%
Boise City, ID	1.57%	Provo, UT	2.73%
Casper, WY	0.54%	Salem, OR	2.39%
Cheyenne, WY	1.17%	Sandy, UT	1.69%
Eugene, OR	3.46%	Seattle, WA	11.78%
Everett, WA	3.91%	Spokane, WA	2.08%
Fairbanks, AK	3.28%	Tacoma, WA	6.91%
Great Falls, MT	0.83%	Vancouver, WA	3.18%
Idaho Falls, ID	1.22%	West Valley City, UT	3.96%

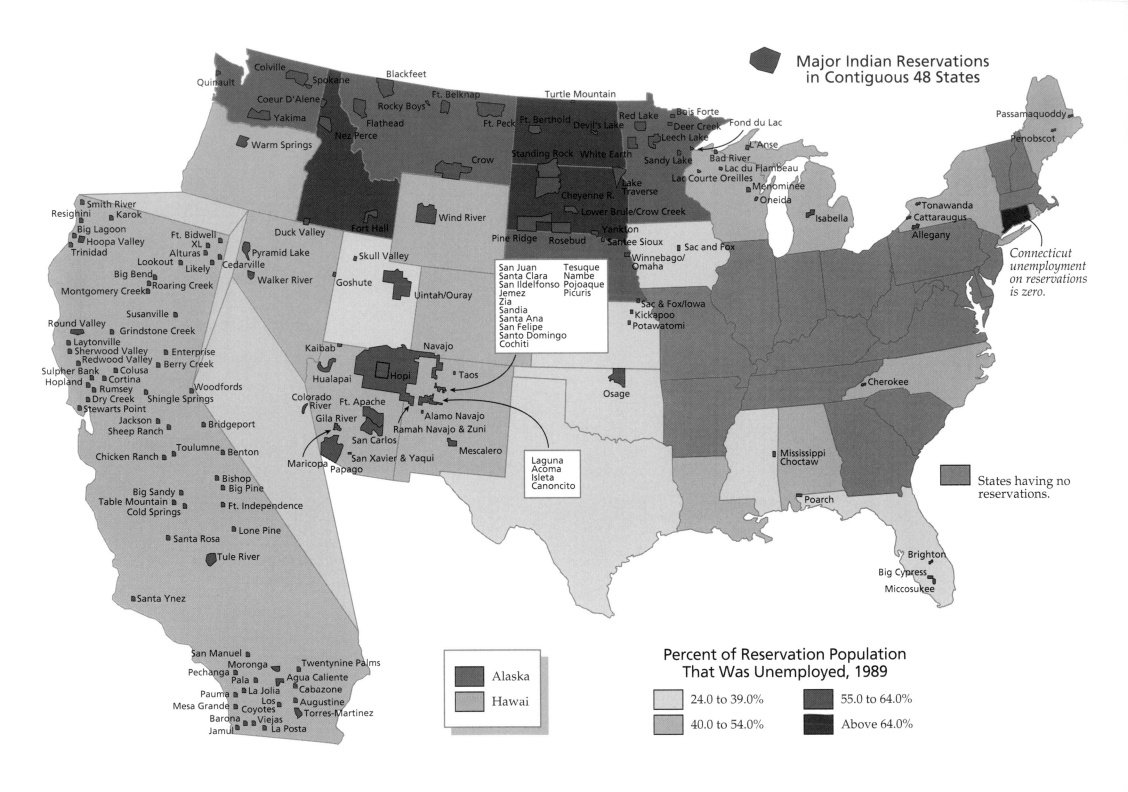

Major Indian Reservations in Contiguous 48 States

Quinault
Colville
Spokane
Blackfeet
Turtle Mountain
Passamaquoddy
Coeur D'Alene
Rocky Boys
Ft. Belknap
Red Lake
Bois Forte
Fond du Lac
Penobscot
Yakima
Flathead
Ft. Peck
Ft. Berthold
Devil's Lake
Deer Creek
Leech Lake
L'Anse
Warm Springs
Nez Perce
Crow
Standing Rock
White Earth
Sandy Lake
Bad River
Lac du Flambeau
Tonawanda
Nez Perce
Lac Courte Oreilles
Menominee
Cattaraugus
Smith River
Duck Valley
Fort Hall
Wind River
Cheyenne R.
Lake Traverse
Oneida
Isabella
Allegany
Resighini
Karok
Big Lagoon
Ft. Bidwell
XL
Skull Valley
Pine Ridge
Rosebud
Yankton
Santee Sioux
Sac and Fox
Winnebago/Omaha
Connecticut unemployment on reservations is zero.
Hoopa Valley
Alturas
Trinidad
Lookout
Likely
Cedarville
Pyramid Lake
Big Bend
Montgomery Creek
Roaring Creek
Walker River
Goshute
Uintah/Ouray
Sac & Fox/Iowa
Kickapoo
Potawatomi
San Juan   Tesuque
Santa Clara   Nambe
San Ildelfonso Pojoaque
Jemez   Picuris
Zia
Sandia
Santa Ana
San Felipe
Santo Domingo
Cochiti
Susanville
Round Valley
Grindstone Creek
Laytonville
Sherwood Valley
Enterprise
Redwood Valley
Berry Creek
Kaibab
Navajo
Sulpher Bank
Colusa
Hopland
Cortina
Rumsey
Woodfords
Hualapai
Hopi
Taos
Osage
Cherokee
Dry Creek
Shingle Springs
Stewarts Point
Jackson
Sheep Ranch
Bridgeport
Colorado River
Ft. Apache
Gila River
Alamo Navajo
Ramah Navajo & Zuni
Chicken Ranch
Toulumne
Benton
San Carlos
Mescalero
Laguna
Acoma
Isleta
Canoncito
Mississippi Choctaw
States having no reservations.
Maricopa
Papago
San Xavier & Yaqui
Big Sandy
Bishop
Big Pine
Table Mountain
Cold Springs
Ft. Independence
Poarch
Lone Pine
Santa Rosa
Tule River
Santa Ynez
Brighton
Big Cypress
Miccosukee
San Manuel
Moronga
Twentynine Palms
Pechanga
Pala
Agua Caliente
Cabazone
Pauma
La Jolia
Los Coyotes
Augustine
Mesa Grande
Barona
Viejas
Torres-Martinez
Jamul
La Posta

Alaska
Hawai

Percent of Reservation Population That Was Unemployed, 1989

24.0 to 39.0%   55.0 to 64.0%
40.0 to 54.0%   Above 64.0%

Native Americans, 1990

United States	1,959,234
Alabama	16,506
Alaska	85,698
Arizona	203,527
Arkansas	12,773
California	242,164
Colorado	27,776
Connecticut	6,654
Delaware	2,019
District of Columbia	1,466
Florida	36,335
Georgia	13,348
Hawaii	5,099
Idaho	13,780
Illinois	21,836
Indiana	12,720
Iowa	7,349
Kansas	21,965
Kentucky	5,769
Louisiana	18,541
Maine	5,998
Maryland	12,972
Massachusetts	12,241
Michigan	55,638
Minnesota	49,909
Mississippi	8,525
Missouri	19,835
Montana	47,679
Nebraska	12,410
Nevada	19,637
New Hampshire	2,134
New Jersey	14,970
New Mexico	134,355
New York	62,651
North Carolina	80,155
North Dakota	25,917
Ohio	20,358
Oklahoma	252,420
Oregon	38,496
Pennsylvania	14,733
Rhode Island	4,071
South Carolina	8,246
South Dakota	50,575
Tennessee	10,039
Texas	65,877
Utah	24,283
Vermont	1,696
Virginia	15,282
Washington	81,483
West Virginia	2,458
Wisconsin	39,387
Wyoming	9,479

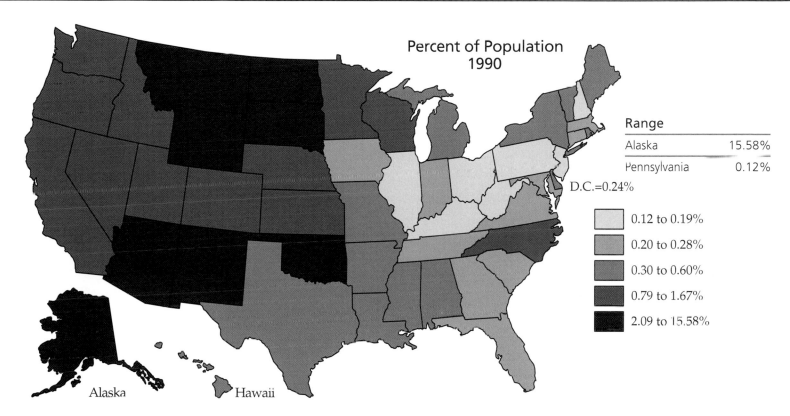

Percent of Population 1990

Range

Alaska	15.58%
Pennsylvania	0.12%

D.C.=0.24%

- 0.12 to 0.19%
- 0.20 to 0.28%
- 0.30 to 0.60%
- 0.79 to 1.67%
- 2.09 to 15.58%

Alaska   Hawaii

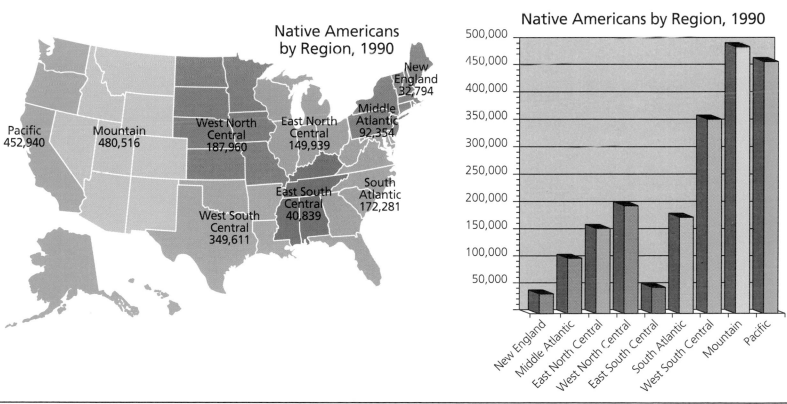

Native Americans by Region, 1990

- New England 32,794
- Pacific 452,940
- Mountain 480,516
- West North Central 187,960
- East North Central 149,939
- Middle Atlantic 92,354
- East South Central 40,839
- South Atlantic 172,281
- West South Central 349,611

Native Americans by Region, 1990

(Bar chart — regions: New England, Middle Atlantic, East North Central, West North Central, East South Central, South Atlantic, West South Central, Mountain, Pacific; y-axis 50,000 to 500,000)

Part Five

ECONOMY

PERSONAL INCOME PER CAPITA

Per capita income varies from region to region in the United States. In 1989, the lowest income was found in the South and the highest in the Northeast. This pattern will probably persist to the year 2000 according to income predictions made by the U.S. Bureau of Economic Analysis. The table below outlines trends in personal income per capita for the years 1979 through 2000.

	Constant 1982 Dollars		
	1979	1989	2000
United States	$11,551	$13,546	$15,345
Northeast	$12,157	$15,931	$17,635
New England	11,989	16,554	18,154
Middle Atlantic	11,977	15,715	15,904
Midwest	$11,828	$13,030	$14,938
East North Central	11,999	13,252	15,098
West North Central	11,412	12,505	14,562
South	$10,330	$12,143	$13,975
South Atlantic	10,559	13,182	15,009
East South Central	9,129	10,526	12,272
West South Central	10,720	11,406	13,206
West	$12,608	$14,125	$15,844
Mountain	10,952	11,983	13,698
Pacific	13,199	14,881	16,607

CHANGE IN INCOME PER CAPITA

Personal per capita income in the United States rose 95.0 percent between 1979 and 1989 when measured in current dollars. In constant 1982 dollars that figure is considerably lower—17.3 percent. The greatest increase in constant dollars occurred in New England and the Middle Atlantic regions. Income was most stagnant in the West South Central.

(Constant 1982 dollars)	1979–1989	1989–2000
United States	17.3%	13.3%
Northeast	31.0%	10.7%
New England	38.1%	9.7%
Middle Atlantic	31.2%	1.2%
Midwest	10.2%	14.6%
East North Central	10.4%	13.9%
West North Central	9.6%	16.4%
South	17.6%	15.1%
South Atlantic	24.8%	13.9%
East South Central	15.3%	16.6%
West South Central	6.4%	15.8%
West	12.0%	12.2%
Mountain	9.4%	14.3%
Pacific	12.7%	11.6%

As the table above shows, the rate of income growth is expected to decrease for the United States as a whole through the 1990s and into the next century. The Northeast will be most heavily hit by a scenario in which income remains the same or just slightly outdistances inflation. Incomes are expected to increase at only one third the rate at which they had between 1979 and 1989. Per capita incomes will rise only 1.2 percent throughout the Middle Atlantic states during the decade of the nineties. Workers in the West South Central and the West North Central will see their incomes rise faster than other regions in the next decade.

MANUFACTURING

Some 19.4 million citizens were employed in manufacturing in 1989. The state that had the largest employment was California. In addition, New York, Pennsylvania, and Ohio had large manufacturing workforces that numbered in the millions.

Manufacturing is changing in the United States. The actual number of employees in manufacturing has decreased and manufacturing establishments have moved south and west from their traditional base in the Middle Atlantic and East North Central rust belt. Manufacturing firms and jobs have also moved out of the country in an effort to avoid unionization and to decrease employee wages.

Value of shipments for firms engaged in manufacturing exceeded $2.5 trillion dollars in 1987. Total payrolls exceeded $476 billion dollars.

RETAIL TRADE

The United States had 17.8 million workers employed in 2.4 million retail trade establishments according to the *Census of Retail Trade, 1987*.

Retail trade is divided into many classifications based on the type of store involved in sales. The largest number of retail outlets are food stores, with 349,811 in 1989. They were followed by automotive dealers with 342,884 establishments. The United States had 153,463 restaurants, 194,808 gas stations, and 34,658 shopping centers in 1989.

Total sales for retail establishments exceeded $1.5 trillion in 1987. Total payrolls exceeded $177.5 billion.

WHOLESALE TRADE

Paid employees in wholesale trade numbered 5.6 million in 1987. 466,680 establishments were engaged in wholesale trade during the same year.

The wholesale trade business is moving south and west. States of the South Atlantic and the Southwest have seen large increases in the number of wholesale trade establishments.

Total receipts for firms engaged in wholesale trade exceeded $2.5 trillion in 1987. Total payrolls exceeded $133.2 billion.

SERVICE INDUSTRIES

The service sector is growing more quickly than any other sector of the U.S. economy. Figures for the years between 1982 and 1987 give credence to the notion that the United States is becoming a service economy. In 1982, 1.3 million service establishments employed 11.1 million U.S. workers. By 1987, those figures increased to 1.6 million establishments and 15.7 million employees. Added to the aforementioned firms who are subject to Federal income taxes were 169,900 health services and membership organizations that were exempt from paying income tax. Firms in this latter category employed 2.8 million workers.

Total receipts for firms engaged in services exceeded $1.1 trillion in 1987. Total payrolls exceeded $407.8 billion.

	Manufacturing		
	Establishments	Employees	Receipts
Northeast	88,287	4,357,000	$483,748,000,000
Midwest	94,278	5,508,000	$787,124,000,000
South	104,500	5,839,000	$800,875,000,000
West	81,871	598,650	$404,325,000,000

	Retail Trade		
	Establishments	Employees	Receipts
Northeast	502,644	13,714,000	$338,198,000,000
Midwest	570,852	4,398,000	$360,239,000,000
South	851,221	6,033,000	$518,423,000,000
West	494,924	3,670,000	$323,404,000,000

	Wholesale Trade		
	Establishments	Employees	Receipts
Northeast	102,542	1,305,900	$678,800,000,000
Midwest	115,662	1,395,500	$627,600,000,000
South	152,412	1,760,600	$726,600,000,000
West	96,064	1,131,800	$415,010,000,000

	Service Industries		
	Establishments	Employees[1]	Receipts
Northeast	1,368,698	3,578,000	$286,682,000,000
Midwest	1,435,564	3,480,000	$236,765,000,000
South	2,019,142	5,200,000	$337,478,000,000
West	1,609,125	3,796,000	$274,912,000,000

[1] Working in firms subject to Federal income tax.

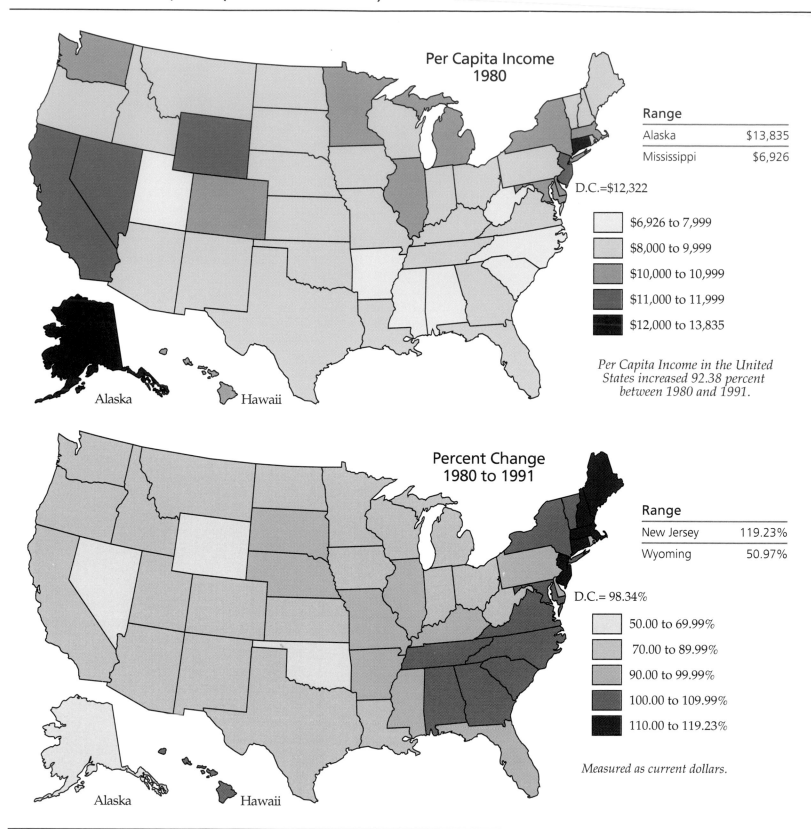

Per Capita Income 1980

Range

Alaska	$13,835
Mississippi	$6,926

D.C.=$12,322

	$6,926 to 7,999
	$8,000 to 9,999
	$10,000 to 10,999
	$11,000 to 11,999
	$12,000 to 13,835

Per Capita Income in the United States increased 92.38 percent between 1980 and 1991.

Alaska   Hawaii

Percent Change 1980 to 1991

Range

New Jersey	119.23%
Wyoming	50.97%

D.C.= 98.34%

	50.00 to 69.99%
	70.00 to 89.99%
	90.00 to 99.99%
	100.00 to 109.99%
	110.00 to 119.23%

Measured as current dollars.

Alaska   Hawaii

Per Capita Income, 1980

United States	$9,919
Alabama	7,704
Alaska	13,835
Arizona	9,172
Arkansas	7,465
California	11,603
Colorado	10,598
Connecticut	12,112
Delaware	10,249
District of Columbia	12,322
Florida	9,764
Georgia	8,348
Hawaii	10,617
Idaho	8,569
Illinois	10,837
Indiana	9,245
Iowa	9,573
Kansas	9,941
Kentucky	8,022
Louisiana	8,682
Maine	8,218
Maryland	10,790
Massachusetts	10,612
Michigan	10,165
Minnesota	10,062
Mississippi	6,926
Missouri	9,298
Montana	8,924
Nebraska	9,274
Nevada	11,421
New Hampshire	9,788
New Jersey	11,573
New Mexico	8,169
New York	10,721
North Carolina	7,999
North Dakota	8,538
Ohio	9,723
Oklahoma	9,393
Oregon	9,866
Pennsylvania	9,891
Rhode Island	9,518
South Carolina	7,589
South Dakota	8,217
Tennessee	8,030
Texas	9,798
Utah	7,952
Vermont	8,577
Virginia	9,827
Washington	10,725
West Virginia	7,915
Wisconsin	9,845
Wyoming	11,339

Per Capita Income, 1991

United States	$19,082
Alabama	15,567
Alaska	21,932
Arizona	16,401
Arkansas	14,753
California	20,952
Colorado	19,440
Connecticut	25,881
Delaware	20,349
District of Columbia	24,439
Florida	18,880
Georgia	17,364
Hawaii	21,306
Idaho	15,401
Illinois	20,824
Indiana	17,217
Iowa	17,505
Kansas	18,511
Kentucky	15,539
Louisiana	15,143
Maine	17,306
Maryland	22,080
Massachusetts	22,897
Michigan	18,679
Minnesota	19,107
Mississippi	13,343
Missouri	17,842
Montana	16,043
Nebraska	17,852
Nevada	19,157
New Hampshire	20,951
New Jersey	25,372
New Mexico	14,844
New York	22,456
North Carolina	16,642
North Dakota	16,088
Ohio	17,916
Oklahoma	15,827
Oregon	17,592
Pennsylvania	19,128
Rhode Island	18,840
South Carolina	15,420
South Dakota	16,392
Tennessee	16,325
Texas	17,305
Utah	14,529
Vermont	17,747
Virginia	19,976
Washington	19,442
West Virginia	14,174
Wisconsin	18,046
Wyoming	17,118

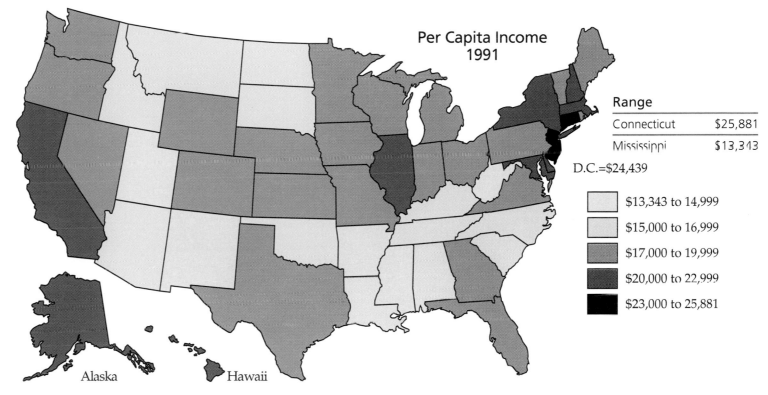

Per Capita Income
1991

Range

Connecticut	$25,881
Mississippi	$13,343

D.C.=$24,439

$13,343 to 14,999
$15,000 to 16,999
$17,000 to 19,999
$20,000 to 22,999
$23,000 to 25,881

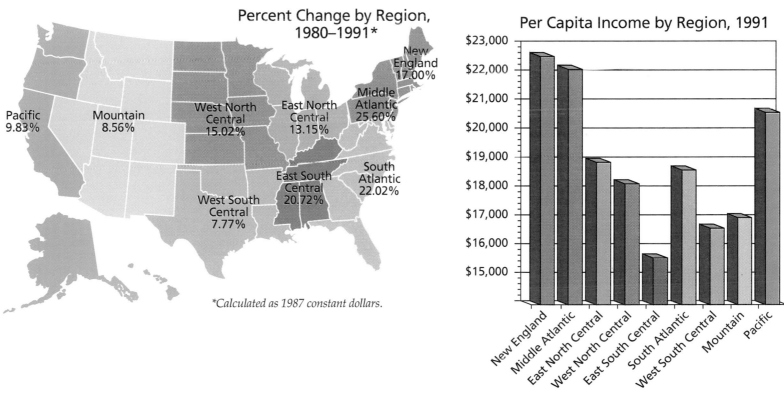

Percent Change by Region, 1980–1991*

New England 17.00%
Middle Atlantic 25.60%
East North Central 13.15%
West North Central 15.02%
Pacific 9.83%
Mountain 8.56%
East South Central 20.72%
West South Central 7.77%
South Atlantic 22.02%

*Calculated as 1987 constant dollars.

Per Capita Income by Region, 1991

Categories: New England, Middle Atlantic, East North Central, West North Central, East South Central, South Atlantic, West South Central, Mountain, Pacific

Major Cities

Boston, MA	$21,676	Paterson, NJ	$20,977
Bridgeport, CT	$31,438	Philadelphia, PA	$15,479
Buffalo, NY	$17,774	Pittsburgh, PA	$19,249
Burlington, VT	$18,937	Portland, ME	$20,383
Elizabeth, NJ	$25,328	Providence, RI	$17,117
Hartford, CT	$24,040	Rochester, NY	$21,192
Jersey City, NJ	$18,440	Springfield, MA	$18,804
Manchester, NH	$22,010	Syracuse, NY	$18,874
New Haven, CT	$21,736	Waterbury, CT	$21,736
New York, NY	$20,829	Worcester, MA	$20,200
Newark, NJ	$21,873	Yonkers, NY	$31,188

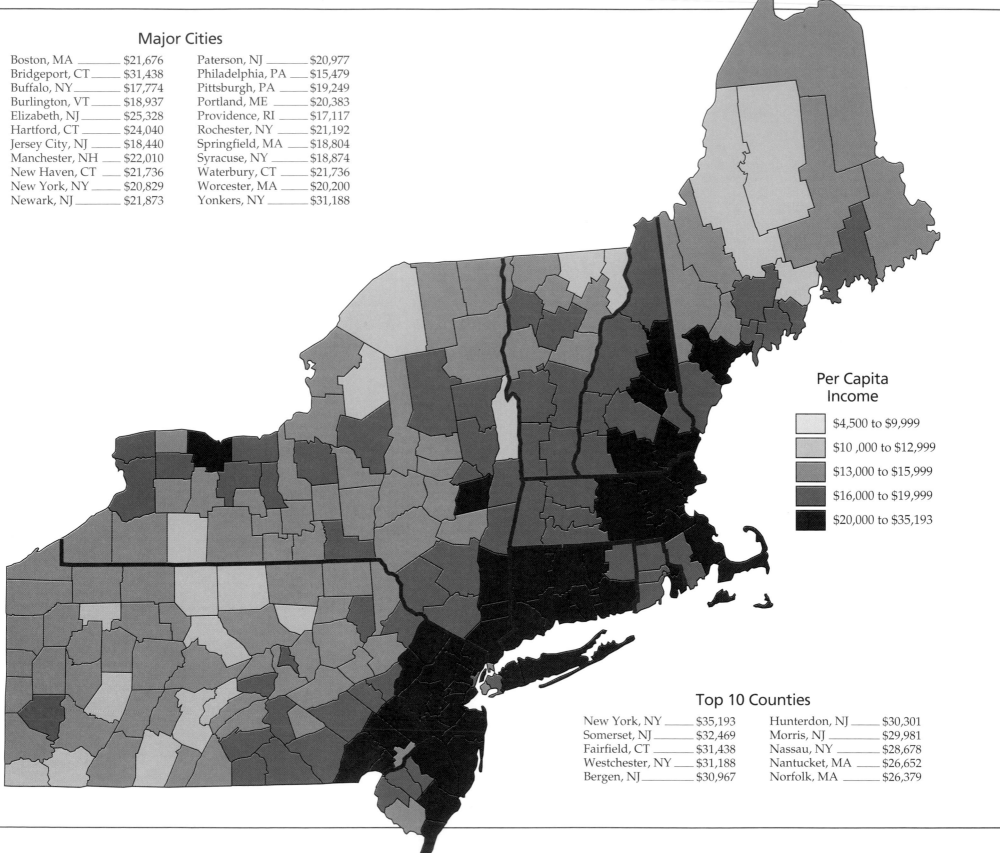

Per Capita Income

- $4,500 to $9,999
- $10,000 to $12,999
- $13,000 to $15,999
- $16,000 to $19,999
- $20,000 to $35,193

Top 10 Counties

New York, NY	$35,193	Hunterdon, NJ	$30,301
Somerset, NJ	$32,469	Morris, NJ	$29,981
Fairfield, CT	$31,438	Nassau, NY	$28,678
Westchester, NY	$31,188	Nantucket, MA	$26,652
Bergen, NJ	$30,967	Norfolk, MA	$26,379

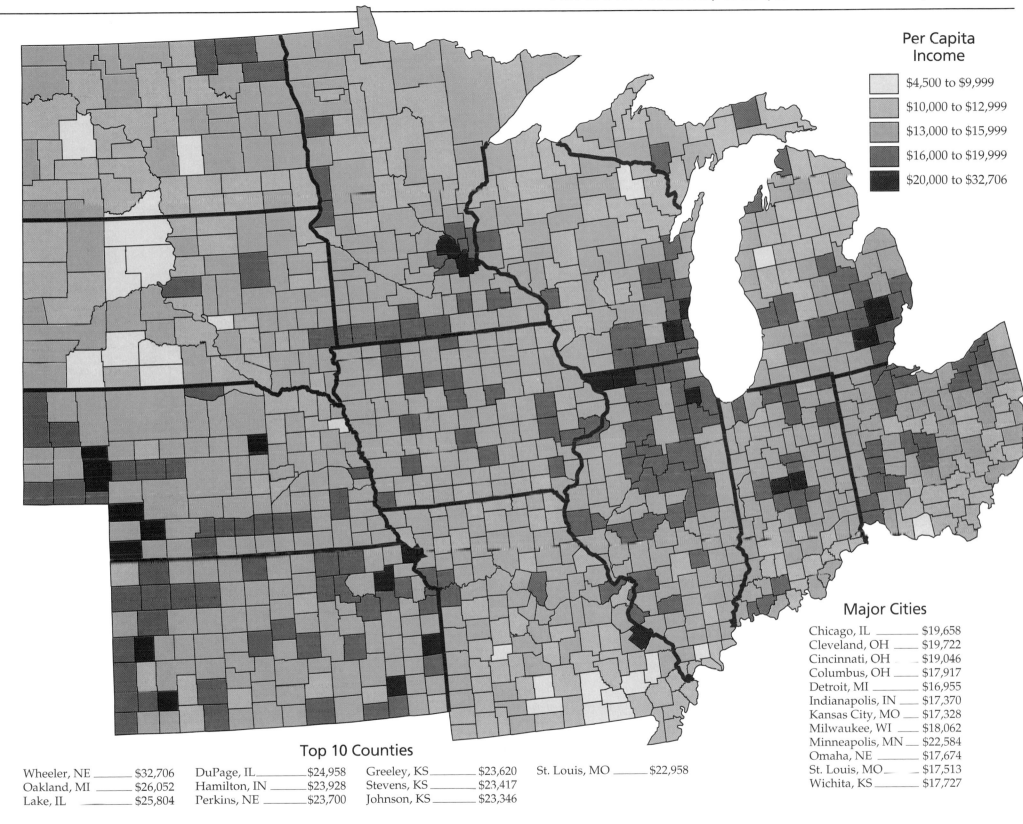

Per Capita Income

- $4,500 to $9,999
- $10,000 to $12,999
- $13,000 to $15,999
- $16,000 to $19,999
- $20,000 to $32,706

Major Cities

Chicago, IL	$19,658
Cleveland, OH	$19,722
Cincinnati, OH	$19,046
Columbus, OH	$17,917
Detroit, MI	$16,955
Indianapolis, IN	$17,370
Kansas City, MO	$17,328
Milwaukee, WI	$18,062
Minneapolis, MN	$22,584
Omaha, NE	$17,674
St. Louis, MO	$17,513
Wichita, KS	$17,727

Top 10 Counties

Wheeler, NE — $32,706	DuPage, IL — $24,958	Greeley, KS — $23,620	St. Louis, MO — $22,958
Oakland, MI — $26,052	Hamilton, IN — $23,928	Stevens, KS — $23,417	
Lake, IL — $25,804	Perkins, NE — $23,700	Johnson, KS — $23,346	

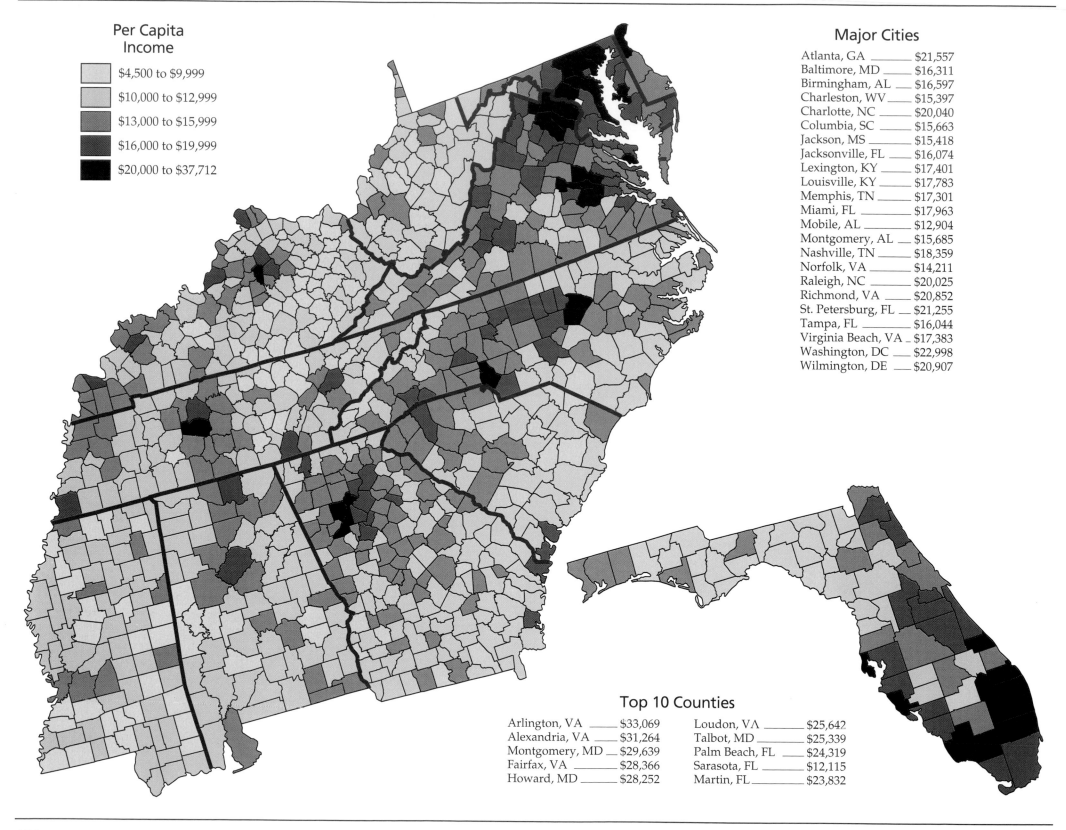

Per Capita Income

- $4,500 to $9,999
- $10,000 to $12,999
- $13,000 to $15,999
- $16,000 to $19,999
- $20,000 to $37,712

Major Cities

Atlanta, GA	$21,557
Baltimore, MD	$16,311
Birmingham, AL	$16,597
Charleston, WV	$15,397
Charlotte, NC	$20,040
Columbia, SC	$15,663
Jackson, MS	$15,418
Jacksonville, FL	$16,074
Lexington, KY	$17,401
Louisville, KY	$17,783
Memphis, TN	$17,301
Miami, FL	$17,963
Mobile, AL	$12,904
Montgomery, AL	$15,685
Nashville, TN	$18,359
Norfolk, VA	$14,211
Raleigh, NC	$20,025
Richmond, VA	$20,852
St. Petersburg, FL	$21,255
Tampa, FL	$16,044
Virginia Beach, VA	$17,383
Washington, DC	$22,998
Wilmington, DE	$20,907

Top 10 Counties

Arlington, VA	$33,069	Loudon, VA	$25,642
Alexandria, VA	$31,264	Talbot, MD	$25,339
Montgomery, MD	$29,639	Palm Beach, FL	$24,319
Fairfax, VA	$28,366	Sarasota, FL	$12,115
Howard, MD	$28,252	Martin, FL	$23,832

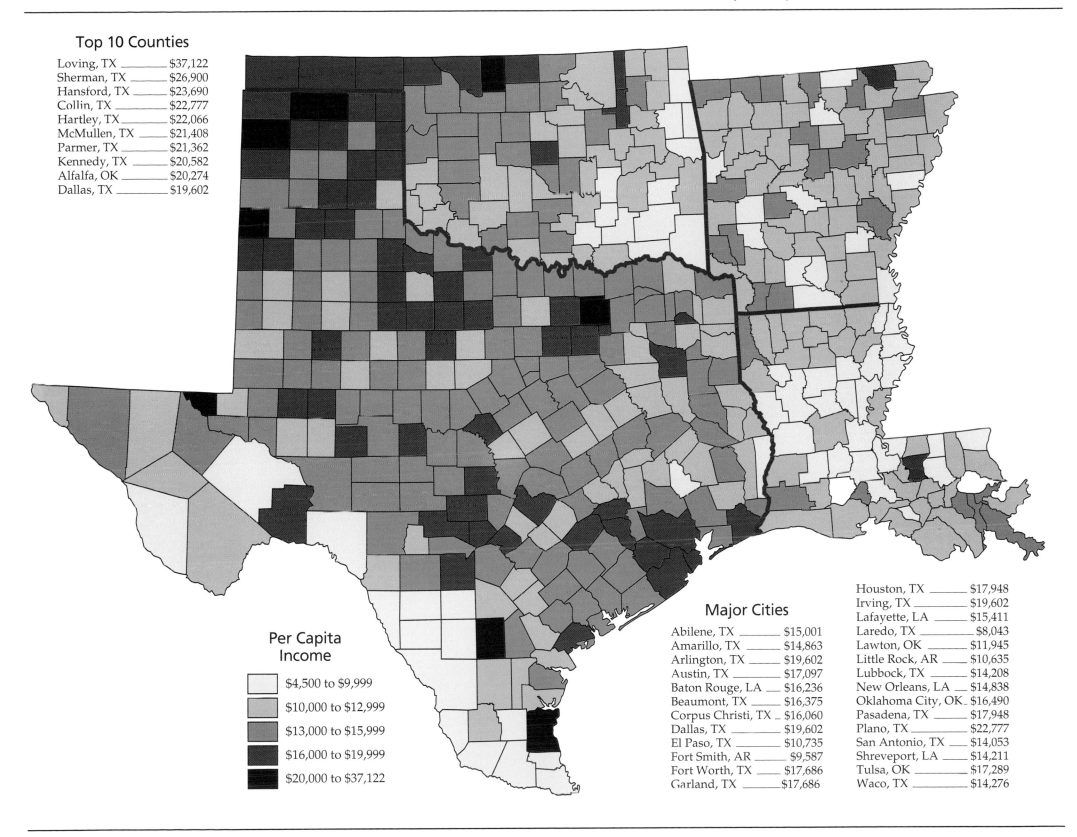

Top 10 Counties

County	Income
Loving, TX	$37,122
Sherman, TX	$26,900
Hansford, TX	$23,690
Collin, TX	$22,777
Hartley, TX	$22,066
McMullen, TX	$21,408
Parmer, TX	$21,362
Kennedy, TX	$20,582
Alfalfa, OK	$20,274
Dallas, TX	$19,602

Per Capita Income

	$4,500 to $9,999
	$10,000 to $12,999
	$13,000 to $15,999
	$16,000 to $19,999
	$20,000 to $37,122

Major Cities

Abilene, TX	$15,001
Amarillo, TX	$14,863
Arlington, TX	$19,602
Austin, TX	$17,097
Baton Rouge, LA	$16,236
Beaumont, TX	$16,375
Corpus Christi, TX	$16,060
Dallas, TX	$19,602
El Paso, TX	$10,735
Fort Smith, AR	$9,587
Fort Worth, TX	$17,686
Garland, TX	$17,686
Houston, TX	$17,948
Irving, TX	$19,602
Lafayette, LA	$15,411
Laredo, TX	$8,043
Lawton, OK	$11,945
Little Rock, AR	$10,635
Lubbock, TX	$14,208
New Orleans, LA	$14,838
Oklahoma City, OK	$16,490
Pasadena, TX	$17,948
Plano, TX	$22,777
San Antonio, TX	$14,053
Shreveport, LA	$14,211
Tulsa, OK	$17,289
Waco, TX	$14,276

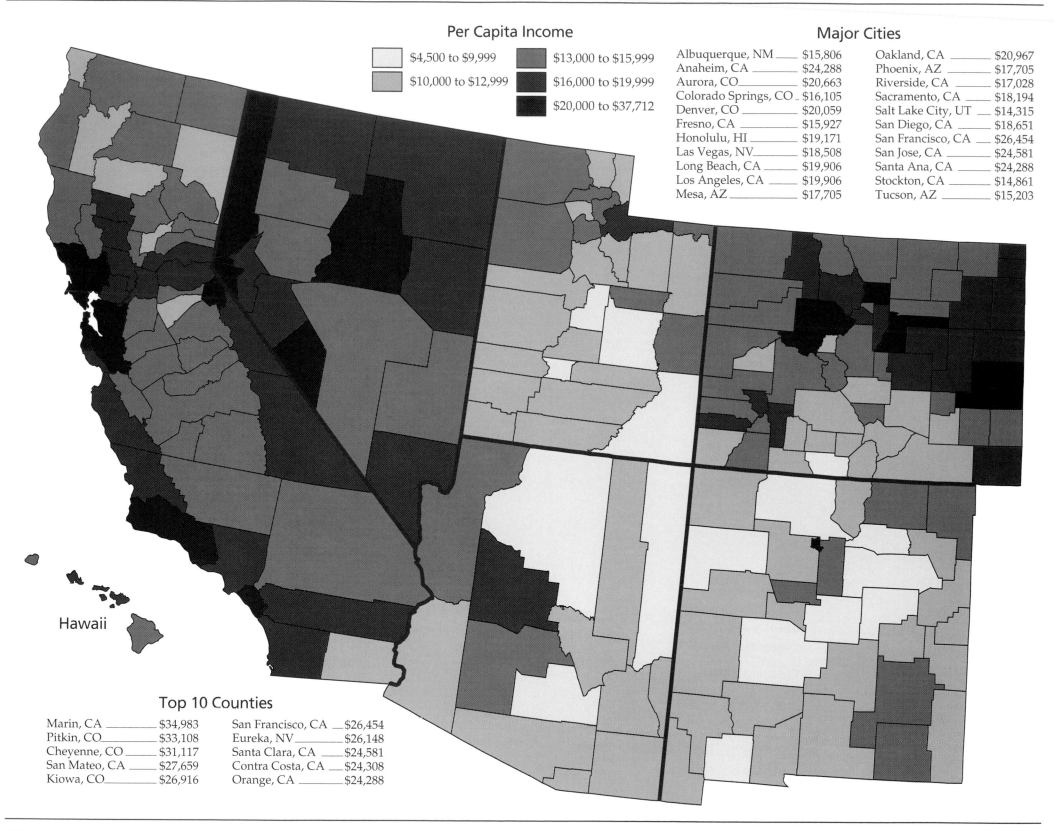

Per Capita Income

$4,500 to $9,999

$10,000 to $12,999

$13,000 to $15,999

$16,000 to $19,999

$20,000 to $37,712

Major Cities

Albuquerque, NM	$15,806	Oakland, CA	$20,967
Anaheim, CA	$24,288	Phoenix, AZ	$17,705
Aurora, CO	$20,663	Riverside, CA	$17,028
Colorado Springs, CO	$16,105	Sacramento, CA	$18,194
Denver, CO	$20,059	Salt Lake City, UT	$14,315
Fresno, CA	$15,927	San Diego, CA	$18,651
Honolulu, HI	$19,171	San Francisco, CA	$26,454
Las Vegas, NV	$18,508	San Jose, CA	$24,581
Long Beach, CA	$19,906	Santa Ana, CA	$24,288
Los Angeles, CA	$19,906	Stockton, CA	$14,861
Mesa, AZ	$17,705	Tucson, AZ	$15,203

Hawaii

Top 10 Counties

Marin, CA	$34,983	San Francisco, CA	$26,454
Pitkin, CO	$33,108	Eureka, NV	$26,148
Cheyenne, CO	$31,117	Santa Clara, CA	$24,581
San Mateo, CA	$27,659	Contra Costa, CA	$24,308
Kiowa, CO	$26,916	Orange, CA	$24,288

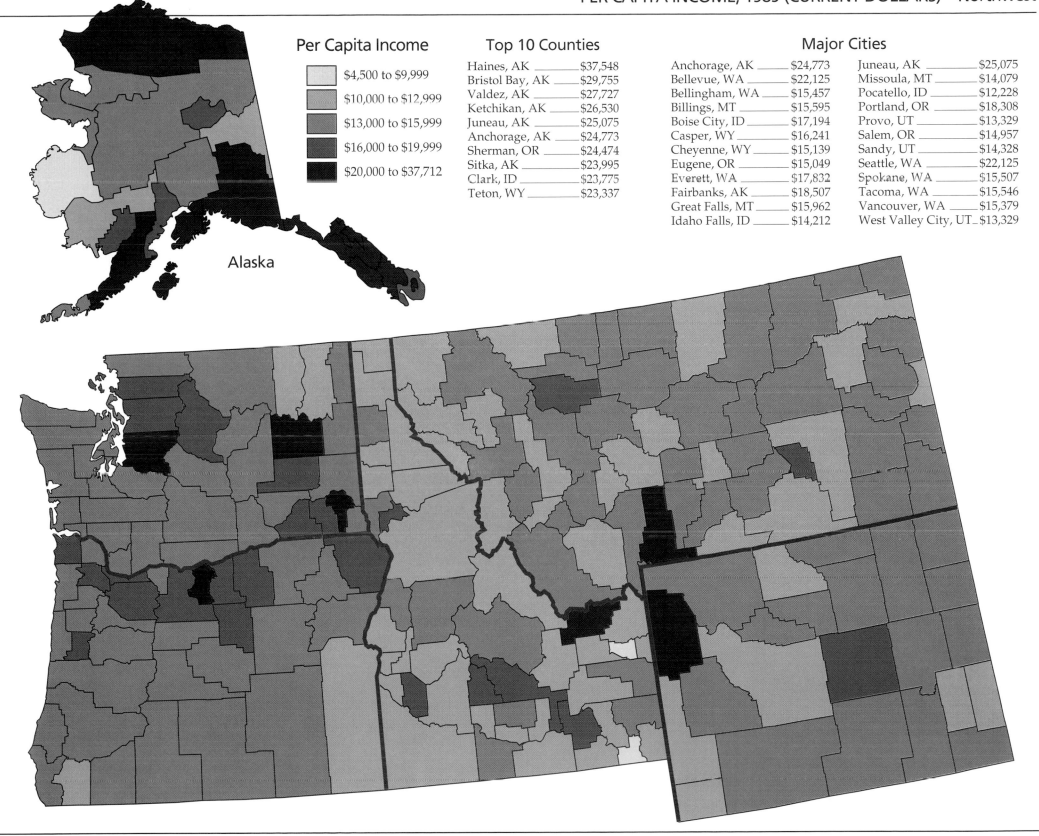

Per Capita Income

- $4,500 to $9,999
- $10,000 to $12,999
- $13,000 to $15,999
- $16,000 to $19,999
- $20,000 to $37,712

Alaska

Top 10 Counties

County	Income
Haines, AK	$37,548
Bristol Bay, AK	$29,755
Valdez, AK	$27,727
Ketchikan, AK	$26,530
Juneau, AK	$25,075
Anchorage, AK	$24,773
Sherman, OR	$24,474
Sitka, AK	$23,995
Clark, ID	$23,775
Teton, WY	$23,337

Major Cities

City	Income	City	Income
Anchorage, AK	$24,773	Juneau, AK	$25,075
Bellevue, WA	$22,125	Missoula, MT	$14,079
Bellingham, WA	$15,457	Pocatello, ID	$12,228
Billings, MT	$15,595	Portland, OR	$18,308
Boise City, ID	$17,194	Provo, UT	$13,329
Casper, WY	$16,241	Salem, OR	$14,957
Cheyenne, WY	$15,139	Sandy, UT	$14,328
Eugene, OR	$15,049	Seattle, WA	$22,125
Everett, WA	$17,832	Spokane, WA	$15,507
Fairbanks, AK	$18,507	Tacoma, WA	$15,546
Great Falls, MT	$15,962	Vancouver, WA	$15,379
Idaho Falls, ID	$14,212	West Valley City, UT	$13,329

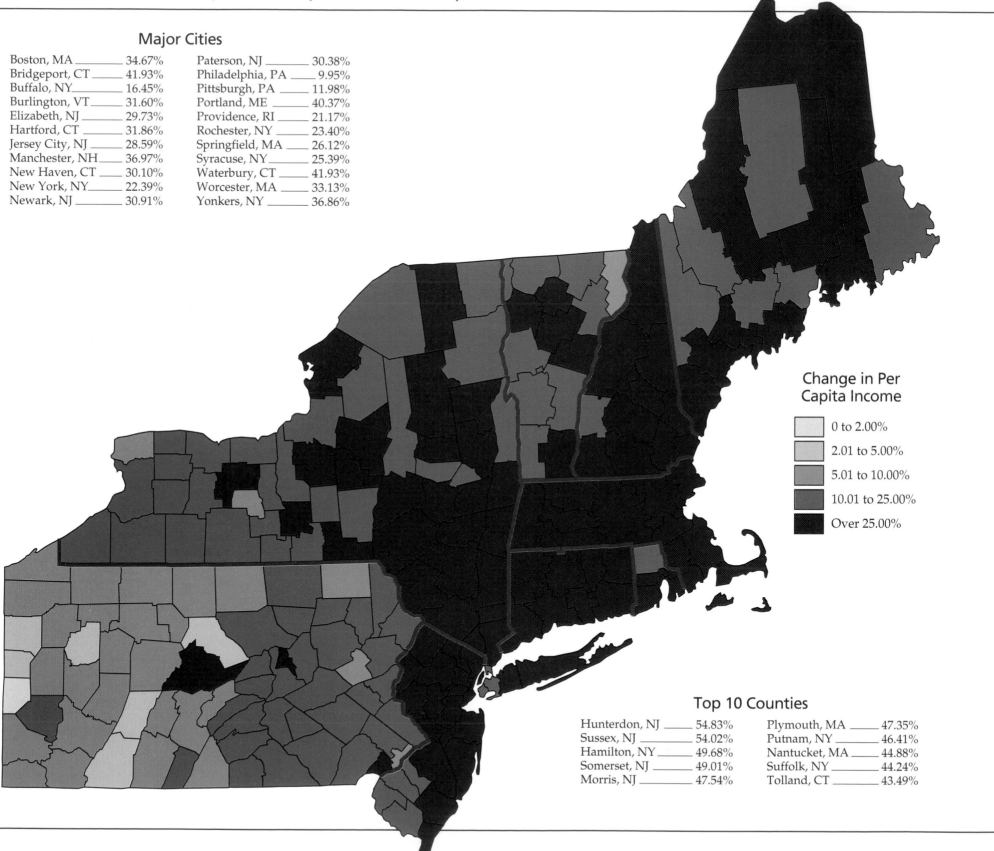

Major Cities

Boston, MA	34.67%	Paterson, NJ	30.38%
Bridgeport, CT	41.93%	Philadelphia, PA	9.95%
Buffalo, NY	16.45%	Pittsburgh, PA	11.98%
Burlington, VT	31.60%	Portland, ME	40.37%
Elizabeth, NJ	29.73%	Providence, RI	21.17%
Hartford, CT	31.86%	Rochester, NY	23.40%
Jersey City, NJ	28.59%	Springfield, MA	26.12%
Manchester, NH	36.97%	Syracuse, NY	25.39%
New Haven, CT	30.10%	Waterbury, CT	41.93%
New York, NY	22.39%	Worcester, MA	33.13%
Newark, NJ	30.91%	Yonkers, NY	36.86%

Change in Per Capita Income

- 0 to 2.00%
- 2.01 to 5.00%
- 5.01 to 10.00%
- 10.01 to 25.00%
- Over 25.00%

Top 10 Counties

Hunterdon, NJ	54.83%	Plymouth, MA	47.35%
Sussex, NJ	54.02%	Putnam, NY	46.41%
Hamilton, NY	49.68%	Nantucket, MA	44.88%
Somerset, NJ	49.01%	Suffolk, NY	44.24%
Morris, NJ	47.54%	Tolland, CT	43.49%

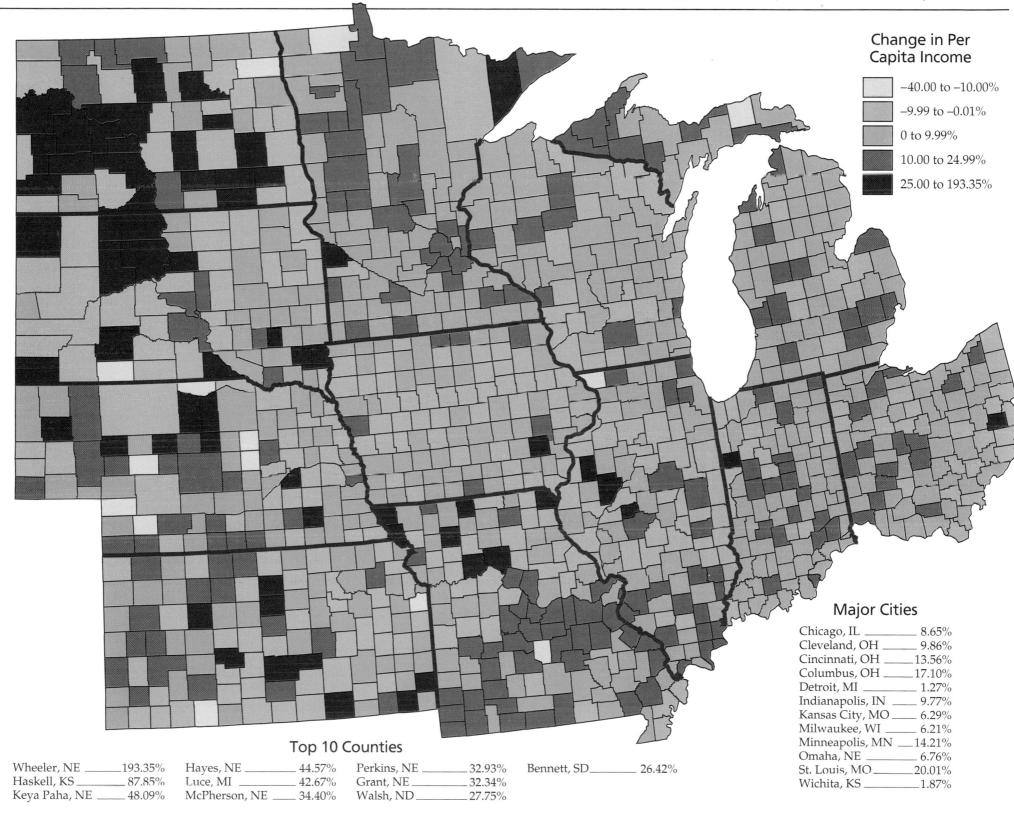

Change in Per Capita Income

- −40.00 to −10.00%
- −9.99 to −0.01%
- 0 to 9.99%
- 10.00 to 24.99%
- 25.00 to 193.35%

Major Cities

Chicago, IL _____ 8.65%
Cleveland, OH _____ 9.86%
Cincinnati, OH _____ 13.56%
Columbus, OH _____ 17.10%
Detroit, MI _____ 1.27%
Indianapolis, IN _____ 9.77%
Kansas City, MO _____ 6.29%
Milwaukee, WI _____ 6.21%
Minneapolis, MN ____ 14.21%
Omaha, NE _____ 6.76%
St. Louis, MO _____ 20.01%
Wichita, KS _____ 1.87%

Top 10 Counties

Wheeler, NE _____ 193.35% Hayes, NE _____ 44.57% Perkins, NE _____ 32.93% Bennett, SD _____ 26.42%
Haskell, KS _____ 87.85% Luce, MI _____ 42.67% Grant, NE _____ 32.34%
Keya Paha, NE _____ 48.09% McPherson, NE _____ 34.40% Walsh, ND _____ 27.75%

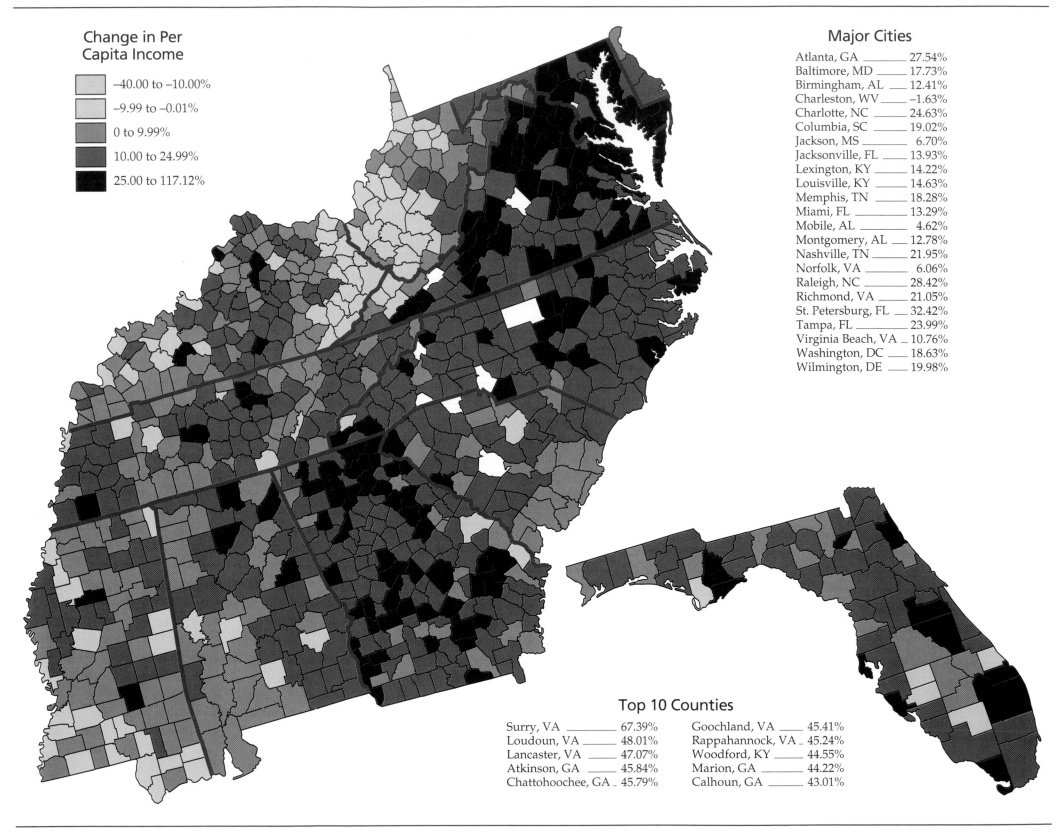

Change in Per Capita Income

- −40.00 to −10.00%
- −9.99 to −0.01%
- 0 to 9.99%
- 10.00 to 24.99%
- 25.00 to 117.12%

Major Cities

Atlanta, GA	27.54%
Baltimore, MD	17.73%
Birmingham, AL	12.41%
Charleston, WV	−1.63%
Charlotte, NC	24.63%
Columbia, SC	19.02%
Jackson, MS	6.70%
Jacksonville, FL	13.93%
Lexington, KY	14.22%
Louisville, KY	14.63%
Memphis, TN	18.28%
Miami, FL	13.29%
Mobile, AL	4.62%
Montgomery, AL	12.78%
Nashville, TN	21.95%
Norfolk, VA	6.06%
Raleigh, NC	28.42%
Richmond, VA	21.05%
St. Petersburg, FL	32.42%
Tampa, FL	23.99%
Virginia Beach, VA	10.76%
Washington, DC	18.63%
Wilmington, DE	19.98%

Top 10 Counties

Surry, VA	67.39%	Goochland, VA	45.41%
Loudoun, VA	48.01%	Rappahannock, VA	45.24%
Lancaster, VA	47.07%	Woodford, KY	44.55%
Atkinson, GA	45.84%	Marion, GA	44.22%
Chattohoochee, GA	45.79%	Calhoun, GA	43.01%

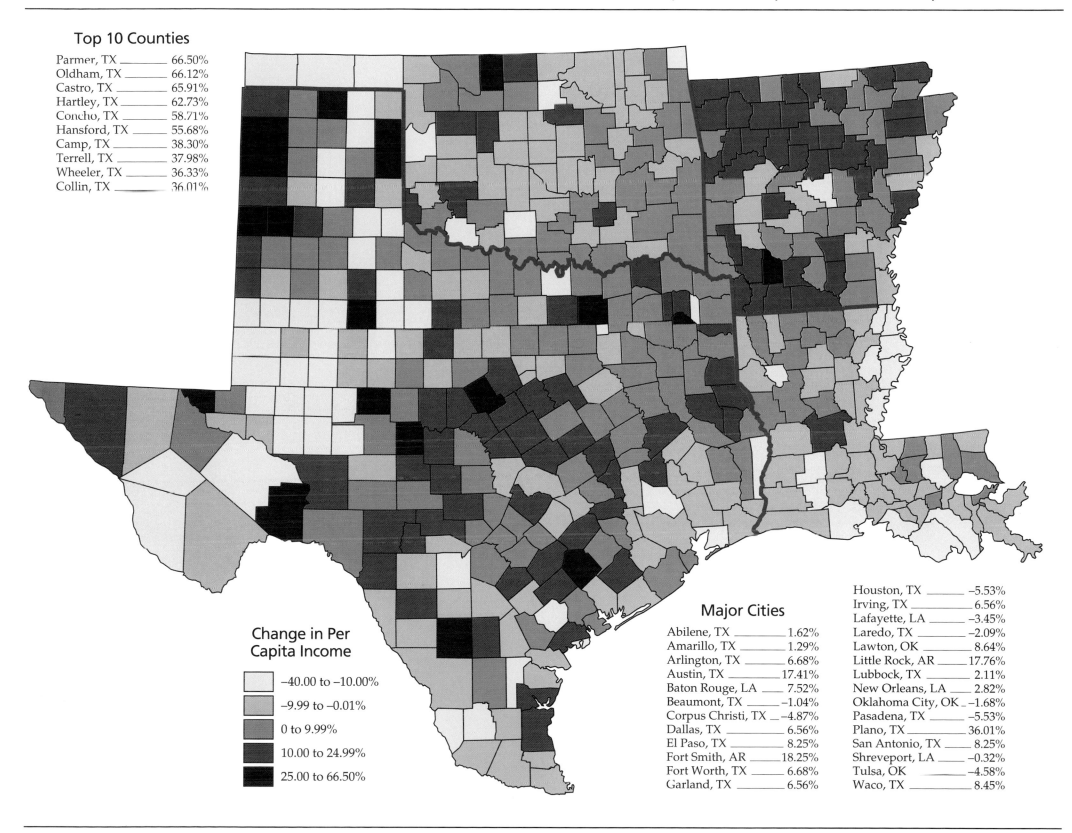

Top 10 Counties

Parmer, TX	66.50%
Oldham, TX	66.12%
Castro, TX	65.91%
Hartley, TX	62.73%
Concho, TX	58.71%
Hansford, TX	55.68%
Camp, TX	38.30%
Terrell, TX	37.98%
Wheeler, TX	36.33%
Collin, TX	36.01%

Change in Per Capita Income

- −40.00 to −10.00%
- −9.99 to −0.01%
- 0 to 9.99%
- 10.00 to 24.99%
- 25.00 to 66.50%

Major Cities

Abilene, TX	1.62%
Amarillo, TX	1.29%
Arlington, TX	6.68%
Austin, TX	17.41%
Baton Rouge, LA	7.52%
Beaumont, TX	−1.04%
Corpus Christi, TX	−4.87%
Dallas, TX	6.56%
El Paso, TX	8.25%
Fort Smith, AR	18.25%
Fort Worth, TX	6.68%
Garland, TX	6.56%
Houston, TX	−5.53%
Irving, TX	6.56%
Lafayette, LA	−3.45%
Laredo, TX	−2.09%
Lawton, OK	8.64%
Little Rock, AR	17.76%
Lubbock, TX	2.11%
New Orleans, LA	2.82%
Oklahoma City, OK	−1.68%
Pasadena, TX	−5.53%
Plano, TX	36.01%
San Antonio, TX	8.25%
Shreveport, LA	−0.32%
Tulsa, OK	−4.58%
Waco, TX	8.45%

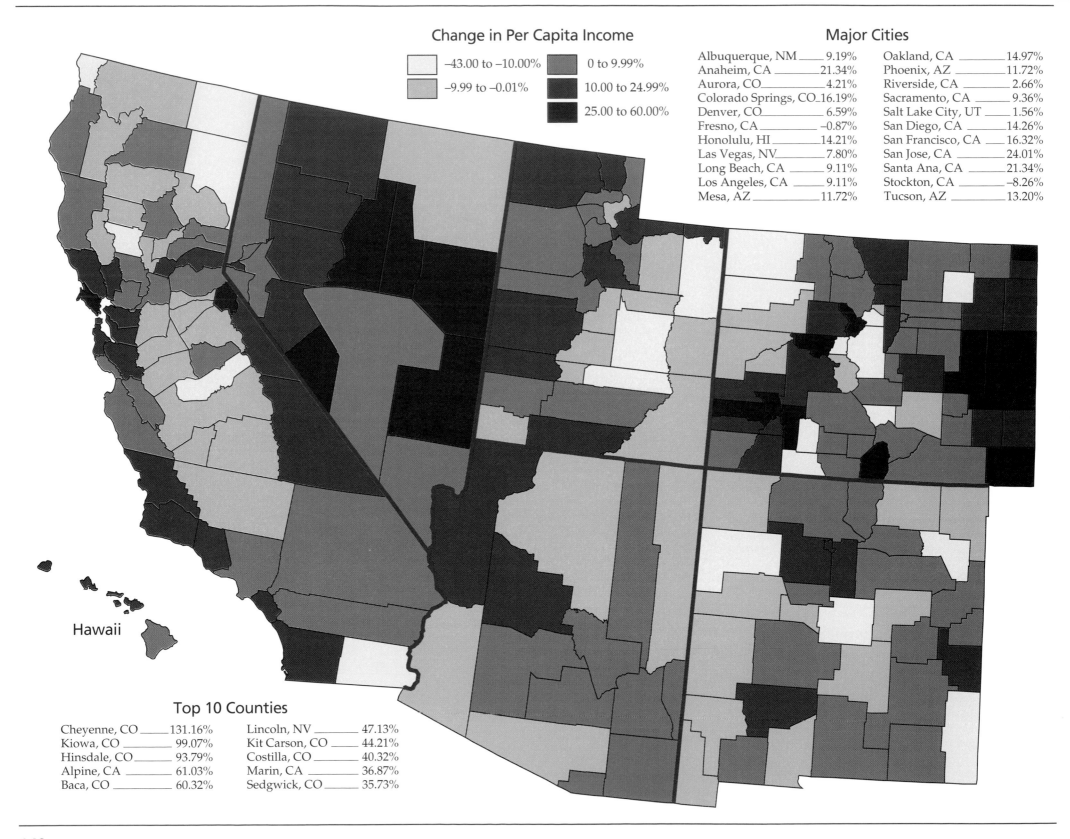

Change in Per Capita Income

- −43.00 to −10.00%
- −9.99 to −0.01%
- 0 to 9.99%
- 10.00 to 24.99%
- 25.00 to 60.00%

Major Cities

City	Change	City	Change
Albuquerque, NM	9.19%	Oakland, CA	14.97%
Anaheim, CA	21.34%	Phoenix, AZ	11.72%
Aurora, CO	4.21%	Riverside, CA	2.66%
Colorado Springs, CO	16.19%	Sacramento, CA	9.36%
Denver, CO	6.59%	Salt Lake City, UT	1.56%
Fresno, CA	−0.87%	San Diego, CA	14.26%
Honolulu, HI	14.21%	San Francisco, CA	16.32%
Las Vegas, NV	7.80%	San Jose, CA	24.01%
Long Beach, CA	9.11%	Santa Ana, CA	21.34%
Los Angeles, CA	9.11%	Stockton, CA	−8.26%
Mesa, AZ	11.72%	Tucson, AZ	13.20%

Hawaii

Top 10 Counties

County	Change	County	Change
Cheyenne, CO	131.16%	Lincoln, NV	47.13%
Kiowa, CO	99.07%	Kit Carson, CO	44.21%
Hinsdale, CO	93.79%	Costilla, CO	40.32%
Alpine, CA	61.03%	Marin, CA	36.87%
Baca, CO	60.32%	Sedgwick, CO	35.73%

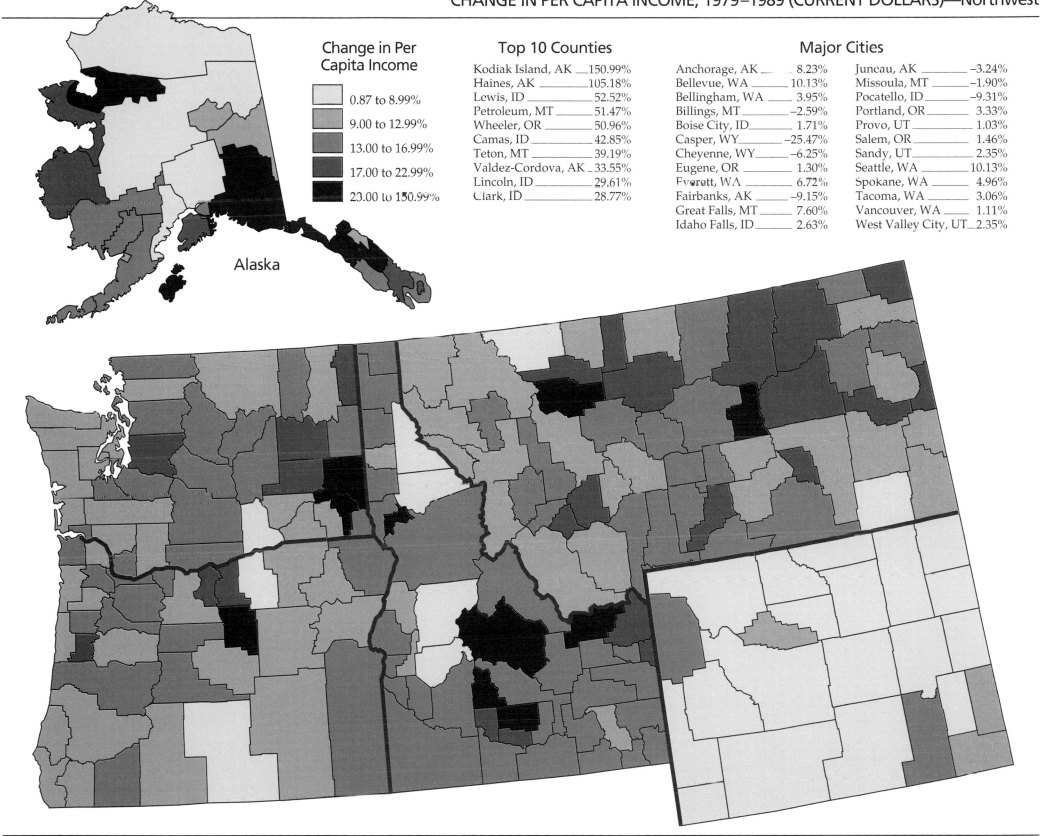

Change in Per Capita Income

- 0.87 to 8.99%
- 9.00 to 12.99%
- 13.00 to 16.99%
- 17.00 to 22.99%
- 23.00 to 150.99%

Alaska

Top 10 Counties

Kodiak Island, AK	150.99%
Haines, AK	105.18%
Lewis, ID	52.52%
Petroleum, MT	51.47%
Wheeler, OR	50.96%
Camas, ID	42.85%
Teton, MT	39.19%
Valdez-Cordova, AK	33.55%
Lincoln, ID	29.61%
Clark, ID	28.77%

Major Cities

Anchorage, AK	8.23%	Juneau, AK	–3.24%
Bellevue, WA	10.13%	Missoula, MT	–1.90%
Bellingham, WA	3.95%	Pocatello, ID	–9.31%
Billings, MT	–2.59%	Portland, OR	3.33%
Boise City, ID	1.71%	Provo, UT	1.03%
Casper, WY	–25.47%	Salem, OR	1.46%
Cheyenne, WY	–6.25%	Sandy, UT	2.35%
Eugene, OR	1.30%	Seattle, WA	10.13%
Everett, WA	6.72%	Spokane, WA	4.96%
Fairbanks, AK	–9.15%	Tacoma, WA	3.06%
Great Falls, MT	7.60%	Vancouver, WA	1.11%
Idaho Falls, ID	2.63%	West Valley City, UT	2.35%

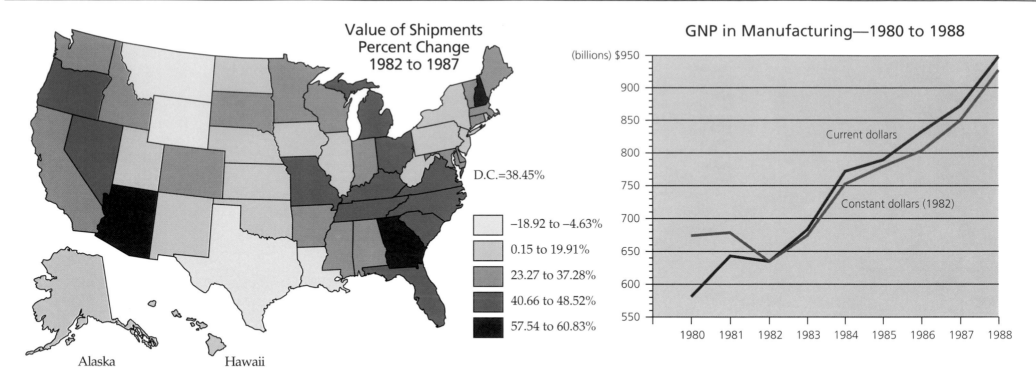

Value of Shipments Percent Change 1982 to 1987

D.C.=38.45%

- −18.92 to −4.63%
- 0.15 to 19.91%
- 23.27 to 37.28%
- 40.66 to 48.52%
- 57.54 to 60.83%

Alaska   Hawaii

GNP in Manufacturing—1980 to 1988

(billions) $950

Current dollars

Constant dollars (1982)

1980 1981 1982 1983 1984 1985 1986 1987 1988

Source: U.S. Bureau of Economic Analysis, *The National Income and Product Accounts of the United States, 1929–1982,* and *Survey of Current Business,* July issues.

Employees in Manufacturing, 1989

State	(000's)	State	(000's)
United States	19,426	Missouri	439
Alabama	384	Montana	22
Alaska	16	Nebraska	95
Arizona	188	Nevada	25
Arkansas	230	New Hampshire	114
California	2,159	New Jersey	654
Colorado	193	New Mexico	42
Connecticut	360	New York	1,192
Delaware	73	North Carolina	868
Dist. of Columbia	16	North Dakota	16
Florida	541	Ohio	1,123
Georgia	568	Oklahoma	163
Hawaii	21	Oregon	217
Idaho	61	Pennsylvania	1,050
Illinois	982	Rhode Island	109
Indiana	642	South Carolina	391
Iowa	234	South Dakota	32
Kansas	185	Tennessee	524
Kentucky	284	Texas	970
Louisiana	174	Utah	103
Maine	106	Vermont	48
Maryland	209	Virginia	428
Massachusetts	563	Washington	361
Michigan	968	West Virginia	88
Minnesota	399	Wisconsin	556
Mississippi	243	Wyoming	9

Source: U.S. Bureau of Labor Statistics, *Employment and Earnings,* monthly. Compiled from data supplied by cooperating State agencies.

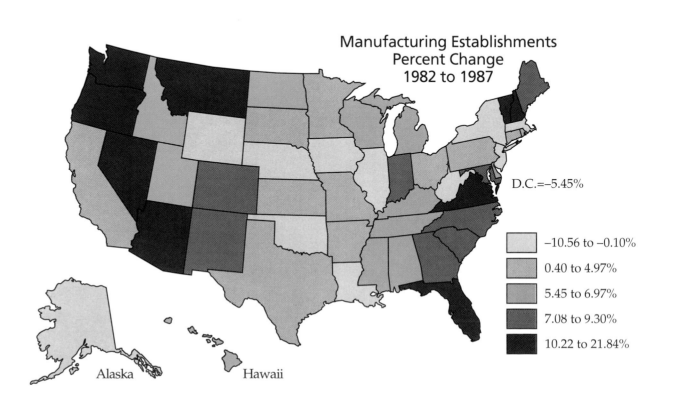

Manufacturing Establishments Percent Change 1982 to 1987

D.C.=−5.45%

- −10.56 to −0.10%
- 0.40 to 4.97%
- 5.45 to 6.97%
- 7.08 to 9.30%
- 10.22 to 21.84%

Alaska   Hawaii

Revenue Percent Change 1982 to 1987

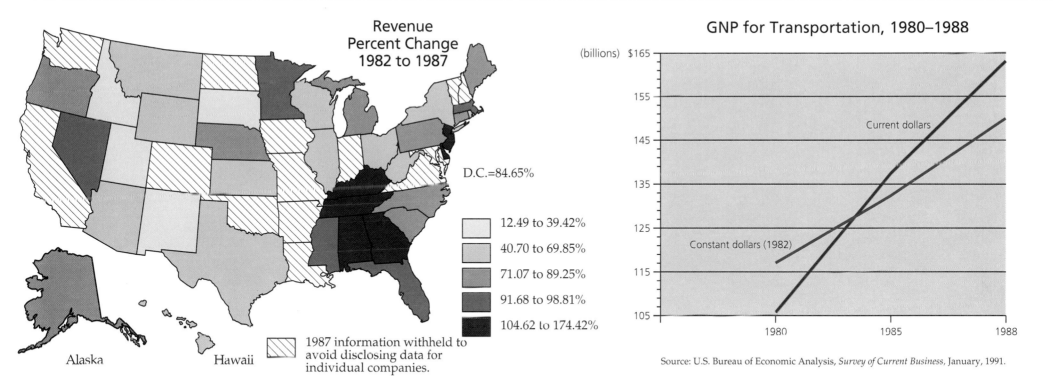

D.C.=84.65%

- 12.49 to 39.42%
- 40.70 to 69.85%
- 71.07 to 89.25%
- 91.68 to 98.81%
- 104.62 to 174.42%

1987 information withheld to avoid disclosing data for individual companies.

Alaska   Hawaii

GNP for Transportation, 1980–1988

(billions)

Current dollars

Constant dollars (1982)

Source: U.S. Bureau of Economic Analysis, *Survey of Current Business*, January, 1991.

Employees in Transportation and Public Utilities, 1989

State	(000's)	State	(000's)
United States	5,648	Missouri	151
Alabama	80	Montana	20
Alaska	21	Nebraska	46
Arizona	77	Nevada	31
Arkansas	55	New Hampshire	18
California	600	New Jersey	242
Colorado	93	New Mexico	29
Connecticut	73	New York	407
Delaware	15	North Carolina	152
Dist. of Columbia	25	North Dakota	17
Florida	266	Ohio	216
Georgia	184	Oklahoma	65
Hawaii	40	Oregon	63
Idaho	19	Pennsylvania	254
Illinois	304	Rhode Island	15
Indiana	128	South Carolina	64
Iowa	56	South Dakota	13
Kansas	66	Tennessee	115
Kentucky	77	Texas	401
Louisiana	106	Utah	41
Maine	22	Vermont	10
Maryland	101	Virginia	149
Massachusetts	128	Washington	108
Michigan	152	West Virginia	36
Minnesota	105	Wisconsin	100
Mississippi	46	Wyoming	14

Source: U.S. Bureau of Labor Statistics, *Employment and Earnings*, monthly. Compiled from data supplied by cooperating State agencies.

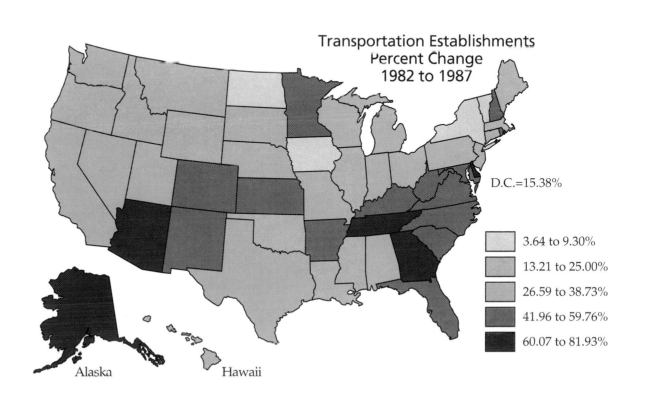

Transportation Establishments Percent Change 1982 to 1987

D.C.=15.38%

- 3.64 to 9.30%
- 13.21 to 25.00%
- 26.59 to 38.73%
- 41.96 to 59.76%
- 60.07 to 81.93%

Alaska   Hawaii

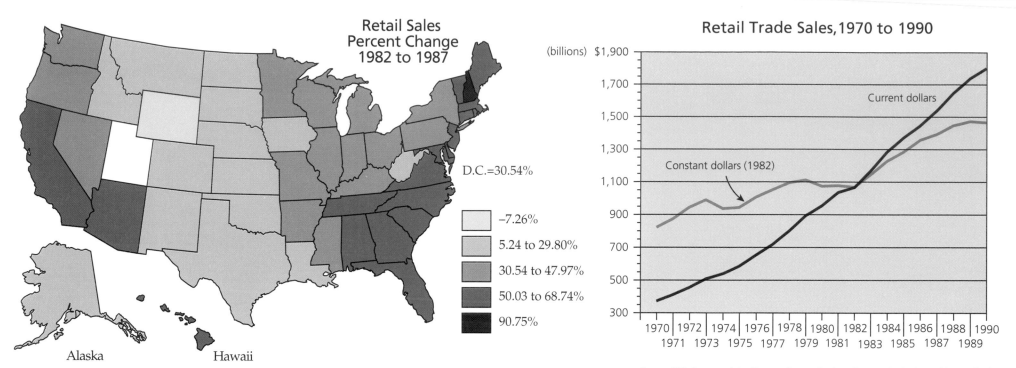

Retail Sales Percent Change 1982 to 1987

D.C.=30.54%

- −7.26%
- 5.24 to 29.80%
- 30.54 to 47.97%
- 50.03 to 68.74%
- 90.75%

Alaska   Hawaii

Retail Trade Sales, 1970 to 1990

(billions) $1,900

Current dollars

Constant dollars (1982)

Source: U.S. Bureau of the Census, *Current Business Reports, Revised Monthly Retail Sales and Inventories, January 1981 Through December 1990,* (BR/90–R), prior issues, and un-published data.

Paid Employees in Retail Sales, 1987

State	(000's)	State	(000's)
United States	17,780	Missouri	376
Alabama	250	Montana	57
Alaska	36	Nebraska	118
Arizona	261	Nevada	81
Arkansas	139	New Hampshire	102
California	2,022	New Jersey	566
Colorado	268	New Mexico	105
Connecticut	268	New York	1,150
Delaware	56	North Carolina	465
Dist. of Columbia	55	North Dakota	48
Florida	1,023	Ohio	804
Georgia	487	Oklahoma	207
Hawaii	102	Oregon	204
Idaho	63	Pennsylvania	848
Illinois	820	Rhode Island	76
Indiana	412	South Carolina	237
Iowa	204	South Dakota	49
Kansas	175	Tennessee	338
Kentucky	244	Texas	1,174
Louisiana	278	Utah	109
Maine	92	Vermont	47
Maryland	378	Virginia	453
Massachusetts	530	Washington	329
Michigan	673	West Virginia	109
Minnesota	347	Wisconsin	372
Mississippi	140	Wyoming	33

Source: U.S. Bureau of the Census, *1987 Census of Retail Trade,* Geographic Area Series, RC87–A–1 to 52; and Nonemployer Statistics Series, RC87–N–1 to 4.

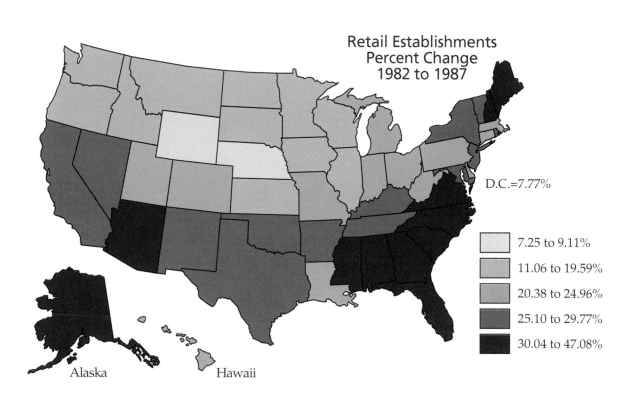

Retail Establishments Percent Change 1982 to 1987

D.C.=7.77%

- 7.25 to 9.11%
- 11.06 to 19.59%
- 20.38 to 24.96%
- 25.10 to 29.77%
- 30.04 to 47.08%

Alaska   Hawaii

Wholesale Sales Percent Change 1982 to 1987

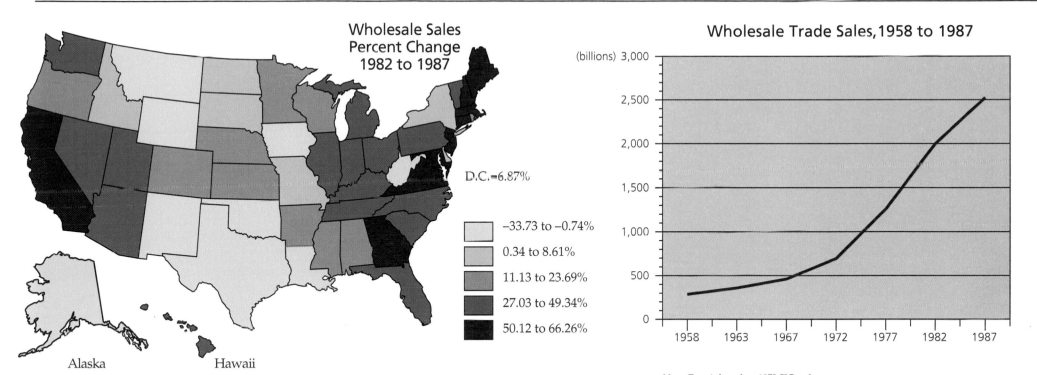

D.C.=-6.87%

- −33.73 to −0.74%
- 0.34 to 8.61%
- 11.13 to 23.69%
- 27.03 to 49.34%
- 50.12 to 66.26%

Alaska   Hawaii

Wholesale Trade Sales, 1958 to 1987

(billions)

Note: Data is based on 1972 SIC code.

Source: U.S. Bureau of the Census, *U.S. Census of Business: 1958*, vol. III; *1963*, vol. IV; *1967*, vol. III; and *Census of Wholesale Trade: 1972*, vol. I; *1977*, WC77–A–52; *1982*, WC82–A–52; and *1987*, WC87–A–52.

Paid Employees in Wholesale Trade, 1987

State	(000's)	State	(000's)
United States	5,593.8	Missouri	124.8
Alabama	77.3	Montana	14.8
Alaska	7.1	Nebraska	43.0
Arizona	64.5	Nevada	17.6
Arkansas	38.8	New Hampshire	22.5
California	682.4	New Jersey	270.7
Colorado	76.1	New Mexico	22.0
Connecticut	84.6	New York	465.4
Delaware	15.5	North Carolina	139.8
Dist. of Columbia	8.8	North Dakota	17.5
Florida	261.0	Ohio	247.5
Georgia	177.8	Oklahoma	54.7
Hawaii	20.1	Oregon	63.7
Idaho	20.7	Pennsylvania	247.2
Illinois	318.9	Rhode Island	22.2
Indiana	107.8	South Carolina	54.3
Iowa	65.8	South Dakota	15.3
Kansas	60.6	Tennessee	115.8
Kentucky	63.3	Texas	395.2
Louisiana	80.3	Utah	34.1
Maine	22.6	Vermont	10.2
Maryland	99.3	Virginia	114.6
Massachusetts	160.5	Washington	102.3
Michigan	178.7	West Virginia	24.2
Minnesota	114.1	Wisconsin	101.4
Mississippi	39.9	Wyoming	6.3

Source: U.S. Bureau of the Census, *1987 Census of Wholesale Trade*, Geographic Area Series, WC87–A–1 to 52.

Wholesale Establishments Percent Change 1982 to 1987

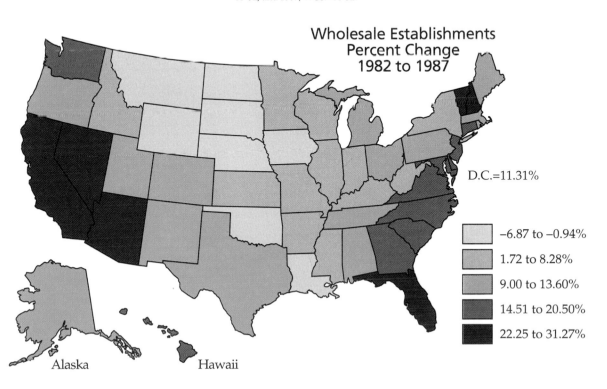

D.C.=11.31%

- −6.87 to −0.94%
- 1.72 to 8.28%
- 9.00 to 13.60%
- 14.51 to 20.50%
- 22.25 to 31.27%

Alaska   Hawaii

Service Receipts Percent Change 1982 to 1987

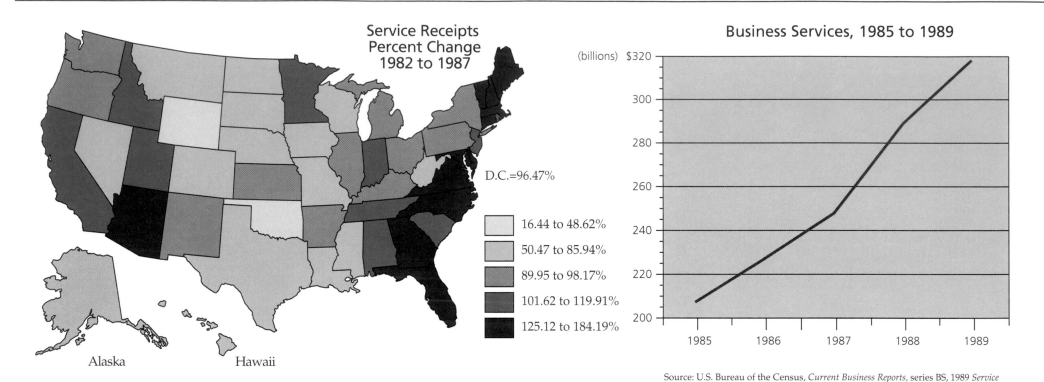

D.C.=96.47%

- 16.44 to 48.62%
- 50.47 to 85.94%
- 89.95 to 98.17%
- 101.62 to 119.91%
- 125.12 to 184.19%

Alaska   Hawaii

Business Services, 1985 to 1989

(billions) $320

300

280

260

240

220

200

1985   1986   1987   1988   1989

Source: U.S. Bureau of the Census, *Current Business Reports,* series BS, 1989 *Service Annual Survey.*

Paid Employees in Service Industries, 1987

State	(000's)	State	(000's)
United States	16,055	Missouri	324
Alabama	190	Montana	36
Alaska	28	Nebraska	89
Arizona	244	Nevada	206
Arkansas	94	New Hampshire	68
California	2,248	New Jersey	596
Colorado	256	New Mexico	88
Connecticut	250	New York	1,293
Delaware	46	North Carolina	331
Dist. of Columbia	121	North Dakota	28
Florida	975	Ohio	648
Georgia	415	Oklahoma	149
Hawaii	92	Oregon	157
Idaho	48	Pennsylvania	694
Illinois	730	Rhode Island	61
Indiana	282	South Carolina	170
Iowa	131	South Dakota	27
Kansas	128	Tennessee	283
Kentucky	166	Texas	1,061
Louisiana	241	Utah	94
Maine	58	Vermont	37
Maryland	369	Virginia	439
Massachusetts	523	Washington	277
Michigan	533	West Virginia	67
Minnesota	295	Wisconsin	265
Mississippi	84	Wyoming	22

Source: U.S. Bureau of the Census, *1987 Census of Service Industries,* Geographic Area Series, SC87–A–1 to 52; and Nonemployer Statistics Series, SC87–N–1 to 4.

Service Establishments Percent Change 1982 to 1987

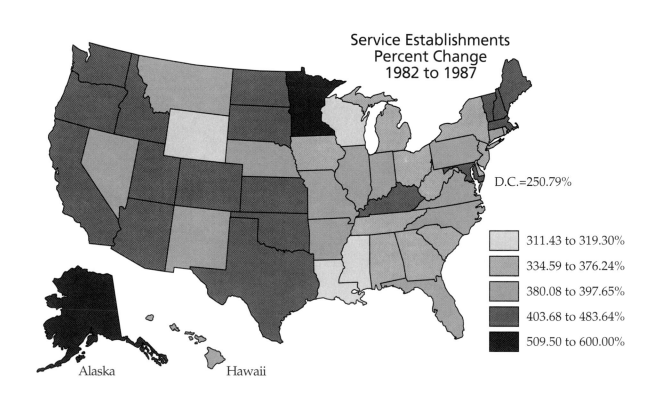

D.C.=250.79%

- 311.43 to 319.30%
- 334.59 to 376.24%
- 380.08 to 397.65%
- 403.68 to 483.64%
- 509.50 to 600.00%

Alaska   Hawaii

Farm Income Percent Change 1986 to 1989

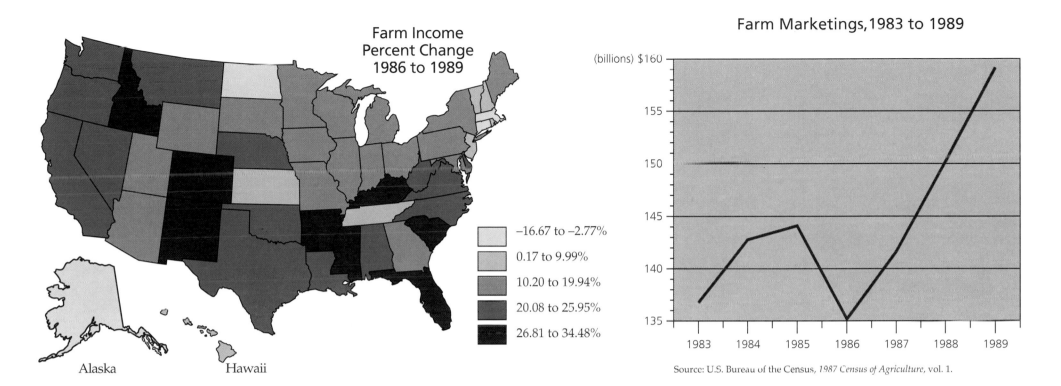

	−16.67 to −2.77%
	0.17 to 9.99%
	10.20 to 19.94%
	20.08 to 25.95%
	26.81 to 34.48%

Alaska   Hawaii

Farm Marketings, 1983 to 1989

Source: U.S. Bureau of the Census, *1987 Census of Agriculture*, vol. 1.

Farm Operator Tenure and Characteristics, 1987

Characteristic	(000's)	Characteristic	(000's)
Total	2,088	Principal Occupation:	
White	2,043	Farming	1,138
Black	23	Other	950
American Indian, Eskimos, and Aleuts	7		
Asian or Pacific Islander	8	Place of Residence:	
Other	7	On farm operated	1,488
Operators of Hispanic origin	17	Not on farm operated	443
Female	132		
Under 25 years old	36	Years on present farm:	
25 to 34 years old	243	2 years or less	114
35 to 44 years old	411	3 to 4 years	135
45 to 54 years old	455	5 to 9 years	304
55 to 64 years old	496	10 years or more	1,163
65 years old or older	447		
Average age (years)	52.0	Days worked off farm:	
Full owner	1,239	None	844
Part owner	609	Less than 100 days	200
Tenant	240	100 to 199 days	178
		200 days or more	737

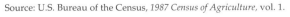

Source: U.S. Bureau of the Census, *1987 Census of Agriculture*, vol. 1.

Farm Acreage Percent Change 1980 to 1990

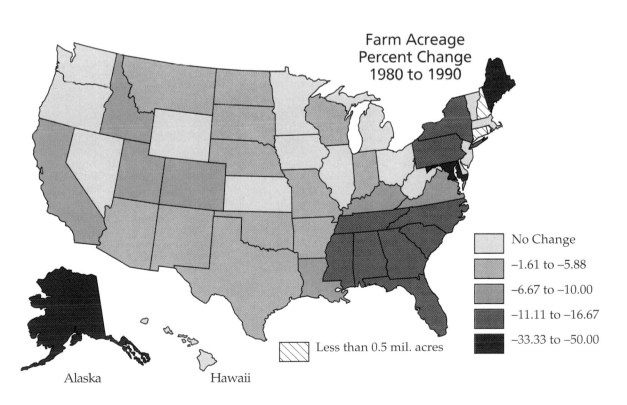

	No Change
	−1.61 to −5.88
	−6.67 to −10.00
	−11.11 to −16.67
	−33.33 to −50.00
	Less than 0.5 mil. acres

Alaska   Hawaii

Part Six

EDUCATION

AMERICA'S SYSTEM OF EDUCATION

During the 1989–90 school year, 83,425 public elementary and secondary schools were administered to by 15,367 school districts. The majority of schools were regarded as "regular schools" serving 98.6 percent of a school–age population between the ages of 5 and 17 years. 2.1 percent of all schools served students with special needs. Another 1.5 percent taught vocational skills.

School sizes varied wildly during the same time period as above. 9.1 percent of all schools had between 1 and 99 members. 2.5 percent had over 1,500 students. 50.7 percent of all public schools had between 300 and 750 students.

In 1990, 40,529,372 students attended public school. Of that number, 56.0 percent attended grades pre–kindergarten through six (PK–6). 22.3 percent of students were enrolled in grades seven through nine (7–9). 19.7 percent attended grades ten through twelve (10–12). 2.0 percent were ungraded. 47.9 percent of all public schools were engaged in the instruction of students PK–6. 5.4 percent were devoted to students 7–9. And 13.9 percent were involved in the education of students in grades 9–12.

Only twenty districts, of the 15,367 reported in 1990, had memberships of more than 100,000 students. The largest school district in the United States was New York City, having 930,440 students during the 1989–90 school year. The second largest was the Department of Education in Hato Rey, Puerto Rico, with 650,720 students, followed by Los Angeles with 609,746 members. The following table shows the twenty largest school districts and the populations of their associated urban centers.

School District	City/State	Enrollment
New York City	Brooklyn, NY	930,440
Department of Education	Hato Rey, PR	650,720
Los Angeles	Los Angeles, CA	609,746
Chicago	Chicago, IL	408,201
Dade County	Miami, FL	279,357
Houston	Houston, TX	191,282
Philadelphia	Philadelphia, PA	189,451
Detroit City	Detroit, MI	175,329
Hawaii Dept of Education	Honolulu, HI	169,507
Broward County	Ft. Lauderdale, FL	148,739
Dallas	Dallas, TX	132,256
Fairfax County	Fairfax, VA	126,713
Hillsborough County	Tampa, FL	119,810
San Diego	San Diego, CA	119,314
Clark County	Las Vegas, NV	111,460
Baltimore	Baltimore, MD	107,782
Prince Georges County	Landover, MD	106,974
Duval County	Jacksonville, FL	106,961
Memphis City	Memphis, TN	105,604
Montgomery County	Rockville, MD	100,261

SCHOOL FINANCES

In 1989, the gross national product (GNP) of the United States was 5.2 trillion dollars. Education cost $358.7 billion or 6.9 percent of the GNP.

Education is the largest single expenditure for all states. On the average, $725 was spent per capita on education in the United States in 1990. Each student received $5,208 for education in the 1990–91 school year. The table below shows expenditures per student for 1990–91 in the United States.

State Expenditures

State	Direct General Per Capita	For K–12 Per Capita	Percent of Direct General	Per Pupil
United States	$2,857	$690	24	$5,208
Alabama	2,230	461	21	3,648
Alaska	9,546	1,660	17	6,952
Arizona	2,980	751	25	4,196
Arkansas	1,948	552	28	3,419
California	3,240	666	21	4,826
Colorado	2,889	743	26	4,702
Connecticut	3,264	774	24	8,455
Dist.of Columbia	3,294	711	22	6,016
Delaware	5,785	838	14	8,221
Florida	2,555	616	24	5,003
Georgia	2,595	687	26	4,852
Hawaii	2,970	513	17	5,008
Idaho	2,226	547	25	3,211
Illinois	2,611	613	23	5,062
Indiana	2,294	630	27	4,398
Iowa	2,650	656	25	4,877
Kansas	2,562	668	26	5,044
Kentucky	2,271	499	22	4,390
Louisiana	2,525	508	20	4,041
Maine	2,693	680	25	5,894
Maryland	2,953	687	23	6,184
Massachusetts	3,286	683	21	6,351
Michigan	3,122	783	25	5,257
Minnesota	3,470	799	23	5,360
Mississippi	2,245	556	25	3,322
Missouri	2,139	593	28	4,479
Montana	2,814	785	28	4,794

State Expenditures (continued)

State	Direct General Per Capita	For K–12 Per Capita	Percent of Direct General	Per Pupil
Nebraska	2,597	676	26	4,080
Nevada	2,931	617	21	4,677
New Hampshire	2,441	675	28	5,474
New Jersey	3,297	828	25	8,451
New Mexico	2,841	686	24	4,446
New York	4,200	934	??	8,680
North Carolina	2,271	609	27	4,635
North Dakota	2,921	661	23	3,685
Ohio	2,580	693	27	5,269
Oklahoma	2,307	586	25	3,835
Oregon	2,961	779	26	5,291
Pennsylvania	2,518	699	28	6,534
Rhode Island	3,056	654	21	6,989
South Carolina	2,293	628	27	3,843
South Dakota	2,355	612	26	3,730
Tennessee	2,242	475	21	3,707
Texas	2,458	696	28	4,326
Utah	2,535	667	26	2,767
Vermont	2,928	765	26	5,740
Virginia	2,637	700	27	5,335
Washington	2,869	743	26	5,042
West Virginia	2,282	632	28	4,695
Wisconsin	2,947	786	27	5,946
Wyoming	4,279	1,122	26	5,255

SCHOOL–AGE POPULATION

In 1990, there were 44,782,688 children of school age in the United States. States with the largest populations had the largest numbers of children. While this seems quite predictable, it is interesting to note that many larger states like Florida, California, Pennsylvania, and New York had less than 18 percent of their citizenship in this category. Minnesota had the smallest percentage of its population between 5 and 17 years of age.

The number of Americans of school age is expected to drop by the year 2000. The tables on page 50 indicate that many states will have fewer children.

Cities do not seem to be the homes for many of the nation's children. In the Northeast, the Midwest, the West, and the Southwest, metropolitan areas have relatively small numbers of school–age children when compared to their total populations. While 18 percent is common in most cities, numbers in the high twenties to the mid–thirties are the norm in more rural areas.

School–Age Population, 1990

United States	44,782,688
Alabama	775,493
Alaska	117,447
Arizona	688,260
Arkansas	456,464
California	5,353,010
Colorado	608,373
Connecticut	521,225
Delaware	114,517
District of Columbia	79,741
Florida	2,016,641
Georgia	1,231,768
Hawaii	196,903
Idaho	228,212
Illinois	2,098,225
Indiana	1,057,308
Iowa	525,677
Kansas	473,224
Kentucky	703,223
Louisiana	892,619
Maine	223,280
Maryland	804,423
Massachusetts	940,602
Michigan	1,756,211
Minnesota	336,800
Mississippi	551,396
Missouri	987,780
Montana	162,847
Nebraska	309,406
Nevada	204,731
New Hampshire	194,190
New Jersey	1,266,825
New Mexico	320,863
New York	3,003,785
North Carolina	1,147,194
North Dakota	127,540
Ohio	2,014,595
Oklahoma	610,484
Oregon	522,709
Pennsylvania	1,997,752
Rhode Island	158,721
South Carolina	663,870
South Dakota	143,958
Tennessee	883,189
Texas	3,445,785
Utah	457,811
Vermont	101,822
Virginia	1,061,583
Washington	878,291
West Virginia	336,918
Wisconsin	928,252
Wyoming	100,745

School–Age Population Projected to Year 2000 (in thousands)

	Ages 5–17	Ages 5–13	Ages 14–17
United States	44,186	30,754	13,432
Alabama	762	546	216
Alaska	139	97	43
Arizona	793	556	237
Arkansas	441	306	135
California	5,691	3,917	1,774
Colorado	652	443	209
Connecticut	520	373	147
Delaware	112	79	32
Dist. of Columbia	79	53	26
Florida	2,191	1,543	648
Georgia	1,375	994	382
Hawaii	192	121	71
Idaho	208	144	64
Illinois	1,868	1,303	565
Indiana	944	658	286
Iowa	430	291	139
Kansas	440	303	137
Kentucky	599	424	175
Louisiana	784	556	227
Maine	230	162	68
Maryland	839	585	254
Massachusetts	920	647	273
Michigan	1,602	1,132	470
Minnesota	791	540	251
Mississippi	515	367	148
Missouri	871	603	268
Montana	144	98	46
Nebraska	268	185	83
Nevada	211	144	67
New Hampshire	222	157	65
New Jersey	1,308	926	382
New Mexico	394	265	128
New York	2,655	1,783	872
North Carolina	1,212	852	360
North Dakota	110	73	37
Ohio	1,744	1,205	538
Oklahoma	594	403	191
Oregon	477	326	150
Pennsylvania	1,639	1,107	532
Rhode Island	150	105	45
South Carolina	664	468	196
South Dakota	133	92	42
Tennessee	829	589	240
Texas	3,675	2,620	1,055
Utah	496	352	145
Vermont	105	75	29
Virginia	1,167	825	342
Washington	836	564	271
West Virginia	285	200	85
Wisconsin	787	529	258
Wyoming	96	66	30

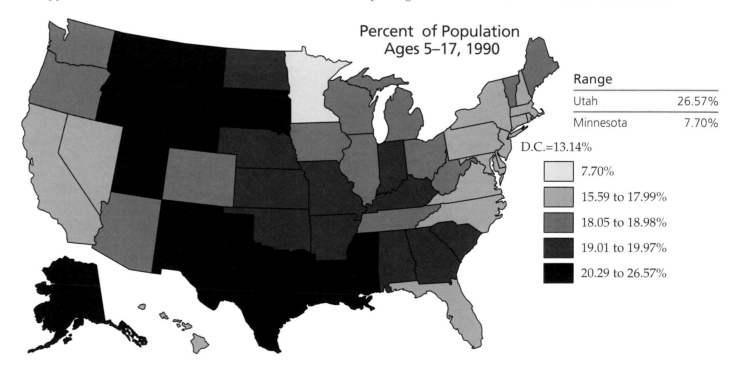

Percent of Population Ages 5–17, 1990

Range

Utah	26.57%
Minnesota	7.70%

D.C.=13.14%

- 7.70%
- 15.59 to 17.99%
- 18.05 to 18.98%
- 19.01 to 19.97%
- 20.29 to 26.57%

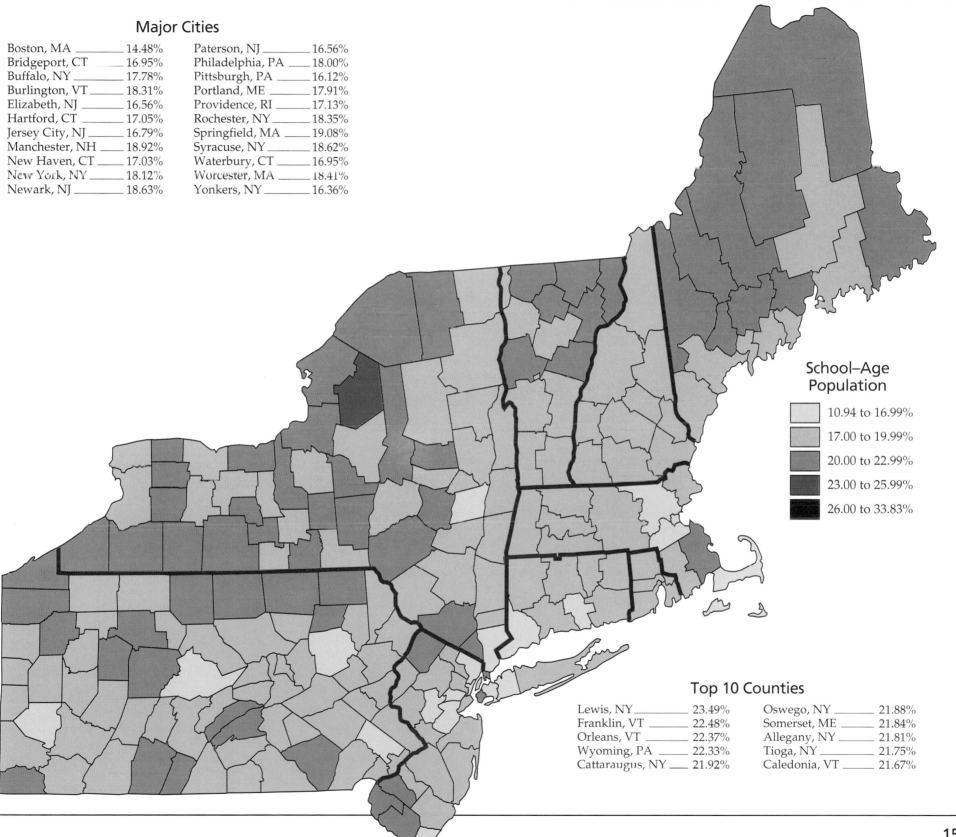

Major Cities

City	%	City	%
Boston, MA	14.48%	Paterson, NJ	16.56%
Bridgeport, CT	16.95%	Philadelphia, PA	18.00%
Buffalo, NY	17.78%	Pittsburgh, PA	16.12%
Burlington, VT	18.31%	Portland, ME	17.91%
Elizabeth, NJ	16.56%	Providence, RI	17.13%
Hartford, CT	17.05%	Rochester, NY	18.35%
Jersey City, NJ	16.79%	Springfield, MA	19.08%
Manchester, NH	18.92%	Syracuse, NY	18.62%
New Haven, CT	17.03%	Waterbury, CT	16.95%
New York, NY	18.12%	Worcester, MA	18.41%
Newark, NJ	18.63%	Yonkers, NY	16.36%

School–Age Population

- 10.94 to 16.99%
- 17.00 to 19.99%
- 20.00 to 22.99%
- 23.00 to 25.99%
- 26.00 to 33.83%

Top 10 Counties

County	%	County	%
Lewis, NY	23.49%	Oswego, NY	21.88%
Franklin, VT	22.48%	Somerset, ME	21.84%
Orleans, VT	22.37%	Allegany, NY	21.81%
Wyoming, PA	22.33%	Tioga, NY	21.75%
Cattaraugus, NY	21.92%	Caledonia, VT	21.67%

School–Age Population

	10.94 to 16.99%
	17.00 to 19.99%
	20.00 to 22.99%
	23.00 to 25.99%
	26.00 to 33.83%

Major Cities

Chicago, IL	19.03%
Cleveland, OH	18.14%
Cincinnati, OH	19.55%
Columbus, OH	18.50%
Detroit, MI	20.44%
Indianapolis, IN	18.88%
Kansas City, MO	19.10%
Milwaukee, WI	19.15%
Minneapolis, MN	16.80%
Omaha, NE	20.24%
St. Louis, MO	18.68%
Wichita, KS	20.44%

Top 10 Counties

Buffalo, SD	33.83%	Sioux, ND	32.65%	Dewey, SD	29.22%	Corson, SD	28.58%
Shannon, SD	33.11%	Ziebach, SD	32.34%	Haakon, SD	28.93%		
Todd, SD	32.91%	Menominee, WI	30.18%	Rolette, ND	28.74%		

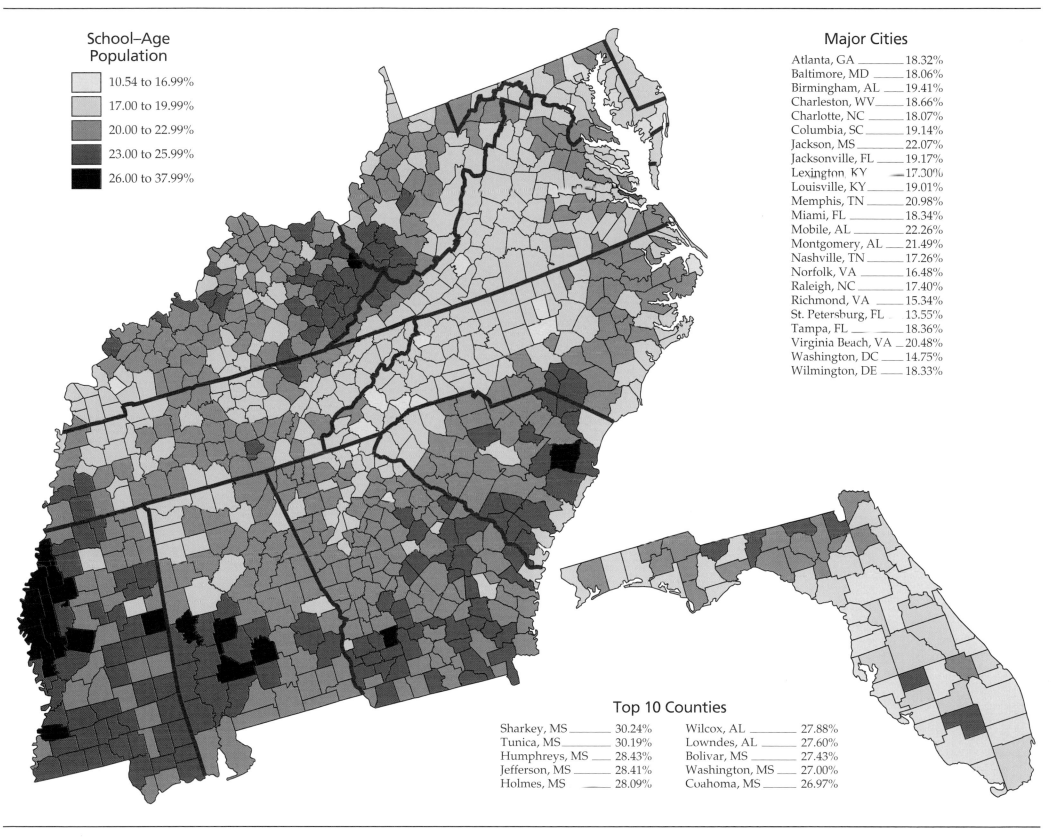

School–Age Population

☐	10.54 to 16.99%
☐	17.00 to 19.99%
☐	20.00 to 22.99%
☐	23.00 to 25.99%
■	26.00 to 37.99%

Major Cities

Atlanta, GA	18.32%
Baltimore, MD	18.06%
Birmingham, AL	19.41%
Charleston, WV	18.66%
Charlotte, NC	18.07%
Columbia, SC	19.14%
Jackson, MS	22.07%
Jacksonville, FL	19.17%
Lexington, KY	17.30%
Louisville, KY	19.01%
Memphis, TN	20.98%
Miami, FL	18.34%
Mobile, AL	22.26%
Montgomery, AL	21.49%
Nashville, TN	17.26%
Norfolk, VA	16.48%
Raleigh, NC	17.40%
Richmond, VA	15.34%
St. Petersburg, FL	13.55%
Tampa, FL	18.36%
Virginia Beach, VA	20.48%
Washington, DC	14.75%
Wilmington, DE	18.33%

Top 10 Counties

Sharkey, MS	30.24%	Wilcox, AL	27.88%
Tunica, MS	30.19%	Lowndes, AL	27.60%
Humphreys, MS	28.43%	Bolivar, MS	27.43%
Jefferson, MS	28.41%	Washington, MS	27.00%
Holmes, MS	28.09%	Coahoma, MS	26.97%

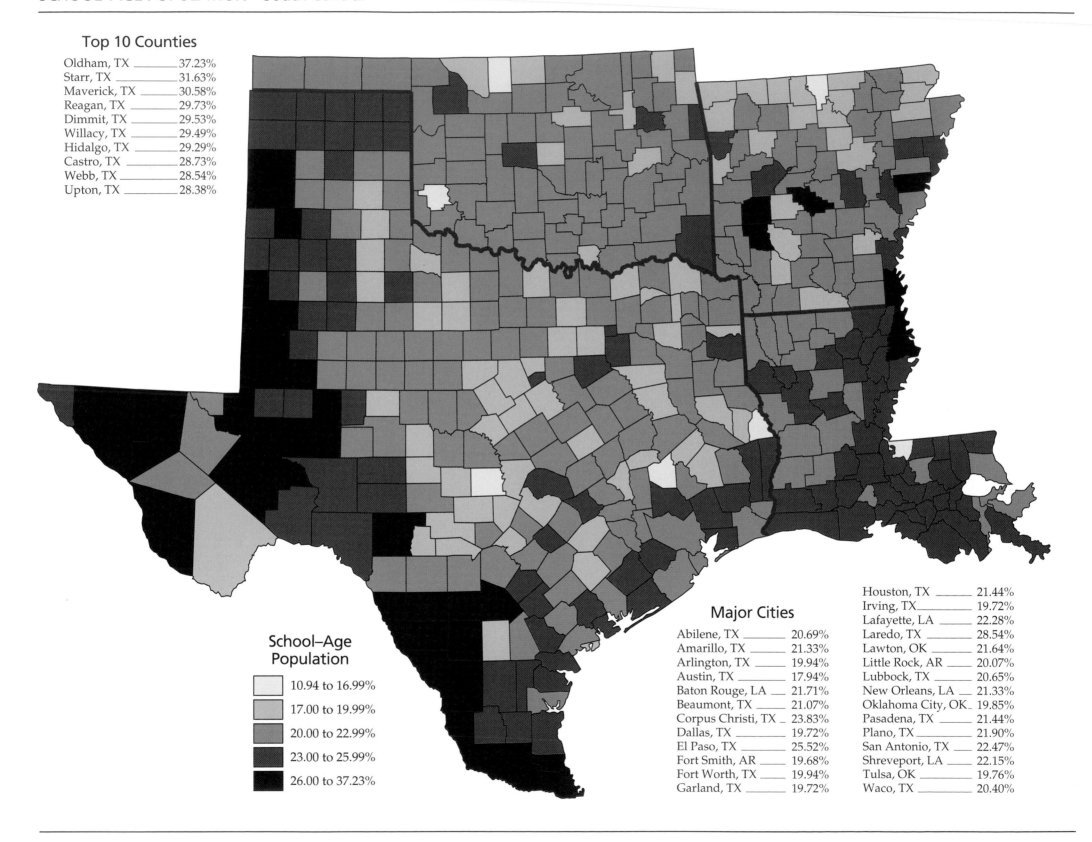

Top 10 Counties

County	Percentage
Oldham, TX	37.23%
Starr, TX	31.63%
Maverick, TX	30.58%
Reagan, TX	29.73%
Dimmit, TX	29.53%
Willacy, TX	29.49%
Hidalgo, TX	29.29%
Castro, TX	28.73%
Webb, TX	28.54%
Upton, TX	28.38%

School–Age Population

Color	Range
	10.94 to 16.99%
	17.00 to 19.99%
	20.00 to 22.99%
	23.00 to 25.99%
	26.00 to 37.23%

Major Cities

City	Percentage	City	Percentage
Abilene, TX	20.69%	Houston, TX	21.44%
Amarillo, TX	21.33%	Irving, TX	19.72%
Arlington, TX	19.94%	Lafayette, LA	22.28%
Austin, TX	17.94%	Laredo, TX	28.54%
Baton Rouge, LA	21.71%	Lawton, OK	21.64%
Beaumont, TX	21.07%	Little Rock, AR	20.07%
Corpus Christi, TX	23.83%	Lubbock, TX	20.65%
Dallas, TX	19.72%	New Orleans, LA	21.33%
El Paso, TX	25.52%	Oklahoma City, OK	19.85%
Fort Smith, AR	19.68%	Pasadena, TX	21.44%
Fort Worth, TX	19.94%	Plano, TX	21.90%
Garland, TX	19.72%	San Antonio, TX	22.47%
		Shreveport, LA	22.15%
		Tulsa, OK	19.76%
		Waco, TX	20.40%

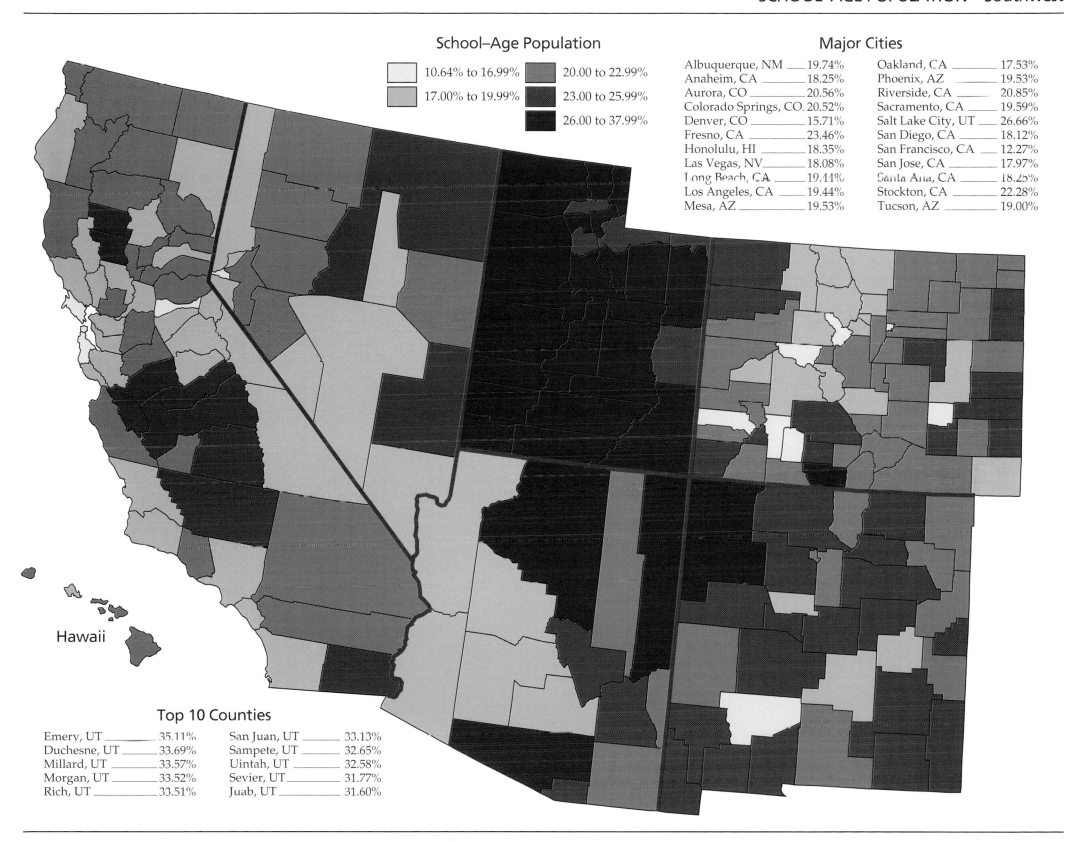

School–Age Population

10.64% to 16.99%	20.00 to 22.99%
17.00% to 19.99%	23.00 to 25.99%
	26.00 to 37.99%

Major Cities

Albuquerque, NM	19.74%	Oakland, CA	17.53%
Anaheim, CA	18.25%	Phoenix, AZ	19.53%
Aurora, CO	20.56%	Riverside, CA	20.85%
Colorado Springs, CO	20.52%	Sacramento, CA	19.59%
Denver, CO	15.71%	Salt Lake City, UT	26.66%
Fresno, CA	23.46%	San Diego, CA	18.12%
Honolulu, HI	18.35%	San Francisco, CA	12.27%
Las Vegas, NV	18.08%	San Jose, CA	17.97%
Long Beach, CA	19.11%	Santa Ana, CA	18.25%
Los Angeles, CA	19.44%	Stockton, CA	22.28%
Mesa, AZ	19.53%	Tucson, AZ	19.00%

Hawaii

Top 10 Counties

Emery, UT	35.11%	San Juan, UT	33.13%
Duchesne, UT	33.69%	Sampete, UT	32.65%
Millard, UT	33.57%	Uintah, UT	32.58%
Morgan, UT	33.52%	Sevier, UT	31.77%
Rich, UT	33.51%	Juab, UT	31.60%

155

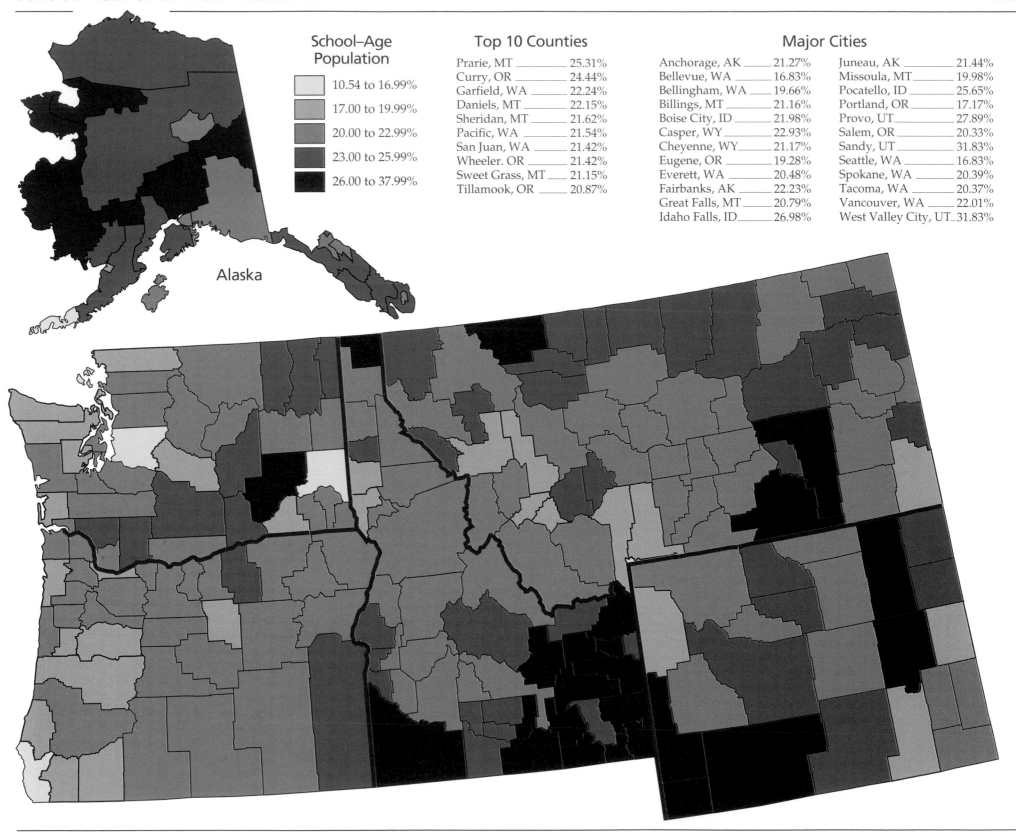

School–Age Population

- 10.54 to 16.99%
- 17.00 to 19.99%
- 20.00 to 22.99%
- 23.00 to 25.99%
- 26.00 to 37.99%

Alaska

Top 10 Counties

County	%
Prarie, MT	25.31%
Curry, OR	24.44%
Garfield, WA	22.24%
Daniels, MT	22.15%
Sheridan, MT	21.62%
Pacific, WA	21.54%
San Juan, WA	21.42%
Wheeler. OR	21.42%
Sweet Grass, MT	21.15%
Tillamook, OR	20.87%

Major Cities

City	%	City	%
Anchorage, AK	21.27%	Juneau, AK	21.44%
Bellevue, WA	16.83%	Missoula, MT	19.98%
Bellingham, WA	19.66%	Pocatello, ID	25.65%
Billings, MT	21.16%	Portland, OR	17.17%
Boise City, ID	21.98%	Provo, UT	27.89%
Casper, WY	22.93%	Salem, OR	20.33%
Cheyenne, WY	21.17%	Sandy, UT	31.83%
Eugene, OR	19.28%	Seattle, WA	16.83%
Everett, WA	20.48%	Spokane, WA	20.39%
Fairbanks, AK	22.23%	Tacoma, WA	20.37%
Great Falls, MT	20.79%	Vancouver, WA	22.01%
Idaho Falls, ID	26.98%	West Valley City, UT	31.83%

Maine

Aroostook

Piscataquis

Penobscot

Somerset

Washington

Franklin

Grand Isle

Franklin

Orleans

Essex

Coos

Oxford

Hancock

Waldo

Clinton

Lamoille

Kennebec

Knox

St. Lawrence

Chittenden

Washington

Caledonia

Lincoln

Sagadahoc

Franklin

Essex

Vermont

Addison

Orange

Grafton

Carroll

Cumberland

Jefferson

New Hampshire

New York

Lewis

Hamilton

Warren

Windsor

Belknap

York

Rutland

Oswego

Harkimer

Fulton

Saratoga

Bennington

Windham

Sullivan

Merrimack

Strafford

Oneida

Washington

Rockingham

Niagara

Orleans

Monroe

Wayne

Hillsborough

Genesee

Onondaga

Madison

Montgomery

Schenectady

Cheshire

Erie

Ontario

Cayuga

Albany

Rensselaer

Franklin

Essex

Wyoming

Livingston

Yates

Cortland

Schoharie

Worcester

Middlesex

Massachusetts

Seneca

Chenango

Berkshire

Hampshire

Suffolk

Schuyler

Tompkins

Otsego

Columbia

Norfolk

Chautauqua

Cattaraugus

Allegany

Steuben

Delaware

Greene

Hampden

Plymouth

Chemung

Tioga

Broome

Windham

Providence

Bristol

Erie

Ulster

Litchfield

Hartford

Tolland

Barnstable

Warren

McKean

Potter

Tioga

Bradford

Susquehanna

Wayne

Sullivan

Dutchess

Connecticut

Kent

Newport

Crawford

Forest

Elk

Cameron

Sullivan

Wyoming

Lackawanna

Putnam

New London

Dukes

Nantucket

Mercer

Venango

Clinton

Lycoming

Luzerne

Pika

Orange

Fairfield

New Haven

Middlesex

Washington

Rhode Island

Lawrence

Clarion

Jefferson

Clearfield

Centre

Union

Monroe

Carbon

Westchester

Suffolk

Butler

Armstrong

Indiana

Pennsylvania

Mifflin

Snyder

Northumberland

Northampton

Warren

Morris

Rockland

Bergen

Bronx

Nassau

Beaver

Cambria

Blair

Juniata

Schuylkill

Lehigh

Hunterdon

Essex

New York

Queens

Allegheny

Perry

Dauphin

Lebanon

Berks

Bucks

Somerset

Union

Hudson

Kings

Richmond

Westmoreland

Huntingdon

Mercer

Middlesex

Washington

Bedford

Fulton

Cumberland

Lancaster

Chester

Montgomery

Monmouth

Fayette

Somerset

Franklin

Adams

York

Delaware

Philadelphia

Burlington

Ocean

New Jersey

Greene

Camden

Gloucester

Salem

Atlantic

Cumberland

Cape May

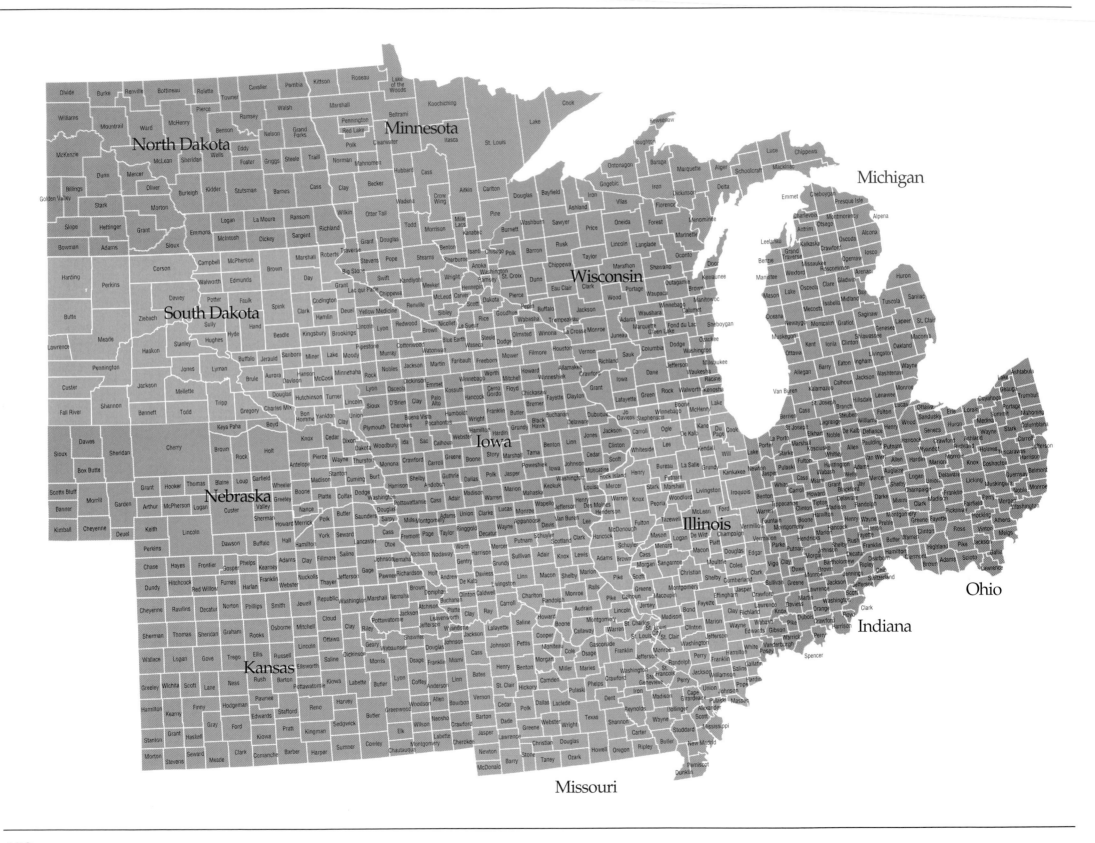

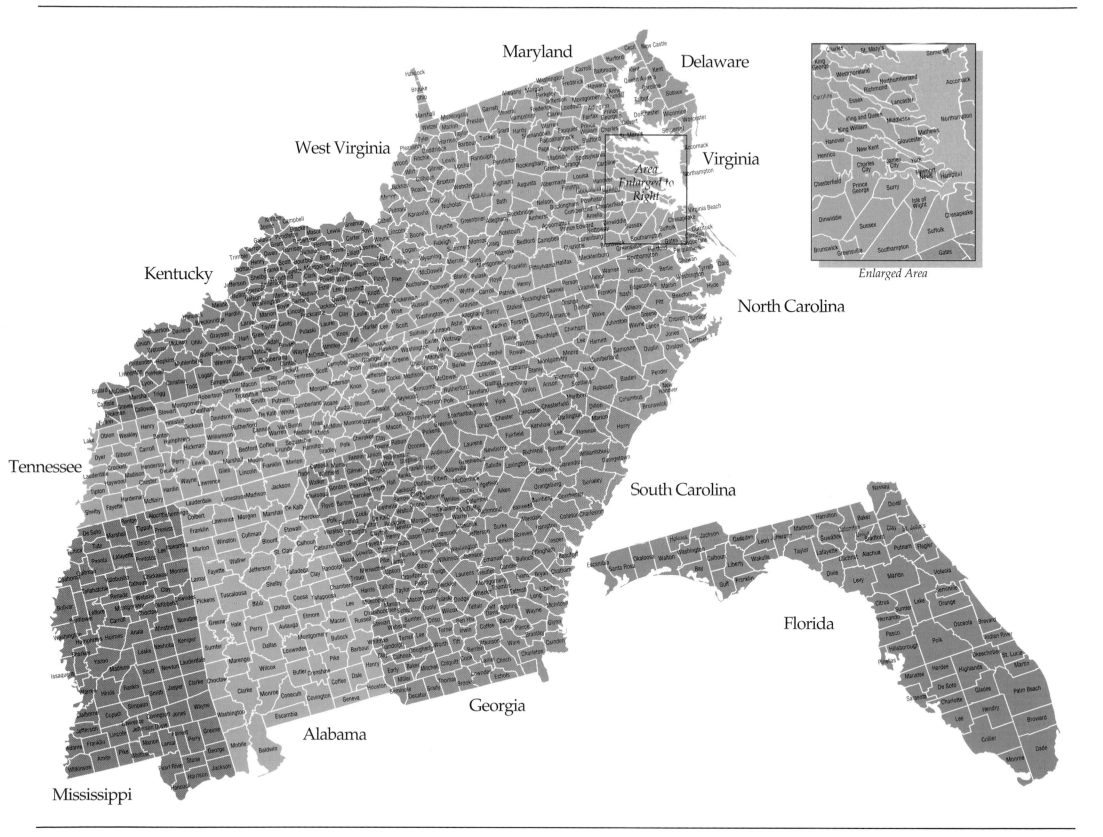

Maryland

Delaware

West Virginia

Virginia

Kentucky

Area Enlarged to Right

North Carolina

Enlarged Area

Tennessee

South Carolina

Florida

Georgia

Alabama

Mississippi

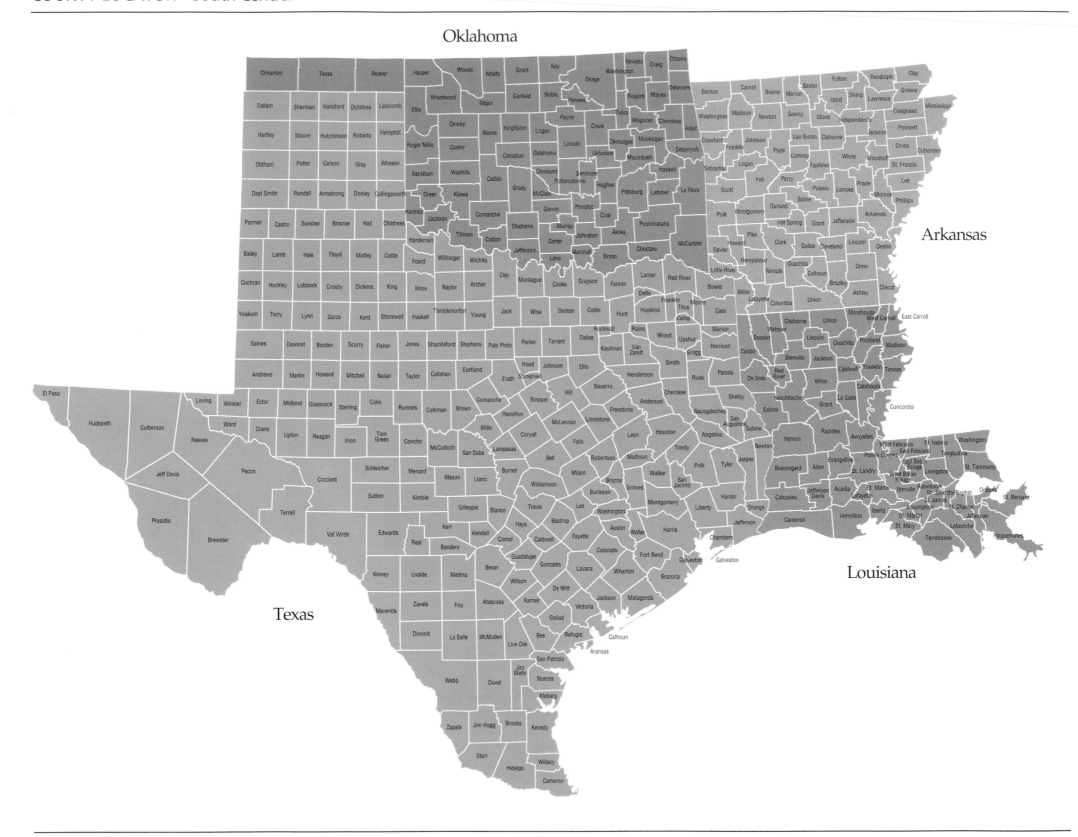

Oklahoma

Arkansas

Louisiana

Texas

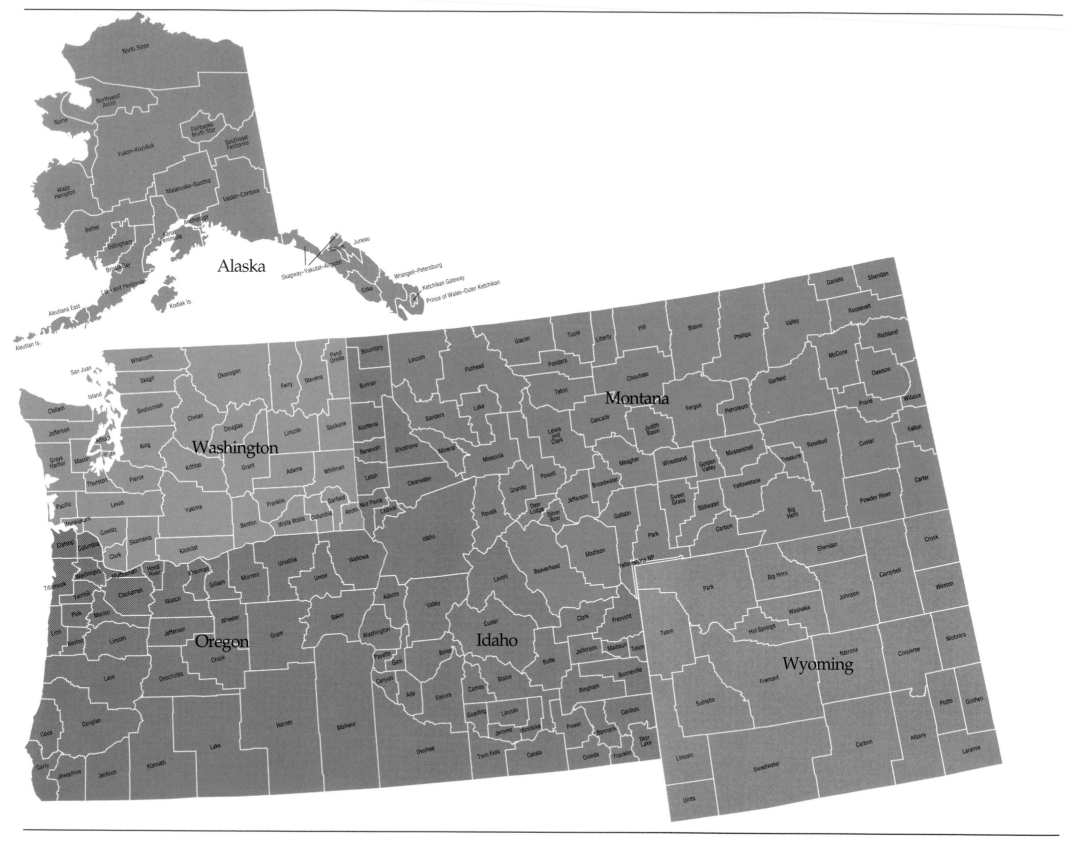

Alaska

North Slope

Northwest
Arctic

Fairbanks
North Star

Nome

Yukon–Koyukuk

Southeast
Fairbanks

Wade
Hampton

Matanuska–Susitna

Valdez–Cordova

Bethel

Kenai
Peninsula

Anchorage

Dillingham

Juneau

Haines

Bristol Bay

Skagway–Yakutat–Angoon

Wrangell–Petersburg

Lake and Peninsula

Sitka

Ketchikan Gateway

Aleutians East

Kodiak Is.

Prince of Wales–Outer Ketchikan

Aleutian Is.

Washington

San Juan

Whatcom

Okanogan

Boundary

Pend
Oreille

Ferry

Stevens

Lincoln

Skagit

Island

Clallam

Snohomish

Chelan

Douglas

Spokane

Jefferson

Kitsap

King

Lincoln

Grant

Mason

Pierce

Kittitas

Adams

Whitman

Grays
Harbor

Thurston

Pierce

Yakima

Franklin

Garfield

Columbia

Asotin

Pacific

Lewis

Benton

Walla Walla

Wahkiakum

Cowlitz

Skamania

Klickitat

Clatsop

Columbia

Clark

Hood
River

Sherman

Gilliam

Morrow

Umatilla

Union

Tillamook

Washington

Multnomah

Wasco

Wallowa

Yamhill

Clackamas

Wheeler

Grant

Baker

Polk

Marion

Jefferson

Oregon

Crook

Washington

Linn

Lincoln

Deschutes

Payette

Gem

Benton

Lane

Ada

Harney

Malheur

Owyhee

Coos

Douglas

Lake

Josephine

Jackson

Klamath

Curry

Idaho

Boundary

Bonner

Kootenai

Benewah

Shoshone

Latah

Clearwater

Nez Perce

Lewis

Idaho

Adams

Valley

Custer

Lemhi

Clark

Fremont

Boise

Butte

Jefferson

Madison

Teton

Canyon

Camas

Blaine

Bonneville

Elmore

Bingham

Gooding

Lincoln

Caribou

Jerome

Minidoka

Power

Bannock

Twin Falls

Cassia

Oneida

Franklin

Bear
Lake

Montana

Glacier

Toole

Liberty

Hill

Blaine

Phillips

Valley

Daniels

Sheridan

Roosevelt

Pondera

Flathead

Teton

Choteau

Richland

McCone

Lewis
and
Clark

Cascade

Judith
Basin

Fergus

Petroleum

Garfield

Dawson

Prairie

Wibaux

Sanders

Lake

Meagher

Wheatland

Golden
Valley

Musselshell

Rosebud

Custer

Fallon

Mineral

Missoula

Powell

Broadwater

Sweet
Grass

Stillwater

Treasure

Carter

Granite

Deer
Lodge

Jefferson

Yellowstone

Big
Horn

Powder River

Ravalli

Silver
Bow

Gallatin

Park

Carbon

Beaverhead

Madison

Park

Yellowstone NP

Wyoming

Teton

Park

Big Horn

Sheridan

Campbell

Crook

Washakie

Johnson

Weston

Hot Springs

Teton

Fremont

Natrona

Niobrara

Converse

Sublette

Lincoln

Sweetwater

Carbon

Albany

Platte

Goshen

Uinta

Laramie

Metro Fact Finder

City/State	Population	%White	%Black	%Am Ind	%Asian	%Hisp	%65+
New York, NY	7,322,564	52.3	28.7	0.4	7.0	24.4	13.0
Los Angeles, CA	3,485,398	52.8	14.0	0.5	9.8	39.9	10.0
Chicago, IL	2,783,726	45.4	39.1	0.3	3.7	19.6	11.9
Houston, TX	1,630,553	52.7	28.1	0.3	4.1	27.6	8.3
Philadelphia, PA	1,585,577	53.5	39.9	0.2	2.7	5.6	15.2
San Diego, CA	1,110,549	67.1	9.4	0.6	11.8	20.7	10.2
Detroit, MI	1,027,974	21.6	75.7	0.4	0.8	2.8	12.2
Dallas, TX	1,006,877	55.3	29.5	20.5	2.2	20.9	9.7
Phoenix, AZ	983,403	81.7	5.2	1.9	1.7	20.0	9.7
San Antonio, TX	935,933	72.2	7.0	0.4	1.1	55.6	10.5
San Jose, CA	782,248	62.8	4.7	0.7	19.5	26.6	7.2
Baltimore, MD	736,014	39.1	59.2	0.3	1.1	1.0	13.7
Indianapolis, IN	731,327	75.8	22.6	0.2	0.9	1.1	11.4
San Francisco, CA	723,959	53.6	10.9	0.5	29.1	13.9	14.6
Jacksonville , FL	635,230	71.9	25.2	0.3	1.9	2.6	10.6
Columbus, OH	632,910	74.4	22.6	0.2	2.4	1.1	9.2
Milwaukee, WI	628,088	63.4	30.5	0.9	1.9	6.3	12.4
Memphis, TN	610,337	44.0	54.8	0.2	0.8	0.7	12.2
Wasington, DC	606,900	29.6	65.8	0.2	1.8	5.4	12.8
Boston, MA	574,283	62.8	25.6	0.3	5.3	10.8	11.5
Seattle, WA	516,259	75.3	10.1	1.4	11.8	3.6	15.2
El Paso, TX	515,342	76.9	3.4	0.4	1.2	69.0	8.7
Cleveland, OH	505,616	49.5	46.6	0.3	1.0	4.6	14.0
New Orleans, LA	496,938	34.9	61.9	0.2	1.9	3.5	13.0
Nashville, TN	488,374	73.8	24.3	0.2	1.4	0.9	11.4
Denver, CO	467,610	72.1	12.8	1.2	2.4	23.0	13.9
Austin, TX	465,622	70.6	12.4	0.4	3.0	23.0	7.4
Fort Worth, TX	447,619	63.8	22.0	0.4	2.0	19.5	11.2
Oklahoma City, OK	444,719	74.8	16.0	4.2	2.4	5.0	11.9
Portland, OR	437,319	84.6	7.7	1.2	5.3	3.2	14.6
Kansas City, MO	435,146	66.8	29.6	0.5	1.2	3.9	12.9
Long Beach, CA	429,433	58.4	13.7	0.6	13.6	23.6	10.8
Tucson, AZ	405,390	75.2	4.3	1.6	2.2	29.3	12.6
St. Louis, MO	396,685	50.9	47.5	0.2	0.9	1.3	16.6
Charlotte, NC	395,934	65.6	31.8	0.4	1.8	1.4	9.8
Atlanta, GA	394,017	31.0	67.1	0.1	0.9	1.9	11.3
Virginia Beach, VA	393,069	80.5	13.9	0.4	4.3	3.1	5.9
Albuquerque, NM	384,736	78.2	3.0	3.0	1.7	34.5	11.1
Oakland, CA	372,242	32.5	43.9	0.6	14.8	13.9	12.0
Pittsburgh, PA	369,879	72.1	25.8	0.2	1.6	0.9	17.9
Sacramento, CA	369,365	60.1	15.3	1.2	15.0	16.2	12.1
Minneapolis, MN	368,383	78.4	13.0	3.3	4.3	2.1	13.0
Tulsa, OK	367,302	79.3	13.6	4.7	1.4	2.6	12.7
Honolulu, HA	365,272	26.7	1.3	0.3	70.5	4.6	16.0
Cincinnati, OH	364,040	60.5	37.9	0.2	1.1	0.7	13.9
Miami, FL	358,548	65.6	27.4	0.2	0.6	62.5	16.6
Fresno, CA	354,202	59.2	8.3	1.1	12.5	29.9	10.1
Omaha, NE	335,795	83.9	13.1	0.7	1.0	3.1	12.9
Toledo, OH	332,943	77.0	19.7	0.3	1.0	4.0	13.6
Buffalo, NY	328,123	64.7	30.7	0.8	1.0	4.9	14.8
Wichita, KS	304,011	82.3	11.3	1.2	2.6	5.0	12.4
Santa Ana, CA	293,742	68.0	2.6	0.5	9.7	65.2	5.6
Mesa, AZ	288,091	90.1	1.9	1.0	1.5	10.9	12.4
Colorado Springs, CO	281,140	85.9	7.0	0.8	2.4	9.1	9.2
Tampa, FL	280,015	70.9	25.0	0.3	1.4	15.0	14.6
Newark, NJ	275,221	28.6	58.5	0.2	1.2	26.1	9.3
St. Paul, MN	272,235	82.3	7.4	1.4	7.1	4.2	13.7
Louisville, KY	269,063	69.2	29.7	0.2	0.7	0.7	16.6
Anaheim, CA	266,406	71.4	2.5	0.5	9.4	31.4	8.4
Birmingham, AL	265,968	36.0	63.3	0.1	0.6	0.4	14.8
Arlington, TX	261,721	82.6	8.4	0.5	3.9	8.9	5.0
Norfolk, VA	261,229	56.7	39.1	0.4	2.6	2.9	10.5
Las Vegas, NV	258,295	78.4	11.4	0.9	3.6	12.5	10.3
Corpus Christi, TX	257,453	76.1	4.8	0.4	0.9	50.4	10.1
St. Petersburg, FL	238,629	78.0	19.6	0.2	1.7	2.6	22.2
Rochester, NY	231,636	61.1	31.5	0.5	1.8	8.7	12.1
Jersey City, NJ	228,537	48.2	29.7	0.3	11.4	24.2	11.1
Riverside, CA	226,505	70.8	7.4	0.8	5.2	26.0	8.9
Anchorage, AL	226,338	80.7	6.4	6.4	4.8	4.1	3.6
Lexington-Fayette, KY	225,366	84.5	13.4	0.2	1.6	1.1	9.9
Akron, OH	223,019	73.8	24.5	0.3	1.2	0.7	14.9
Aurora, CO	222,103	82.4	11.4	0.6	3.8	6.6	6.8
Baton Rouge, LA	219,531	53.9	43.9	0.1	1.7	1.6	11.5
Stockton, CA	210,943	57.5	9.6	1.0	22.8	25.0	10.5
Raleigh, NC	207,951	69.2	27.6	0.3	2.5	1.4	8.8
Richmond, VA	203,056	43.4	55.2	0.2	0.9	0.9	15.4
Shreveport, LA	198,525	54.3	44.8	0.2	0.5	1.1	13.7
Jackson, MS	196,637	43.6	55.7	0.1	0.5	0.4	11.6
Mobile, AL	196,278	59.6	38.9	0.2	1.0	1.0	13.7
Des Moines, IA	193,187	89.2	7.1	0.4	2.4	2.4	13.4
Lincoln, NE	191,972	94.5	2.4	0.6	1.7	2.0	10.9
Madison, WI	191,262	90.7	4.2	0.4	3.9	2.0	9.3
Grand Rapids, MI	189,126	76.4	18.5	0.8	1.1	5.0	13.1

City/State	Population	%White	%Black	%Am Ind	%Asian	%Hisp	%65+
Yonkers, NY	188,082	76.2	14.1	0.2	3.0	16.7	16.4
Hialeah, FL	188,004	89.9	1.9	0.1	0.5	87.6	14.0
Montgomery, AL	187,106	56.5	42.3	0.2	0.7	0.8	11.7
Lubbock, TX	186,206	77.6	8.6	0.3	1.4	22.5	9.8
Greensboro, NC	183,521	63.9	33.9	0.5	1.4	1.0	11.8
Dayton, OH	182,044	58.4	40.4	0.2	0.6	0.7	13.1
Huntington Bea., CA	181,519	86.1	0.9	0.6	8.3	11.2	8.3
Garland, TX	180,650	79.7	8.9	0.5	4.5	11.6	5.5
Glendale, CA	180,038	74.0	1.3	0.3	14.1	21.0	13.3
Columbus, GA	178,681	58.9	38.1	0.3	1.4	3.0	10.8
Spokane, WA	177,196	93.3	1.9	2.0	2.1	2.1	16.2
Tacoma, WA	176,664	78.1	11.4	2.0	6.9	3.8	13.7
Bakersfield, CA	174,820	72.7	9.4	1.1	3.6	20.5	9.2
Fremont, CA	173,339	70.6	3.8	0.7	19.4	13.3	6.7
Fort Wayne, IN	173,072	80.5	16.7	0.3	1.0	2.7	13.3
Arlington, VA	170,936	76.6	10.5	0.3	6.8	13.5	11.4
Newport News, VA	170,045	62.6	33.6	0.3	2.3	2.8	9.3
Worcester, MA	169,759	87.1	4.5	0.3	2.8	9.6	16.1
Knoxville, TN	165,121	82.7	15.8	0.2	1.0	0.7	15.4
Modesto, CA	164,730	80.6	2.7	1.0	7.9	16.3	10.5
Orlando, FL	164,693	68.8	26.9	0.3	1.6	8.7	11.4
San Bernardino, CA	164,164	60.6	16.0	1.0	4.0	34.6	10.0
Syracuse, NY	163,860	75.0	20.3	1.3	2.2	2.9	14.9
Providence, RI	160,728	69.9	14.8	0.9	5.9	15.5	13.6
Salt Lake City, UT	159,936	87.0	1.7	1.6	4.7	9.7	14.5
Huntsville, AL	159,789	72.6	24.4	0.5	2.1	1.2	10.0
Amarillo, TX	157,615	82.7	6.0	0.8	1.9	14.7	12.0
Springfield, MA	156,983	68.6	19.2	0.2	1.0	16.9	13.7
Irving, TX	155,037	78.7	7.5	0.6	4.6	16.3	5.4
Chattanooga, TN	152,466	65.0	33.7	0.2	1.0	0.6	15.3
Chesapeake, VA	151,976	70.7	27.4	0.3	1.2	1.3	8.5
Kansas City, KS	149,767	65.0	29.3	0.7	1.2	7.1	13.0
Metairie, LA	149,428	91.6	4.9	0.2	1.8	6.2	14.1
Fort Lauderdale, FL	149,377	69.6	28.1	0.2	0.9	7.2	17.8
Glendale, AZ	148,134	85.0	3.0	0.9	2.1	15.5	7.9
Warren, MI	144,864	97.3	0.7	0.5	1.3	1.1	14.9
Winston-Salem, NC	143,485	59.5	39.3	0.2	0.8	0.9	14.2
Garden Grove, CA	143,050	67.3	1.5	0.6	20.5	23.5	8.7
Oxnard, CA	142,216	58.7	5.2	0.8	8.6	54.4	7.7
Tempe, AZ	141,865	86.8	3.2	1.3	4.1	10.9	6.6
Bridgeport, CT	141,686	58.5	26.6	0.3	2.3	26.5	13.6
Paterson, NJ	140,891	41.2	36.0	0.3	1.4	41.0	9.6
Flint, MI	140,761	49.6	47.9	0.7	0.5	2.9	10.7
Springfield, MO	140,494	95.7	2.5	0.7	0.9	1.0	15.2
Hartford, CT	139,739	40.0	38.9	0.3	1.4	31.6	9.9
Rockford, IL	139,426	81.1	15.0	0.3	1.5	4.2	14.7
Savannah, GA	137,560	46.8	51.3	0.2	1.1	1.4	13.8
Durham, NC	136,611	51.7	45.7	0.2	2.0	1.2	11.3
Chula Vista, CA	135,163	67.7	4.6	0.6	8.9	37.3	11.7
Reno, NV	133,850	86.1	2.9	1.4	4.9	11.1	11.8
Hampton, VA	133,793	58.4	38.9	0.3	1.7	2.0	9.6
Ontario, CA	133,179	64.6	7.3	0.7	3.9	41.7	6.4
Torrance, CA	133,107	73.0	1.5	0.4	21.9	10.1	11.9
Pomona, CA	131,723	57.0	14.4	0.6	6.7	51.3	7.0
Pasadena, CA	131,591	57.3	19.0	0.4	8.1	27.3	13.2
New Haven, CT	130,474	53.9	36.1	0.3	2.4	13.2	12.3
Scottsdale, AZ	130,069	96.0	0.8	0.6	1.2	4.8	16.3
Plano, TX	128,713	88.5	4.1	0.3	4.0	6.2	3.6
Oceanside, CA	128,398	74.7	7.9	0.7	6.1	22.6	14.0
Lansing, MI	127,321	73.9	18.6	1.0	1.8	7.9	9.6
Lakewood, CO	126,481	93.2	1.0	0.7	1.9	9.1	10.5
E. Los Angeles, CA	126,379	42.2	1.4	0.4	1.3	94.7	7.6
Evansville, IN	126,272	89.6	9.5	0.2	0.6	0.6	17.2
Boise City, ID	125,738	96.4	0.6	0.6	1.6	2.7	11.9
Tallahassee, FL	124,773	68.2	29.1	0.2	1.8	3.0	8.8
Paradise, NV	124,682	86.5	4.9	0.6	4.0	10.5	12.7
Laredo, TX	122,899	70.8	0.1	0.2	0.4	93.9	8.2
Hollywood, FL	121,697	88.2	8.5	0.2	1.3	11.9	23.1
Topeka, KS	119,883	84.7	10.6	1.3	0.8	5.8	14.7
Pasadena, TX	119,363	83.7	1.0	0.5	1.6	28.8	7.7
Moreno Valley, CA	118,779	67.4	13.8	0.7	6.6	22.9	4.0
Sterling Hgts, MI	117,810	96.3	0.4	0.2	2.9	1.1	9.2
Sunnyvale, CA	117,229	71.6	3.4	0.5	19.3	13.2	10.4
Gary, IN	116,646	16.3	80.6	0.2	0.2	5.7	11.4
Beaumont, TX	114,323	55.0	41.3	0.2	1.7	4.3	13.8
Fullerton, CA	114,144	74.7	2.2	0.5	12.2	21.3	10.2
Peoria, IL	113,504	76.5	20.9	0.2	1.7	1.6	14.4
Santa Rosa, CA	113,313	89.4	1.8	1.2	3.4	9.5	16.3
Eugene, OR	112,669	93.4	1.3	0.9	3.5	2.7	12.7
Independence, MO	112,301	96.2	1.4	0.6	1.0	2.0	14.4
Overland Park, KS	111,790	95.4	1.8	0.3	1.9	2.0	9.9
Hayward, CA	111,498	61.8	9.8	1.0	15.5	23.9	10.7
Concord, CA	111,348	84.0	2.4	0.7	8.7	11.5	9.5
Alexandria, VA	111,183	69.1	21.9	0.3	4.2	9.7	10.3
Orange, CA	110,658	83.0	1.4	0.5	7.9	22.8	8.7
Santa Clarita, CA	110,642	87.3	1.5	0.6	4.2	13.4	6.3
Irvine, CA	110,330	77.9	1.8	0.2	18.1	6.3	5.8

City/State	Population	%White	%Black	%Am Ind	%Asian	%Hisp	%65+
Elizabeth, NJ	110,002	65.5	19.8	0.3	2.7	39.1	12.1
Inglewood, CA	109,602	17.4	51.9	0.4	2.5	38.5	6.8
Ann Arbor, MI	109,592	82.0	9.0	0.4	7.7	2.6	7.2
Vallejo, CA	109,199	50.5	21.2	0.7	23.0	10.8	10.9
Waterbury, CT	108,961	79.6	13.0	0.3	0.7	13.4	16.5
Salinas, CA	108,777	54.6	3.0	0.9	8.1	50.6	8.3
Cedar Rapids, IA	108,751	95.5	2.9	0.2	1.0	1.1	13.2
Erie, PA	108,718	86.1	12.0	0.2	0.5	2.4	16.1
Escondido, CA	108,635	85.2	1.5	0.8	3.7	23.4	13.0
Stamford, CT	108,056	76.3	17.8	0.1	2.6	9.8	13.3
Salem, OR	107,786	91.2	1.5	1.6	2.4	6.1	14.5
Citrus Heights, CA	107,439	91.2	2.3	1.1	3.3	6.9	9.6
Abilene, TX	106,654	82.4	7.0	0.4	1.3	15.5	11.8
Macon, GA	106,612	47.1	52.2	0.1	0.4	0.6	14.6
El Monte, CA	106,209	62.2	1.0	0.6	11.8	72.5	6.4
South Bend, IN	105,511	76.0	20.9	0.4	0.9	3.4	16.8
Springfield, IL	105,227	85.6	13.0	0.2	1.0	0.8	14.9
Allentown, PA	105,090	86.2	5.0	0.2	1.3	11.7	16.9
Thousand Oaks, CA	104,352	90.4	1.2	0.4	4.8	9.6	9.0
Portsmouth, VA	103,907	51.2	47.3	0.3	0.8	1.3	13.9
Waco, TX	103,590	67.6	23.1	0.3	0.9	16.3	14.9
Lowell, MA	103,439	81.1	2.4	0.2	11.1	10.1	12.1
Berkeley, CA	102,724	62.1	18.8	0.6	14.8	8.4	11.0
Mesquite, TX	101,484	87.2	5.8	0.5	2.6	8.8	5.3
Ran. Cucamonga, CA	101,409	78.6	5.9	0.6	5.4	20.0	5.1
Albany, NY	101,082	75.5	20.6	0.3	2.3	3.1	15.3
Livonia, MI	100,850	98.0	0.3	0.2	1.3	1.3	13.1
Sioux Falls, SD	100,814	96.8	0.7	1.6	0.7	0.6	11.7
Simi Valley, CA	100,217	88.2	1.5	0.6	5.5	12.7	5.3
New Bedford, MA	99,922	87.6	4.1	0.4	0.4	6.7	17.4
Grand Prairie, TX	99,616	75.8	9.7	0.8	3.0	20.5	6.4
Aurora, IL	99,581	74.1	11.9	0.2	1.3	23.0	8.6
Manchester, NH	99,567	97.0	1.0	0.2	1.1	2.1	13.7
Brownsville, TX	98,962	84.8	0.2	0.1	0.3	90.1	8.7
Clearwater, FL	98,784	89.1	9.0	0.2	1.0	2.9	25.6
Pueblo, CO	98,640	83.0	2.2	0.8	0.6	39.5	16.0
Columbia, SC	98,052	53.7	43.7	0.3	1.4	2.0	11.8
Lancaster, CA	97,291	79.4	7.4	0.9	3.7	15.2	7.9
Green Bay, WI	96,466	94.2	0.5	2.5	2.3	1.1	12.6
Roanoke, VA	96,397	74.6	24.3	0.2	0.7	0.7	17.1
Costa Mesa, CA	96,357	84.3	1.3	0.5	6.6	20.0	8.2
Wichita Falls, TX	96,259	80.4	11.2	0.7	1.8	10.0	12.6
West Covina, CA	96,086	59.8	8.5	0.5	17.2	34.6	8.7
Cambridge, MA	95,802	75.3	13.5	0.3	8.4	6.8	10.5
Youngstown, OH	95,732	59.3	38.1	0.2	0.3	4.0	18.2
Sunrise Manor, NV	95,362	81.1	9.7	1.0	4.2	9.9	9.5
Davenport, IA	95,333	89.1	7.9	0.4	1.0	3.5	12.7
Lafayette, LA	94,440	70.8	27.2	0.2	1.3	1.7	9.5
Norwalk, CA	94,279	55.8	3.2	0.9	12.4	47.9	8.6
Burbank, CA	93,643	82.6	1.7	0.5	6.8	22.6	14.5
Santa Clara, CA	93,613	73.7	2.6	0.5	18.6	15.2	10.0
Brockton, MA	92,788	80.2	13.0	0.3	1.7	6.3	12.4
Fall River, MA	92,703	97.2	1.0	0.1	1.3	1.7	18.1
Miami Beach, FL	92,639	88.3	5.2	0.2	1.2	46.8	30.1
San Buenaventura, CA	92,575	86.1	1.7	1.1	2.7	17.6	12.5
Daly City, CA	92,311	39.5	7.7	0.4	43.8	22.4	10.5
Arden-Arcade, CA	92,040	89.1	3.9	1.0	4.0	6.9	16.0
Downey, CA	91,444	72.5	3.4	0.6	8.8	32.3	13.4
Chandler, AZ	90,533	85.2	2.6	1.2	2.4	17.3	5.0
Compton, CA	90,454	10.6	54.8	0.3	1.9	43.7	5.7
Odessa, TX	89,699	75.4	6.0	0.5	0.7	31.1	10.1
Midland, TX	89,443	79.8	9.1	0.4	1.0	21.3	9.4
Dearborn, MI	89,286	97.6	0.6	0.3	0.9	2.8	18.0
Arvada, CO	89,235	94.3	0.6	0.5	2.0	7.4	7.6
El Cajon, CA	88,693	87.4	2.9	1.0	2.8	14.0	10.9
Edison, NJ	88,680	79.5	5.6	0.1	13.7	4.3	10.7
Trenton, NJ	88,675	42.2	49.3	0.3	0.7	14.1	12.7
Parma, OH	87,876	97.9	0.7	0.1	1.1	0.9	19.1
Fort Collins, CO	87,758	93.3	1.0	0.5	2.4	7.1	7.7
Fontana, CA	87,535	67.7	8.7	0.9	4.5	36.1	5.5
Camden, NJ	87,492	19.0	56.4	0.4	1.3	31.2	8.4
Richmond, CA	87,425	36.2	43.8	0.6	11.8	14.5	11.3
Kendall, FL	87,271	89.9	4.7	0.1	3.0	31.4	9.4
West Valley City, UT	86,976	90.8	0.8	1.1	4.0	7.1	4.2
Santa Monica, CA	86,905	82.8	4.5	0.4	6.4	14.0	16.5
Bellevue, WA	86,874	86.5	2.2	0.4	9.9	2.5	10.4
Provo, UT	86,835	94.1	0.3	1.1	2.7	4.2	6.5
Bloomington, MN	86,335	94.7	1.6	0.3	3.1	0.9	10.3
South Gate, CA	86,284	41.6	1.7	0.4	1.6	83.1	7.3
Clinton, MI	85,866	95.4	3.0	0.3	1.1	1.2	10.8
Santa Barbara, CA	85,571	77.7	2.2	0.9	2.3	31.5	16.2
Duluth, MN	85,493	95.9	0.9	2.1	0.9	0.6	17.1
San Mateo, CA	85,486	78.6	3.6	0.4	13.3	15.5	16.3
Warwick, RI	85,427	98.0	0.8	0.2	0.8	1.0	16.8
Naperville, IL	85,351	92.6	2.1	0.1	4.8	1.8	5.6
Quincy, MA	84,985	91.7	1.1	0.2	6.6	1.4	16.7
Gainesville, FL	84,770	73.4	21.4	0.2	3.9	4.4	9.4

City/State	Population	%White	%Black	%Am Ind	%Asian	%Hisp	%65+
Westland, MI	84,724	94.7	3.3	0.6	1.0	1.9	10.8
San Angelo, TX	84,474	78.8	4.8	0.4	1.1	28.0	13.1
Cheektowaga, NY	84,387	98.3	1.1	0.1	0.4	0.5	18.7
Racine, WI	84,298	76.4	18.4	0.3	0.5	8.1	13.1
Hammond, IN	84,236	84.8	9.2	0.2	0.4	11.8	14.3
Canton, OH	84,161	80.7	18.2	0.5	0.3	1.1	16.4
McAllen, TX	84,021	70.9	0.3	0.2	0.7	77.0	10.4
Carson, CA	83,995	34.7	26.1	0.6	25.0	27.9	8.0
Decatur, IL	83,885	82.5	16.7	0.1	0.5	0.5	16.1
Boulder, CO	83,312	92.5	1.3	0.5	3.9	4.8	7.8
Newton, MA	82,585	92.8	2.1	0.1	4.6	2.0	14.9
Carrollton, TX	82,169	83.1	4.9	0.4	6.8	10.2	3.4
Alhambra, CA	82,106	40.9	2.0	0.4	38.1	36.1	13.0
Scranton, PA	81,805	97.2	1.6	0.1	0.9	0.7	21.9
Lynn, MA	81,245	83.1	8.1	0.3	3.7	9.1	15.1
Billings, MT	81,151	94.6	0.5	3.2	0.6	3.1	13.6
Lawton, OK	80,561	70.8	19.3	3.3	3.3	6.3	9.2
Sioux City, IA	80,505	92.6	2.3	2.0	1.5	3.3	14.7
Charleston, SC	80,414	57.2	41.6	0.1	0.9	0.8	12.8
Kenosha, WI	80,352	89.8	6.4	0.4	0.6	5.9	13.5
Kalamazoo, MI	80,277	77.3	18.8	0.6	1.9	2.7	10.9
Norman, OK	80,071	87.5	3.6	4.8	3.2	2.4	8.2
Nashua, NH	79,662	95.2	1.6	0.2	1.9	3.0	10.1
Coral Springs, FL	79,443	93.1	3.5	0.2	2.1	7.1	7.0
Reading, PA	78,380	78.6	9.7	0.1	1.4	18.5	16.6
Norwalk, CT	78,331	79.3	15.5	0.1	1.6	9.4	12.6
Albany, GA	78,122	44.2	55.0	0.2	0.4	0.8	10.8
Westminster, CA	78,118	69.6	1.1	0.6	22.5	19.1	9.4
Tuscaloosa, AL	77,759	62.8	35.5	0.1	1.3	0.8	11.7
Whittier, CA	77,671	73.4	1.3	0.6	3.3	39.0	13.9
Fairfield, CA	77,211	68.2	13.8	1.0	10.7	13.2	6.4
Elgin, IL	77,010	77.8	7.3	0.2	3.5	18.9	10.5
Joliet, IL	76,836	69.2	21.6	0.2	1.0	12.7	14.5
Alameda, CA	76,459	69.9	6.7	0.7	19.2	9.1	11.8
Somerville, MA	76,210	88.7	5.6	0.1	3.7	6.3	12.3
Corona, CA	76,095	75.9	2.8	0.8	7.1	30.4	5.8
Cranston, RI	76,060	95.1	2.4	0.2	1.8	2.0	18.6
Silver Spring, MD	76,046	65.2	22.7	0.3	5.5	13.0	14.4
Columbia, MD	75,883	75.8	18.5	0.2	4.8	2.5	4.7
Southfield, MI	75,728	67.9	29.1	0.3	2.4	1.7	17.0
Fayetteville, NC	75,695	57.6	38.3	1.3	1.5	3.1	10.7
Visalia, CA	75,636	74.8	1.5	1.0	6.4	25.1	11.1
Clarksville, TN	75,494	75.0	20.9	0.4	2.2	3.9	7.1
New Britain, CT	75,491	81.6	7.6	0.2	1.8	16.3	16.9
Arlington Heights, IL	75,460	94.8	0.6	0.1	3.7	2.7	12.2
Tyler, TX	75,450	66.1	28.2	0.3	0.5	8.9	14.8
Sandy, UT	75,058	97.1	0.2	0.3	1.7	2.5	3.5
Cape Coral, FL	74,991	97.5	1.0	0.2	0.6	3.7	22.0
Richardson, TX	74,840	86.8	4.7	0.3	6.6	4.3	7.5
Farmington Hills, MI	74,652	93.9	1.9	0.2	3.8	1.2	11.8
Westminster, CO	74,625	90.6	1.0	0.6	3.7	11.5	4.8
Fargo, ND	74,111	97.1	0.4	1.1	1.3	0.7	10.1
Lakewood, CA	73,557	81.1	3.7	0.7	9.4	14.6	12.1
East Orange, NJ	73,552	7.2	89.9	0.4	0.6	4.1	11.5
Evanston, IL	73,233	70.6	22.9	0.2	4.8	3.7	12.4
Troy, MI	72,884	91.5	1.3	0.2	6.8	1.3	8.4
Mission Viejo, CA	72,820	90.3	0.9	0.3	6.3	7.7	7.9
Pawtucket, RI	72,644	89.3	3.6	0.3	0.6	7.2	16.3
Pompano Beach, FL	72,411	70.0	28.5	0.1	0.6	5.4	25.2
Rialto, CA	72,388	57.9	20.4	0.9	3.5	31.5	6.6
Kenner, LA	72,033	77.4	18.1	0.3	1.7	10.1	6.6
Vista, CA	71,872	80.7	4.5	0.8	4.0	24.8	12.2
St. Joseph, MO	71,852	95.0	3.6	0.3	0.4	2.2	17.1
Clifton, NJ	71,742	92.8	1.4	0.1	3.5	6.8	20.9
Wilmington, DE	71,529	42.1	52.4	0.2	0.4	7.1	14.8
Vacaville, CA	71,479	78.8	8.9	1.0	3.8	15.9	6.8
Bethlehem, PA	71,428	87.6	2.9	0.1	1.7	13.0	17.2
Hawthorne, CA	71,349	42.3	28.3	0.5	11.0	31.1	7.3
Lorain, OH	71,245	78.2	13.8	0.4	0.3	16.9	13.4
Pontiac, MI	71,166	51.3	42.2	0.8	1.4	8.0	8.7
Muncie, IN	71,035	89.1	9.5	0.3	0.7	0.9	13.3
Taylor, MI	70,811	93.2	4.2	0.6	1.3	2.8	8.0
Rochester, MN	70,745	94.2	1.0	0.3	4.1	1.2	11.0
Lake Charles, LA	70,580	57.3	41.6	0.2	0.5	1.1	13.2
Lakeland, FL	70,576	78.1	20.2	0.2	0.9	3.3	22.9
Springfield, OH	70,487	81.6	17.4	0.2	0.5	0.6	15.4
Longview, TX	70,311	76.6	19.9	0.4	0.6	4.1	13.0
North Charleston, SC	70,218	62.7	34.3	0.5	1.6	2.5	5.9
Lawrence, MA	70,207	65.0	6.4	0.5	1.9	41.6	12.6
Everett, WA	69,961	91.7	1.7	1.7	3.9	2.8	13.0
Saginaw, MI	69,512	52.3	40.3	0.5	0.4	10.5	11.9
High Point, NC	69,496	68.1	30.2	0.5	0.9	0.8	14.1
Waukegan, IL	69,392	64.3	19.8	0.4	3.1	23.7	11.0
Baldwin Park, CA	69,330	55.6	2.4	0.7	12.3	70.8	5.6
Cherry Hill, NJ	69,319	89.8	3.2	0.1	6.1	2.0	14.1
Columbia, MO	69,101	85.1	9.9	0.3	4.1	1.3	8.7
Palmdale, CA	68,842	75.7	6.4	0.9	4.4	22.0	4.8
Buena Park, CA	68,784	70.9	2.5	0.7	14.4	24.5	8.0
Utica, NY	68,637	86.7	10.5	0.3	1.1	3.4	19.4
Schaumburg, IL	68,586	90.6	2.1	0.1	6.5	2.7	7.3
Gresham, OR	68,235	93.8	1.1	1.0	2.7	3.3	10.0
San Leandro, CA	68,223	74.1	5.8	0.7	13.8	15.2	19.3
St. Clair Shores, MI	68,107	98.7	0.2	0.3	0.6	0.9	18.6
Sandy Springs, GA	67,842	89.6	7.6	0.1	1.6	2.9	9.8
West Palm Beach, FL	67,643	63.4	32.6	0.1	0.9	14.2	18.2
Orem, UT	67,561	96.4	0.1	0.8	1.5	3.0	6.2
Federal Way, WA	67,554	86.7	4.0	0.9	7.2	3.3	6.2
Mountain View, CA	67,460	72.7	5.0	0.6	14.7	16.0	9.8
Cicero, IL	67,436	75.2	0.2	0.4	1.6	37.0	13.7
New Rochelle, NY	67,265	76.0	18.1	0.1	2.9	10.8	17.3
Mount Vernon, NY	67,153	39.8	55.3	0.4	1.8	7.8	14.9
Plantation, FL	66,692	90.7	6.2	0.1	1.8	8.1	14.4
Waterford, MI	66,692	96.9	1.1	0.6	0.7	2.3	9.7
Newport Beach, CA	66,643	95.8	0.3	0.3	2.9	4.0	15.5
Brick Township, NJ	66,473	97.8	0.6	0.1	0.8	2.6	17.3
Waterloo, IA	66,467	86.6	12.1	0.2	0.7	0.8	15.7
Redding, CA	66,462	92.6	1.1	2.2	3.3	4.0	14.5
Denton, TX	66,270	82.0	9.5	0.5	2.8	9.0	8.1
Redwood City, CA	66,072	82.8	3.6	0.5	6.3	24.1	11.5
Lynchburg, VA	66,049	72.5	26.4	0.2	0.8	0.7	16.4
Dundalk, MD	65,800	92.9	6.1	0.4	0.4	0.9	16.1
Appleton, WI	65,695	96.6	0.2	0.4	2.4	0.9	11.9
Largo, FL	65,674	97.6	1.0	0.2	0.8	1.9	32.4
Lawrence, KS	65,608	87.1	4.9	3.0	3.9	3.0	7.0
Danbury, CT	65,585	86.8	6.6	0.2	3.9	7.7	11.6
Schenectady, NY	65,566	88.6	8.7	0.3	1.1	2.7	17.1
Pembroke Pines, FL	65,452	91.3	5.3	0.2	2.0	11.5	19.4
Royal Oak, MI	65,410	97.9	0.5	0.2	1.1	1.1	15.7
Tonawanda, NY	65,284	97.9	0.7	0.2	1.0	0.8	20.0
Framingham, MA	64,994	90.1	3.7	0.2	2.9	8.1	12.3
Henderson, NV	64,942	91.4	2.7	1.0	2.0	8.1	8.3
Sunrise, FL	64,407	89.3	7.4	0.1	1.9	8.6	23.0
Portland, ME	64,358	96.6	1.1	0.4	1.7	0.8	15.0
Ogden, UT	63,909	87.4	2.7	1.1	1.8	12.0	14.6
Wyoming, MI	63,891	93.5	2.7	0.5	1.5	3.5	9.7
Baytown, TX	63,850	73.0	12.0	0.3	0.8	23.2	9.7
Killeen, TX	63,535	58.1	30.1	0.5	5.8	14.0	4.0
Champaign, IL	63,502	80.7	14.2	0.2	4.1	1.9	8.2
Upland, CA	63,374	78.9	5.3	0.5	7.0	17.5	9.2
Olathe, KS	63,352	94.3	3.0	0.4	1.7	1.8	5.2
West Allis, WI	63,221	98.2	0.3	0.5	0.6	1.5	17.9
Carlsbad, CA	63,126	89.8	1.2	0.5	3.2	13.8	13.1
Bethesda, MD	62,936	89.3	3.0	0.1	6.6	5.9	18.5
El Toro, CA	62,685	85.6	1.8	0.4	9.2	10.3	6.9
Palm Bay, FL	62,632	89.3	7.5	0.3	1.8	5.3	11.4
Antioch, CA	62,195	85.4	2.6	1.1	4.8	15.6	7.6
Las Cruces, NM	62,126	88.2	1.9	0.9	1.1	46.9	11.3
Lynwood, CA	61,945	24.0	23.7	0.4	2.2	70.3	5.1
Daytona Beach, FL	61,921	67.4	30.7	0.2	1.1	2.5	21.4
Napa, CA	61,842	90.3	0.4	0.8	2.1	15.2	14.9
Niagara Falls, NY	61,840	82.2	15.6	1.6	0.3	1.2	19.2
Bellflower, CA	61,815	69.8	6.3	0.9	10.1	23.9	10.8
Rochester Hills, MI	61,766	95.0	1.4	0.2	3.2	1.4	8.7
Asheville, NC	61,607	79.1	19.8	0.3	0.6	0.9	20.1
Boca Raton, FL	61,492	94.4	2.9	0.1	1.9	5.6	21.5
Bayonne, NJ	61,444	90.4	4.7	0.1	1.8	9.5	18.7
Hamilton, OH	61,368	91.9	7.3	0.2	0.4	0.5	14.2
Santa Maria, CA	61,284	61.6	2.2	0.9	6.1	45.7	12.0
Town 'n' Country, FL	60,946	90.5	4.3	0.2	2.1	17.9	9.0
Dearborn Heights, MI	60,838	97.3	0.5	0.4	1.3	2.3	16.8
Monterey Park, CA	60,738	26.7	0.6	0.3	57.5	31.3	13.8
Bristol, CT	60,640	96.0	2.1	0.2	0.8	2.7	13.6
Bloomington, IN	60,633	91.2	4.0	0.2	4.0	1.6	6.9
Walnut Creek, CA	60,569	90.6	1.0	0.3	6.7	4.7	22.8
Kettering, OH	60,569	97.8	0.7	0.1	1.2	0.8	16.9
Greeley, CO	60,536	89.1	0.7	0.6	1.0	20.4	11.2
Redlands, CA	60,394	79.6	3.8	0.7	4.4	19.0	11.9
Redondo Beach, CA	60,167	87.0	1.6	0.5	6.8	11.5	7.2
West Hartford, CT	60,110	94.0	2.2	0.1	2.8	3.1	22.1
Irvington, NJ	59,774	22.6	69.9	0.2	2.2	10.6	9.4
Iowa City, IA	59,738	91.1	2.5	0.2	5.6	1.7	6.6
Lakewood, OH	59,718	97.5	0.8	0.2	1.0	1.5	13.5
Chino, CA	59,682	67.3	9.8	0.5	3.4	36.2	5.0
Melbourne, FL	59,646	87.4	9.5	0.3	2.1	3.5	17.0
Montebello, CA	59,564	47.0	1.0	0.5	15.1	67.6	11.9
Meriden, CT	59,479	89.7	4.3	0.2	0.7	13.7	14.7
Anderson, IN	59,459	84.9	14.2	0.3	0.4	0.6	16.1
Skokie, IL	59,432	81.2	2.2	0.1	15.6	4.1	20.7
Pico Rivera, CA	59,177	58.8	0.7	0.6	3.2	83.2	9.6
Galveston, TX	59,070	61.5	29.1	0.2	2.3	21.4	13.5
Port Arthur, TX	58,724	49.3	42.2	0.3	4.8	8.2	17.1
Lakewood, WA	58,412	74.5	12.7	1.4	9.5	5.5	10.7
Greenville, SC	58,282	63.6	35.2	0.1	0.8	1.0	15.9
Pensacola, FL	58,165	65.7	31.9	0.5	1.6	1.6	16.4
Broken Arrow, OK	58,043	91.7	3.1	3.6	1.0	2.1	5.5
Passaic, NJ	58,041	45.3	20.6	0.5	7.1	50.0	10.4
Union City, NJ	58,012	74.7	5.1	0.2	2.1	75.6	10.0
Brandon, FL	57,985	93.0	3.8	0.3	1.7	6.9	7.7
Waltham, MA	57,878	91.4	3.1	0.1	3.6	5.6	13.1
Burke, VA	57,734	85.5	4.1	0.2	9.0	4.6	2.6
Dubuque, IA	57,546	98.4	0.6	0.1	0.6	0.6	16.0
Terre Haute, IN	57,483	88.6	9.4	0.4	1.1	1.3	16.9
Medford, MA	57,407	93.4	4.1	0.1	2.0	1.7	16.8
Charleston, WV	57,287	84.1	14.2	0.2	1.3	0.6	18.4
Florence-Graham, CA	57,147	20.4	24.0	0.3	0.4	77.2	5.5
Canton, MI	57,047	92.9	2.0	0.3	4.5	1.4	4.8
Waukesha, WI	56,958	95.4	0.6	0.3	1.3	5.9	9.8
Eau Claire, WI	56,856	95.1	0.4	0.6	3.8	0.6	12.7
Elyria, OH	56,746	85.0	13.7	0.2	0.5	1.5	11.8
Livermore, CA	56,741	89.4	1.5	0.7	4.6	9.8	7.1
Chicopee, MA	56,632	95.4	1.8	0.1	0.6	3.6	17.2
Brooklyn Park, MN	56,381	90.6	4.9	0.6	3.4	1.2	3.3
Merced, CA	56,216	61.7	6.9	0.9	15.2	29.9	9.0
Oak Lawn, IL	56,182	98.3	0.1	0.1	1.1	2.4	20.2
Huntington Park, CA	56,065	31.2	1.1	0.5	1.8	91.9	5.6
South Augusta, GA	55,998	48.2	48.8	0.3	1.9	2.0	8.4
Palo Alto, CA	55,900	84.9	2.9	0.3	10.4	5.0	15.5
Port St. Lucie, FL	55,866	94.2	3.8	0.2	0.9	4.0	17.2
Santa Fe, NM	55,859	81.2	0.6	2.2	0.6	47.4	12.8
Lancaster, PA	55,551	70.9	12.2	0.2	2.0	20.6	12.2
Wilmington, NC	55,530	64.9	33.9	0.3	0.6	0.9	15.9
Encinitas, CA	55,386	89.4	0.6	0.4	2.9	15.2	9.1
Levittown, PA	55,362	97.4	1.4	0.1	0.8	1.2	11.1
Spring Valley, CA	55,331	73.6	8.5	0.8	7.9	18.9	8.4
Great Falls, MT	55,097	93.1	1.0	4.6	0.8	1.7	14.5
Victoria, TX	55,076	76.9	7.9	0.3	0.4	37.9	11.4
Thornton, CO	55,031	89.7	1.3	0.9	1.7	16.9	5.3
Oshkosh, WI	55,006	96.3	0.8	0.5	2.2	0.8	14.1
Bryan, TX	55,002	69.9	17.2	0.2	1.5	19.8	9.8
Yuma, AZ	54,923	73.0	3.8	1.1	1.7	35.6	12.0
Monroe, LA	54,909	43.3	55.6	0.1	0.8	0.8	13.4
Euclid, OH	54,875	82.9	16.0	0.1	0.9	0.8	22.2
Huntington, WV	54,844	92.5	6.7	0.1	0.5	0.5	19.9
West Bloomfield, MI	54,843	92.5	2.0	0.1	5.2	1.2	9.8
Yakima, WA	54,827	82.5	2.4	2.0	1.3	16.3	16.4
Vineland, NJ	54,780	73.0	11.5	0.3	0.9	23.6	14.1
Gastonia, NC	54,732	74.0	24.9	0.2	0.7	0.5	14.4
Brookline, MA	54,718	87.4	3.1	0.1	8.4	2.9	15.4
St. Charles, MO	54,555	95.9	2.8	0.3	0.7	1.0	9.9
Rapid City, SD	54,523	88.2	1.3	8.9	1.0	2.2	11.5
Redford, MI	54,387	98.1	0.7	0.4	0.6	1.5	16.5
Council Bluffs, IA	54,315	97.8	0.8	0.3	0.4	2.4	13.7
S. San Francisco, CA	54,312	61.5	4.0	0.7	24.6	27.1	11.4
Troy, NY	54,269	88.3	7.6	0.2	3.0	2.1	14.0
National City, CA	54,249	40.9	8.5	0.7	17.7	49.6	9.4
Weymouth, MA	54,063	97.6	1.0	0.1	0.9	1.0	13.8
Cleveland Hgts, OH	54,052	60.2	37.1	0.2	2.1	1.1	12.8
West Haven, CT	54,021	84.1	12.4	0.2	2.0	3.6	14.8
Malden, MA	53,884	89.4	4.2	0.2	5.2	2.6	15.3
Union City, CA	53,762	43.9	8.6	0.6	33.4	25.1	7.1
Wheat'n-Glenm't, MD	53,720	67.0	16.2	0.3	11.1	12.1	11.9
Fountain Valley, CA	53,691	78.2	0.9	0.6	17.7	8.1	7.3
Diamond Bar, CA	53,672	63.7	5.7	0.4	24.9	17.0	4.2
Oak Park, IL	53,648	77.0	18.3	0.1	3.3	3.6	11.5
Dothan, AL	53,589	71.5	27.3	0.3	0.8	0.7	12.7
Owensboro, KY	53,549	93.0	6.4	0.1	0.3	0.4	15.0
Battle Creek, MI	53,540	80.7	16.5	0.6	1.3	1.8	14.4
Sparks, NV	53,367	88.4	2.4	1.4	4.5	8.6	9.3
Carol City, FL	53,331	38.9	54.5	0.2	0.6	36.0	5.9
Beaverton, OR	53,310	89.4	1.0	0.5	7.7	3.3	9.1
Levittown, NY	53,286	97.4	0.3	0.1	1.8	4.1	10.8
Cerritos, CA	53,240	42.3	7.4	0.3	45.2	12.5	5.7
Des Plaines, IL	53,223	92.0	0.6	0.1	4.7	6.6	15.4
Mount Prospect, IL	53,170	90.2	1.1	0.1	6.4	6.4	11.9
Danville, VA	53,056	62.7	36.6	0.1	0.5	0.5	18.7
Binghamton, NY	53,008	91.9	4.9	0.3	2.1	1.8	19.1
Coon Rapids, MN	52,978	97.3	0.5	0.8	1.1	0.9	4.6
La Mesa, CA	52,931	90.2	3.0	0.5	3.1	9.8	18.3
Santee, CA	52,902	91.1	1.7	0.8	3.0	10.7	8.3
Bossier City, LA	52,721	79.3	18.1	0.4	1.5	2.6	8.9
College Station, TX	52,456	83.0	6.3	0.2	6.5	8.9	2.8
Yorba Linda, CA	52,422	85.7	1.1	0.4	10.1	9.4	5.0
Harrisburg, PA	52,376	42.6	50.6	0.3	1.8	7.7	13.0
Hacienda Heights, CA	52,354	59.1	2.1	0.6	27.3	32.0	7.7
Taylorsville-Bennion, UT	52,351	93.6	0.7	0.6	2.9	5.6	4.3
Irondequoit, NY	52,322	97.4	1.3	0.2	0.6	1.4	23.3
Edmond, OK	52,315	91.8	3.1	2.5	2.0	1.8	7.0
Camarillo, CA	52,303	86.3	1.6	0.5	6.3	12.1	16.7
Midwest City, OK	52,267	77.1	16.3	3.9	1.7	2.7	11.3
Bellingham, WA	52,179	93.8	0.8	1.8	2.8	2.4	14.1
Suffolk, VA	52,141	54.7	44.6	0.2	0.4	0.6	12.9

City/State	Population	%White	%Black	%Am Ind	%Asian	%Hisp	%65+
Janesville, WI	52,133	98.1	0.6	0.2	0.8	1.1	11.9
Bloomington, IL	51,972	90.9	6.7	0.2	1.5	1.6	12.0
Altoona, PA	51,881	98.0	1.5	0.1	0.3	0.4	18.6
Lodi, CA	51,874	89.3	0.3	0.9	4.7	16.9	15.7
Spring Valley, NV	51,726	89.3	3.1	0.5	5.1	6.9	9.1
Rosemead, CA	51,638	35.4	0.6	0.5	34.3	49.7	9.0
Longmont, CO	51,555	92.7	0.4	0.7	1.2	11.1	9.9
Wheaton, IL	51,464	93.0	2.5	0.1	3.8	2.0	9.3
Penn Hills, PA	51,430	83.9	15.5	0.1	0.4	0.5	16.3
Haverhill, MA	51,418	94.9	2.0	0.2	0.8	5.3	14.2
Roseville, MI	51,412	97.3	1.0	0.5	1.1	1.2	13.7
Burnsville, MN	51,288	94.8	2.3	0.3	2.3	1.0	3.9
La Habra, CA	51,266	76.6	0.9	0.7	4.1	33.9	10.7
Florissant, MO	51,206	95.0	4.1	0.2	0.5	1.0	13.9
La Crosse, WI	51,003	93.8	0.7	0.4	4.9	0.9	15.7
Annandale, VA	50,975	82.7	3.8	0.2	11.2	6.9	10.0
Sarasota, FL	50,961	82.0	16.2	0.2	0.7	4.7	25.2
Plymouth, MN	50,889	95.7	1.6	0.4	2.0	1.0	5.0
Deltona, FL	50,828	93.8	3.3	0.3	0.7	10.1	18.6
Warren, OH	50,793	77.9	21.3	0.2	0.3	0.7	16.9
Tustin, CA	50,689	73.2	5.7	0.5	10.4	20.7	7.5
Milpitas, CA	50,686	52.1	5.9	0.9	34.7	18.6	4.9
East Lansing, MI	50,677	84.6	6.9	0.3	7.0	2.5	4.5
Mansfield, OH	50,627	80.7	18.1	0.2	0.6	0.9	15.0
Peoria, AZ	50,618	86.9	2.2	0.6	1.4	15.5	14.9
Pleasanton, CA	50,553	90.7	1.4	0.4	5.8	6.7	5.4
East Hartford, CT	50,452	86.8	8.4	0.2	2.2	6.0	15.6
Hesperia, CA	50,418	85.7	2.5	0.9	1.4	19.0	11.3
East Providence, RI	50,380	92.1	4.4	0.5	0.6	1.7	18.9
Clovis, CA	50,323	83.2	1.7	1.4	5.5	16.3	7.9
Palm Harbor, FL	50,256	98.5	0.4	0.2	0.6	2.1	23.1
Union, NJ	50,024	86.5	9.4	0.1	3.3	4.5	21.6
Cheyenne, WY	50,008	89.6	3.1	0.7	1.2	11.8	12.0
North Miami, FL	49,998	62.4	31.9	0.2	2.4	24.6	15.1
Gardena, CA	49,847	32.2	23.5	0.5	33.2	23.1	10.9
Taunton, MA	49,832	95.3	2.0	0.2	0.5	4.7	14.1
Lauderhill, FL	49,708	58.6	38.5	0.1	1.5	6.8	21.3
Sheboygan, WI	49,676	94.4	0.2	0.4	3.9	2.5	17.0
South Whittier, CA	49,514	67.2	1.2	0.7	4.2	51.8	7.8
Hempstead, NY	49,453	32.4	58.8	0.5	1.7	19.1	8.5
Towson, MD	49,445	93.7	4.0	0.1	2.0	1.3	23.3
Grand Forks, ND	49,425	95.5	0.8	2.3	1.1	1.2	9.2
Stratford, CT	49,389	90.1	7.9	0.1	0.8	3.6	19.7
Johnson City, TN	49,381	93.1	5.9	0.2	0.7	0.6	15.9
Wauwatosa, WI	49,366	97.3	1.2	0.2	1.0	1.0	19.8
Alexandria, LA	49,188	49.6	49.3	0.2	0.7	1.0	14.3
Santa Cruz, CA	49,040	85.9	2.3	0.9	4.6	13.6	10.1
Rocky Mount, NC	48,997	49.6	49.6	0.2	0.4	0.5	13.1
Cuyahoga Falls, OH	48,950	98.1	1.1	0.1	0.6	0.4	15.3
Jackson, TN	48,949	59.1	40.3	0.1	0.4	0.5	15.5
St. Cloud, MN	48,812	96.8	1.0	0.6	1.3	0.6	10.2
Decatur, AL	48,761	82.4	16.5	0.3	0.6	0.8	12.0
Harlingen, TX	48,735	80.1	0.8	0.2	0.4	71.0	13.2
Rancho Cordova, CA	48,731	78.9	10.1	1.1	7.3	7.8	8.0
White Plains, NY	48,718	73.7	19.0	0.2	3.1	14.2	15.5
Carmichael, CA	48,702	92.3	2.2	0.8	3.2	5.0	13.7
Shelby, MI	48,655	98.0	0.3	0.3	1.2	1.0	7.4
Pittsfield, MA	48,622	95.5	3.1	0.2	0.8	1.1	17.3
Castro Valley, CA	48,619	85.9	2.9	0.5	8.6	9.2	15.0
Reston, VA	48,556	81.8	11.0	0.2	5.3	5.2	6.1
Kendale Lakes, FL	48,524	88.8	3.2	0.1	2.4	63.6	8.5
Parsipp'ny-Troy H., NJ	48,478	85.1	3.6	0.1	10.1	4.2	9.0
North Bergen, NJ	48,414	84.2	2.1	0.2	4.8	41.2	15.1
San Rafael, CA	48,404	83.5	2.9	0.3	5.5	14.4	13.9
Minnetonka, MN	48,370	97.1	0.9	0.2	1.6	0.8	9.8
Arcadia, CA	48,290	71.5	0.8	0.4	23.4	10.7	16.1
Milford, CT	48,168	96.8	1.5	0.1	1.0	2.3	13.9
Roswell, GA	47,923	92.2	4.9	0.1	1.8	2.7	6.9
West Seneca, NY	47,866	98.8	0.4	0.2	0.4	0.6	14.9
Glendora, CA	47,828	88.5	1.1	0.5	5.6	15.2	10.6
North Las Vegas, NV	47,707	45.2	37.4	1.0	2.4	22.2	6.8
Paramount, CA	47,669	48.2	10.7	0.7	5.8	60.8	6.2
Novato, CA	47,585	89.6	2.8	0.5	5.0	7.3	9.8
Pittsburg, CA	47,564	58.6	17.6	0.8	12.2	23.7	7.7
Wilkes-Barre, PA	47,523	96.1	2.9	0.1	0.6	0.7	21.0
Eagan, MN	47,409	93.7	2.4	0.3	3.1	1.3	2.1
Mentor, OH	47,358	98.6	0.3	0.1	0.9	0.6	9.4
Davie, FL	47,217	92.8	3.9	0.2	1.7	10.0	9.0
Ames, IA	47,198	89.9	2.4	0.1	6.9	1.6	6.8
Delray Beach, FL	47,181	72.0	26.3	0.1	0.7	6.1	31.7
Dale City, VA	47,170	76.6	17.5	0.4	4.0	5.3	1.9
Peabody, MA	47,039	96.8	1.2	0.0	1.1	2.9	14.1
Wayne, NJ	47,025	95.0	1.1	0.1	3.1	3.1	13.2
Medford, OR	46,951	94.8	0.3	1.2	1.2	5.1	17.4
Downers Grove, IL	46,858	93.2	1.7	0.1	4.2	2.4	12.2
Casper, WY	46,742	96.5	0.9	0.5	0.5	3.9	11.4
Laguna Hills, CA	46,731	91.1	1.0	0.3	6.3	5.8	39.6
Plainfield, NJ	46,567	26.5	65.7	0.5	1.1	15.0	9.9
Hoffman Estates, IL	46,561	87.2	2.9	0.2	8.0	5.5	4.3
Lewisville, TX	46,521	88.6	4.6	0.6	1.9	8.7	4.5
Lee's Summit, MO	46,418	96.9	1.7	0.3	0.6	1.0	10.9
Vancouver, WA	46,380	92.3	2.3	1.3	3.2	3.0	16.3
Deerfield Beach, FL	46,325	81.6	16.7	0.1	0.8	3.9	36.3
Biloxi, MS	46,319	74.6	18.6	0.3	5.7	2.8	11.4
Davis, CA	46,209	79.7	3.0	0.7	13.2	7.4	6.2
Boynton Beach, FL	46,194	77.7	20.1	0.1	0.6	6.8	30.3
Temple, TX	46,109	72.8	17.1	0.4	0.9	13.7	16.4
Pocatello, ID	46,080	94.1	0.9	1.4	1.3	4.5	10.9
Apple Valley, CA	46,079	86.8	3.9	1.0	2.5	12.6	9.9
Edina, MN	46,070	97.2	0.7	0.1	1.7	0.7	20.4
Middletown, OH	46,022	88.3	11.0	0.1	0.4	0.4	14.5
N. Richland Hills, TX	45,895	93.6	1.8	0.5	1.6	5.8	6.8
Flagstaff, AZ	45,857	79.6	2.5	9.2	1.4	15.2	4.3
St. Peters, MO	45,779	96.4	2.2	0.2	1.0	1.1	4.5
Athens, GA	45,734	66.4	29.6	0.1	3.3	1.6	10.2
Potomac, MD	45,634	84.4	3.7	0.1	11.1	5.4	8.5
Lima, OH	45,549	74.5	24.0	0.2	0.5	1.5	13.4
Aspen Hill, MD	45,494	73.3	14.5	0.4	9.2	7.8	8.8
Berwyn, IL	45,426	95.6	0.1	0.1	1.7	7.9	21.4
Enid, OK	45,309	91.0	4.4	2.3	1.3	2.1	15.8
Greenville, MS	45,226	39.8	59.6	0.1	0.4	0.6	12.3
Brentwood, NY	45,218	73.0	13.4	0.4	2.0	34.7	7.0
Fort Myers, FL	45,206	64.2	32.2	0.2	0.8	7.7	16.1
Bloomfield, NJ	45,061	89.1	4.3	0.1	5.0	5.1	18.0
Greenville, NC	44,972	64.2	34.1	0.2	1.2	0.8	8.7
Kokomo, IN	44,962	89.5	8.9	0.3	0.7	1.7	13.6
Murfreesboro, TN	44,922	82.3	14.5	0.2	2.8	0.8	9.9
Rockville, MD	44,835	79.2	8.3	0.3	9.8	8.6	10.5
Tamarac, FL	44,822	96.0	2.3	0.1	0.9	5.4	47.6
Corvallis, OR	44,757	89.1	1.2	0.7	8.0	2.8	9.4
Roseville, CA	44,685	91.5	0.9	1.0	3.3	10.8	11.3
Springfield, OR	44,683	95.4	0.7	1.5	1.5	2.9	10.8
Roswell, NM	44,654	81.7	2.6	0.7	0.6	36.5	16.0
Augusta, GA	44,639	43.0	56.0	0.2	0.6	0.8	18.8
Arlington, MA	44,630	95.2	1.3	0.1	3.0	1.7	17.8
Laguna Niguel, CA	44,400	88.5	1.4	0.3	7.8	7.8	6.9
Newark, OH	44,389	96.0	3.2	0.2	0.4	0.7	15.1
Rome, NY	44,350	89.4	8.0	0.2	1.3	3.9	13.7
Marietta, GA	44,129	76.3	20.5	0.3	1.8	3.2	10.4
Idaho Falls, ID	43,929	95.3	0.6	0.6	1.2	4.2	10.3
Woonsocket, RI	43,877	93.3	2.6	0.2	3.0	2.6	16.2
Cary, NC	43,858	89.8	5.5	0.3	3.8	1.6	4.4
St. Louis Park, MN	43,787	95.3	1.9	0.4	2.1	1.0	16.1
Bradenton, FL	43,779	82.9	14.4	0.2	0.6	5.4	28.5
Lafayette, IN	43,764	95.8	2.1	0.3	1.1	1.7	13.2
Bedford, TX	43,762	92.8	2.6	0.4	2.5	4.6	4.7
Warner Robins, GA	43,726	72.7	25.0	0.3	1.4	1.8	8.2
Holyoke, MA	43,704	73.1	3.6	0.2	0.8	31.1	16.8
Elkhart, IN	43,627	84.0	14.0	0.4	0.8	2.0	13.2
East Brunswick, NJ	43,548	88.1	2.2	0.1	9.1	2.9	8.7
Poway, CA	43,516	89.9	1.4	0.5	6.2	6.9	7.0
Spartanburg, SC	43,467	53.1	45.6	0.1	0.9	0.8	15.3
Pinellas Park, FL	43,426	96.1	1.0	0.3	1.9	3.3	23.1
Covington, KY	43,264	91.5	7.7	0.2	0.4	0.7	14.3
Covina, CA	43,207	80.3	4.1	0.5	7.6	25.6	10.8
Moline, IL	43,202	94.1	2.0	0.2	0.9	6.8	16.0
Petaluma, CA	43,184	92.1	1.3	0.6	3.3	9.2	11.6
Southglenn, CO	43,087	96.5	0.8	0.3	1.9	3.1	6.8
Margate, FL	42,985	93.1	3.7	0.2	1.5	7.7	30.4
Missoula, MT	42,918	95.5	0.3	2.4	1.4	1.3	12.3
West Jordan, UT	42,892	94.0	0.3	0.6	1.9	6.5	2.7
Revere, MA	42,786	93.2	1.4	0.2	3.7	3.8	17.0
Belleville, IL	42,785	92.1	6.8	0.2	0.6	1.3	19.0
Middletown, CT	42,762	85.4	11.1	0.2	1.9	3.3	12.0
E. Hill-Meridian, WA	42,696	88.9	2.5	0.8	6.6	2.9	5.6
Altadena, CA	42,658	49.0	38.8	0.5	4.2	14.1	11.9
Cypress, CA	42,655	79.2	2.0	0.5	13.7	13.5	7.5
Rowland Heights, CA	42,647	53.8	5.2	0.4	29.3	29.7	6.8
Tuckahoe, VA	42,629	92.7	4.7	0.1	2.2	1.3	15.6
Mishawaka, IN	42,608	97.1	1.6	0.4	0.7	1.1	14.8
Gadsden, AL	42,523	70.8	28.2	0.1	0.7	0.4	20.3
West Babylon, NY	42,410	88.1	9.9	0.2	1.0	4.7	11.0
Bell Gardens, CA	42,355	38.2	0.5	1.2	1.3	87.5	4.2
Salina, KS	42,303	93.1	3.5	0.5	1.2	2.7	14.4
Turlock, CA	42,198	82.5	1.2	0.9	4.4	21.0	12.5
York, PA	42,192	72.5	21.3	0.2	1.1	7.7	13.5
Kennewick, WA	42,155	89.9	1.1	0.8	2.0	8.7	9.1
Bloomfield, MI	42,137	91.7	2.4	0.1	5.6	1.3	13.4
N. Highlands, CA	42,105	77.8	10.0	1.5	6.7	9.3	8.7
Ocala, FL	42,045	74.9	23.8	0.3	0.6	2.2	20.8
Elmhurst, IL	42,029	95.9	0.4	0.1	3.0	2.7	14.3
Perth Amboy, NJ	41,967	59.8	11.8	0.4	1.6	55.5	13.8
San Luis Obispo, CA	41,958	88.7	1.9	0.8	5.1	9.4	12.2
Sumter, SC	41,943	59.8	38.2	0.3	1.2	1.6	10.4
Hattiesburg, MS	41,882	58.2	40.4	0.1	1.1	1.0	12.7
Chester, PA	41,856	32.0	65.2	0.2	0.4	3.8	13.9
Lincoln Park, MI	41,832	97.3	0.9	0.5	0.4	3.8	14.4
Layton, UT	41,784	92.7	2.1	0.7	2.3	5.6	4.5
New Brunswick, NJ	41,711	57.4	29.6	0.3	4.0	19.3	9.3
Renton, WA	41,688	83.5	6.6	1.2	7.7	3.0	10.5
Rancho Palos Ver., CA	41,659	76.2	1.9	0.2	20.5	5.3	12.0
Rock Hill, SC	41,643	60.4	38.1	0.4	0.8	0.6	12.4
Port Charlotte, FL	41,535	94.1	4.4	0.2	1.0	3.5	33.4
Ellicott City, MD	41,396	88.2	5.2	0.1	6.2	1.4	8.8
Azusa, CA	41,333	66.0	3.8	0.7	6.6	53.4	6.9
Placentia, CA	41,259	76.2	1.9	0.5	8.2	24.7	7.2
Fitchburg, MA	41,194	89.4	3.4	0.2	2.6	9.6	15.4
Germantown, MD	41,145	80.4	12.1	0.3	5.6	5.1	2.0
San Clemente, CA	41,100	91.6	0.7	0.4	2.7	12.9	13.0
Portage, MI	41,042	94.3	2.8	0.4	2.1	1.4	8.5
Meridian, MS	41,036	54.0	45.4	0.1	0.4	0.6	16.5
Joplin, MO	40,961	95.0	2.1	1.9	0.6	1.2	17.2
East St. Louis, IL	40,944	1.6	98.1	0.1	0.1	0.4	10.8
Essex, MD	40,872	90.0	8.4	0.4	0.9	1.3	12.2
Bolingbrook, IL	40,843	76.8	15.6	0.3	5.0	5.9	3.5
Texas City, TX	40,822	67.1	25.1	0.4	1.1	15.9	11.3
Gulfport, MS	40,775	69.9	28.6	0.3	0.9	1.5	14.4
Manteca, CA	40,773	89.5	1.5	1.2	3.5	17.8	8.2
Goldsboro, NC	40,709	50.3	47.4	0.3	1.3	1.5	11.0
Victorville, CA	40,674	73.1	9.6	1.1	3.7	23.0	11.6
Miramar, FL	40,663	79.3	15.7	0.2	2.3	17.3	9.7
Bowling Green, KY	40,641	86.4	12.2	0.2	1.1	0.7	13.1
Rock Island, IL	40,552	80.7	17.2	0.2	0.6	3.8	17.3
La Mirada, CA	40,452	81.2	1.4	0.6	8.2	25.9	11.4
Carson, NV	40,443	90.7	1.7	2.7	1.4	7.7	14.9
Charlottesville, VA	40,341	76.1	21.2	0.1	2.3	1.2	12.2
Moore, OK	40,318	90.2	1.8	5.3	1.3	3.4	5.0
Muskegon, MI	40,283	69.9	27.1	1.0	0.3	3.5	14.7
Cupertino, CA	40,263	74.4	0.9	0.3	23.0	4.9	8.8
Colton, CA	40,213	58.2	8.7	0.9	4.3	49.7	6.6
Palm Springs, CA	40,181	83.2	4.5	0.7	3.3	18.7	25.8
Hicksville, NY	40,174	93.8	0.8	0.1	4.4	4.9	14.8
Blue Springs, MO	40,153	95.6	2.4	0.4	1.1	1.6	5.9
Frederick, MD	40,148	84.3	12.8	0.3	1.9	2.1	12.1
Coral Gables, FL	40,091	93.0	3.4	0.1	1.7	41.8	17.4
University City, MO	40,087	49.1	48.2	0.1	2.2	1.1	13.9
Chico, CA	40,079	89.5	1.8	1.1	4.0	8.7	9.0
Kirkland, WA	40,052	92.8	1.5	0.6	4.3	2.4	9.6
Normal, IL	40,023	92.4	5.0	0.1	1.9	1.5	6.3
Freeport, NY	39,894	56.5	32.3	0.4	1.3	21.2	10.4
Valdosta, GA	39,806	55.2	43.5	0.2	0.9	1.1	10.8
Woodland, CA	39,802	77.5	1.3	1.3	3.1	26.2	11.2
Hoover, AL	39,788	95.2	3.3	0.1	1.2	0.9	9.8
Lewiston, ME	39,757	98.2	0.7	0.2	0.7	0.7	16.4
Fairfield, OH	39,729	95.0	3.3	0.1	1.4	0.7	8.5
Quincy, IL	39,681	94.9	4.1	0.2	0.5	0.4	20.2
Gaithersburg, MD	39,542	72.2	12.9	0.4	10.2	9.3	6.4
Burlington, NC	39,498	76.3	22.6	0.2	0.8	0.6	17.2
Lakeside, CA	39,412	94.0	0.7	0.8	1.4	9.3	10.0
Lombard, IL	39,408	93.4	1.3	0.1	4.4	2.8	12.7
Titusville, FL	39,394	87.3	11.0	0.4	0.8	2.8	15.9
Grand Island, NE	39,386	96.0	0.3	0.3	1.3	4.8	14.6
Eden Prairie, MN	39,311	96.4	1.1	0.2	2.1	0.7	3.3
Hutchinson, KS	39,308	91.5	4.1	0.6	0.4	5.4	16.6
Palatine, IL	39,253	94.2	0.9	0.1	3.2	3.6	8.9
Burlington, VT	39,127	96.8	1.0	0.3	1.5	1.2	10.6
West Orange, NJ	39,103	87.6	5.7	0.1	5.6	4.4	18.9
Blaine, MN	38,975	97.2	0.3	0.8	1.4	1.0	3.1
San Marcos, CA	38,974	84.7	1.5	0.8	2.9	27.5	14.7
San Bruno, CA	38,961	71.6	4.1	0.8	17.9	18.6	10.5
Bay City, MI	38,936	93.6	2.4	0.8	0.4	5.6	15.4
State College, PA	38,923	88.5	3.4	0.1	7.3	2.0	4.7
Seaside, CA	38,901	52.7	23.5	1.0	13.5	17.4	5.4
Culver City, CA	38,793	69.2	10.4	0.6	12.0	19.8	13.3
Maple Grove, MN	38,736	97.1	0.9	0.3	1.6	0.8	2.4
Chapel Hill, NC	38,719	82.3	12.5	0.3	4.3	1.6	8.6
Richmond, IN	38,705	89.6	9.2	0.3	0.6	0.7	16.6
Huber Heights, OH	38,696	90.7	6.9	0.2	1.7	1.5	5.9
Boardman, OH	38,596	98.1	1.1	0.1	0.6	0.9	19.3
Leavenworth, KS	38,495	79.8	15.8	0.7	2.0	4.7	9.7
Petersburg, VA	38,386	26.6	72.1	0.2	0.8	1.2	15.0
Attleboro, MA	38,383	95.5	1.0	0.2	2.4	2.9	12.1
Westfield, MA	38,372	96.5	0.9	0.1	0.8	4.1	13.8
Beverly, MA	38,195	97.6	0.9	0.1	1.0	1.1	15.0
McLean, VA	38,168	88.3	1.7	0.2	9.2	4.2	13.9
Euless, TX	38,149	86.5	4.6	0.6	5.1	7.9	4.0
Leominster, MA	38,145	93.1	2.3	0.2	1.6	8.3	13.0
Bremerton, WA	38,142	83.9	7.1	1.7	5.3	4.8	13.6
Sun City, AZ	38,126	99.6	0.2	0.1	0.1	0.5	84.6
West New York, NJ	38,125	76.7	4.0	0.4	1.9	73.3	13.7
Salem, MA	38,091	93.0	2.7	0.3	1.4	6.7	15.2

City/State	Population	%White	%Black	%Am Ind	%Asian	%Hisp	%65+
Midland, MI	38,053	95.6	1.7	0.4	1.9	1.7	11.9
Shawnee, KS	37,993	94.9	2.1	0.4	1.7	2.6	7.1
Chesterfield, MO	37,991	93.7	2.4	0.1	3.6	1.2	9.2
Atlantic City, NJ	37,986	35.4	51.3	0.5	4.0	15.3	19.2
Kent, WA	37,960	89.2	3.8	1.4	4.4	3.9	6.5
Newark, CA	37,861	68.6	4.3	0.6	15.9	22.9	5.3
Calumet City, IL	37,840	73.3	23.7	0.1	0.6	6.4	15.5
Kentwood, MI	37,826	91.3	5.6	0.4	2.0	2.0	9.6
Teaneck, NJ	37,825	66.6	26.2	0.2	5.6	6.3	14.5
Hilo, HA	37,808	26.6	0.6	0.6	70.2	8.5	14.6
Olympia Heights, FL	37,792	93.3	0.9	0.1	1.3	79.2	14.5
Fond du Lac, WI	37,757	97.8	0.3	0.5	0.8	1.5	16.3
Montclair, NJ	37,729	65.5	31.0	0.2	2.3	3.3	15.2
Manhattan, KS	37,712	90.1	5.0	0.5	3.3	2.8	8.1
Muskogee, OK	37,708	69.0	18.9	11.0	0.5	1.5	18.6
Pacifica, CA	37,670	76.3	5.2	0.7	13.6	13.5	7.4
Lompoc, CA	37,649	70.5	7.8	1.3	5.4	26.8	8.5
Bowie, MD	37,589	91.4	5.7	0.3	2.3	2.2	6.3
Hillsboro, OR	37,520	88.6	0.5	0.6	2.2	11.2	8.7
Jackson, MI	37,446	80.2	17.7	0.6	0.4	2.5	14.1
Kingwood, TX	37,397	95.2	1.3	0.2	1.9	4.4	3.2
Norwich, CT	37,391	91.3	5.3	0.6	1.1	3.1	15.7
Loveland, CO	37,352	94.9	0.3	0.5	0.7	6.8	13.0
Glen Burnie, MD	37,305	86.3	11.3	0.3	1.7	1.3	10.9
Tinley Park, IL	37,121	96.2	1.6	0.1	1.4	2.5	8.9
San Gabriel, CA	37,120	48.0	1.1	0.5	32.4	36.3	13.4
Glenview, IL	37,093	91.0	0.8	0.1	7.4	2.4	12.8
Wausau, WI	37,060	93.1	0.1	0.7	6.0	0.7	17.3
Hackensack, NJ	37,049	66.4	24.8	0.2	3.7	15.1	14.3
La Puente, CA	36,955	63.9	3.5	0.6	7.8	74.9	6.0
Wilson, NC	36,930	52.4	46.9	0.1	0.3	0.7	13.8
East Meadow, NY	36,909	90.3	5.0	0.1	3.5	3.9	13.2
Fort Pierce, FL	36,830	53.7	42.4	0.3	0.5	6.4	19.2
Kailua, HA	36,818	57.7	1.4	0.5	39.1	5.5	10.8
Indio, CA	36,793	54.5	4.0	0.8	1.6	68.1	8.1
Camp Lejeune, NC	36,716	67.6	24.7	0.7	2.0	8.4	0.0
Linden, NJ	36,701	76.8	20.0	0.1	1.5	7.4	19.3
Stillwater, OK	36,676	87.6	3.7	3.4	4.6	1.8	8.2
Marrero, LA	36,671	51.9	45.0	0.5	1.9	2.9	9.3
Bountiful, UT	36,659	98.2	0.1	0.3	0.9	1.6	10.8
Buffalo Grove, IL	36,427	94.2	1.0	0.1	4.4	2.0	5.5
Florence, AL	36,426	82.1	17.1	0.3	0.4	0.5	16.6
Kingsport, TN	36,365	94.8	4.4	0.1	0.6	0.3	20.0
Urbana, IL	36,344	75.7	11.4	0.2	11.7	2.7	9.0
Rohnert Park, CA	36,326	89.2	2.6	1.0	4.8	8.9	7.5
New Albany, IN	36,322	93.2	6.2	0.2	0.3	0.5	16.5
Willingboro, NJ	36,291	39.7	56.1	0.3	1.9	5.3	6.9
Missouri City, TX	36,176	60.6	29.4	0.3	6.3	9.2	4.1
Park Ridge, IL	36,175	97.4	0.1	0.1	2.2	1.3	19.0
Commack, NY	36,124	96.1	0.6	0.0	2.9	2.5	8.5
West Hollywood, CA	36,118	90.2	3.4	0.4	3.1	8.7	18.3
Hemet, CA	36,094	90.9	0.7	0.9	1.2	14.9	42.1
Campbell, CA	36,048	83.6	2.0	0.6	9.5	10.6	9.3
Concord, NH	36,006	98.2	0.6	0.3	0.7	1.0	14.0
Woburn, MA	35,943	96.6	1.0	0.2	1.5	2.3	12.7
Redmond, WA	35,800	91.1	1.3	0.5	6.3	2.5	6.9
Oxon H.-Glassm., MD	35,794	18.2	77.9	0.3	2.8	1.9	4.9
Monrovia, CA	35,761	69.7	10.1	0.5	4.5	28.5	10.8
Duncanville, TX	35,748	82.5	12.1	0.3	2.1	6.7	6.8
Orland Park, IL	35,720	95.4	0.4	0.1	3.6	2.3	9.9
Richfield, MN	35,710	93.5	2.6	0.6	2.8	1.1	16.9
Findlay, OH	35,703	95.9	1.3	0.2	0.8	3.4	13.6
Everett, MA	35,701	93.5	3.2	0.3	1.8	3.8	16.4
South Valley, NM	35,701	61.4	1.3	1.7	0.4	72.5	9.2
Fort Hood, TX	35,580	54.9	33.9	0.8	3.5	12.4	0.1
Beloit, WI	35,573	81.8	15.7	0.3	1.2	1.9	13.4
Jefferson City, MO	35,481	88.8	10.1	0.3	0.5	0.8	15.8
Kaneohe, HA	35,448	31.2	1.2	0.4	65.6	6.9	10.9
Hagerstown, MD	35,445	92.5	6.3	0.1	0.7	0.8	16.0
Shelton, CT	35,418	97.1	1.0	0.2	1.3	2.5	12.6
N. Miami Beach, FL	35,359	71.6	21.8	0.2	3.4	22.1	19.9
Pine Hills, FL	35,322	72.2	22.8	0.3	2.1	8.4	8.8
Port Orange, FL	35,317	97.7	1.0	0.3	0.8	2.0	22.6
Strongsville, OH	35,308	96.6	0.8	0.1	2.4	1.0	7.9
San Ramon, CA	35,303	87.1	2.0	0.3	9.0	5.8	4.3
East Detroit, MI	35,283	98.7	0.2	0.4	0.6	0.8	18.8
Catonsville, MD	35,233	88.7	9.3	0.2	1.7	1.0	20.4
Brookfield, WI	35,184	96.9	0.4	0.2	2.4	0.7	12.6
Suitland-Silver H., MD	35,111	13.6	84.3	0.3	1.3	1.4	5.8
N. Tonawanda, NY	34,989	98.9	0.2	0.3	0.4	0.8	14.5
Sayreville , NJ	34,986	93.1	3.2	0.1	3.0	4.0	12.3
North Chicago, IL	34,978	56.7	34.4	0.5	3.6	9.2	5.2
De Kalb, IL	34,925	88.9	4.7	0.1	4.5	4.1	6.9
Wheeling, WV	34,882	94.7	4.5	0.1	0.7	0.3	21.9
Altamonte Springs, FL	34,879	89.9	5.9	0.3	1.8	8.5	9.6
Kearny, NJ	34,874	90.5	1.2	0.2	4.7	17.1	13.3
Fort Bragg, NC	34,744	60.9	29.1	0.9	2.6	10.3	0.1
Pennsauken, NJ	34,733	80.5	14.7	0.4	1.8	4.9	15.8
Jamestown, NY	34,681	94.9	2.6	0.5	0.5	3.0	17.2
Apple Valley, MN	34,598	96.7	0.9	0.2	1.9	1.0	2.6
Blacksburg, VA	34,590	87.4	4.3	0.1	7.7	1.8	4.2
Minot, ND	34,544	95.8	1.1	2.1	0.8	0.8	13.9
Lancaster, OH	34,507	98.8	0.5	0.2	0.4	0.5	15.7
Brighton, NY	34,455	92.1	3.0	0.1	4.3	1.6	19.7
Highland, CA	34,439	73.1	11.0	1.1	4.8	22.8	6.6
Cape Girardeau, MO	34,438	90.2	8.0	0.2	1.3	0.6	14.6
East Point, GA	34,402	31.6	66.3	0.2	0.7	1.9	11.6
Panama City, FL	34,378	75.5	21.8	0.6	1.7	1.3	17.0
Bell, CA	34,365	42.0	1.0	0.8	1.4	86.1	6.5
Prichard, AL	34,311	20.1	79.4	0.4	0.0	0.3	11.2
Cedar Falls, IA	34,298	96.9	1.1	0.2	1.4	0.8	11.1
Aloha, OR	34,284	90.7	0.7	0.7	6.4	3.8	5.0
Bartlesville, OK	34,256	88.6	3.3	6.4	1.1	1.8	16.7
Belleville, NJ	34,213	86.1	3.7	0.2	6.0	10.1	14.6
North Olmsted, OH	34,204	97.1	0.7	0.1	1.7	1.2	12.9
Ewing, NJ	34,185	78.7	18.3	0.1	1.8	2.7	16.8
Upper Arlington, OH	34,128	97.3	0.3	0.1	2.3	0.7	18.7
Marion, OH	34,075	94.7	4.2	0.3	0.5	0.8	13.0
Lenexa, KS	34,034	94.6	2.4	0.4	2.0	1.7	5.8
Dunedin, FL	34,012	98.1	1.1	0.2	0.4	1.8	33.3
Farmington, NM	33,997	77.1	0.8	13.8	0.4	16.0	8.7
Valley Stream, NY	33,946	94.9	0.4	0.0	3.6	4.5	17.1
East Chicago, IN	33,892	38.0	33.6	0.2	0.2	47.8	13.2
Parkersburg, WV	33,862	97.7	1.7	0.2	0.3	0.3	19.9
Tamiami, FL	33,845	92.5	0.8	0.1	0.7	82.6	9.4
Olympia, WA	33,840	92.0	1.2	1.2	4.8	2.6	14.5
Braintree, MA	33,836	97.4	0.6	0.1	1.6	0.9	17.1
Auburn, AL	33,830	79.9	16.3	0.2	3.4	0.9	5.6
Danville, IL	33,828	78.3	19.1	0.2	1.1	2.1	17.5
Bethel Park, PA	33,823	98.1	1.0	0.1	0.8	0.5	13.6
Michigan City, IN	33,822	75.8	22.5	0.3	0.7	1.8	13.9
Martinez, GA	33,731	89.6	6.2	0.2	3.7	1.4	5.3
Elmira, NY	33,724	85.4	12.3	0.3	0.6	2.7	15.0
Port Huron, MI	33,694	90.1	6.8	0.8	0.6	3.5	13.9
Torrington, CT	33,687	96.7	1.7	0.2	1.2	1.1	18.6
Littleton, CO	33,685	96.1	0.9	0.6	1.4	5.2	12.1
New City, NY	33,673	92.4	2.7	0.1	4.2	3.6	7.1
Beavercreek, OH	33,626	96.3	0.9	0.2	2.3	1.0	9.1
New Berlin, WI	33,592	98.4	0.2	0.2	1.0	0.8	8.5
West Little River, FL	33,575	27.7	68.0	0.1	0.3	29.4	8.1
Hurst, TX	33,574	93.4	2.6	0.5	1.2	5.2	8.9
Tracy, CA	33,558	86.3	2.5	1.0	4.6	24.3	8.1
Galesburg, IL	33,530	88.6	8.4	0.2	0.9	3.8	18.0
Long Beach, NY	33,510	87.0	7.8	0.3	1.7	10.8	18.6
Bessemer, AL	33,497	41.4	58.4	0.1	0.1	0.2	17.5
Roseville, MN	33,485	95.1	1.6	0.3	2.6	1.1	16.8
Ross Township, PA	33,482	97.9	1.1	0.0	0.9	0.4	18.5
Elk Grove Village, IL	33,429	91.5	0.8	0.1	6.8	3.6	7.2
Greenfield, WI	33,403	97.6	0.4	0.4	1.0	2.0	17.1
Hoboken, NJ	33,397	79.0	5.5	0.2	4.4	30.1	11.1
Mount Lebanon, PA	33,362	97.7	0.5	0.0	1.7	0.8	18.4
Butte-Silver Bow, MT	33,336	97.3	0.1	1.6	0.4	2.4	17.0
Watertown, MA	33,284	96.1	1.3	0.1	2.2	2.0	17.1
Tulare, CA	33,249	65.6	6.2	1.1	2.5	33.8	10.7
Annapolis, MD	33,187	64.9	33.0	0.2	1.3	1.5	12.2
Bangor, ME	33,181	97.1	0.9	0.7	1.0	0.6	13.6
Spring, TX	33,111	88.7	5.8	0.4	1.3	9.4	3.0
Auburn, WA	33,102	92.4	1.4	2.1	3.0	3.1	11.6
East Cleveland, OH	33,096	5.3	93.7	0.1	0.7	0.6	10.5
Chicago Heights, IL	33,072	55.0	35.1	0.2	0.3	15.0	12.6
Novi, MI	32,998	96.0	0.8	0.3	2.6	1.1	8.0
Sierra Vista, AZ	32,983	77.4	12.0	0.6	5.2	11.8	7.3
Pharr, TX	32,921	70.2	0.1	0.2	0.1	88.4	11.4
Woodlawn, MD	32,907	70.0	24.5	0.2	4.9	1.5	11.1
Alton, IL	32,905	75.6	23.1	0.5	0.3	1.1	17.3
Hanover Park, IL	32,895	85.5	3.6	0.2	7.4	11.0	3.0
Germantown, TN	32,893	95.2	1.9	0.2	2.7	0.8	5.4
Merritt Island, FL	32,886	92.4	5.4	0.4	1.3	2.8	15.3
Brea, CA	32,873	87.0	1.1	0.4	6.2	15.4	9.3
Granite City, IL	32,862	98.4	0.2	0.4	0.5	1.8	15.3
Haltom City, TX	32,856	89.8	1.3	0.7	4.8	8.5	12.0
Yucaipa, CA	32,824	92.6	0.5	0.9	1.0	11.0	24.0
Willowbrook, CA	32,772	11.0	55.2	0.2	0.6	44.6	9.6
Logan, UT	32,762	91.4	0.6	1.3	5.1	3.1	8.8
Marion, IN	32,618	82.6	14.8	0.4	0.7	3.2	16.6
Manitowoc, WI	32,520	96.4	0.2	0.5	2.5	1.1	19.8
Rio Rancho, NM	32,505	84.1	2.6	2.1	1.2	21.8	12.0
Claremont, CA	32,503	82.2	5.0	0.4	8.5	10.3	12.4
Oceanside, NY	32,423	97.3	0.4	0.1	1.4	3.9	12.9
San Dimas, CA	32,397	81.7	3.8	0.5	8.6	17.3	9.4
Chelmsford, MA	32,388	96.1	0.5	0.1	3.1	1.0	9.7
Sanford, FL	32,387	68.8	28.5	0.4	0.9	4.9	12.9
Austintown, OH	32,371	96.5	2.6	0.2	0.5	1.1	14.4
Richland, WA	32,315	93.0	1.4	0.7	3.3	3.0	12.6
Montgomery, MD	32,315	78.7	11.3	0.3	6.6	7.3	4.9
Northbrook, IL	32,308	93.0	0.2	0.0	6.4	1.6	14.6
Moorhead, MN	32,295	95.3	0.5	1.4	1.1	2.8	11.1
Pekin, IL	32,254	99.2	0.1	0.2	0.4	0.6	15.6
Millcreek, UT	32,230	93.2	1.1	1.0	2.7	5.6	13.0
Madison Heights, MI	32,196	95.9	0.9	0.5	2.4	1.2	11.6
Hendersonville, TN	32,188	96.7	2.3	0.2	0.6	0.8	8.3
North Providence, RI	32,090	97.1	1.0	0.1	1.2	1.8	18.7
Manhattan Beach, CA	32,063	93.5	0.6	0.3	4.4	5.1	8.6
Addison Village, IL	32,058	87.9	1.7	0.1	5.9	13.4	6.7
Trumbull, CT	32,000	96.8	1.3	0.1	1.7	1.8	15.6
Fort Lee, NJ	31,997	77.2	1.3	0.1	20.3	5.6	20.1
Beverly Hills, CA	31,971	91.3	1.7	0.2	5.5	5.4	20.3
Monterey, CA	31,954	86.6	2.9	0.6	7.3	7.8	12.9
Williamsport, PA	31,933	92.3	6.7	0.2	0.5	0.8	15.0
So. Sacramento, CA	31,903	51.9	18.8	1.8	12.8	25.2	10.0
Dana Point, CA	31,896	89.6	0.6	0.6	2.3	13.9	10.0
Chalmette, LA	31,860	97.7	0.3	0.3	1.1	4.9	11.7
Garden City, MI	31,846	98.6	0.2	0.4	0.5	1.5	9.9
New Iberia, LA	31,828	64.2	33.3	0.2	2.0	2.3	12.4
Marlborough, MA	31,813	94.8	1.8	0.2	1.9	4.2	11.2
Martinez, CA	31,808	87.7	3.3	0.8	5.7	8.4	9.0
Columbus, IN	31,802	95.4	2.5	0.2	1.6	0.9	14.0
Oakville, MO	31,750	98.7	0.2	0.1	0.7	0.9	6.5
Garfield Heights, OH	31,739	84.4	14.8	0.1	0.5	0.8	19.4
Carol Stream, IL	31,716	88.4	3.4	0.2	5.8	5.7	5.2
West Des Moines, IA	31,702	96.3	1.3	0.1	1.6	1.9	10.6
Texarkana, TX	31,656	63.0	35.9	0.4	0.5	1.1	17.1
Parkville, MD	31,617	85.2	12.7	0.1	1.7	1.2	18.2
Sherman, TX	31,601	83.2	12.6	0.9	0.8	4.4	16.4
Pleasant Hill, CA	31,585	89.3	1.4	0.6	7.0	6.6	11.7
Longview, WA	31,499	94.7	0.5	1.5	2.1	2.0	15.5
Gilroy, CA	31,487	68.2	1.2	0.7	4.0	47.3	7.7
Mankato, MN	31,477	96.3	0.7	0.3	2.3	1.1	10.9
Waipahu, HA	31,435	11.6	2.0	0.5	83.8	11.5	10.5
El Centro, CA	31,384	60.0	4.5	0.7	2.5	65.3	8.0
Chillum, MD	31,309	21.5	69.1	0.3	3.7	9.8	10.0
Danville, CA	31,306	91.6	0.8	0.3	6.5	4.1	8.4
Fairborn, OH	31,300	92.4	4.1	0.4	2.6	1.3	9.4
North Brunswick, NJ	31,287	80.0	11.1	0.2	6.8	5.8	9.2
Murray, UT	31,282	95.8	0.7	0.5	1.5	4.2	10.3
Auburn, NY	31,258	91.9	6.8	0.3	0.5	2.2	18.3
Spring Hill, FL	31,117	97.7	1.3	0.1	0.4	4.0	33.5
Temple City, CA	31,100	71.9	0.6	0.4	19.5	18.8	14.9
Watsonville, CA	31,099	55.1	0.7	1.0	5.6	60.9	12.6
Allen Park, MI	31,092	98.0	0.5	0.2	0.7	3.2	20.3

Source: U.S. Bureau of the Census, *Census of Population and Housing, 1990.*

Glossary

African American (Black)

A person having origins in any of the Black racial groups in Africa. Normally excludes persons of Hispanic origin except for noted tabulations produced by the Bureau of the Census.

American Indian or Alaskan Native

A person with origins in any of the original peoples of North America and maintaining cultural identification through tribal affiliation or community recognition.

Asian or Pacific Islander

A person having origins in any of the original peoples of the Far East, Southeast Asia, the Indian subcontinent, or the Pacific Islands. This area includes China, India, Japan, Korea, the Philippine Islands, and Samoa.

Birth Rate

The number of births per 1,000 of resident population.

Census (Decennial)

A survey of the population taken every 10 years, primarily to establish a basis for apportionment of members of the House of Representatives among the States.

Constant Dollars

Dollar amounts that have been adjusted by means of price and cost indexes to eliminate inflationary factors and allow direct comparison across years.

Consumer Price Index (CPI)

This price index measures the average change in the cost of a fixed market basket of goods and services purchased by consumers.

Country of Origin

The county from which a person emigrated from to the United States.

Current Dollars

Dollar amounts that have not been adjusted to compensate for inflation.

Death Rate

The number of deaths per 1,000 of resident population.

Employees (Paid)

All full or part-time employees, including management. Employees on paid sick leave, paid holidays, and paid vacations are included. Proprietors and partners of unincorporated businesses are not included.

Employment

Includes civilian, noninstitutional persons who (1) worked during any part of the survey week as paid employees; worked in their own business, profession, or farm; or worked 15 hours or more as unpaid workers in a family-owned enterprise; or (2) were not working but had jobs or businesses from which they were temporarily absent due to illness, bad weather, vacation, labor–management dispute, or personal reasons—whether or not they were seeking another job.

Expenditures

Charges incurred, whether paid or unpaid, which are presumed to benefit the current fiscal year.

Family

A group of two persons or more (one of whom is the householder) related by birth, marriage, or adoption and residing together. All such persons (including related subfamily members) are considered as members of one family.

Family Household

Consists of two or more persons, including the householder, who are related by birth, marriage, or adoption and who live together as one household; all such persons are considered as members of one family.

Farm Income

Comprises cash receipts from farm marketings of crops and livestock, Federal government payments made directly to farmers for farm–related activities, rental value of farm homes, value of farm products consumed in farm homes, and other farm–related income such as machine hire and custom work. Farm marketings represent agricultural products sold by farmers, multiplied by prices received per unit of production at the local markets.

Federal Funds

Amounts collected and used by the Federal Government for the general purposes. There are four types of Federal fund accounts: the general fund, special funds, public enterprise funds, and intragovernmental funds. The major Federal fund is the general fund, which is derived from general taxes and borrowing. Federal funds also include certain earmarked collections, such as those generated by and used to finance a continuing cycle of business–type operations.

Fiscal Year

The yearly accounting period for the Federal Government, which begins on October 1 and ends on the following September 30. The fiscal year is designated by the calendar year in which it ends; e.g., fiscal year 1988 begins on October 1, 1987, and ends on September 30, 1988.

Gross National Product (GNP)

The total national output of goods and services valued at market prices. GNP can be viewed in terms of expenditure categories which include purchases of goods and services by consumers and government, gross private domestic investment, and net exports of goods and services. The goods and services included are largely those bought for final use in the market economy.

Group Quarters

All persons not living in households are classified by the Census Bureau as living in group quarters. Two general categories of persons in group quarters are recognized: (1) institutionalized persons and (2) other persons in group quarters.

Hispanic (Latino)

A person of Mexican, Puerto Rican, Cuban, Central or South American, or other Spanish culture or origin, regardless of race.

Homeowner Vacancy Rate

The percentage relationship between the number of vacant units for sale and the total homeowner inventory. It is computed by dividing the number of vacant units for sale only by the sum of the owner–occupied units and the vacant units that are for sale.

Household

All the persons who occupy a housing unit. A house, an apartment, another group of rooms, and a single room, are regarded as housing units when they are occupied or intended for occupancy as separate living quarters, that is, when the occupants do not live and eat with any other persons in the structure, and there is direct access from the outside or through a common hall.

Householder

The person (or one of the persons) in whose name the home is owned or rented. If a home is owned or rented jointly by a married couple, either the husband or the wife may be listed first. Prior to 1980, the husband was always considered the household head (householder) in married–couple households.

Housing Unit

A house, an apartment, or a mobile home or trailer, a group of rooms or a single room, occupied as separate living quarters or, if vacant, intended for occupancy as separate living quarters.

Immigrants

Aliens admitted for legal permanent residence in a country.

Immigration

The act of migrating into a country for the purpose of permanent residence.

Inflation

Upward movement in general price levels that results in a decline of purchasing power.

Labor Force

Persons employed as civilians, unemployed (but looking for work), or in the armed services during the survey week. The civilian labor force comprises all civilians classified as employed or unemployed.

Married Couple

A husband and wife living together in the same household, with or without children and/or other relatives.

Median Age

This measure divides age distribution into two equal parts: one–half of the cases falling below the median value and one–half above. Generally, median age is computed on the basis of more detailed age intervals than are shown in some census publications; thus, a median based on a less detailed distribution may differ slightly from a corresponding median for the same population based on more detailed distribution.

Metropolitan Population

The population residing in Metropolitan Statistical Areas (MSAs).

Metropolitan Statistical Area (MSA)

A large population nucleus and the nearby communities which have a high degree of economic and social integration with that nucleus. Each MSA consists of one or more entire counties (or county equivalents). Similar to MSA is CMSA (Consolidated Metropolitan Statistical Area).

Migration

Geographic mobility involving a change of usual residence between clearly defined geographic units, that is, between counties, States, or regions.

Nonfamily Household

Consists of a person living alone or of a householder living with other unrelated individuals. A one–person household consists of one person living alone.

Nonresident Alien

A person who is not a citizen of the United States and who is in this country on a temporary basis and does not have the right to remain indefinitely.

Nonmetropolitan Residence Group

The population residing outside Metropolitan Statistical Areas (MSAs).

Owner–Occupied (Housing Unit)

A housing unit is owner–occupied if the owner or co–owner lives in the unit even if it is mortgaged or not fully paid for.

Per Capita Income

A figure derived by dividing aggregate money income by total resident population.

Personal Income

Current income received by persons from all sources minus their personal contributions for social insurance. Personal income includes transfers (payment not resulting from current production) from government and business such as social security benefits, military pensions, etc., but excludes transfers among persons.

Persons Per Household

Obtained by dividing the number of persons in households by the number of households or householders.

Persons Per Family

This measure is obtained by dividing the number of persons in families by the total number of families or family householders.

Racial (ethnic) Group

Classification indicating general racial or ethnic heritage based on self–identification.

Renter–Occupied (Housing Unit)

Non–owner occupied housing units rented for cash or occupied without payment of cash rent.

Rental Vacancy Rate

This is the percentage relationship of the number of vacant units for rent to the total rental inventory. It is computed by dividing the number of vacant units for rent by the sum of the renter–occupied units and the number of vacant units for rent.

Residence

The place where one usually lives and sleeps.

Resident Population

Includes civilian population and armed forces personnel residing within the United States. Excludes armed forces personnel residing overseas.

Revenues

All funds received from external sources, net of refunds, and correcting transactions. Noncash transactions such as receipt of services, commodities, or other receipts in kind are excluded as are funds received from the issuance of debt, liquidation of investments, and nonroutine sale of property.

Salary

The total amount regularly paid or stipulated to be paid to an individual, before deductions, for personal services rendered while on the payroll of a business or organization.

Sex Ratio

A measurement derived from dividing the total number of males by the total number of females and multiplying by 100.

Taxes (Income)

Taxes levied on net income, that is, on gross personal income minus certain deductions permitted by law. These taxes can be levied on individuals or businesses.

Unemployed

Civilians who had no employment but were available for work and (1) had engaged in any specific job–seeking activity within the past 4 weeks, (2) were waiting to be called back to a job from which they had been laid off, or (3) were waiting to report to a new wage or salary job within 30 days.

White

A person having origins in any of the original peoples of Europe, North Africa, or the Middle East. Normally excludes persons of Hispanic origin except for tabulations produced by the Bureau of the Census.